GRAVEYARD HARBOR

ROBERT GRAYSMITH

MONKEY'S PAW PUBLISHING, INC. - LOS ANGELES

Books by Robert Graysmith

Zodiac
The Sleeping Lady
Auto Focus
Unabomber
The Bell Tower
Zodiac Unmasked
Amerithrax
The Laughing Gorilla
The Girl in Alfred Hitchcock's Shower
Black Fire
Shooting Zodiac
Graveyard Harbor

Audio Books

Zodiac
Zodiac Unmasked
Black Fire

Film Adaptations

Zodiac
Auto Focus

GRAVEYARD HARBOR:
Treasure, Murder, and Vigilantes in the Gold Rush's Fantastic Floating City of One Thousand Abandoned Ships

Copyright ©2023 by Robert Graysmith.

All rights reserved.
No part of this book may be reproduced or used in any manner without written permission of the publisher or copyright owner except for the use of brief quotations in a book review.

Illustrated by the author.

Book & Cover design by Aaron Smith

ISBN: 978-1-7365800-9-7

Monkey's Paw Publishing, Inc.
Los Angeles, CA

www.monkeyspawpublishing.com

The "Monkey Paw" design is a trademark of Monkey's Paw Publishing, Inc.

*To the Wonderful Janet Randall
Who Took Me to Mark Twain's Home
And Inspired a Book*

UNDER BRIGHT MOONLIGHT Capt. Coffin saw Jesus Christ walking along San Francisco's Long Wharf as if on a sunny day in Nazareth. A resurrected Messiah was striding into a floating city of nearly a thousand abandoned ships filled with ten thousand fugitives. Slender as a stalk of wheat, nearly six-feet tall, the familiar figure walked in a slow, measured stride swinging his arms pendulum-like. Every few steps, he stopped, lowered his head, and peered out from under the broad brim of his low-crowned hat. Then, his head, sharp-featured and dark-complected, would fly up like a snake about to strike. His chin beard was twin-pointed as fangs. His rich, dark-brown hair was fine, wavy, and worn shoulder length like the traditional portraits of Jesus. His nose was aquiline, his heavy-lidded eyes, blue-black and glistening as anthracite, perpetually brightened under the luminous light. His face had an intellectual and thoughtful cast, a feature belied by the wicked smile that played about his lips.

The same Spanish settlers who had renamed Yerba Buena Cove "Graveyard Harbor" called him, "Creeping Jesus." To Capt. Coffin, unofficial master of the port, he was English Jim—the Sacramento shop breaker and horse thief, the Foster's Bar murderer and robber of Dodge. He was an escaped convict off the Sacramento prison brig, the prime suspect in Auburn Sheriff Echols's murder, and for a fact had shot-gunned Charlie Moore to death on the ragged trail to Marysville and nearly bludgeoned Jansen to death.

There was something mystical about English Jim. No jail could hold him. He could not die. More than once he had stood beneath the gallows with a rope around his neck, yet still lived. More than once an innocent man who was English Jim's identical twin would stand in his place on the gallows. Jim and his loose-knit gang of eight ruthless apostles—arsonists, robbers, cutthroats, corrupt officials and inside men (including the man who built the city vault) were planning to rob San Francisco of three million dollars in gold. The innumerable lives lost and a city destroyed multiple times were only collateral damage in carrying out English Jim's cunning scheme.

First, more men would have to die.

Contents

Author's Note

Prologue
(1)

— I —

Black Water and Shallows
(3)

— II —

The Zenith of Incandescence
(107)

— III —

The Covenant of Promise
(239)

Epilogue
(331)

Appendix
Selected References

AUTHOR'S NOTE

THIS IS A WORK OF NONFICTION. All the characters are real. All their dialogue is based on letters, personal diaries, journals, memoirs, autobiographies, biographies, historical records, and published newspaper reports and interviews. For further verification, I turned to public speeches, civil and criminal trials, illegal Vigilante Committee tribunals, official transcripts, and handwritten and dictated confessions. I reviewed birth, marriage and death records, ship passenger lists, ship arrivals and departures, immigration reports, shipwrecks and survivors, fleet records, and local newspapers of the period. I consulted San Francisco City directories, street guides, maps, census reports, weather reports, wind and tidal conditions, eyewitness reports, illustrations done at the scenes, rare period photos of the actual Ghost Fleet, early city views and city records of the great landfill into water lots. For the first time in one hundred and fifty years in a book, the name and motive of the mastermind of the blazes that laid waste to San Francisco six times in eighteen months is revealed. This is the story of torchlight manhunts through the corridors of Graveyard Harbor, the lynching of men on the docks, and two identical twins, one good and one evil who were mistaken for each other. It is a story of passion and fire upon the water. This is the first story of the Ghost Fleet of Graveyard Harbor from birth to burial under San Francisco to its unexpected rebirth over a century later when many of the spectral ships with all their secrets and treasure rose to the surface again and brought still unsolved mysteries with them. This is a story about the good that still exists in the worst of men.

Robert Graysmith, San Francisco, June 2023

PROLOGUE

A YEAR EARLIER, ONLY THE frail reed canoes of the Coastal Miwoks had broken the calm surface of Nature's most perfect natural harbor. With James Marshall's discovery of a dime-sized nugget in his mill race on January 24, 1848, all that had changed. On December 6, a battle-shocked, exhausted, and heavily disguised US Navy scout, Lt. Edward Beale, had galloped cross country on a secret mission to burst into President Polk's office with an official dispatch clutched in one hand and a saddlebag packed with $3000 worth of California gold in the other. The President introduced Beale to the US Senate as he was, rawboned and filthy and red-eyed. To a standing ovation, the scout announced the news to the world. After that, steamers and frigates in ever-increasing numbers furrowed the harbor like a plowed field and the world rushed into Graveyard Harbor. That is, if one could find it without any maps.

Capt. George B. Coffin, a last minute choice, was one of these men.

For once the winds were on his side. This afternoon, it was the fog which was his enemy.

— I —
BLACK WATER AND SHALLOWS

The whole coast, as far as the eye could reach, was, in a moment, spread out to the rapturous gaze of one hundred passengers, who had not seen the land but once for one hundred and fifty-five days. The scene was transporting beyond description.

—William Taylor, *California Life Illustrated*

T HE GLOW OF HIS pipe highlighted Capt. Coffin's broad features. He was a bluff man with the hard lines of a brig as if built entirely of oak and Indian teak, copper-covered and copper-bolted like a sturdy ship. He was a fathom deep at his high-water mark. His nose and wide chin were rounded as if the sea wind had worn away their edges. His clear blue eyes were deep-set and his low, steady voice carried the natural tone of a man used to command. Against the wind's howl, blinded by coastal fog, Capt. Coffin found his hearing oddly enhanced. He heard the tap of a slatting halliard, the howl of wind, and the sound of his own footsteps as he paced the deck of his *Alhambra*, but nothing more.

There was not a sound from his 93 passengers, nor a murmur from his exhausted crew. Somewhere, in the heavy banks of fog, buried deep behind a deceptive passage was one of the most magical, mystical and mysterious places in the world—and it was filled with gold. But Coffin had no map to guide him there. Between bouts of anger and confusion and disorientation, he had to fight through layers of vapor to uncover this strange land. To his mind, it was like peeling an onion. You peel back one layer revealing the next, then the layer beneath, and another and another until you have . . . nothing.

Certainly, that was it, nothing. So far it had been a voyage of mistakes. A mistake had brought him here and away from his family for years, and a mistake by the government and one authoritarian official in particular who had abandoned him floating along the unexplored West Coast without a damned map. He looked to the ragged and dirty scrap of paper in his hand that was his map. He clenched his pipe in his teeth and thought back to what had led him to this spot halfway between possibilities and impossibilities. Yes, it had been maps to begin with or rather lack of maps.

"Shame!" Capt. Coffin cursed, gripping the wheel harder. "Eternal shame on the existing Government!"

Unbelievably, the maps of the government's famous and extraordinarily expensive expedition of eight to nine years earlier were still not widely available. He had tried to find a map at Rio and attempted again at Valparaiso and been rebuffed each time. Coffin was not a man to ever give up. Finally, he inquired at the British frigate *Inconstant*. They had no maps either, not even a lithographic copy. But her sailing master was considerate enough to draw him a rough sketch of the approaches to San Francisco Bay. So Coffin had that. Pacific Squadron Commander Thomas Catesby Jones had been in charge of the mapping project and steadfastly produced few maps. Coffin wished he and his ilk were before him now so he could tell them in person—with his fists. He ventured that if these maps had been important to any political party, be it Whig or be it Tory, there would have been stacks of them at every port. They would be raining from the sky and he would have been fishing them from the surf with a grappling hook.

Coffin's eyes strayed to the words he had carved over the main hatch, words passed down from father to son. He spoke them aloud—as if he ever needed a reminder. "Be honest. Be firm. Be resolute." Unlike himself, the government had been dishonest, pliant, and irresolute by not delivering their promised maps of the jagged California coast. With no chart to guide him to his harborage, locating the headlands at the Golden Gate would be a tricky proposition. Lined along the starboard rail was a row of frozen statues colored a uniform gray. Coffin imagined some phantom sculptor having fashioned the immobile figures and posed them while he was hopelessly scanning the coastline for his port.

These passengers had been grasping the starboard rail for most of the day, waiting, hoping, and praying, one leg over the rail. Their hands must be pretty tired by now, Coffin thought. They were clutching pans, shovels, pickaxes, retorts, crucibles, and twenty-pound capacity buckskin bags to hold the huge gold nuggets they expected to trip over in the streets of San Francisco. For security, one passenger had an ingenious box with a secret lock. Another had a false bottom to his trunk to hold his gold. He must be dead on his feet, Coffin thought, after holding so large a trunk for so long.

Coffin himself was fatigued. Normally, he was an iron man who never tired, but today, for some reason, was different. It must be the weather, he told himself, that had to be it. If only it would clear.

Early last month, "a thundering black cloud had come driving along, darting forth intensely vivid forks of lightning, and looking as though it was going to blow the *Alhambra* out of the water." Never give up, keep your word ran through his mind. It was the family credo. It was his credo. But this time he knew he might fail. His temper today was sharp, abrupt, and so unlike his normally reasonable and pleasant nature, that of a poet and artist and bold adventurer.

"On breaking into the after-hold to get at a reserve of water, " Coffin recalled, "I was startled to find half the casks empty and put the passengers and crew on rations." Tom Reid's ship was two days ahead of the *Alhambra*, but Coffin lost her when he put in for water.

At 2:00 PM, there was movement among the frozen, gray statues to starboard. A passenger, Mr. Cumstock had torn himself away from the tableau. Coffin watched him as he drifted to his side like a wisp of ghostly fog.

"I hope you do not take offense, Captain," he said meekly, still holding his shovel, "but do you not think you are still too far *south*? It is the opinion of myself and some of the passengers that the harbor is much further north." Three other passengers who possessed that same point of view joined Cumstock as a Greek chorus who repeated his advice word for word. For most of the voyage these "experts," these know-it-alls, had been subject to the jeers and gibes of the other passengers for their ill-conceived opinions. Thus, Coffin took their advice with a grain of salt, but now he had had enough.

"Go to the devil!" he roared at this self-appointed Committee on

Navigation. "And give my compliments to his associates, and tell them to follow him."

By 2:30 PM, conditions had turned favorable. Coffin could hardly believe it. Tantalized with unexpected light head-winds and pig in a poke calms, Coffin took full advantage of them. He kept his ship on the tack which would place her head nearest his port. The fog began to thin, and he could see again, not well, but in silhouette could make the shape of the guardian mountain he was seeking. That was enough. Coffin's heart began to beat rapidly. They were going to make it.

At 2:45 PM, the *Alhambra* passed through a large school of dolphins which brought a rare smile to his face. Momentarily, they grasped his attention as he knocked the ashes from his pipe. He considered them the most beautiful of all fishes. "When caught and lying in the sun," he rhapsodized, "the colors of its skin are changeable violet, green, yellow, blue, orange, and red. It is the marine chameleon." Flocks of boobies, sea birds, were alighting on the *Alhambra's* yards and rigging. It was a sign.

He consulted his ragged scrap of paper again, folded it, replaced it in his pocket, and winked at the self-appointed Committee. He had just discerned a landmark a half-mile distant. Placing his best helmsman at the wheel, he stationed himself on the topgallant forecastle to shape his course for Fort Point, the southern boundary of a land so hidden that Spanish explorers had sailed past without a glance.

At 3:00 PM, he got sight of a mountain which forms the boundary of the entrance to San Francisco Bay. Gingerly, he put the helm slightly to starboard. On each side, a rocky bluff covered with green moss climbed nearly three hundred feet to the sky. He craned his neck. These must be "The Heads" he thought—Point Lobos and Point Bonita which form the vestibule of the Golden Gate. Point Lobos, one half-mile off the southern head and a mile south of the main ship channel, was barely visible in the miasma. Point Bonita on the northwestern side of the Gate was now invisible and no help at all.

"At 4:00 PM, October 10, 1849," Coffin wrote, "I glimpsed the brown hills of the headlands as a rapid flood tide swept my freighter *Alhambra* through the Golden Gate." Seal Rocks, then Point Lobos and north Lobos Rock flashed by. Then he rushed past Lands End at a forty-five degree angle on a close reach. As he swung fine on the starboard bow, he observed two wide ebony stones, the likes of which he had never seen. Black Rock and Little Mile Rock were known together as Mile Rocks, so named because they are a mile south of the main shipping channel leading into the Bay. They rose twenty-feet above the water attracting mist and unwary hulls to their demise. Unmarked by light or bell buoy, they remained a constant threat to vessels entering and leaving Nature's most perfect harbor, though in 1849, you could count those ships leaving on the fingers of one hand. The Southern side of the entrance to the Golden Gate was spotted with a group of dangerous wave-swept rocks. Some were minor, but all were dangerous and able to sink the *Alhambra*.

Coffin was cautious. He had a right to be. There was peril everywhere, including eleven species of shark in the Cove. The dim shapes of Mile Rocks slipped past to the stern as he caught the wind. There were more such rocks, and he began counting to keep them in mind when he left the Harbor and returned home. There was Black Head Rock, Lobos Rock, and Pyramid Rock, even an East Pyramid Rock. But these deadly obstacles were only a few of those beneath the surface of the Golden Gate. There were great submarine cavities, where the Gate tides have washed the channel floor to a depth of four hundred feet and pushed up the excess. He was headed toward Pyramid Rock when he encountered another dense fog bank. Now where had that come from? He looked astern and was shocked.

Heavy fog was funneling in from seaward like an express train. The hairs on his neck rose. These vaporous barriers of growing depth and crushing thickness were the "The Diablo," which is what the Spanish called the Devil, the daily northwester which channels morning and late afternoon fog through the Golden Gate. Shaped like an arrow of vapor, the Devil swept over the *Alhambra* and shrouded her as it swept toward the shore. The Devil was leading the way and Coffin was following, unable to see a foot ahead.

His greatest fear was that once he had broken through the walls of vapor, battered and kicked and pummeled like a prizefighter to the other side there would be naught there. Then, silence. Coffin was stunned. The *Alhambra* had entered an area of inaudibility and Coffin found himself not only blind, but deaf to all around him. The odd configuration of the shoreline and cliffs at the Gate deflect sound waves and make any signals such as fog bells ineffective. It was too dangerous to proceed and he anchored for the night. He knew he was close. He heard a strange clanking and groaning—the Ghost Fleet was breathing and beckoning to him to come and join it—forever.

BY LAMPLIGHT IN HIS CABIN, Coffin busied himself while keeping an ear cocked for activity at the Gate. He heard nothing. He waited for the fog to clear but would have to wait for dawn so he could be sure of his location and the myriad obstacles ahead. He got out his colors and inks. A skillful artist, he had painted a watercolor of his 694-ton freighter departing the Mississippi on April 14. It was his way of remembering the ship if the worst happened. Eight months earlier, when speculators bought the *Alhambra* and engaged him as skipper, the freighter had been in poor shape. He had fixed that.

On an earlier February day this year of 1849, he had arrived at New Orleans in command of the *Ocean Queen* of Newburyport from Liverpool for New Orleans having on board 350 steerage passengers. The passage had been long the first part of it exceedingly boisterous, but nothing like this one. "At New Orleans, Capt. Henry Shoof had come on board to relieve me as being part owner. As I was leaving for home I received an application of a ship about to leave, fitted out for California with freight and passengers. I felt it was my duty to accept the situation and I was placed in charge of the old ship, *Alhambra*, to put her in condition for the voyage, and to fit her for 200 passengers."

"That first day in New Orleans I found her completely run out of tackle," he recalled, "and rotten fore and aft. I put the vessel in dry dock to replace the copper sheathing and ship's rigging for $10,000. Everything was done and furnished that I could think of to make passengers comfortable during the long voyage," he said. Of an orderly bent, he also drew a detailed plan of his intended alterations and good intentions. He had dipped his pen in India ink and captioned the design, "Plan of Berth Deck, Ship *Alhambra*." With a flourish, he signed it: "By Capt. George Coffin." It was good enough to frame.

Following his plan, builders constructed thirty-eight double staterooms, each six-foot-square, in two rows and provided new mattresses, extra blankets, spare bedding and sets of dishes. They added a kitchen on deck and quarters for the crew and first class passengers and placed four long dining tables between the main mast and mizzen mast. The smaller cabin was for the crew who were usually crammed below deck in the noisy forecastle. Coffin and the supercargo would occupy the aft portion of the larger cabin. Six passengers, who had paid extra, were to live in the forward portion. Below decks at the stern, they installed quarters for a surgeon and servants, six-foot-square staterooms with ample ventilation along the starboard and port bulkheads.

During the outward voyage, Coffin had written four issues of a shipboard newspaper, *The Emigrant*, and composed amusing doggerel for it. The first two issues consisted of two pages of foolscap written out in full by Dr. Moss, a passenger. One motto began, "We can all of us preach patience to others, but to practice this virtue ourselves is quite another and far more difficult matter."

For certain, Coffin was learning the lesson of patience.

The next morning, Thursday, October 11, the fog began lifting. Bit by bit, Coffin realized he was at the entrance of a huge bay extending to the eastward about three to five miles. A high, steep promontory was on the southern shore. On all sides distant mountains at the Gate hid the Cove from the prying eyes of passing ships. As a man of strong will, a man of iron, Capt. Coffin intended to shove aside one clouded wall after another until he had reached his goal. But now the morning Diablo came sweeping shoreward. The wind behind Coffin was as the rumbling of a train. The decibels were shaking his balance at the wheel. The fog kept coming and hurled over his head. He watched it head shoreward. The Diablo is usually much worse in the morning though it rarely covers the entire city. Some areas of San Francisco are always still visible. Coffin hoped the unseen shore might be one of these.

The mist cleared, backing away from Coffin at such speed that he felt he was flying backwards. He put his anger to work. Punching, battering his way ahead—nothing was going to stop him—another blow—through the mist, he could see bits and pieces of the seaside scattered like a shattered mirror.

As the *Alhambra* veered northeast, then rushed through the Gate on a tidal wave of ocean fog, his passengers and crew gave the thirty-five year old captain three lusty cheers—well-deserved after a 180-day voyage in which he had spent much of his own money to refurbish the ship so that his passengers and crew would be comfortable.

"If I possessed a taste for it," Coffin remembered, "I might have received a warm embrace from every lady on board."

A magnificent harbor opened before his eyes. As if to welcome the *Alhambra*, the sky filled with white gulls, ducking, soaring, and spreading their wings, their *ha, ha, ha* echoing across bright blue water. Coffin began drawing his own map of Graveyard Harbor since he had none. He was gazing upon a land of overlapping half-circles: from the narrow crescent rim constituting the beach to a chain of wild and terrible mountains forming an insurmountable half-circle from the Presidio to the Mission to Rincon Point. Such an anchorage was beyond measurement. Coffin attempted it anyway.

The main part of the freshwater estuary, the largest in the country, measured three to four miles east-to-west. Five miles southeast of the Gate, the Ghost Fleet spread for two square-miles. Graveyard Harbor's considerable length from north to south was far more difficult to ascertain. Coffin visualized its silhouette as a bright blue salamander with a tail some sixty miles long, its tiny feet representing tributaries. Because fog covered the southern end, he reached no definite conclusion as to its length.

He looked for landmarks above, and found only lofty sand hills, naked brown slopes, and pitched tents of denim. As for the shoreline itself, it was thickly studded with dark hulks of all descriptions riding at anchor both north and south. Strain as he might, Coffin could not see beyond the forest of masts in the eastern portion of the Cove. "I never saw so many ships at anchor in one port in my life," one observer whispered. "I went up the masthead and tried to count them, but they were so thick I found it impossible. Ships, ships and ships beyond ships stretching away to the southeastward of every craft of sail, of every grade, of every shape of spar, of every rig of vessel, representing every nation that has deep water craft bearing the symbol and stamp of different countries. Ships, ships, and ships beyond ships stretching away to the South until they were shut out by the hills the city was to be built upon." Coffin thought of the sandy beaches, inlets, rivers, and jagged cliffs, which if counted as part, would triple the Harbor's length.

News of the California Gold Rush had overtaken many ship's captains who altered their course to sail to San Francisco and more coming every day.

To his right, the sand hills of San Francisco rolled away, rising and falling in gentle slopes. Only Signal Hill stood in bold, jagged relief at the turn of the Bay. Hundreds of windjammers, square-riggers and craft from every port carelessly littered the Cove. Vessels of all nations were here, from the Oregon coast, down through the Spanish Main and from all parts of Europe, and even the Orient, some recently arrived, some castoff for six months and all without much hope. A phantom, floating city lacking any settled form of government fronted the new city of San Francisco like a necklace.

Had shipbuilders ever expected their fine vessels to meet such a fate? After that, steamers and frigates anchored before Yerba Buena Cove, "Hitherto a glassy expanse ruffled only by the tide and breeze. [Now it] was thickly studded with dark hulks," historian Hubert H. Bancroft writes, "[presenting a forest of masts and bearing the symbol and stamp of different countries."

Capt. Coffin hove up anchor and kedged his freighter up on a flood tide in a calm.

And to repay him? At 8:00 AM, every-man-Jack, seized by gold fever, showed their heels as they went over the side in their well-varnished hats, flowing ribbons, and white duck pants. And those ninety-three passengers, whom he had coddled, advised, and looked after like a father? Conforming to established local custom, they leaped the rail with their picks and shovels and swam for shore. They had left him alone in a city of forsaken ships on a sinking vessel full of cargo with a storm on the horizon. Soon, all had departed except for Dr. Tappe, his fair, fat spouse, and plump black dog.

Slowly water began to rise in the hold. The sky began to blacken.

"Gloom! Eternal gloom on my existence," Coffin snapped in one his rare instances of self-pity. "Many of the ships, idle, worthless, and with no prospect of ever leaving, must go down at their anchors," he predicted as he surveyed the young, but ever-growing Ghost Fleet. Was this the fate of his beloved *Alhambra* and his dreams and those of his investors to whom he had given his promise to deliver the paid cargo into the proper hands and the passengers safely onto shore? He had never failed to keep his word before, but it had come to that.

On those rolling, turning ships with their up-straining masts, no crew remained to clear the cables at the turn of the tide. No faithful watch stood ready to tumble out and cry, "All hands!" when the wind picked up a choppy sea. Who would man the pumps as water crept up in leaky hulls, and strong currents caused an anchor to drag. No one, but a few tenacious skippers like Capt. Coffin. All the rest had deserted in a mad, wild exodus of golden-eyed greed. The day passed.

Squinting, Coffin studied the hundreds of ship's lanterns glimmering and swinging all around him in the fog. Had any man ever been as lonely as he? Was he to be interred in Graveyard Harbor (as the Spanish had named Yerba Buena Cove) beneath the crushing tonnage of the Ghost Fleet?

Many obstacles were working against the packet-trade veteran, ranging from the desertion of his crew and passengers to the weather swirling madly around him and growing stronger on the horizon. Who was to unload his merchandise? Even if he could find dockhands, he had no money to pay their excessive fees. Everyone was elsewhere, getting rich.

He looked to the darkening sky and shivered. Puffing out fog of his own from his pipe, Coffin tried to pierce the chilling mist shrouding the shoreline. Strain as he might, he could not see beyond the "rickety Venice hemmed in by a forest of masts." Now, everyone had deserted, gone to dig gold, leaving him alone in a city of forsaken ships on a sinking vessel with worse to come.

Coffin went below. "Brought the ship to anchor," he wrote in his *Log*, "and moored her in a good berth and unbent the sails. The next day not an individual was left on board."

COFFIN BECAME AWARE OF an excited hubbub in the thick fog hugging the shore. It was dark although it had to be late afternoon. Above the creak of hulls, came the thump of oarlocks and drip of oars. He could hear men moving along the shadowed canyons of decaying wood and rusting metal of earlier ships which had brought their own darkness. He heard excited voices. He peered toward shore, but could see nothing of the land portion of Graveyard Harbor. Of course, he realized, others were not chained to their vessels as he was and were free to roam the fleet as he was not and that was what they were doing now. A great rush of boat-hotel keepers and floating restaurateurs beset him on all sides, shouting and begging all in the name of making a fortune off the backs of new arrivals.

"They bid as high as $300 a month for the services of Margaret my cook," Coffin said. "The poor wretch was fairly bewildered and didn't know what to do, so when she came to me for advice, I chose for her a position in the family of a New England gentleman, one of the very few that had a family there and one of the few I felt would treat her right." Treat her right. That was what he prayed for. She would live on one of the ships in the Cove that had been converted into lodgings, a refuge from the sandblasted and muddy shore. "By that afternoon, the fine gentleman agreed to give Margaret a $100 a month salary, with the promise of all his wife's cast-off clothing, if she pleased her." Coffin had done that much for someone else, but in every other way he had never felt so inadequate or miserable and downright angry. Studying his deserted ship, he considered how many others he had let down. October 11, passed and he still heard strange, furtive noises, and frantic activity moving all around him and closing in. This most ethical of men had arrived in a most unethical port—Coffin, a very moral man, entered the very model of a city of immorality.

It was midnight, a new day. He dated his log entry, "Friday, October 12, 1849," in advance, put out the lamp, and wearily climbed on deck to consider his situation and a way out of it, if there was one. The wind nearly swept him away. Loose pages from his *Log* fanned out over the dark waters. He would have to rewrite those from memory for he was determined to make a record of this strange, unworldly venue. Coffin was lightheaded. He had gone without eating to preserve what provisions he had onboard for his passengers. He dared not leave his vulnerable ship and valuable cargo to go ashore and fetch supplies. In the faint moonlight, he tracked the wavering green patina of water lines. Overlapping stains indicated this or that ship around him had settled, then risen and settled again. Crates of cargo inside a hold had swollen and caused this or that ship to rise and list creating a series of other waterlines. In some cases, stoves, prefab metal homes and other cargo had burst explosively through the sides and sunk another vessel. Sprouting weeds grew out of the rotting timbers like snakes.

Even if he could find dockhands, he had no money to pay their excessive fees. The $30 a day cost of labor for each man was so high it would not pay him to unload his cargo for that was more than it was worth. And what man wanted to unload lading when he could be picking up gold nuggets in the Plaza and on every street. He shook his head. No way existed to compel men to forsake such riches and sail ships back home. As for the *Alhambra*, the flood of ships behind her had sealed her fate, that of a lifer. Pacific trade winds whipped the Bay waters around the *Alhambra*. Bordering the Bay were mud flats, salt and freshwater marshlands, and tall tule reed swamps. The Cove was stranger at night. He went to the rail. The East Bay flats were an eerie place where seven-foot high reeds advanced and explosions of flying birds blackened the sky.

At 2:00 AM, Coffin walked his ship, bailing where it was necessary and looking for leaks to patch. He had put so much love and expense into the *Alhambra* that he would hate to lose her. Yes, he would hate to lose his wonderful vessel, and his memories of his passengers. He was as fond of them as his ship. He had posted these "Rules and Regulations" on his wall to guide him:

> "The Commander and Officers of this ship will endeavor to promote the comfort and welfare of the passengers. Should any passenger feel himself aggrieved, he is requested to make his complaint to the Commander in person, with the assurance that all reasonable complaints shall be attended to and promptly redressed."

His First Mate, William Higgins, had done that. He had been the last of his crew to leave, but only because he needed Capt. Coffin to officiate in his wedding with the fearsome Widow Lathrop. The Widow had begged Coffin to wed them in Valparaiso, midway on the long coastline of Chile, but he had refused because he foresaw only disaster ahead for any spouse of hers.

"Wait until we arrive in San Francisco," he had told her placatingly. He knew the Widow's capricious nature. "If Higgins still wants to marry you then I will give my blessings." Mrs. Lathrop had resumed her seat at the table by Coffin's right hand. "She took especial care to look neat and tidy, fresh and new," he said, "and to a stranger might appear a modern Octavia." As expected, Higgins developed qualms about marrying her and ignited her fury. With determination, she set out to win him back. By the time they reached San Francisco Bay, she had succeeded. A parson spliced the couple on the deck of the nearby brig *Arabian*. Coffin gave the union little hope and he was right. Shortly afterward, she became infatuated with a well-known debauchee and had her marriage to Higgins annulled. She got his money, and the authorities got his horse and cart. All Higgins got was peace of mind. As far as Coffin was concerned that was more than enough.

He laughed in his empty cabin, recalling how fond Mrs. Tappe was of cabbage cut into small strips and salting them. "She was a rosy-cheeked corpulent lady," he recalled. "On sauerkraut days, Mrs. Tappe would seize the dish and fill her plate and eat it as fast as she could, keeping her eyes fixed all the time upon the main dish, and appearing to be mentally saying. 'Now, don't anybody empty that dish till I can get another chance at it.' The sauerkraut had a tendency to keep her body corporate in a condition to please the doctor, her husband. Oh, sauerkraut, nothing like sauerkraut!"

ONSHORE, THE PERPETUAL MOAN of sand down newly carved streets had been the city's background music.

No more—the ceaseless bumping of hulls had become a constant gray noise. Each morning, San Franciscans woke to a mournful flapping of sails and groan of ships straining at their cables. Each night, San Franciscans drifted to sleep to the lullaby of an icy wind whistling through slack rigging. Southeasterly breezes set the abandoned vessels—floating and still seaworthy, beached and mud-bound and bursting with cargo, to dragging their anchors as they struggled to free themselves from the shallow Cove. Coffin could have told them it was useless. Was he to be buried beneath the crushing tonnage of the Ghost Fleet? He listened all night to the rhythmical thumping of hulls and howl of wind—the siren song of Graveyard Harbor which lulled him to sleep at half hour intervals and awakened him at equal intervals. Coffin was not only an artist, but a poet. These lines from "The Tempest" came to the highly educated skipper:

> "The music crept upon me upon the waters, Allaying both their fury and my passion with its sweet air; thence I have follow'd it; or it hath drawn me rather. But tis' gone. No, it begins again."

During the outward voyage, Coffin had written four issues of a shipboard newspaper, *The Emigrant*, and composed amusing doggerel for it. The first two issues consisted of two pages of foolscap written out in full by Dr. Moss, a passenger. One motto began "We can all of us preach patience to others, but to practice this virtue ourselves is quite another and far more difficult matter." For certain, Coffin was learning the lesson of patience.

As waves threatened to sweep over the *Alhambra*, Coffin gazed mournfully toward the still invisible shore. He had no way to reach it. His ship needed him, for bailing and guarding the valuable merchandise. While puffing out clouds of his own fog from his pipe, he tried to pierce the chilling mist shrouding the shoreline. The fog was unique to San Francisco. Strain as he might, he could not see beyond a beach hemmed in by a forest of masts.

When the haze cleared and vessels slowly swung about with the tide, a narrow aperture was created through which Coffin could see a slice of the shore. There was movement there. It took him awhile to figure out what he was seeing. A crowd of men, trousers tucked tightly into their high boots like pantaloons, were swarming about Montgomery St, swimming for their lives in the mud shore of the bold amphitheater. No sooner had they begun trudging along the mud flats, than they sank up to their knees and, cursing, sank to their hips. Then, they had to call upon their friends to save them. In turn, those friends needed to save themselves by calling on another set of friends, and so it went.

Huddled on his canting vessel, Coffin eyed the muddy battlefield. It stood in contrast to the cool refuge of Graveyard Harbor, a city upon the water where he had always wanted to live. It was outrageous that he had made the long trip here but could not travel the last 200 yards to shore, or make out any but a small portion of it beyond the fog.

On MONDAY AFTERNOON, OCTOBER 15, bad weather and heavy winds were nipping at the surface of the Cove, and because of this Coffin began to make out the ships surrounding the *Alhambra*. It was as if a curtain had pulled back and he was the audience. He had not realized that he had shipboard neighbors within speaking distance. He was glad of the company and felt less alone. There might be someone who could run the occasional errand for him since he could not leave his *Alhambra* as it was now. He began to recognize faces and place names to them. He saw Capt. Edward King visiting the *Susan S. Owens*. King was the newly appointed Harbor Master of the Port. It made Coffin wonder how anyone could call this crowded disarray of abandoned ships, piles of cargo, and shallow water a "port."

The *Owens* had arrived a day earlier with eight women aboard. "Ladies of the Lake," Coffin called them until he learned their names. One such "Lady of the Lake" was Sophia Eastman, a dark-haired, eighteen-year old teacher from Massachusetts. "I can perform all kinds of labor," she said, "but teaching would be preferable to any other kind." She and her companion, Mrs. Wright, had arrived in Graveyard Harbor aboard the *Colorado* a week before Capt. Coffin. When Mrs. Wright, who had brought a portable tavern house with her, died, Sophia became a nurse at the city hospital.

The City Council's first official order to Harbor Master King was to untangle the packed mass of ships on the waterfront. An impossible job, a miserable job, Coffin thought, and one he doubted King would attempt, though he might make furtive attempts simply for show. There were now over five hundred ships in the harbor with more arriving every day. The Council's second command to King was to remove all vessels not receiving or discharging cargoes to Wood Island or to the southern side of Rincon Point. Coffin watched as King, his spouse, and Dr. Hardy left the *Susan S. Owens*, and rowed to the merchant ship *Andalusia* where Dr. Hardy was a passenger.

Twenty-one days earlier, Capt. Codman out of Baltimore had guided the *Andalusia* to her berth with difficulty and with considerable ease managed to entangle her bow with several ships. Once he had extricated the *Andalusia*, Codman safely moored her just to the north of the *Alhambra*.

All around the *Andalusia*, vessels floated in such close proximity that Anne Willson Booth, another of Dr. Hardy's fellow passengers and the young niece of the ship's owner, Wesley F. Willson, was able to chat amiably over her clothesline with them. As Coffin gazed upon the same rolling swells as she did, he watched Dr. Hardy assist the Harbor Master and his wife aboard the *Andalusia*. Capt. Codman had some time ago told Anne that King should be pleased to bring his wife to see her, and she had begun to fear he had forgotten his promise.

"I was very much pleased with Mrs. King," Anne told Coffin later, "whom I found a pleasing, intelligent person. She is from Massachusetts, and has resided in this country upwards of three years. She tells me that there were but two houses when she first came and there were but two vessels lying in the harbor."

Coffin made coffee and went to the bridge. Leaning on the rail, he watched steam drift off his cup into the fog. He parted the steam with a wave of his hand and saw Anne's Uncle Wes at the *Andalusia's* stern. "Come to breakfast in the morning," Wes was calling out to several gentlemen passing in a skiff. His words echoed over the gray waters. Coffin wished he was speaking to him. He yearned to join them, but could not, not yet. He watched as Uncle Wes rowed to morning marketing ashore and disappeared into the fog. Upon Wes's return in much worse condition, Coffin wasn't sure he wanted to go ashore—ever. Soaked and shivering, Uncle Wes, who had coveted boots and oiled clothing as much as fresh fruit, had returned nearly empty-handed. Begrudgingly, he had paid eleven dollars for a leg of mutton and a handkerchief full of potatoes and onions. He climbed back aboard the *Andalusia,* filled with disgust at the high prices and deep mud.

"Pedestrians have to be careful to retain their foothold," Uncle Wes cautioned. "In places the mud is four-feet deep. A few evenings ago, I dined at William Buckler's City Hotel and judged the fare very ordinary indeed and badly cooked."

Caroline Stoddard, who resided on a ship near Capt. Galagher's schooner, *A. Emery*, had a different outlook, a far brighter one. "Mr. Sanford called," she said, "and accompanied Anne and I in our boat onshore. [We] landed at his residence, which is on the wharf—very convenient to the business part of the city. We found a cheerful bright coal fire in a grate in his parlor. We took a peep into his and Mr. Morgan's bedroom, where everything is in perfect order and neatness. It looked much more like home comfort than anything I had seen."

As families moved ashore and housing became more difficult to find, more and more passengers decided to remain aboard the vessels which had brought them to the Cove. "Contributing to women's apparent absence were the numbers of San Francisco women living unseen aboard ships," historian JoAnn Levy observed. It was estimated that more than half the women of San Francisco lived upon the water. Coffin could see why. Any ship was heaven compared to the howling sand and fleas of the shore. Some lived in relative luxury in fine, paneled staterooms filled with beautiful furniture, their every need attended to by servants. None lived more comfortably than Mrs. Smith, a commodities dealer. When she heard about a vegetable shortage on her way to San Francisco, she used her junk jewelry to buy onions and quinces at a Pacific Isle, then sold the onions for $1800 and the quinces for a profit inside Graveyard Harbor.

Onboard the *Balance*, John McCrackan, a sociable young lawyer and aspiring artist from New Haven, Connecticut, described Mrs. Smith's home as a "beautifully fitted up...inlayed with—rose wood, her state room large and convenient and indeed the whole vessel in perfect order." Passengers had remodeled the salon and cabin and hung them with paintings. Her winsome servant girl brought a lump of fresh-made butter over to his ship. "It was from the cream of pure milk furnished by her cow which she still retains onboard her ship, and I assure you a good cow, for a lady living in the bay, is one of the most expensive and greatest luxuries one could ask." Onboard the *Andalusia*, Anne and Uncle Wes also kept dairy cows and other livestock. They frequently consumed fresh meat—steaks and fried liver for breakfast, roast for supper, and a killed pig every Saturday. Some nights the cook made plum pudding and taffy and Anne made puffs filled with preserves. She sent some to Coffin.

For a change, the sun had risen clearly in the morning, promising a beautiful day, but then Graveyard Harbor, cranky as ever, returned to its old ways. By midmorning, when Capt. Codman and Mr. West breakfasted with Anne, the sky had become overcast, then dark. When Anne first arrived in the Cove, she believed she had a firm grasp on the constants and alterations in the weather: the mornings were always damp and cool, the noons always very, very hot, dusty and sultry, and the evenings consistently cold, foggy, and unwholesome enough to make thick clothing a necessity. At 11:00 AM, fat drops of rain began to splat on deck and changed her mind for her.

BEFORE THE BEGINNING OF the rainy season rudimentary piers were creeping out into the Bay. William Squire Clark's Point served as Graveyard Harbor's first wharf for hundreds of arriving vessels in the Cove. Clark, ex-Army scout and Indian fighter, had lengthened his stone pier at the foot of Broadway. Visualizing "a magnificent city rising out of the sea," he felled giant trees for piles. Unable to find a pile-driver, he lifted 1200-pounds of iron from a whaler, ballasted it with pig iron from Sausalito, and lashed the works together into a giant hammer. With the windless of a wrecked ship, he made a pile-driver to sink timbers around the rocky ledge of *Punta de la Loma Alto*. One drawback—passengers were compelled to wade through the boggy marsh at the foot of Broadway to shore and emerge on the other side as muddy scarecrows.

"His success was great at first," Coffin learned, "and he went on and built a pier from the ship to the foot of Sacramento Street, and erected warehouses on it at a great outlay, hiring money at the usual rate, which was ten percent a month." Clark kept three deserted ships permanently docked at his wharf for storage, but could not tame the treacherous marsh surrounding them. When a financial reverse overtook him, he could not pay his bankers and they seized his property.

Clark's Point sufficed until June 24, 1849, when Capt. Weare moored his 513-ton sail-ship *Philadelphia* there to dump a cargo of coal and have its hold refitted with tiers of bunks. When an arsonist set the ship afire at the wharf, Clark let the *Philadelphia* burn at the water's edge, ordered the cables cut, and allowed her to drift away with the tide like a Viking funeral. Now, he not only had damage to repair, but competition from a new and improved landing. Dispirited, he took to drink, and died alone in one of the storeships he had so built in confident expectation of becoming a millionaire.

Skippers had begun rowing passengers to Capt. William Alexander Leidesdorff's new seventy-foot landing at the foot of Clay Street where smaller ships could safely tie up and unload. Coffin was concerned about both wharves' longevity. Without a seawall how far could these crude piers stretch into deep water before the rushing tides ripped them apart?

The water city had much to recommend it over the treeless hills, and seasonal mire pits of downtown San Francisco. In those days pioneers kept careful records of their day-to-day adventures and drew maps and illustrations to illuminate them. Coffin decided to do just that in his *Log*. Why not? It was something to do while he was stuck in place. Like a reporter, he could cover Graveyard Harbor, learn its history and that of its people, and leave his children his story—if he ever got back home.

He then went below to patch another leak.

"If this should be the commencement of the rainy season," Anne called over to Capt. Coffin, "we shall have a dreary time of it, as it continues throughout the winter months. Those who know from experience say these are mere showers, that when the regular rains set in we shall begin to think of a regular deluge." Anne, Mrs. King, and the rest of the *Andalusia's* passengers scanned the threatening skies apprehensively.

Anne recalled the day the *Andalusia* sailed round the point, and she and her husband, Lucius, had gotten their first glimpse of Graveyard Harbor. "Just as the morning fog dispersed," she recalled. "I saw such a fleet as I never saw before, upwards of three hundred vessels there. The harbor, filled with all kinds of shipping, from war vessel down to the sloop, was a beautiful sight." Her first evening, she observed pitched tents and tiny fires burning all along the hillsides. In the twilight, she discerned small figures moving about like ants in a tiny village. She considered it the most picturesque scene she had ever beheld. That first night, the uniqueness of being safely moored in the harbor kept her from sleeping. When she went on deck the next morning, she saw an odd world encircling her.

"High hills covered with a low green herbage," she wrote in her own illuminated *Log*. "The harbor, filled with all kinds of shipping, looks beautiful." She dwelled on the white sails glistening in the sun, then darkening as the motion of the tide lessened. "I think I can never grow weary of living on the water, and feel as much reluctance to quit it as if it were my native element."

Coffin felt the same way.

The weather hadn't improved by noon when he observed Anne's party headed toward shore again in a narrow boat. An icy fog, a devil fog, was rolling back in as Capt. Smith's schooner arrived from Bodega and Uncle Wes, Dr. Hardy, and Mr. Effinger went onboard to buy a bag of potatoes for $25. When nobody was looking, they secretly filled their pockets with apples and made their getaway over the side like deserters. Returning to the beach, they fell in with Capt. Smith who was to dine with them that evening. Coffin watched as they were rowed back to the *Andalusia*, eager to be away from the quicksand of the land and its fierce winds. The late afternoon was so dark that Anne could scarcely see without the aid of a lamp.

ON OCTOBER 20, THE *Andalusia* began taking in ballast. Optimistic Uncle Wes estimated that in another week or two or three he would have all the cargo out and all the ballast in. He rubbed his hands together briskly. "Then, I can drop further out and make ready for sailing," he called out. He changed his plans when a fierce gale commenced blowing through a gap in the hills, quavering half-begun frame houses, ripping tents from their pegs, and filling the streets with dust which quickly became mud. As rain began to fall, the shore became fat and indolent with sludge. At low tide, Coffin gazed over a large range of mud flats trapping unwary pedestrians in the shallows. The mud plains extended far out into the Bay to the abandoned ships. Coffin was topside when he heard of a melancholy occurrence in the harbor. It struck close to home—"Capt. Proctor of the ship *Capitol* of New Bedford has jumped overboard in a temporary fit of derangement and was drowned."

Coffin was not surprised. Capt. Proctor had been sick for weeks because of difficulties between himself and his passengers. "It is said they were a very unruly set and harassed the poor man out of his wits," Coffin wrote in his *Log*, as if he was writing one of his ship newspapers. "All the ships in the harbor had their flags at half-mast in token of respect."

Outside the sky was bleak. The sea picked up and began to beat against the side of the *Alhambra* as if it had singled her out for punishment. Ghost Fleet ships were rolling and pitching and trying to leap from the water. Flags were shredding into tiny fragments, marking the path of the currents, and dressed Graveyard Harbor in mourning clothes. Word was passed from ship to ship that more death was coming: five crew members were to be hung inside the Ghost Fleet.

"Five seamen belonging to the frigate *Savannah* are condemned to be hung for a crime committed a short time previous to our arrival," Coffin heard. "They attempted to drown a midshipman belonging to the US schooner *Ewing* by knocking him into the sea, deserting in a long boat, and rowing over him. Their exhausted victim's cries attracted people on shore and they saved him. The next day, the deserters were captured."

Pacific Squadron Commander Thomas Catesby Jones, the man who had failed to make the maps available, and thus rankled Capt. Coffin to fury, was in his office writing a letter to Secretary of the Navy J. J. Mason. "It is impossible to maintain any naval force in California," he wrote Mason, "because of constant desertion." The US bark *Anita*, armed with two guns to patrol the upper California Coast, was down to six crewmen in a single minute. The *Huntress's* recruits had deserted in an equal amount of time. A huge number of soldiers at San Francisco and Sonoma had abandoned their ships. "Among the deserters from my squadron are some of the best petty officers," Jones wrote in exasperation in a second letter to Mason, "and men having only a few months to serve and a large balance due them amounting in the aggregate to ten thousand dollars."

Jones already had any deserter caught ashore flogged through the fleet. Now, he saw an opportunity to further enforce harsh discipline. He sentenced the five captured sailors to death by court-martial and ordered all sailors in the Bay to witness the execution from the decks of their vessels.

"Jones is a fool," Coffin called over to Anne. "He will be remembered as the officer who occupied Monterey eight years ago and demanded that Mexico surrender California to the United States. He had the Mexican flag lowered, raised the American flag in its place, then two days later, ran the Mexican flag up again. For shame."

TUESDAY, THE DAY OF the execution, boats plied about in every direction; spectators filled the surrounding sand hills. All eyes were fixed on the Cove, all except Coffin's who had no taste for such things.

"Poor, misguided men," Anne said as she watched from her ship. "Oh, how my heart bleeds for them." Onboard the three war vessels where the "horrid affair" was to be consummated, Reverend William "Father" Taylor administered the ordinance of baptism and sacrament. His face was lined with sorrow. So was that of Capt. Coffin, who had turned away and refused to watch the most bizarre execution in his experience.

Just before noon, the first deserter was noosed and a heavy weight tied to the other end of a hanging rope. It was fixed so that the discharge of a cannon would part it. At noon, Anne heard the gun fire. The condemned man twitched up like a hooked trout caught on the end of a line, flying high above the yardarm in one smooth arc and breaking his neck. Anne waited, her teeth clenched, for the next man to die. In a few minutes, another gun was fired. A second body flew up kicking and flailing higher than the other, then falling as a stone.

She held her breath.

She waited.

There were no more explosions.

Thank goodness, she thought.

When Anne's friends rowed back from the naval vessel, they told her that only two condemned men had been executed. Commander Jones had reprieved the remaining three and sentenced them to work in irons for three years without pay. Three days later, the bodies of the two deserters were still hanging from the yardarms, an abject lesson and grim reminder of the folly of desertion and that of some commanders.

In the distance new storms of unusual violence and duration were crawling toward the *Alhambra*. Alone, Coffin listened to the machine gun-like banging on his roof and endured the downpour in mute agony. Would the rain never end? He went below. "During the winter," he wrote in his *Log*, "we had frequent gales of wind and storms from the southeast, which had a reach of twenty-five miles down San Jose Bay, which on a flood tide raised a very heavy sea." Storms swept the Cove clear of small boats and mercilessly battered the orphaned fleet.

At 9:00 AM, when Capt. Codman and Mr. West breakfasted with Anne again, the sky became overcast. Codman remained all afternoon as they greeted land visitors who were appreciative of the comparable luxury they enjoyed aboard ship. Having kept house onboard for weeks, Anne yearned for a real home. There was little to choose from onshore— only makeshift lodging houses and hotels of canvas with cloth ceilings, paper walls, and a few warped planks. Narrow, uncomfortable pine bunks were tiered one above another in rooms measuring two-and-a-half-feet wide by six-feet long. Lucius went ashore to shop for a suitable lot, though most of the properties and better structured homes had been sold by midsummer and the few available were extraordinarily expensive. A very small room cost $100 a month. In July, a vacant lot on Montgomery Street near Washington had sold for $10,000 and the following month, with the addition of a tiny cabin, gone for the princely sum of $27,000. Anne was "ready and anxious to embark upon almost anything that might be profitable." In the afternoon, Lucius returned from house-hunting quaking and burning with fever from exposure. Anne rushed him to bed and sat up with him all night. She feared he might die. The next day, Lucius was better. He had gotten good news— an offer on a 21-foot X 120-foot lot for $500 not far from the business section of the city. He needed a few days to make his decision. After buying the lot, the expense of getting up even the tiniest house would be enormous and they would need a spare room or two to accommodate paying borders. Uncle Wes offered him four of the state rooms put up between decks for the use of the passengers, but they would make "a frail tenement."

"It is a very pretty location," Anne reported in beautiful, flowing script, "being elevated considerably above the business part of the town, is healthy, free of dust, and overlooks the harbor." On shore, the tiniest of tiny rooms, if available, currently rented for $150 per month. The Booths got their fashionable lot for $200 less than asked, though lesser corner lots were selling briskly for $10,000. That night Lucius began tearing down their state room on the *Andalusia* while Anne prowled for useful items that no one might miss.

Sly Johnny Cole, watching her every moment, said, "I know you want to pilfer things that aren't yours." His arched brows went up. His little pink tongue flicked out.

"There are some items stowed aft on top of the sails," she ordered. "Climb up and get them down for me." She looked around. Sly Johnny wasn't there any more. She ended up doing the climbing herself. How they would laugh at home, she thought, to see her prowling about the ship's hold on her hands and knees in search of prey till nearly midnight. Anne got down the ship's mizzen topgallant sail, and in the morning went on deck to stretch and paint it and make it rain resistant.

Anne listened to the rain beat against the deck, and watched the sea begin to kick up.

"It will be our roof," she told Coffin confidently.

San Francisco rain was not like rain anywhere else, he thought, "and wondered how their makeshift roof of canvas would fare against such endless pounding once they were on the mud shore. He was doubtful such a roof would serve them well.

"It does rain in style!" was all he replied.

"We were led to believe there were but a very few ladies, if any, in this place," Anne continued. "On the contrary, we find there are some three or four hundred, of a class one would scarcely expect to meet with in this far off place. I have met several ladies myself, that would do credit to, and highly adorn, any society however fastidious in its demands ... The ladies, with a very few exceptions, are all married. To them, I admit, it is a sufficiently serious undertaking: but without the protection of a husband or father, I think it madness."

Coffin excused himself. All the darkening day, he lit the lamps, and watched the water rise in the *Alhambra's* hold. It had become a ritual.

Anne's husband, Lucius finished dismantling their stateroom and had the last of the usable lumber carried ashore so they could start building their own little cottage. After living for so long in the floating city, they were eager to move into their new home where the ground was solid under their feet. The weather refused to cooperate, like everything else about Graveyard Harbor.

On Saturday, October 20, the *Andalusia* began taking in ballast. Uncle Wes estimated that it would take him another week to have all the cargo out and all the ballast in. Then, he could drop further out and make ready for sailing. The beginning of November arrived and with it sharp storms that slashed and swept the Cove clear of small boats and mercilessly battered the orphaned fleet. As the day waned, the storm increased in intensity and hopes began to dwindle that those ships would survive.

Coffin feared for his large freighter. Many vessels like his, called out of retirement and refitted, had battled high seas and headwinds across half-a-world only to sink within sight of a dock. It was as if the sheer will which had carried them so far had evaporated at the last minute. Such faltering of purpose was common and wasted the hardiest among them. Seven months earlier, during a Bay squall, the *Flora* had sunk and its captain, S. C. Reeves, a former Columbia Bar pilot, had drowned within sight of the Central Wharf. In August, the bark *San Francisco* out of Beverly, Massachusetts, weighted down with 63,000-feet of lumber and 10,000 bricks, sank as it entered Graveyard Harbor. On November 1, the *Tonquin* struck Whalesman Shoal and sank to the bottom, though her cargo of bricks, lumber, and stoves was salvaged.

That afternoon, a large schooner lying near Anne's party dragged its anchor, drifted down upon the *Andalusia* and plunged its jib boom into the vessel's side like a sword. The schooner caused little damage but, in shearing off from the *Andalusia*, nearly ran down a craft full of Chileans.

"Some fell upon their knees," Anne said, "and commenced counting their beads."

Uncle Wes rowed over and demanded the captain pay for the accident, which he did.

At night in the lonely hours, Coffin heard the echo of his own solitary footsteps striking the deck. He mistook them for his crew and passengers who must still be onboard, but of course were not. He stood stock still and listened. He heard the tap of a slatting halliard, and the creaking of half a thousand abandoned ships, their hulls thumping against each other like so many hearts beating at once. But he knew the *Alhambra* would hold up.

NINE INCHES OF RAIN fell on Tuesday night, November 6. By Friday morning, the storms had temporarily abated. From the quarterdeck, Coffin saw more of the land portion of Graveyard Harbor. The streets were alive with a busy crowd of people who had just arrived. The sun was flashing on the hilltops where various tenements, hastily constructed warehouses, and small huts were interspersed with flimsy tents that would be gone by noon to be replaced by new ones.

"At dawn the next day," Coffin wrote in his *Log*, "I was sitting in my cabin ruminating upon my situation and thinking of the dear family that I was, as it seemed, abandoning, when the Nantucket ship *Canada* parted mooring in the midst of thunderous rain, and drove down foul of the *Alhambra*." Feverishly, he lashed the runaway vessel alongside his own, and for two days and one night, the two ships lay side by side, gutting their channels away and pitching the bow to the water with tremendous force.

"Securely lashed on each side," he said, "we blowed, and snorted, roared and bellowed *through*, not over the bar."

On the third night of unusually fierce rain, Coffin peered into the pitch blackness aware danger was approaching. But he could see nothing. He raised his lantern just as he felt a terrible crash. A British ship on the flood tide, against the force of the storm, had been brought up against the *Alhambra* and *Canada*. She had no sooner run her stem out into the current than she flew round like the fan of a windmill and drove down foul of the other two, and 'jibbooms' and mainsails snapped off like joss sticks." The Britisher's starboard bow cut under the *Alhambra's* larboard quarter like a saw and its starboard quarter crashed against the *Canada's* stern and stove-in her bows and quarter. Coffin estimated that in a short time the *Canada* would go to the bottom and pull him and his beloved *Alhambra* below with her.

He began to pray and bail. His heart was throbbing. As the tide turned, Coffin saw the possibility of salvation. He began to pound and pry. The British vessel, having no moorings, drifted off, hung tantalizingly in the air, and crashed broadside onto the bow of the *Xylon*, which was pitching and rolling wildly not far from the *Alhambra*. The cutwater of the *Xylon* rose with the high harsh sea and like a huge cleaver slashed down on the rail. Once! Twice! It cut deep into the British vessel amidships. The Britisher, crushed, immediately sank. The *Canada* followed upon her heels. The *Alhambra* almost joined her, but Coffin had wrenched her free only minutes before they plunged to the floor of the Cove.

Taking advantage of a short break in the storm, he turned the *Alhambra* through the new opening toward Long Wharf. He ran her aground on the mud flats among fifty other abandoned craft on the shores of Graveyard Harbor.

W HEN THE RAINS LET up on Sunday morning, December 2, Coffin decided to attend Divine Services and pray for deliverance from the dire predicament in which he found himself through no fault of his own. He left the *Alhambra* angled on a mud flat, and trudged west toward the Square where today the first religious services in Graveyard Harbor were to be held. "The first time I went onshore," he observed, "I was like a countryman in London, completely bewildered. The next thing that struck me was the extravagant price of marketing. In this region where cattle were last year slaughtered for the hide alone, beef was now selling in the market at fifty cents a pound and pork and mutton seventy-five cents a pound. And here vegetables of a quality superior to all grown anywhere else yield one hundred percent more than New England. I had to buy potatoes at the rate of twenty-five cents per pound. Butter, cheese and lard was one dollar each for one pound. Eggs were ten dollars per dozen or one dollar for one egg. Yet, numerous restaurants were crowded with customers."

The first thing he had to learn was to walk all over again.

"I saw that those who had been in Graveyard Harbor longer, the more experienced, were wearing boots that reached up to their thighs. They went dashing about, taking enormous strides that I could never hope to equal. My waders were puny alongside their mighty boots. Every few feet, I had to stop and shake mud from my shoes. The ground was so soft and so cut up by trucks and carts, it was impossible for me to get along without sinking up to my knees."

The dust of fall had become the mud of winter during long rainy weeks until all of San Francisco was a slough. Rushing streams poured down mud streets into the shallow Cove making it even shallower with its silt and garbage and keeping the bigger ships at length where they could not tie up. "Men go about plunging into mud and puddles for there are no pavements," commented one observer. Snorting horses, braying mules, and drunken men were dragged eyeball-deep. Water rushed beneath the temporary city creating sinkholes, quagmires, bogs, and mud pits that sucked everything below. In desperation animal carcasses and unsalable goods were chucked into the quicksand along Clay and Jackson, anything to fill the insatiable mud. The filling-in had begun on Montgomery St. because the harbor's shallowness prevented deep-draft brigs, colliers, brigantines, schooners, and windjammers from unloading directly onto the waterfront. Coffin looked around. New arrivals staggering along unpaved arteries rarely made it to the end. Coffin heard that three men who had only tripped into the mud, were sucked beneath. The following spring, their corpses would be discovered sliding along under Montgomery St. as if on a toboggan run. Heavy wagons—mule team, cargo, and drivers still furiously whipping their teams, disappeared beneath the quicksand and became part of Graveyard Harbor.

Coffin stepped from plank to mud hill to crate, and back to plank again. While performing his clumsy tiptoe ballet, he saw "the wonders of the place." There were few. In carefully passing along the waterfront where abandoned ships were pulled up onto dry land to become homes, he wasn't careful enough. He stubbed his boot against a bundle of sharp mill saws their owner could not be bothered to see after. His disgust at this perfect desert of mud brought about a change of mind. It made him pine for his watery home aboard a freighter. To him, that was the most wonderful life possible—when conditions permitted.

From the water, the Gold Rush town had appeared small, meager, and impossible to decipher because of the dense forest of masts between the *Alhambra* and shore. Today had been a gold-like dawn in the midst of so much destruction. Yet, real gold had also brought San Francisco so much loss of life and misfortune. Unimpeded by obstructions and in the cold light of this brighter day, he saw that San Francisco had grown in just the few days he had been there. Named streets were springing up and rudimentary attempts at piers were being made at the ends of those streets to go with established piers—to reach out and interconnect and form a latticework for a city. Now the piers were in a race with each other. He looked to the surrounding hills. Squatters had pitched hundreds of tents a mile from the city on the eastern portion of the semicircular Cove and given the sandy level, over a mile and half square, the improbable name of Happy Valley.

"It is neither a valley," he snorted, "nor is it happy. It is a region of gloom and the birthplace of all pestilence that afflicts Graveyard Harbor."

He sat down on a barrel of beans to take in the vast expanse of the Ghost Ships for the first time drifting around him. They were nudging against each other like one huge family. Discarded cargo lay everywhere. Every by-place, cranny, and cave was filled with discards. Such was the case with a large portion of the goods brought to this anomalous place. Bills of lading provided that goods not called for in thirty days were to be sold at auction of the ship master or consignees. Unsold and uncalled for, such cargo was chucked into the insatiable maw of the Cove as fill. The citizens of Graveyard Harbor were doing their all to move the shore out to deeper water.

While the western side of the Bay was wide, its continental portion was scarcely deep enough to float a matchstick. The estuary of the Cove was shallower than Charges Harbor—eight feet where the brief inshore bottom sloped to barely eighteen feet from where it met the Bay. Further out, the water deepened a little, to twenty-five feet, but certainly no more than forty feet—ever. Graveyard Harbor's shallowness presented a dilemma to every ships' master. The Cove could not accommodate their large freighters and frigates close enough to unload their heavy cargoes even if willing crews could be found and their masters could afford the excessive unloading fees.

Coffin eyed the garbage and offal floating on the water, a kind of oily slick that he could smell. He suspected disease was going to be an ongoing problem in the Cove and especially in Happy Valley, and worried how it would affect his neighbors. At least, Anne and her husband were transitioning to a home on land high above the shore where they would be safe. He saw her now and waved. She had weathered the storm as he had and was headed in a Whitehall boat for the divinities just as he was. He inquired of the progress of her new home.

"When the *Andalusia's* cooks deserted for the gold fields," she said, "Lucius, who has been working sick from dysentery, decided we had to reduce the number of family onboard. The children are a great annoyance. It generally happens, when Uncle Wes has company in the cabin, they both have a spell of crying, which makes it anything else than agreeable."

Coffin wished her good luck, but said nothing of his own dilemma. There was no reason to burden her. She had enough to worry about. Still unable to unload his cargo, Coffin was dancing 'impatient attendance' onboard the *Alhambra*, not in the water, but in a saltless sea of mud. The Sunday services in the Square were not to begin until 3:00 PM, though in the future they would start at 9:00 AM. This gave Coffin time to commit to memory the names of ships scattered topsy-turvy about him on the shore. Some had been called out of retirement, refitted, and remade. Others, patched and held together with spit and nails, had battled high seas and headwinds across half a world only to sink within the confines of Graveyard Harbor within a few feet of a pier.

He had plenty to occupy himself now that he was writing again. He remembered what enormous pleasure he had derived from filling four issues of his own shipboard newspaper with his poetry, anecdotes, and descriptive narrative. So well-received was his journalism that the *Alhambra* passengers nearly rioted waiting for the second issue and Dr. Clark had to read the handwritten paper aloud to them. Coffin had written of the graceful demeanor, superb carriage, and elegant movement of the Valparaiso women he loved and in a piece, "Precision," had cautioned that, "precision is an excellent quality, when it is not too precise, but extremes in all things are unnatural." He thought to himself how much more satisfying a book would be than a newspaper, even if it had to be published later just for his children. It was very important to him that any project he began, be finished. The Ghost Fleet deserved a biography, and so he began filling a book he dubbed his *Log*.

At each ship Coffin reached, he asked questions of the becalmed and bewildered skippers. In this way, he learned their stories, their successes, and failures, their sins and transgressions, and of the faithless passengers and ungrateful crews who had abandoned them. Graveyard Harbor, he vowed, would never get the *Alhambra*. By God, he would sell her before he would let that happen. He shook an imaginary fist at the ghostly armada, then went to find shelter from a sudden brief shower. Under the prow of a ship extending onto a mud street, he leaned back and surveyed a world unlike any other. He began with the facts. San Francisco Bay is at once mysterious, lovely and vast—450 square miles of water within its one hundred mile shoreline. Though the Bay was capacious enough to hold the world's navies, its shoreline remained a coastal Sahara. Essentially everything south of indestructible Telegraph Hill, east of Montgomery between Broadway and California Streets, was underwater.

From the high tide line, Montgomery St, to the base of Nabob Hill five blocks away, San Francisco was a wasteland of sand mountains. Steadfastly, they trooped over the instant city, tripping over the occasional dwarf tree, and cursing all the way. A necklace of towering dunes ringed downtown. One eighty foot high sand mountain loomed on Market at Third St, and reached halfway to Fourth. A second dune towered fifty-feet at the intersection of Bush and Kearny. At the southwestern corner of Geary and Stockton, a third sand peak stretched its way back to Market and Fourth. Finally, a sixty foot high sand alp straddled Second and Market. This amphitheater of fearful summits was flanked by a range of low hills southward separating it from Hayes Valley.

The ground sloped most dramatically upward to Nabob Hill's precipice of 376 feet. The terrain was too steep to permit horses to pull wagons from ships to warehouses where cargo could be unloaded and too solid to be pancaked. Below, the commercial district pushed tight against the pebbly beach, but no further. The city yearned to move a mile out into the Cove to a depth of thirty-five feet where deep water vessels could anchor and relieve the congestion of the water city, but got no further. Thus, in its quest for flat land, San Francisco restlessly spread not only sideways and across dunes and hillocks, but crept piecemeal into the shallows of Graveyard Harbor where the Ghost Fleet rocked and in turn began to crawl upon land itself.

To prevent the endless desertions to the gold fields, prudent civilian captains had begun anchoring further out in the stream and allowing local lighters to ferry passengers and freight to the northernmost end of the Cove. During Bayard Taylor's first sunrise in the Cove he had watched as lighters "warped out from ship to ship," and to Clay Street to meet "carts and porters busy on the beach." Flat barges poling along the shallows carried the bulk of freight. Bay taxies and coasting schooners were created, but grew more expensive in the day-to-day discharging of animals, vegetables, and hay for the market in an atmosphere of insatiable greed.

Coffin reached the Square. Not long ago, it had been a scraggly potato patch tended by a Mexican local, Candelario Miramontes. "Three sides of the Square were mostly occupied by buildings," one pioneer recalled, "which served the double purpose of hotels and gambling houses, the later being regarded at the time as a very reputable profession." Nearly all the gambling houses, the best houses in the city, fronted on that square. "Crowds were going in and out, fortunes were being lost and won, and terrible imprecations and blasphemies were let loose," wrote Wilson Flint, who was there.

Gamblers were the most powerful and influential organization in the city. Such was their power, that though they shot a man almost every week, there were no arrests nor investigations—no power of law dared to touch them. The walls of these gambling houses were hung with splendid French paintings. Rough tables were piled with gold and silver, and all night, these houses, each with its band, "were crowded with moving masses of humanity of every age."

Coffin was attracted by a superannuated building on the fourth and upper side of the Square. By the rows of plank benches in front, he assumed this was the site of the church—sin on three sides of the

Plaza, and salvation on the other. The long, dark one-story of unburnt brick stood at a 30-degree angle to Dupont Ave adorned by two brass cannon and a flagpole in front. The spacious *Casa Grande* was the oldest building in San Francisco and the original Mexican Custom House. In its lengthy life, it had been a barracks, a quartermaster's depot, a schoolhouse, and now a Custom House again. Established to stop foreign trading ships from evading payment of taxes on goods left at San Francisco, it had failed in every respect. Widespread smuggling continued at all of the California ports. One tax dodge traders used was to stop at one of the islands off the southern coast when they first arrived, unload most of their cargo, then go to Monterey and pay tax on the partial load. After receiving clearance papers, they picked up the cached goods, and sold them at various coastal settlements.

There was a murmur in the crowd. People were being pushed aside. Coffin saw why. Striding toward the Custom House was a dark, glaring twenty-eight year old giant. His forehead was high, his eyebrows black, and the thick hair above his ears was flying back like eagle's wings. But it was his wide beard, like the base of a pyramid, that struck Coffin as that of a biblical prophet. The stranger was robust, handsome, and effortlessly shoving aside anyone and anything in his path. He could have been mistaken for one of those newfangled, New England locomotives seen around Pittsfield where great things in literature were being accomplished. Coffin made way. So did everyone else like the parting of the Red Sea. This giant was the preacher and the mud pit was his cathedral and a whiskey crate his pulpit. For such a fiery prophet of gloom, Rev. William "Father" Taylor was in good spirits this drizzly morning of his first sermon. En route by ship to San Francisco, his wife, Isabelle, had given birth on June 21 to a daughter they named *Corriente* (Spanish for "current"). Privately, he called her "my little Oceana." Oceana would not be lonely. While she had been born at sea, young children in Graveyard Harbor had been born within a water city in its infancy, and knew no other home.

The fearless Baltimorian Methodist had spoken at the funerals of a thousand nameless outcasts, and often walked as their sole mourner. Father Taylor had been taken aback by the lack of a proper house of worship, but took it in stride. When he needed a proper home, he did something about it. After his arrival in September, he had crossed to the East shore of the Bay and hacked his own lumber from the stately redwoods behind San Antonio Creek. He had bartered and bought cut-rate, and in this way built his own house, a roughhewn, board-frame, multi-shingled affair both elegant and picturesque in its way. Though Father Taylor meant well, his plans did not always work out. On a visit to Australia he shipped his wife a box of eucalyptus seeds which she planted behind the San Francisco dunes and sowed on a dozen ranches in the East Bay. The slender trees transformed the landscape and with their shallow roots and oil soaked leaves became a serious fire hazard to this day.

Yesterday, he had announced that he would preach in the open air at 3:00 PM in the Square. His supporters regarded this as a very dangerous experiment. The Square was the gamblers and saloon keepers' principal rendezvous, and Sunday was the best of seven for their businesses. Any interruption in income was a hindrance that had to be removed by violence if necessary. Before his service, Father Taylor made certain that Mrs. Taylor and her two friends were comfortably seated in the first row of plank benches. Theirs were the only bonnets there and stood out in a sea of felt hats and checkered shirts.

"Many of the rough-looking parishioners were men of intelligence and respectability," he said. Soon, he had them rocking the Square with hymns. Their lusty singing rebounded between five hundred vessels, one for every member of the flock singing.

"Jesus reigns," Father Taylor sang loudly. "He reigns victorious; Over heaven and earth most glorious."

His was not a particularly good voice. No one seemed to mind. His obvious sincerity made up for it. The ground was so infirm that he had planned on standing on a work-bench (such as Jesus as a carpenter of ploughs and yokes, and of men, might have used) to keep from sinking to perdition. Someone had stolen the bench. That was Graveyard Harbor for you. Taylor settled for next best and incorporated his strange choice into his text.

"I have for my pulpit today, as you see, a barrel of whisky," he preached. "I presume this is the first time this barrel has ever been appropriated to a useful purpose. The 'critter' contained in it will do me no harm while I keep it under my feet." He looked down at the barrel beneath his feet. It was empty. "I am very afraid that my timely warning, as is too often the case, was not heeded and its contents have gone down the throats of some of our fellow citizens." He would preach in the year ahead probably a hundred times on the heads of liquor barrels which stood on the wharf. He saw the irony. The following Sabbath when he preached in the same place he intended to replace it with a barrel of pork, which he said, was "literally less of the spirit and more of the flesh."

"I took my stand in front of their largest saloon," he said later, "and sang before, I suppose five hundred gamblers and as many more 'excitables' of all sorts, in less than ten minutes. I so committed them to my cause, that so far from disturbing them, they received the word kindly, and although I often preached on gambling and drinking, showed it up with all its withering consequences.

"In San Francisco gamblers and thieves are an aristocracy," he preached and all believed, even the gamblers outside setting up their crude wagering tents and the gamblers inside who were just waking for their night's work. So believed the deserters, thieves, and even murderers within the Ghost Fleet which was lapping at the pebbly shore close enough to engulf the pious and sinners alike.

"The way of the transgressor is hard," Father Taylor concluded, his booming voice and that of his flock quavering the fragile Old Adobe behind. "I hope to labor on to the time when these dens of iniquity around me shall be swept away. 'By swearing and lying, and killing, and stealing, and committing adultery, they break out, and blood toucheth blood. Let the wicked forsake his way because the way of the wicked is exceedingly offensive to God. It is most hideous and hateful in itself.'" He paused. "I have never lost a congregation." he assured them. "What is your purpose here in California? For what have left your parents and friends, your wives and children, and braved the dangers of the deep, and of the desert? For what have you endured so much privation, and pain, and toil, in the rugged mountains of California? Is it all to 'lay up treasure in heaven, where moth and rust doth not corrupt, and where thieves do not break through nor steal?' Not a word of it."

When a gambler was shot dead at the midnight hour, Father Taylor was asked to say a few words over him. He was laid out just where he was killed—in the Parker House. His sermon was this, "What are you doing here in California? Look at that bloody corpse! What will his mother say? What will his sisters think of it? To die in a distant land, among strangers, is bad. To die unforgiven in a gambling house,—Oh, horrible! Yet this is the legitimate fruit of the excitement and dissipation, chagrin, a business fatal to your best interests of body and soul, for the times and for eternity."

"Generally after that," he recalled, "whenever they shot a fellow they sent for me to preach his funeral."

Father Taylor had made up his mind to accept all the tribulations that went with being a street preacher including the sin of pride. He would steel himself "to be called a fool for Christ's sake and to be grinned at by the scorner . . . sighted by the gentlemen through handglasses, double-barreled spy glasses, and large telescopes, to be sworn at by ruffians, and to be slandered by many you call your friends. But never mind, trust in God and do your duty."

Coffin realized he had found another strong, ethical man like himself. At heart, Father Taylor was a good man, perhaps the good man Coffin was hoping to be and to meet and to guide others and who would join him in this new country to show him the way. But Taylor's sermon had ultimately left a bad taste in his mouth because of its hellfire and brimstone. When the bellowing and eye-rolling was over, he felt he had not achieved the deliverance and salvation for which he had yearned.

It had begun to pour again. The Old Adobe's roof of thick, secondhand red tiles was leaking. Its big window was cracked. In the window's reflection, Coffin saw something interesting. A man riding a burro and holding an umbrella over his head was approaching his whisky barrel pulpit from behind. Another umbrella hung from his saddlebag next to a canteen. He was soaked and waterlogged at the same time, outside and inside. His legs were extended to their full length in the stirrups. He was covered with pine needles and burrs and about as tired a man as Coffin had ever seen.

"Who is that?" Coffin asked the preacher of the older man.

"He's the new Port Collector," Father Taylor informed Coffin as he and his wife left to prepare his next sermon. Coffin turned his eyes to the office. He might find aid there.

ON NOVEMBER 12, Col. James Collier of Litchfield had arrived in Graveyard Harbor after a long, hazardous overland journey, one he was not eager to repeat. He had followed the Southern route out from the Carrizo Corridor, via a canyon and over the mountains to take possession of the *Casa Grande*. President Zachary Taylor had appointed the Connecticut man to the office of Port Collector of Customs for San Francisco Bay. As far as the former attorney and failed politician was concerned, the President had done him an ill turn. He had been instructed to act as a depository for public monies, but even as Father Taylor concluded his first day of preaching on the steps of the *Casa Grande*, the growing criminal element was eyeing the city's poorly protected stores of gold. The situation had put Collier into a panic from his very first hour of his very first day. This was the man who could possibly solve Coffin's problem.

Coffin moved aside Father's Taylor's whisky barrel pulpit with his foot, stepped forward, and knocked on the door of the Old Adobe. It made quite a racket. He could be heavy-fisted in all but his poetry and drawing in which his light touch made him superior in skill. "I have come to ask you about clearing the harbor," he began through the closed door, "and about my ship, and..."

"Come in, come in," Collier said.

Coffin entered a sixteen-by-twenty foot room with two low windows. It was oppressive inside. Both windows were dirty and cracked as an earthquake fault. The floors were cluttered and dirty. Inside, Collier was ignoring him. He was going about emptying old buckets from under old leaks and putting new buckets under new leaks. Every chair was crowded with stacks of papers to keep them off the floor and dry. Coffin was shocked by the torrent of complaints which issued from the older man the moment he stepped inside and tried to ask his question. He could only stand and listen to Collier as he opened his heart to anyone within earshot.

"The first time I opened the door to the Custom House," Collier said without looking up from his overflowing buckets, "it crashed to the floor. The other doors were off their hinges, too. Rats were plentiful with tangled tails, and swimming for their lives. The walls were so dilapidated by time as to render the rats inside liable to be crushed by the heavy roof. A person so disposed could, with a knife, make such a breach in the wall as to enter the room in twenty minutes. The Custom House has no vault for securing the public money, and in every possible way, it is susceptible to theft. I had only been inside this last sad relic a few hours before I leapt up and rushed into the streets to search for a more secure building. The first property offered me cost $2400 a month to rent. Then, I considered making repairs on the *Casa Grande*, until I discovered they would cost as much as renting another building. Nor were there any secure warehouses available."

Collier next considered those Gold Rush ships put back into "wobbly service" on the fly, such as old whalers cobbled together specifically for the Gold Rush, and fitted with tiers of hammocks for the crew. From his window, he had seen them beached on the mud flats below. He invited Coffin to come down to the shore which lapped at Montgomery Street which contained most businesses and crossing thoroughfares such as a dry goods center on nearby Clay Street. Two streets crowded with warehouses had been built on piles across the front of Montgomery Street, the dividing line separating the solid portion of the city from the floating part, each reaching out to the other. North of this street, offices stood on piles driven into the mud flats. At high water, the sea would rise around and under these streets and buildings and make pedestrians and lodgers feel as if they were sailing.

Collier asked Coffin to follow him. They headed down a slope. Wading into the water, they looked over nineteen Ghost Fleet hulks being made ready for conversion to storehouses. Collier climbed aboard and looked them over. "They will not do," he hollered down to Coffin. "Their use was hazardous, and a most inconvenient practice since it opens a broad door for smuggling."

Smuggling was the original reason Collier had come to San Francisco. He had immediately written Treasury Secretary William Meredith to request that a prefab, cast-iron house be shipped to him around the Horn. Collier, who could not abide sloth in others, had gotten right to work. Cursing his weak-willed predecessor, Edward Harrison, for his poor record keeping, he spread out a stack of soggy documents on his desktop, pounded them dry with his fist, flattened them with his palm, and began to refine and rewrite his reports on dry paper. Outside, the rain increased as Collier carted documents about the room dodging raindrops and sidestepping puddles and figuring out what to do. "I will need help," Collier pleaded to Meredith. His small office on a busy day could not contain any additional clerks, but he had asked anyway. Meredith had replied by instructing him to hire personnel at a certain pay scale. Fat chance! Clerks in San Francisco (when they could be found) were getting $3000 a year. "It is impossible to retain clerks or other officers without the payment of salaries corresponding with the expense of living," Collier replied. It rankled him that clerks were making twice as much money as he was as Port Collector. Collier barely knew Dr. Andrew Randall, a former naval gunner and self-appointed medic, but begged him to take over the job of deputy collector at the Monterey Custom House for a trifling $1000 per year.

"Why that would not even pay my board," sniffed Randall, a sickly, old man with a ludicrously long beard.

Collier doubled the salary offer and Randall accepted. One of the doctor's shady associates was John "Long Ghost" Troy, whom Herman Melville later immortalized in his book *Typee*. Long Ghost, like many slippery characters whose temperament did not make for solid citizenship, had also found his way to San Francisco looking for gold and easy ways to get it without working.

Collier had dipped his pen in an inkwell half-filled with rainwater, and wrote out the history of the harbor. The first sailing vessel to put into the Cove had been the *Mary and Ellen* (formally the *Zemo*). Capt. John H. Eagleston had bought a brig from Salem, Massachusetts, for $7,000 and renamed it for his daughters. While in Salem, he heard gold had been discovered in California and sailed for San Francisco on October 28, 1848. He reached the Cove in March 1849, but after disposing of his cargo of flour and passengers, could not raise a crew to sail on to Oregon. Sailors wanted $300 per month, much more than captains made, and as much ham, eggs, butter, soft tack, and canned meats as they could obtain, and unlimited liberty in port. Eagleston was forced to sell the *Mary and Ellen*. He was sad to do this, but not too sad. He sold it for an eight thousand dollar profit.

Collier inaugurated the bumpy transition from the chaos of his unofficial predecessor to his own iron-fisted reign. A stickler for rules, On November 15, he had revoked all licenses for ships carrying on Bay trade and prohibited further importation of bottled liquor. To curtail smuggling along the unguarded coast he chartered a small schooner, the *Argus*, and bought another vessel, the *Catherine*, to act as auxiliary cutters for the revenue marine. He overhauled and outfitted both with armament. While the revenue cutter *C. W. Lawrence* (named after the Collector of the Port of New York) rode in San Francisco Bay at his disposal, the cutter did so with a skeleton crew. Most of her men had deserted too. Fighting to establish his authority without a proper custom house or vault and with so much gold under his care, Collier was so overwhelmed it began to affect his sensibilities and honesty. After earlier methods to curtail desertions had failed, San Francisco's powerful cabal of merchants and captains passed a law imposing jail terms of six months at hard labor for ship desertion and tacked on a fine of $500 and thirty days in jail for harboring any deserter. They would need enforcers.

Next, he updated Secretary Meredith with another report on the Cove's history. "On June 17, 1849, William Robert Prince had estimated one hundred ships in the harbor. In July there were 500 square-rigged vessels, 233 of them from the Atlantic states. People arriving by sea in that month alone totaled 3,565 men and 49 women. By mid-August, 3000 sailors had jumped ship and left 200 vessels abandoned in the Cove. In October, the number of orphaned ships had risen from 308 at the beginning of the month to 500 at the last of the month. As of November 1, he estimated there were 526 abandoned vessels left to swing at anchor in the Cove, "Almost all without guard." By the following week, upward of 647 vessels had entered the harbor, including 401 of American registry. The amount of tonnage in the shallow Cove now totaled 120,000 tons of which 87,469 tons were of American shipping. From April 12, 1849, until the end of January, the aggregate tonnage of the 805 arrivals in the Cove equaled 300,000-tons. Over half the ships were American, the rest foreign.

To trace the earliest desertions in the Cove from arriving ships, Collier returned to his predecessor's files—stacks of mildewed papers encircling Collier like a whirlpool. Over four thousand men from 697 ships littering the Cove, had taken "leg bail." Without a backward glance, deserting officers left behind tens of thousands of dollars of back pay. Drying a page with his sleeve, he noticed the ink had run, but was still legible. It read: "In December 1848, the US line-of-battle ship *Ohio* sailed into the Bay, all 120 guns blazing, her rigging hanging with white smoke. Once the Man 'O War dropped anchor, crimps with drugged rum surrounded the *Ohio* and enticed eighteen men to jump ship.

"Now lads, give me a harbor full," the *Ohio's* mate said to his men, "but over the side first." They had escaped under fire from other military vessels in the harbor.

"Seamen, gold-hungry, are deserting by the hundreds every month," Collier had written his boss. When most of Capt. Alex Fraser's crew deserted, he kept the remaining few only by raising their wages to match his own meager pay—$35 a month. They abandoned vessels which had safely carried dreamers over a five or six-month, eighteen thousand-mile voyage. Ships from Central and South America, China, Hawaii, Europe, and Australia had come all this way only to be discarded in the Cove. A water city which rivaled Venice had been born, but what of its population? The marvelous timberland of petrified spars rocking in Graveyard Harbor was still growing. Many types lived onboard the landlocked, listing, and still-floating ships: thieves planning their next robbery, gamblers who had welched on bets, and fugitives from the law. He took a deep breath and went on. There were mutineers, murderers, actual pirates from Asia, ex-convicts, naval deserters, struggling captains like Coffin, and respectable families waiting for a home on land. Collier estimated a total of 40,000 immigrants, including 800 women, had immigrated to San Francisco in 1849. It would be his job to document them.

As the wind howled through cracks in the windows, Collier had begun entering and clearing vessels, and preparing a first census of the huge abandoned fleet. Stepping around a puddle, he went to the broken window, and looked directly out onto the gray, rain-swept Cove with its haunted fleet. He studied the rows of ships left to rot in the Cove, then returned to documenting the unparalleled amount of tonnage bobbing at his front door. Listening to a steady *drip-drip-drip*, he swam on among the chairs and stacks of papers until he felt he must drop. There had to be easier ways.

IT WAS DARK NOW. Both Coffin and Collier were tired. Dispirited, Collier bid Coffin goodnight, and watched as the rugged skipper trudged toward his lonely ship on the flats. He noticed that the captain's fists were clenched as he stalked toward his abandoned ship. That night, Coffin added this inscription on the flyleaf of his *Log*: "Should you be called to encounter disappointment and losses, remember your Grandfather and your Father: be honest, be firm, be resolute. Remember this *Log* is intended only as a family souvenir."

Collier wanted to quit for the day, but worked through the night, excited that he might make a change, and by morning knowing he would not. The problem of deserters was insurmountable. Capt. R. H. Pearson of the *Oregon*, knew how to deal with deserters. He anchored across the channel at Sausalito under a Man O' War's guns and immediately after the first three gold-fevered crewmen vaulted the rail, clapped any prospective mutineers and their ringleaders in irons for two weeks, well into the *Oregon's* return run to Panama. By then, he had compelled them to endure a raise in pay from $12 to $112.

To protect shipowners from costly abandonments, the Council created the Regulators, a quasi-military unit drawn from Col. Jonathan Drake's idled ragtag regiment of 750 First New York Volunteers. The Regulators were to be paid $50 a head for each runaway sailor they apprehended. But they were uncontrollable. When they attacked a Chilean encampment on Telegraph Hill in an orgy of robbery, rape, and murder, two hundred angry citizens gathered to arrest them. In a single day, wealthy merchant Sam Brannan dragged the prisoners aboard the *USS Warren*, deported twenty, and sentenced the ringleaders to one to ten years at hard labor. At the time, the city had not a single police officer to enforce the law nor adequate jails to confine the offenders for an hour, and they were released. At loose ends, the vindictive Regulators renamed themselves the Hounds and became a worse problem than the deserting sailors. They set fires for protection money, and robbed the merchants they were hired to protect of hundreds of thousands of dollars of gold dust.

In the leaking adobe, Collier rubbed his eyes in weariness and tried to shake the chill from his bones. Hands locked behind his back, he rocked back on his heels, and scanned the growing fleet in the rain-swept Cove. It was rocking back and forth like himself. "How," he wondered, "could this orphaned fleet be put to practical use?" He wondered what to do about the shallow Cove which was nothing more than a watery barricade to keep large ships from tying up, unloading, and clearing the harbor. Then, he had a creative idea. The finest steamers, frigates, clippers, and whalers brought only a fraction of their worth at auction, but they could be beached and used as lodgings, warehouses, and public buildings. Collier returned to his desk and eyed his plans for a Custom House vault, his third insurmountable problem. Outside, rough men, emboldened by drink and the spilling of blood by the Hounds, were loitering, whispering, laughing, and greedily eyeing the vulnerable Old Adobe. Yes, he needed a strong vault that no Hound could crack, one that would hold millions. He had little time before his political enemies forced him out. He had to make certain the growing fortune in city gold was secure.

"Now," Collier muttered, "in the limited time remaining, who could I get to make that a certainty?" In his rush, he made the worst decision possible. He hired a professional criminal to build the new vault of the Custom House. Fifty-year-old John Morris Morgan (John Morris or, for short, "Old Jack") had a criminal past, but was an experienced stone mason. Old Jack got to work right away, making certain to keep a copy of the combination to the safe and the vault plans.

As Collier dried the last of his papers, he was reminded that while traveling overland to San Francisco, he had been the first to alert Secretary Meredith to a fearful havoc on the horizon. "We encountered disease and death at almost every step," Collier had cautioned him. "Many left their bones to bleach. In some places there was a road of skulls. It followed the emigrants. It will be here soon."

THE SHALLOW COVE was still as death. Capt. Coffin heard the mournful wail of a horn and removed his sharkskin cap in respect. The death cart was making its routine morning visit to collect those who had died during the night. It was square and clumsy, joined together with rawhide and wooden splints on two chisel-hewed, elongated wooden wheels. Coffin went down on Long Wharf to see. He watched as a ship towing several black boats with American flags at half-mast sailed past bound for the grave and the trench. Outside, the sky grew bleaker, the sea began to pick up, and the city of ships began to roll and pitch. On shore, new refuse was being carried by rain down into the Cove to breed more illness.

"When the rains come again," he said, "they will sweep the Ghost Fleet clean of filth and pestilence and make it safe again."

On December 5, young Gardiner from *Salem* onboard the Ghost Fleet ship *Magnolia* had been sent to the hospital during the fiercest part of the storm. No one knew what was wrong with him. At first, Coffin feared Gardiner was insane, but two days later learned the true cause. The young man had died raving from brain fever. It had taken two men to hold him down as he twisted and turned and raved.

E. A. Upton, another *Magnolia* passenger, was ill too. A week earlier, a land flea had bitten him on the ankle and the bite had become inflamed. "Every little scratch or bruise received in this country is apt to become infected," Upton said. "In scratching the place, I started up the skin, causing the blood to start a little. It is now a very bad running sore and my entire leg is affected." Upton limped below deck, preferring his cabin to the infectious fleas and stinging wind of the shore. Fresh water was almost impossible to find because the city had no infrastructure to clean and filter the water. So Upton soaked his leg in Cove water, a miasma of garbage, rotted fish, and discarded bodies, the worst possible thing he could have done. The tainted water contained bacterium which causes diarrhea, dysentery, cramps and burning thirst. He was effectively bedridden and helpless.

After the first mate and crew went ashore, only Upton and the steward, a stout, double-fisted Irishman with red cheeks, remained onboard. At midnight, Upton heard a violent banging at his door. Splinters of wood showered onto the interior planks. Lantern light blazed through widening cracks. The steward, roaring, a wild look on his face, small yellow teeth moving side to side, burst through the door. Upton recognized the signs from past encounters with the man. He had gotten very drunk on the *Magnolia's* cargo of wines and liquors and was very savage indeed when inebriated. Upton cowered in his bed, drawing his legs up after him and pulling his covers up to his chin as if that would save him. "From the bottom of my heart do I pity the wife of a drunken husband," Upton said, "which she is obliged to live and bear with continually." For the rest of the night, he recoiled in his bunk as the steward raged and howled, smashing things about the cabin, and lunging at him until he collapsed into a stupor at the foot of the bed and lay there until morning.

Saturday, the agreeable Capt. Codman breakfasted with Anne Booth who was still living onboard the *Andalusia* while her ailing husband taxed himself to complete their house and load their goods. Each night she nursed him back to health. Each morning he staggered to work gasping for air. On Sunday, Anne accompanied Codman ashore to hear Father Taylor's sermon. She hoped she might find renewed strength there. She paused in the center of the Square, surrounded by iniquity and gambling on three sides, and lifted her gaze to the surrounding hills. Surprise showed on her face. Four months earlier, the lofty slopes had been covered with a kind of scraggly live-oak bush which she had accepted as permanent embellishments to the landscape. The sandy soil didn't seem capable of producing anything else. Now grass was growing luxuriantly in place of tangled brush. Now, twice as many houses as before were trooping up the hillsides, including a lopsided shanty with "gaudy verandahs and balconies."

During a break in the bleak weather, the *Andalusia's* steward, a more gentle sort than the sadistic bully Upton had encountered onboard the *Magnolia*, had decided that now was a good opportunity to clean out Anne's former cabin and put everything to rights for the new tenants. The Hardys were leaving too. He would be able to use their empty cabin as storage for trunks and wardrobe. When Capt. Hugg of Baltimore called on the *Andalusia* that night, Uncle Wes placed linen tablecloths on the dining table, a rare luxury. Hugg told Anne that she had acted wisely in remaining onboard the ship as long as she had.

"And why is that?" she asked.

"There is no place on shore half as comfortable. Or as safe. Earlier in the evening, a man started to go to the Post Office from the beach and fell dead instantly, another victim of cholera."

"It is reported there are six deaths from cholera on board of a vessel just arrived from Panama," Anne added. That might be the *Falcon*, she ventured, but wasn't sure. "If it should gain a footing in the Cove, great will be its havoc." In 1832 the country had suffered such a scourge and now cholera was killing at least half of those infected as it swiftly spread to New Orleans, then to Panama. Encouraged by wet, hot weather and poor sanitary conditions in Panama City, the disease sickened thousands of gold seekers waiting for transit to San Francisco. They had few laws in the boom town, but there was one which was taken seriously. If you shot a vulture, you would be jailed. Vultures were too beneficial in cleaning the filthy streets.

Onboard the *Andalusia*, Mrs. Taylor was sick again. At first, Anne believed her illness was due to living so long on shipboard. Then, she recalled how Mrs. Taylor had allowed her mischievous little son, Morgan, to put his dirty fingers among everyone's food. Acute bacterial infection is spread by unwashed hands, impure drinking water, and fecal-oral contact.

"Such a thing as washing his face and hands after eating was never done," Anne fumed to Capt. Hugg. "I suspect much of the illness in the Cove is caused by eating with dirty hands. As Mr. Wright, one of the passengers, was suffering from a severe attack of diarrhea, burning thirst, and cramps, Anne instinctively linked the Cove's disease to the impure drinking water. "The water is thought to be unwholesome and should not be drunk . . . without a little brandy," she advised. "Five to ten deaths per day can be linked to the city's poor water supplies. Dr. Hardy is better today. He is constantly begging me to write to his mother and inform her of his illness. I tell him it would be cruel to do so, before she would receive the letter, he will be quite well."

Anne had heard of one man being found dead in his tent. "Circumstances being such as to induce the belief he had been dead three days."

"He died from starvation, not cholera," Capt. Hugg informed her.

"Oh," she said. "There is much more dissipation about town now than there was when we first arrived—mostly confined to sailors. When they accumulate a sum of money they knock off work, and become victims of the various means devised by others to dispossess them of it. When their funds are exhausted, they are cared for by nobody, and if sickness overtakes them, they are left to die and suffer."

Anne awoke at midnight to hear her husband, Lucius, sobbing and moaning piteously in his sleep. He had been sick since October. Thinking Lucius was having a nightmare, she roused him. "And it was with difficulty that he told me he had been dreaming about our poor, little George," Anne said. "He thought he saw him strangling and he was unable to assist him. So full of agitation was he on waking, that he could scarcely realize it being all a dream. We laid awake till morning talking about the darling fellow—Oh! How we both long for him."

The following night, Anne dreamed her son had come down with symptoms of scarlet fever. It put her in mind of the many children living with their families on the water and life there. She could always identify the water families by the lines of clothing drying on their decks of canting vessels. She recalled the Erie Canal barges she had seen. On those barges, families lived three steps down from the aft deck in ten-by-ten foot cabins above the main hold. They slept in narrow bunks at the forward end, and kept a coal stove glowing all day. The children were all schooled, "canaled," onboard. One Erie canal mother lost four children—the oldest from sunstroke, the second by drowning, another in an explosion and the last, an infant, in an accidental fall. Another mother tied all her children to various objects on deck.

"Why, yes," she said nonchalantly, cinching a knot in her teeth and hanging laundry with her other hand, "they are always falling in."

Housing remained a problem in Graveyard Harbor. As an experiment, the lumber-scarce city had broken up a few Ghost Fleet ships for lumber. From this salvaged wood, they built houses such as the one at 825 Francisco Street. Charles Hare, the town's first ship undertaker, was hired to take a few abandoned vessels to pieces which he did—all but the *Candace*. Glaring, he surveyed that stubborn vessel. She had sailed as a Pacific trade ship before being transformed into a three-masted whaler—two-fisted and full of fight and with enough spirit to take on a dozen Hares. After a hunting trip to the Arctic, the *Candace* had set sail for her homeport of New London, Connecticut, loaded with 400 barrels of whale oil and 2,000 pounds of whale bone. Leaking badly, the *Candace* had temporarily docked in San Francisco and, as happened with most Gold Rush vessels, never left. Pity poor Hare. Her tough oak ribs and multiple layers of two-inch planks were too much for him. A century later, excavators found the Indestructible *Candace*, still whole, still defiant, hidden deep beneath Hare's shop where no one could see it.

One enterprising man made brandy casks from Ghost Fleet planks. Equipment-poor Volunteer Firefighters, including young Tom Sawyer, a runner, local hero of the *Independence* sinking, and later friend of Mark Twain, looted the picturesque windjammers for scarce pieces of hose, rusted axes, and leaky leather buckets. Men sawed away masts to store or burn for winter fuel.

Ever since the *Philadelphia* had burned at the water's edge on June 24, there had but one pilot boat in the harbor, the Boston boat *Anonyma* operated by two former passengers. In early July, the *Anonyma* had come alongside the *Niantic*.

"Do you want a pilot?" two captains had hallowed up to Capt. Henry Cleaveland, skipper of the *Niantic*.

"Are you a regularly organized Board of Pilots," Capt. Cleaveland replied.

"No, but we expect to be."

"Expectations won't save my ship. What do you charge?"

"Ten dollars a foot."

"Tell him to go to Hell," yelled Mate Freeman. "I have been in here before and can do it again."

The novice pilots were turned away by other captains, too. Discouraged, they withdrew the *Anonyma* for river trade, leaving San Francisco without a licensed pilot for the rest of 1849.

Capt. Henry Cleaveland had plenty of experience in making tough harbors. He had sailed the 450-ton, bluff-bowed sperm-whaler *Niantic* from Liverpool to Valparaiso. At Paita, Chile, he was notified about the Gold Rush and lashed his "bluff-bowed," extraordinarily wide ship all the way to Panama where thousands of gold seekers who had crossed the Isthmus were clamoring for passage to San Francisco.

"She came into Panama with a clean, whitewashed height between decks of seven-feet in the clear," one *Niantic* passenger recalled. "The good old ship brought her in sixty-four days, and in all that time never a pump brake manned or called for, never a creak of timber joints and never a smell of rottenness." Moorhead, Whitehead & Waddington, a Chilean merchant firm, spent several weeks fitting the *Niantic* out for a more profitable trade than whaling. Capt. Cleaveland shoehorned 248 passengers aboard, sent an extra $45,000 in gold coin back to the ship's owners, and set sail for San Francisco on May 2. Several hours out from Panama, she becalmed, and dysentery, scurvy and cholera broke out aboard.

On July 3, when the summer fogs cleared, Cleaveland fixed his position at sixty miles off San Francisco. Mt. Tamalpais was visible. Weeds and logs floated alongside. Passengers perched on the rail arms full of tin pans, shovels, pickaxes, retorts, crucibles, and twenty pound capacity buckskin bags to hold the huge gold nuggets they expected to find. For security, one passenger had an ingenious box with a secret lock. Another had a false bottom to his trunk. Conforming to established local custom, the passengers jumped ship. The crew deserted piecemeal—

five on the first day, nine on the second, three on the third—all except the ship's cook. He was excused because he was arrested for attempted murder.

Without a crew and the impossibility of finding one, the *Niantic's* owner and her consignees, Cook, Baker & Company, had been left with a "useless elephant." Capt. Cleaveland advertised the *Niantic* for sale as a fast sailer. Gildmeister, De Fremesy & Company snapped her up for an entirely different purpose. Their unusual plan for the *Niantic* involved Capt. Coffin's clever nephews, Capt. George Noyes and Capt. Eben Noyes.

In mid-August 1849, George Noyes had been contracted to relocate the *Niantic* by beaching her on the mud flats. After he, and two young Spanish sailors, Felix and Miguel, swept out a family of harmless Darien cockroaches, they removed some ballast and rigging, lashed some empty oil casks found in the hold to the ship's bottom, and at high tide, floated her by slow stages. They allowed her to drift snugly into place on the northwestern corner of Clay and Sansome streets to water lot No. 129 which was only a couple of feet above sea level. At low tide the *Niantic* remained dry above the water, enabling them to make repairs and alterations to her at their leisure.

On one side, where the *Niantic's* hull curved up from the bottom, the pier hugged tight against the ship. On the opposite side, they drove piles and sank one of her masts alongside to sturdy the former whaler and tea carrier. They used an old pumping as a pile to complete the ship's fastening. As the pumping was pounded down through its stern below the saltwater line, something very queer happened.

They struck a stream of *fresh* water forming an artesian well in the midst of the brackish and filthy water. Sensing their good fortune, George and Eben Noyes built a shed at the *Niantic's* stern to house the pump house and arranged to sell the water in the freshwater-scarce town. Soon, the *Niantic's* pump accounted for two consecutive days of ten thousand gallons of the best fresh water in town.

They constructed a sturdy stage around the *Niantic's* port side and stern, built a large wooden barn to shield the weather deck, and erected a low-pitched plank shingle roof leading to stores, offices, and an accounting house for commission merchants on the poop deck. Plummer and Brewster moved their merchant business upstairs on deck as more concerns left their preordered metal warehouses for the security and practicability of a floating storehouse. Then, they built a few houses on the deck, rented these out as sleeping quarters, and divided the hull into warehouses. Carpenters cut two large doors for carts to access the new subdivided warehouses in its hull and for lighters on the starboard side. On the ground floor a stage and a ramp led up from the Clay Street Wharf to between a deck above the subdivided hold and hung at its midsection as a hoisting beam. A wide balcony surmounted by a verandah offered a splendid view of the Cove.

The *Niantic* floated so far inland that buildings sprouted around her as the shore began to fill in. In those days, if such a vessel could find a permanent mooring place and be arranged as a warehouse with doors and staircases, it suddenly became prosperous. Refurbished, the ex-blubber hunter would earn its owners $20,000 a month in rental income over the next twelve months. Success was contagious. Even the forty-foot-square store on the wharf next to the *Niantic* was bringing in $600 a month.

The cry of gulls awakened Coffin from his afternoon nap. He stretched, washed his face, and went on deck to smoke his pipe. The Cove was shrouded in a fog bank. A friend invited him for supper. The fog was burning off by the time they finished eating and he had gotten back into his boat. A distance away, he pulled alongside a charred boat that had burned some months earlier in a blaze so hot it had consumed part of a neighboring ship's hull. The tear amidship was bigger than a sea lion. Through the rent, Coffin glimpsed ceramic bowls and unopened crates with oriental writing bobbing and swirling. Then, about sixty feet away, Coffin noticed a tall, silhouetted figure surveying him from another deck.

He instantly looked the other way. He came to a deserted whaler close to the Clay Street Wharf which was lit up with candles. The frigate was a stage to minstrels and touring actor companies. Scattered vibrations of applause skittered across the waters from a small crowd in boats. A clown in black and white makeup was holding a large hoop through which a small dog was jumping tirelessly back and forth.

Coffin shivered in the cold night air and adjusted his sharkskin cap. The long silhouettes of anchored vessels stood out against the hearth-like glimmer of lights across the Bay. On ships further out, he glimpsed twinkling green and red lights. Behind and all around the *Niantic*, loomed the shadows of transplanted buildings. He came out into a clearing washed in blue light. The first thing he glimpsed was the biggest American flag he had ever seen. The wind was whipping the banner so fiercely the stars and bars stood straight out from a main mast. The tip of the *Niantic's* bowsprit jutted into a third-story window across the street where a man in his long johns was washing up at a basin. He dried his hands, took up his lantern, and ducked under the bowsprit on the way to his bed as if it was the most natural thing in the world to do.

Felix and Miguel had built a temporary footbridge to the street and constructed tents from part of the whaler's sails on an upper deck. Coffin climbed to the upper deck where he encountered George and Eban Noyes. Glad-handing and backslapping Coffin, George Noyes went to a trunk and spread out a large blueprint he had prepared on the deck. The designs were proposed additions to the Niantic storeship. "Someday," George said, "the *Niantic* Hotel will be one of the most romantic sites in all San Francisco . . . the hull of a stranded Ghost Ship built right into a block of rugged tenements. It will be bigger, more inventive and more unusual than all the rest. Think of the contrast."

Coffin had no difficulty imagining the *Niantic* as a finished hotel—the upper decks painted, a restaurant erected on deck, and old whaling equipment converted into functional items—oil casks into chairs and tables, longboats as flower beds and harpoons and lances arranged above the doors like crossed swords in a British castle. Guests might slumber in a hammock at the head of the stairs. In the history of the city of ships the *Niantic* had staying power and adaptability, like himself. Multistory buildings, two, or three stories high, so uncommon in the rapid-fire city before, were becoming common. Wheeler and dealer Sam Brannan planned to erect a stone building an unbelievable four stories high on Montgomery Street between California and Sacramento Streets.

"I was interested in the bark *Byron* and her cargo of lumber a while back," Capt. George Noyes told his Uncle. "She had unfortunately come here too late. Had the wise gentlemen who own the *Byron* sent her out here early, at a time when they were not willing to believe the stories that were told about San Francisco, they might have realized a profit of $50,000, whereas it is now doubtful if they come out without loss."

Coffin paused. He was lamenting what might have been if his freighter *Alhambra* had been loaded with lumber. Why, her owners would have cleared $250,000 and himself $30,000. When he arrived in Graveyard Harbor in October, lumber was worth four hundred dollars a thousand, pork was fifty cents a barrel, and commission was fixed at ten-percent. "Oh! That abominable *IF*!" Coffin thought. Timing was everything as dishonest "Honest Harry" Meiggs knew. He had arrived with a cargo of lumber and sold it for twenty times what it cost him in New York. In three months he had five hundred men felling redwoods for him in Mendocino and sending the logs down in "chain-bound raft" to his sawmill near his own wharf.

On December 26, The *Daily Alta California* advertised:

"STORAGE—in the *Niantic*-Warehouses, foot of Clay Street. The whaler's owners of the ship *Niantic* announce to the public of San Francisco, that said vessel is ready to receive upon the most favorable terms. From the facilities offered of receiving and delivering goods, both afloat and on shore, with security against rain and fire."

Ten dollars a month per ton bought forty cubic feet of storage space.

Uncle Wes's ship, the *Andalusia*, was being disassembled too, a few boards at a time. Capt. Codman had sold the house over the main hatchway to a passenger for $60. He could have gotten $500 for it now, but he had given his word and, like Capt. Coffin, never broke it.

"Mrs. Taylor continues poorly," Anne said. "I think, however, when she becomes settled in her house, and interested in the management of it, she will be better."

After dinner Anne and Mrs. Reed went ashore to arrange things in the new Taylor house onshore. After a difficult ascent from the beach to the hill to first visit Col. Myers that evening, the two women ran into a friend who had gone ashore the night before and had not returned. He had a wild look in his eye. That worried Anne. She stood swaying with him a long time in the high winds, begging him to come back with them.

"Try and calm yourself," she begged. Finally, he agreed and accompanied her and Mrs. Reed to the house where he dutifully swept the chips and shavings out of the rooms. By the time he had come to his senses, Anne had to leave and temporarily return to her floating home. Dr. Hardy called to take her aboard, but when they reached the beach they discovered their boat was gone.

"Boat, sir?" a lighterman asked. "Carry you out and back for three dollars?"

"Three dollars! We are lying not more than two hundred yards from the shore!" Anne complained. "The charge is really exorbitant."

Boatmen got one dollar for each passenger they took from shore to ship and Anne knew that. The doctor ended the argument by paying the boatman what he asked, scooping Anne up in his arms, and unceremoniously dropping her into the boat. Her nerves were jangling by the time they reached the *Andalusia*. A very quiet tea in her cabin without the noise of children and scolding of their mothers soothed her. That racket was something she would not miss. Soon, they would be land people like normal folks with a yard and flowers.

William Smith Jewett sailed into the Cove and contributed a bold description of Graveyard Harbor—"Ships, ships and ships beyond ships stretching away to the southeastward until they shut out by the hills the city is to be built upon . . . and gold enough for all!"

Among the respectable immigrants came an influx of ex-convicts, thieves, and murderers so brutal they had been deported from the penal colonies of Australia. Their migratory customs caused them to be named the "Sydney Ducks."

"Neither life nor property were secure against their depredations," according to a local man, J. M. Letts, "[The Ducks] felt themselves so secure in their strength and numbers, that they did not seek the protection of night, but frequently committed the most revolting crimes at noonday, and under the eye of the public authorities . . . They would plunder houses, commit the most diabolical acts upon the inmates, murder in the case of resistance, then commit the building to the flames to hide their infamy."

Worse yet, the Ducks sent word to their fellows in London, Sydney, and New York to join them post haste.

"There are easy pickings in San Francisco," they wrote gleefully. "We will need robbers, cutthroats, conmen, burglars, an engineer or two, and arsonists, *especially* arsonists. Join us."

"Why?"

"The city needs burning."

At 4:00 AM, CHRISTMAS EVE, Upton was asleep on the *Magnolia* near the *Balance* and *Globe*, suffering ill effects from his infected leg, when the first mate shook him awake. At first he thought it was the drunken Steward come back for another pass at him. It was worse than that.

"The city is on fire!" the mate shouted.

Upton hobbled on deck, where he saw a vast sheet of flame burning everything in its path. "But unlike any such occasion in the Atlantic cities," he said, "not a bell was to be heard, not a single stream from an engine to be seen ... so many thousands of men compelled to stand still, look on, and see the fire burn, not having a single engine, hook or ladder at their command to work." Nor had they the slightest inclination to fight the flames unless their own property was threatened. By the time Upton rowed ashore, the fire had spread rapidly down the Square to Montgomery Street where there were equally silent watchers.

In the Cove, travel-writer Bayard Taylor was making another attempt to escape the City of Golden Promise when the fire broke out. So far he had experienced a mutiny onboard the Peruvian brig he had hoped would take him to Mazatlan, and now a huge fire. Scampering into the rigging, he watched a tiny spark burn its way through the fog, and burst into a broad, flickering column of red. Within fifteen minutes every roof, rafter, and foundation beam shot unwavering jets of fire out over Graveyard Harbor. Flames surged into spiral folds high above the city. A cascade of flame thundered downslope, a waterfall of flame. For hours, they tacked offshore. As the brig dashed toward Alcatraz rock, he finally heard noise—gongs, bells, trumpets, falling roofs, and terrible cries. The Parker House burned to the ground. The townsfolk, slow to panic until their own property was endangered, finally woke as if doused in cold water. They stayed the fire by exploding buildings with gunpowder to create fire breaks. Shock waves from explosions nearly rocked Upton from his perch. Then, a leak forced the brig to return to the doomed city. Exasperated, Taylor threw up his hands and vowed to give escape one more chance. He would wait until the mail steamer *Oregon* sailed on New Year's Eve. That long and no more.

From the deck of the superannuated *Balance*, John McCrackan saw pandemonium everywhere. He hurried to the Square. "Several wine stores were selected to be blown up. People were invited to enter and help themselves beforehand," he said, "which of course, they accepted without waiting for a second invitation."

The next day, as McCrackan trod the warm ashes of downtown, he was openly optimistic. He predicted the whole destroyed area would be rebuilt before a few weeks passed. He had been floating inside Graveyard Harbor long enough to recognize its fighting spirit and that of its inhabitants. "The gold and silver mines are inexhaustible," he crowed above the clatter of hammers and the laughter and singing of strong men. "Coal mines have been lately discovered and with a rich beautiful country, what can prevent our prosperity?" McCrackan was proven right. The Golden City was rapidly rebuilt with barely a trace of fire left behind and the mines kept producing.

Coffin watched with amusement as townsfolk, bursting with unwarranted pride, hauled a visiting *New York Evening Post* correspondent about in mud up to his ankles. At every sodden step, they held him in place and wildly applauded their wonderful ship-city. Truly there was nothing like it.

"They dragged me," the poor journalist wrote, "from one pine box dwelling to another that was called mansion, hotel, bank, or store, as it may please the imagination."

The reporter's mouth dropped open when he saw a huge storeship, its bow stretching into the road, between the Eagle Saloon and Bubb Grub. A ladder had been drawn up at their sterns. Next to a General Store another huge vessel had been beached as a hotel. Next to the *Niantic* was Boggs Liquor Store, the Tract Society, and a lithography and printing business. Horse drawn carts passed and men on horseback ducked their heads to pass under the prows of ships encroaching on the road."

An assortment of fish swirled near a break in the hold of an iron-hulled ship where crates of goods that once represented the hope of riches of some eastern speculator now lay underwater. The vagaries of San Francisco made items valuable on Tuesday, junk on Wednesday and landfill by Thursday. Discarded crates of tobacco bobbed in submerged holds. Dried beef caught by powerful eddies swirled in a soup of phosphorescent seaweed. Here and there along the shore were discarded shirts—all perfectly good. It was cheaper to buy a new shirt than have the old one cleaned.

The *Niantic* ship hotel at the foot of Clay St.

"In the finest parts of town," the reporter wrote, "foot passengers stumble over old clothes, crockery, boots, bottles, boxes, dead dogs, and cats, and enormous rats. Constantinople itself may really be considered clean in comparison. [They] have told me, with a sincerity that would have done credit to a Bedlamite, that these splendid structures were theirs, and they, the fortunate proprietors, were worth $200,000 to $300,000 a year each."

"What is supposed to be the rental, the yearly value, of this cardboard city?" the scribe inquired of the inhabitants.

"Not less than $12 million," came the serious reply. "Maybe more."

The reporter could barely contain his laughter. But he knew that the townsman was sincere.

San Francisco had embraced this waterborne metropolis as it built slowly outward to meet the landlocked fleet, cannibalizing the Ghost Fleet's cordage, spars, and planks as it went, and filling itself with pride. A third of wood-scarce San Francisco would ultimately be constructed from parts of these spectral ships. There was one deficiency. No secure bank, outside of the Custom House bank (which was so laughable it would have knocked the reporter off his feet), existed in the mining regions. At this time the city's only new commercial bank, an eggshell-like scow floating at the corner of California and Battery was so fragile it could be washed away by a good rain. Presently, rain was in great supply, as was the criminal element in nearby Sydney Town.

By December 31, Collier, the diligent port collector, estimated that a total of 41,000 immigrants, including 800 women, had immigrated to

San Francisco that year. Though the city had burned to the floorboards on Christmas Eve Day, the marvelous timberland of petrified spars rocking in Graveyard Harbor had increased in size. "[The Ghost Fleet is] . . . a Venice built of pine instead of marble," a Chilean gold seeker reported. "It is a city of ships, piers, and tides. Large ships a good distance from the beach serve as lodgings, stores and restaurants."

ON NEW YEAR'S EVE, Bayard Taylor at last escaped from Graveyard Harbor onboard the steamer *Oregon*. Coffin watched the joyful writer go and applauded him for his bravado. As for himself, he saw no reason to celebrate New Year's Day. Why celebrate when so much was so wrong in the instant city of Gold? Why celebrate when so much could be put right in this land of riches where people had been drawn from all lands to work together and yet did not?

On Wednesday, January 2, 1850, the Philadelphia schooner *Samson* made a long, shoreward pull against a strong tide. During her passage into the Cove, she passed ships of every description and nation. Some were ashore, aground, sunk, or capsized, others were hauled up on the mud flats and stripped of their wood to use for land housing or used whole as ship stores. Coffin wondered if this was to be the fate of his *Alhambra*. The *Samson* forced her way to a hulk used as a combination storage and boarding house at the end of a rudimentary pier. Large capitals signs advertising "Boarding & Lodging," "Storage," and "Lumber for sale," were written large against the side.

"I have never experienced shipping in such numbers before," said E. I. Barra, a passenger onboard the *Samson*. "It was as if they were piled on top of the other."

He and his fellow passengers disembarked, mounted a flight of shaky steps, and found themselves inside one of the new ship-hotels. Slumped inside the main cabin, wrung out like a dish rag, was the first elected Harbor Master, James Hagan. His pockets were turned out. He had nearly bankrupted himself by funding all his duties himself in the constant rush of Graveyard Harbor. He was another of the rare ethical men of Graveyard Harbor who kept their word no matter the cost and ruined themselves in the process.

The Ghost Fleet continued to be as restless and vengeful as the storms of '49. The *Thomas H. Benton* had gone ashore in one such storm at Angel Island with a complete loss. Seven days later, ships dragged their anchors so badly several collisions occurred. The *Ceres* was struck very violently by three large vessels and a section of its stern caved in. Coffin worried over newly arriving vessels. They would have a rough go of it. As he sat on Long Wharf, rain pelting him, he looked to the black skies and knew this was going to be a bad one.

ON JANUARY 25, 1850, fifty-foot high seas and a violent storm blew the little brig *Col. Fremont* off course. At the rail stood a slender (one hundred and fifty pound) cowboy of medium height (five-feet, nine-inches) though his dynamic personality made him seem taller. Quiet, self-contained energy seemed to make the wrangler impervious to the driving rain. Broad-shouldered, loose-jointed, slim hipped and bowlegged, he had fitted all those lanky limbs into a simple buckskin outfit. The howling wind spun the wheeled spurs on his tooled cowhide boots. His long brown, wavy hair flew away from his face. Smooth-shaven and sun-bronzed, he had piercing hazel eyes, brushy eyebrows and a light chin beard. The writer O. Henry had once drawn his portrait. He had depicted a deceptively youthful face creased with a thoughtful, careworn expression that made him look as if he was frowning.

Col. John "Coffee Hays," the most famous Texas Ranger of them all, was known far and wide as "Coffee Jack." He had been named after Andrew Jackson's able lieutenant, General John Coffee. Criminals had another name for the relentless lawman—"Devil Jack," the same name the Ranger's hung on his fearless fighting father, Harmon Hays. A Tennessean from the same region as Andy Jackson, he was in his heart a true Texan. Cool, soft spoken with a high-pitched voice, he was utterly without fear. A youthful colonel of the First Texans, the most spirited regiment of General Taylor's army.

On September 22, 1846, he had led two hundred of his San Antonio-based, mounted frontiersmen up the nearly perpendicular cliffs of Cerro del Obispado and captured the stronghold. As a subagent on the Gila, he had put down a Paiute uprising in Nevada. So many things packed in such a small package—soldier, surveyor and commander. His company of volunteers, the most jovial and hearty set of men in all Texas, were master marksmen, master horsemen and master woodsmen. On their full-blooded race horses they could attack, pursue, or escape any enemy. Devil Jack battled Creek Indians with Sam Houston and was Apache chief Flacco's closest comrade during his forays against the Comanches.

"Me and 'Red Wing' aren't afraid to go to hell together," Flacco loved to shout. "Capt. Jack, he's too mucho bravo. He's not afraid to go to hell all by himself!"

At Devil Jack's sides hung the modern equivalent of a magic sword. He had used his twin, well-oiled Colts in combat with Comanches and border bandits, and when seventy Plains Indians jumped him on the Pedernales River, he killed thirty with those guns. A close friend of Samuel Colt, he owned the best Colt revolvers ever made, the Walker-Colt .44-caliber. It had a stout frame (some four and a half pounds), a grip suited to a large hand, a large cylinder to accommodate six heavy rounds, a sturdy trigger guard so it could be worn in a belt, and a lever rammer so it could be reloaded at a gallop without breaking the gun apart.

On deck, Devil Jack was resting his hands reassuringly on the handles of his twin Walker-Colts when he heard Capt. Nason fire a cannon to signal the *Col. Fremont's* arrival in Graveyard Harbor. He barely stirred at the loud retort. There were louder and more raucous noises onboard. The last few days the captain had been reeling about the deck assailing "God Almighty" with bloodcurdling curses for not providing him with fair weather. On the California coast the West Wind blows constantly from March until October. It had lasted longer this year. Beginning at about 9:00 AM, it howls with evil ferocity till sunset. Nason lifted his arms and implored the heavens to aid him. It began to rain harder.

As the lone passenger out of thirty-nine not seasick, Devil Jack was the only one to experience their entrance through the Golden Gate. How wide was the sheltered passage? he wondered. A mile? More? Pacific trade winds whipped the Bay waters around the *Col. Fremont*. "The Diablo" sent Capt. Nason into an apoplectic rage of cursing and throwing his hat to the ground. Finally, the mist cleared. The vastness of the abandoned fleet took Devil Jack's breath away; he estimated nearly a thousand ships, an armada of white and tan sails there. "No harbor in the history of the world has ever sheltered so much deserted tonnage at one time," historian Felix Riesenberg, Jr., observes. "Those ships filled out the bight of the Cove, a ghostly fleet whose abandonment recalled tales of the Sargasso Sea... Here was a fleet far mightier in number than any envisioned by the early explorers." As the *Fremont* weaved past the orphaned fleet, Devil Jack realized that Graveyard Harbor was not dead. It was alive with thousands of squatters roving the dead wood, rusting iron, and rotting canvas that had carried them to the Cove from every deep water port on the globe.

The *Fremont* slowed as it neared North Point allowing Devil Jack to study rows of white houses on the point to his right, possibly a quadrangle of the old Presidio. If the *Fremont* had been on schedule, Nason could have anchored at the Broadway Wharf, a two-hundred and fifty-foot long commercial wharf that enabled square-riggers to discharge cargo directly on the dock. It was filled and he had to anchor further out. Devil Jack and his friends rowed ashore and climbed the shoulder of Signal Hill (also known as Semaphore Hill, Tall Hill, Goat Hill and eventually Telegraph Hill).

A one hundred-foot-long perpendicular flagstaff with wooden semaphore arms extended from the top of the two-story lookout station on the sand hills, its long arms waving darkly against the sky. In place since last September, its zigs and zags announced the approach of any ship and forwarded the message to the peak where a lookout ran a flag up identifying the ship.

Below the peak, only a few scars remained of the Christmas Eve Fire which had burned much of the city. When Devil Jack and his party reached Portsmouth Square, four native Californians' beautiful embroidered jackets and enormous broad-brimmed sombreros galloped into view. Light flashed from their silver-mounted headstalls, silver bridles, and engraved boxed stirrups. *Calconeros* slashed down their leggings. As the quartet leapt from their saddles, their long oversized spurs made a frightful jangling. Miners passing on the broad street were dressed drably in comparison. All wore thick woolen shirts, battered slouch hats, and clay-stained pants cut from canvas tents. They walked carefully in high-legged boots, heads lowered as if a fortune was buried in the mud and they didn't want to miss it. Jack navigated to the Adelphi, a two-room house on the northern side of Clay Street near Montgomery Street. In those days the ocean came up within a few feet on the eastern side of the street. The Adelphi, a slovenly lodging, was sadly one of the best accommodations available. They climbed a narrow, fragile stairway from the street, stomped the mud from their boots, and entered the outer room—the landlord's sitting and dining room. In the center glowed a large stove where several guests were warming themselves. Tiers of plain pine bunks lined both sides of the innermost apartment.

After Devil Jack secured overpriced beds for himself and his friends, they went to eat a supper of pie, coffee and hard-boiled eggs at Marye's Restaurant, a cozy eatery between Kearny and Montgomery streets. As Jack sipped his coffee, he took stock of his fortunes. He was cash poor, having received only the usual compensation for his army service. If he sold his Texas property now it would show little profit. Through the doorway and driving rain, he saw unbridled lawlessness in the street. San Francisco needed a good sheriff to sort this mess out, Devil Jack thought, and decided he might be the man for the job. An election was coming up in April; he needed a new challenge, having conquered every other obstacle in his path so far.

ON WEDNESDAY, JANUARY 30, Coffin was distraught. He had been forced to let his beloved *Alhambra* go to the Pacific Steamship Company for only $13,500. He had spent almost that much in New Orleans to make her fit for the voyage to Graveyard Harbor.

"And what will become of her?" he asked.

"She will be broken up and used as a storeship on land."

Ten days later, Isaac W. Baker, prospector, arrived in the Cove, and noted the crowds of shipping showing flags of all nations discharging cargo and steamers running to and fro like any large Atlantic or European metropolis. The flow was endless and backing up, causing unending difficulties and filling out the Cove as more ships were unable to escape and were abandoned. The *Janet* was leased and moored next to Clark's Wharf to accept storage onboard, but none of the storeships were as successful or as famous as the *Niantic*, the amazing, never-equalled flagship of Graveyard Harbor.

Five days after that, Coffin was back on Long Wharf trying to settle his accounts when a big quake (two sharp jolts worth) rocked San Francisco. He was so deep in misery and self-torment that the tremor went unnoticed. Disgusted, he threw down his ledger without totaling his figures. Why bother? His long, expensive voyage to San Francisco had erased any thought of profit and his tribulations eradicated any sense of calm. To raise money he would have to sell the *Alhambra's* boats, cooking apparatus and expensive furniture. For a man who did not like to fail, this was torture.

"I had a very troublesome time and task in getting clear of my cargo," he complained, "on account of the great number of consignees, many of whom could not be found. Those consignees I did locate had to pay seven dollars per ton to lightermen for taking their goods on shore, a distance of only a half-mile. On land, truckers would not cart the smallest load a few feet for less than a dollar. Lightermen finding no one at hand to receive the goods, would leave them in the mud, their time being too precious to them to waste in hunting up consignees. Many things were lost and ruined in this way and the owners, thinking they had a claim upon the ship, would sue, and I was obliged to obtain a lawyer and dance attendance at court to save the ship from loss."

Begrudgingly, Coffin was forced to pay $2,500 to have the *Alhambra* unloaded.

Around 9:00 PM, he headed into the Cove. The landscape felt empty as his heart. Bordering the Bay were mud flats, salt and freshwater marshlands, and tule reed swamps throbbing with life. At night, the East Bay flats were an eerie place to be when seven foot tall reeds advanced and explosions of flying birds blackened the sky. As he rowed his skiff along one of the long shadowed corridors formed by lines of deserted ships, he parted damp webs of tangled rigging drooping in his path like spider's webbing. He smelled the pungent scent of camphor from carved wooden figureheads and the odor of mildew. The pearl-like mist, sparkling lamps and silver fog bells were an alien world to him.

The storms and prolonged rains, the carpet of green on the surrounding hills had lifted Coffin's spirits, but with the sale of the last item of her cargo, he was once again a captain at large.

"Being now at liberty," Coffin decided, "I began to look about and to ponder upon what I should go about to acquire a share of fortune's favors." Others speculating in merchandise were realizing a profit of 50 per cent in one hour, and those buying lots and selling then the next day, were making a comfortable fortune in a week. "But I had not the courage or rather recklessness to enter that field." As for taking to the mines with a pick and shovel, he had no taste for that either, not a lick, nor the slightest inclination. To get by, he began operating lighters, carrying small orders of clothing, fresh meat and supplies from a ship's chandler. For $600 he bought a sloop he renamed the *Sophronia* after his wife, whom he deeply missed, then hired a boat builder to lengthen and deck the vessel. His new enterprise began well. He hauled coffee from a Pernambuco brig to the shore and earned $60 before breakfast. He first bought a scow of twenty tons capacity, for which he paid $1,300, an extravagant price, but one his new ship earned back in ten days. Coffin then bought another for $1,100, and afterwards a smaller one for $700.

"I had thus invested $3,000 in lighters, beside small boats, costing $500 more, thus costing me $3,600, would not have been worth $1,000. Had I confined myself to this business, I should have probably have done well enough, but, like everybody else, I was not satisfied. I grasped for more."

Infectious greed, the common currency of Graveyard Harbor, tried to beguile Coffin, but at heart it could not. He was not a greedy man. He was only a man who strove to achieve his best and speak the truth. At every turn, he was cheated by the boat purchasers who never paid him the money upon which they had agreed. What was not stolen from him, the crooked courts took when he went to trial to complain. Even when he won his case the defendants never paid him and Coffin had to pay the court costs.

He decided to take a second flyer on the river. Three men had started a large auction establishment, Besse & Co, and mounted a sign above it as large as the *Sophronia*.

"They threatened by their style of opening to clear the field of all the other auctioneers then existing," Coffin said. "They had been under way about a week. I thought it a good opportunity to dispose of some articles which I had on hand, and I put in 25,000 'segars,' two barometers, six spyglasses, and a number of articles left of the *Alhambra's* stores. The auction went off in fine style; bread, cold ham, punch, etc … was profusely provided and everybody was in fine spirits." His things brought satisfactory prices, and he went to his bunk that night relieved. "Settling day was two days afterward, but when I called for my account, I found the store closed. The monstrous sign had disappeared. Besse & Co. had 'absquatulated' and that was the end of that adventure."

Perhaps the *Alhambra's* voyage had been cursed, he thought afterward. All the happy couples he had brought to the Cove onboard the *Alhambra* had separated—the Bogarts, Capt. White and his little Spanish wife, and young Tillman who had been driven mad by unfounded jealousy to leave his laughing wife.

Vicente Perez Rosales, a native of Santiago, Chile, had visited San Francisco on the French bark *Stangueli*, a year earlier. On his return, he was taken aback by the change. "How different was the San Francisco of my second visit!" he said. "The Bay was crowded with ships, all of them deserted. Passengers and crews were raising the unstable population to over thirty-thousand and so intense was the activity of transient and permanent residents alike, that the city was growing and being transformed as if by magic."

The long wharves had been built out and lengthened over huge redwood piles. Slender piers, only half-finished, were rushing from every major street down to the water's edge to carry the thoroughfares deep into the Cove where they were needed. "Long piers, supported on redwood piles were being constructed, or were being further extended at the end of every street that ran down to the beach." Piers were improvised by grounding ships at the ends of streets and laying beams up to them to carry the street out over the tidal flat, and create foundations for new buildings. Macondray and Company had gotten rich accepting and insuring goods for storage aboard the *Panama*. Within days, the newly fitted storeship *Georgian* at the foot of Jackson Street would be put up for sale.

Henry Howison built a successful wharf between Battery and Front streets at the end of Sacramento Street at a depth of fourteen feet at high tide and a length of eleven hundred feet into deeper water. Buildings grew up around such piers and upon them. The *Thomas Bennett* out of Charleston, a live oak and cedar ship known for being exceptionally sturdy, now floated off the southern side of Howison's Pier, her bow pointing toward Battery Street. A pier was built out to her and she was covered and built around with stores. When the Monumental Fire House, a unit composed entirely of Baltimore men, was built the Volunteers began to congregate there.

"C.C. Richmond's wholesale drugstore sat on piles. The sidewalk was several feet above the middle of the street which was a shelving beach covered with tide twice a day." Two doors down, another storeship, the *Garnet,* sailed as imposingly in the midst of normal buildings and homes. The *George Nicolas* had been transformed into a modest floating storeship. Owing to a shortage of material for pier construction, boxes and sacks of earth were piled up at the waterline. Streets and warehouses were improvised by grounding a row of vessels in a line, then building over beams and boards resting upon the ships.

FATHER TAYLOR WAS HAVING a spartan breakfast of cold tea and crusts of dry bread on Long Wharf when there was some excitement in the Cove. The *Victoria* had reached San Francisco on February 18, and been forced to tack off the Farallones for three days because of the over-crowded harbor. When the Australian ship landed after 96 chaotic days at sea, ten crewmen charged as mutineers, inspired by Capt. John Carphin's abusive attitude toward them refitting, ten crewmen were led off the barque in chains and taken aboard the *USS Warren* as prisoners.

Among the 272 passengers from Windsor were John and Elicia Gough (Goff), and Thomas Berdue, an itinerant ex-salesman, ex-sailor, and erstwhile gold hunter. Berdue's real name was Thomas Burdeu, aka Thomas Bardew, aka Thomas Burdenue, aka Thomas Burdue. Though his face was friendly and full, he was later described as having a "peculiar sharp face," probably during one of his periods of extended sickness in the Sierra Nevada Range which had wasted him or simply because he had been mistaken for someone else, which was unlikely. He was a very unusual and striking individual.

Fair-complected, standing five foot, seven and three-quarter-inches tall, with a full oval face and dark brown or auburn hair, he was a well-built, well-proportioned man in his late thirties. His eyes were blue-gray. His auburn hair was long and wavy. A facial scar on his right cheek trailed past a strong jawline and continued down his neck. He also had a finger missing a joint from an accident when he was a sailor, and an India ink tattoo encircling his ring finger. Presently, he was cultivating a light brown beard with twin points to hide the scar. When the beard took and became thick and dark, many compared him to the traditional statues and panel paintings of Jesus Christ.

Frail, sensitive, and shy, Berdue was a hard-luck guy who had decided to get out of the gambling game and hightail it up to the mining country where he intended to hit it rich. His pregnant common-law-wife, Elen, and their children would join him in San Francisco once she and the newborn were fit to travel and he had mined enough gold to make the trip feasible. Afterward, he planned on opening a store. Born October 21, 1819, in Surrey England, the son of a Northumberland farmer who leased 200 acres and employed half-a-dozen farmhands, he left the farm to work as a salesman for a large Newcastle coal company. Convicted of pick-pocketing. Berdue was sentenced to seven years and exiled for life to Australia where he arrived as a convict on the ship *England* on September 28, 1835. Granted a ticket of leave on November 11, 1839, he married Emma Arnold in 1843, and lived in Windsor, New South Wales. Looking to make his fortune, he had sailed from Sydney Australia Harbor aboard the *Victoria*.

Father Taylor put down his crust and cup and took note of the young man leaving the ship and crossing to a gambling den. He first noticed him because he seemed out of place among the slick gamblers in wide, felt hats slouching in doorways after a night of cards. Their Prince Albert coats were carefully unbuttoned to show off gold chains drooping across brocade waistcoats, and diamond studs sparkling on their cuffs. The young man was a plain as a deserted field. Father Taylor now saw the resemblance. He looked like the traditional portraits of Jesus. He was pleased when Tom Berdue turned his back and headed out of town to mine like the others. Father Taylor felt he was a good man worthy of saving. He was rarely wrong. Mrs. Elliot, another *Victoria* passenger, had also gauged the young man. "I recollected him perfectly as a fellow passenger of the voyage and how exceptionally quiet and pleasant he had been onboard. I left Sydney, New South Wales in November and did not see him again after my arrival in San Francisco on February 22. On March 10, I am leaving for Auburn, Sutter County." Tom was headed to Auburn too. Father Taylor, who was interested, learned this because another passenger, Mr. Hughes, saw him in Auburn later.

Shipowners divesting themselves of their vessels kept finding profitable new uses for them. Ghost Fleet ships were converted by cutting a large opening in the topsides on a level with the between deck section. Holes were sawed in the sides for windows and doors, gangplanks added, and vessels transformed into gambling establishments or businesses, insane asylums, or prisons, even a floating city hall. Speculators beached abandoned vessels near the shore. Embedding these orphaned ships in deep mud, they connected them to streets by fragile walkways, pilings and docks, and converted them into ship-houses that stood shoulder to shoulder with conventional land buildings.

Floating ships were anchored alongside lengthening piers to make ship-storehouses, buoyant bordellos, drifting hospitals, and nomadic public offices. Roofed over, some decaying vessels became floating hotels with overcrowded staterooms filled with unwholesome air and six berths each. Lodgers were permitted to sleep only between midnight and 4:00 AM. Coffin was pleased that the veritable, variegated armada of stranded ships were proving a useful, practical solution to the housing shortage.

The next day, February 23, E. Mickle and Co. advertised the *General Harrison* for sale. Because of her size and the hundreds of ships jamming the Cove, she would have difficulty clearing San Francisco. Patiently, the firm waited, then purchased the *General Harrison* themselves, beached her on a water lot at Battery and Clay Streets, and began lightening and dismasting the ship, housing it over, and securing it with pilings just beyond the *Niantic*.

By February 28, the rainy season had officially ended, though occasional showers kept the mud from completely drying out and cease trapping folks in mid-step like flypaper. The Beach brothers had located their *Apollo* a block from the *Niantic* as the second large vessel to beached and housed over as a land store. She had been floating at the northwestern corner of Battery and Sacramento streets with its stern pointed towards Front Street and parallel with Sacramento Street.

On March 1, a Friday, workers floated the *Apollo* over to the northeastern corner of Front and Sacramento streets and refitted it as a lucrative storeship connected to Long Wharf by sturdy bridges. Stripping her of masts and rigging, workers drove loose piles to keep her in place, but still allowing her to gently move up and down with the tides. Now, the *Apollo* pointed west, her bow facing Sansome Street and her stern tight against narrow Battery Street. Because the corners of the streets were on piles, merchants laid little piers just big enough to accommodate the stores forming the junction of the streets. By October she would be earning her owner H. D. Beach a fortune. He advertised that his buoyant stronghold offered uncommon advantages for storage—"safety from fire and all other risks."

"Other risks" included the growing gangs of criminals who were a constant danger. As advancing wharves and piling-supported stores and shops surrounded the *Apollo*, it became an odd-looking vessel, dismasted and dismantled far inland. At high tide, goods could be ferried from the shipping to the stores and from them to the Stockton and Sacramento steamers.

By now, the *General Harrison* had been housed over and secured with pilings just beyond the *Niantic* to convert it into a warehouse and, by May, would be the third storeship of Graveyard Harbor. Coffin saw that four other profitable storeships had been moored across the street. Last November 8, the Lindsays had founded the first *bonded* storeship, but it was the *Niantic*, that odd and beautiful jewel of land and water, which continued to grip the imagination of Graveyard Harbor and capture its soul. The *Tecumseh* and an unidentified brig were berthed southeast of the *Bennett* at the corner of California between Sansome and Battery streets.

Coffin noted all these additions in his *Log*, made sketches of the vessels, and headed home to his temporary bunk while he still had a bunk of any kind. The lessening of storms and prolonged rains, the carpet of green on the surrounding hills had lifted Coffin's spirits. With the sale of the last item of cargo he was once again a captain at large. He began operating lighters, carrying small orders of clothing, fresh meat, and supplies from a ship's chandler. For $600 he bought a sloop he renamed the *Sophronia* after his wife, then hired a boat builder to lengthen and deck the vessel. His new enterprise began well. He hauled coffee from a Pernambuco brig to the shore and earned $60 before breakfast. Encouraged, he decided to take a second flyer on the river.

The *Niantic* was prospering. Its pump log had recently accounted for two consecutive days of ten thousand gallons of the best fresh water in town. Even the forty-foot-square shop next to the *Niantic* on the wharf was bringing in $600 a month. A ship-city was rising from the water. Some decaying vessels, roofed over, became business premises and floating hotels. Overcrowded staterooms, noisy and filled with unwholesome air, contained six berths each and permitted lodgers to sleep only between midnight and 4:00 AM.

Owing to a shortage of material for pier construction, boxes and sacks of earth were piled up at the waterline. Streets and warehouses were improvised by grounding a row of ships in a line from the ends of the city streets and shops then building over beams and boards resting upon the ships.

Across the street four other profitable storeships were moored. The *Thomas Bennett* of Charleston, a live oak and cedar ship known for being exceptionally sturdy, floated off the southern side of Howison's Pier between Battery and Front streets on Sacramento, its bow pointing toward Battery. A pier was built out to it and it was covered and built around with stores. The place had been the Hq for young blades from Baltimore until the Monumental Fire House, a unit composed entirely of Baltimore men, was constructed and the volunteers began to congregate there. The *Tecumseh* and an unidentified brig were berthed southeast of the *Bennett* at the corner of California between Sansome and Battery.

GEORGE B. REED was behind the counter of his nearby store arranging merchandise when ex-Texas Ranger Devil Jack Hays entered. Political boss Sam Brannan was with him, hanging onto his arm like a limpet. Brannan, the richest land developer in town, had created San Francisco's first public school, published its first newspaper, the *California Star*, and built the first flour mill on the American River. When gold nuggets began turning up in his flour and at nearby John Sutter's Mill, he salted San Francisco streets with bits of gold from a quinine bottle so erstwhile prospectors would buy his mining provisions at inflated prices. After fleecing Sutter, Brannan kept up his sly ways and ended up owning a fifth of Sacramento.

"I want you to meet Devil Jack Hays," Brannan told Reed, snaking his arm around the ranger's shoulders like a bear. "He's going to be the business community's candidate for the town's next sheriff." Reed doubted that, but smiled and pumped Devil Jack's hand anyway.

The cowboy was not inclined toward sociability, but never failed to remove his hat for man or woman whenever he spoke. He did that now. They talked about the weather, but the Texas Ranger, who had announced his candidacy in February, refused to give his views on political matters or reveal his party affiliation. Three days later, much to Brannan's discomfort, Devil Jack announced he was running as an

Independent. His two opponents were the appointed sheriff Col. John E. Townes, the choice of the Whigs and the nominee of the Democratic Party, and "Col." J. J. Bryant, the champion of gambling tables and loafers.

All three candidates spent several days riding from one district to another and at each location were cheered by their respective supporters. Devil Jack won the most hearts because he spoke fluent Spanish and considered himself the watchdog for the Hispano Californians, especially the poor who had been deprived of their lands. In San Francisco the streets were filled with noise, confusion and torchlight parades for the upcoming election for sheriff.

Ghost Fleet resident, artist and lawyer John McCrackan was elected judge of the election. He had accepted only out of admiration for the famous Texas Ranger. Two days earlier, Devil Jack had given a short campaign speech in Happy Valley. "Gentlemen," he said briefly, "I never gave a speech in my life. I can only say, should I be elected sheriff, I will perform the duties of the office to the best of my abilities." Next day's rally at the Red House was so packed by excited voters that Devil Jack had to adjourn to the street out front.

The following evening, McCrackan attended a champagne dinner in Devil Jack's honor at the Bay Hotel, a 600-ton ship that had been drawn up on the mud under a high bank, and made into a restaurant-hotel. She was one of the first abandoned ships to be transformed into a land-building. Devil Jack, seated to his left, surprised him. From Devil Jack's adventures, McCrackan had expected him to be a perfect "Joe Mountain" of immense proportions, not such a small, unsophisticated man. Still, as an aspiring portrait painter, he was taken with the Ranger's colorful appearance and asked him to sit for him. Col. Jonathan Drake Stevenson, whose regiment reduced to restless liberty caused chaos as the ravening Hounds, had sat twice for a full-scale oil. Jack declined the honor. Because there were five women, "all brilliant and pretty," at the dinner, McCrackan was not too disappointed as he accepted invitations to visit them all.

He left the party at 8:00 PM and took a boat to the *Balance* where he had a quiet drink with Mr. and Mrs. Brooks and Capt. E. Washborn Ruggles, a fine navigator but unfit to command a ship as eminent as the *Balance*. Mrs. Brooks remained quite happy tied to the *Balance*. "These moonlight nights," McCrackan said, "her husband takes her all about the Bay in their little skiff, calling upon this friend and that, for you must know there are a great many ladies living upon ships in the bay, renting houses is expensive while it costs nothing if you have a ship to live upon."

"I am doing first rate work in my profession," McCrackan complained, "but no one who is anybody thinks of being painted by anyone but Mr. William S. Jewett who gets most of his commissions at his Merchant Street studio. Mrs. William Jewett was at the dinner tonight too. I consider her the most beautiful woman in California."

Spirits deflated, McCrackan left the party and rowed a short distance away so he could observe the ninety-two-year-old brig in its entirety. Built in Calcutta, the British had captured it during the War of 1812. When James DeWolf of the privateer True Blooded Yankee recaptured it, he rechristened it the *Balance* to balance another ship just lost to him by a British cruiser. Though elderly, the live oak and teak ship had safely taken McCrackan, his fellow passengers, and the worst cooks and most impudent stewards of any ship safely around the Horn. Amazingly, the brig's towering masts were the same ones installed nearly a century earlier. McCrackan recalled that the *Balance* once provided an achingly beautiful experience at sea. One bright moonlit night, several sixty-foot-long sulphur-bottom whales had played around the ship, joyfully spouting, sporting and banging her sides with their tails just hard enough not to sink her.

On Election day, McCrackan put his heart into championing the "Gallant Texan Ranger" as the first regularly elected Sheriff in San Francisco history. "The whole town was perfectly alive," he said, beaming, "everybody out, everybody excited. This office is the only one that there is any strife about." While Devil Jack had no money to defray the cost of campaigning, his fame, charisma and popularity drew vast crowds.

His opponent, Col. Bryant, was not popular, but was counting on buying his way into office. As a celebrated gambling house sport he operated the game at the Bryant House (the former Ward House) and had made a fortune. Each morning at four o'clock, he left his new casino with $50 in small change jingling in his coat. In the darkness he felt his way to the vegetable market where street urchins were collecting scraps for their goats and cows. He dipped into his pocket, withdrew a handful of coins and scattered them among the kids. He loved watching them scramble for them.

The colonel showered gold pieces onto those down on their luck, chartered barrooms in every ward to provide free liquor and lunches for everyone, advertised liberally in his Exchange, and filled the Square with banners. His hired costumed horsemen and four wagons of musicians pulled by four mules each marched around town extolling his name and raising an unholy racket that made more enemies than friends. All morning six strolling bands of musicians paraded the Square singing Bryant's praises; donkey carriages in colorful bunting awaited to carry his supporters to the polls.

"As you may imagine," McCrackan said, "dealing out all his wines, dinners and liquors so generously, he made friends."

Bryant was staging a display on the Square when Devil Jack appeared, preceded by rockets, firecrackers and sparklers and riding on a snorting black charger. Prancing and rearing, he galloped back and forth putting on the finest display of expert horsemanship yet seen in San Francisco. Men crowded around to pump the Ranger's hand. With hat in hand, Devil Jack bowed as his horse kneeled. The crowd surged forward, lifted him up and carried him on their shoulders.

By noon, Devil Jack was leading the polls. By afternoon, the Whigs, realizing there was no chance of their candidate John Townes getting in, threw all their votes to Devil Jack to keep Bryant out.

"Col. Jack Hays was elected by over a thousand majority," McCrackan said, "and he swept the field." Bryant not only lost the election and the $10,000 he wagered on himself to win, but the night before the returns his gambling establishment, bar, and household furniture were attached by the city.

McCrackan awoke on the *Balance* the next morning, went topside and watched morning light shining on an East Bay summit. Volcanic Mount Diablo had lately been burning freely and smoke issuing from its mouth was hanging in dark masses in the bright sky. Looking out over the unique floating city in the crisp air, McCrackan heard singing and laughter coming back to him over the lapping water. It was wonderful. The rainy winter, the longest yet recorded, had halted the building of wharves, but with the improved conditions the construction was resumed at a frantic pace.

EARLY SUNDAY MORNING, APRIL 14, Coffin enjoyed one of his few pleasant, cloudless days since the rains, the longest yet recorded. Graveyard Harbor held an almost poetic beauty. The winds died down. The Bay shone like a mirror. The sky was a startling blue. The sun was out, but there was an edge to it—a whisper that bode ill tidings to his practiced ear. The sky was tinged gray now and failing.

"If it be the Devil in possession of your heart," Father Taylor preached, "do you imagine that you can convert the Devil, or free yourself from him without a violent struggle? You can do not one of these any more than you can veil the darkness of the noonday sun." Coffin looked about in wonderment of the changes all around. He looked to his right. The Ghost Fleet was expanding and crowding the land, practically come up on his toes. He looked to his left. A Clay Street firm was accepting goods to be stored aboard the *Salem*, which lay off California St. and Davis next to the *Henry Lee*, and selling off its deckhouse and equipment. John Redmond followed suit by taking on goods for storage on the *Talca* off the foot of Washington Street.

IT WAS STEAMER DAY and the entire city was brimming with excitement. The *Tennessee* with 551 passengers (not counting officers, crew, and stowaways), entered the Gate. This was the largest number ever to arrive at the port in one vessel, Remarkably, Capt. Cole had left 800 more behind in Panama clamoring for passage. John McCrackan was so excited by the event he decided to take a cup of chocolate as luxury as he went ashore to Sunday services. On the beach, he sipped his chocolate and cheered with all the other spectators. As the *Tennessee* from Panama hove into view, the navy fired two salutes.

"In ten minutes after the gun was fired," John McCrackan said, "our beautiful Bay was perfectly alive with boats of all sizes and shapes."

A long-haired man that attracted all eyes ambled onto the deck of the *Tennessee* to enjoy one of the few pleasant days San Francisco had enjoyed since the rains. He inhaled the scent of Graveyard Harbor and felt his heart race. Here was promise and wealth. Jemmy-from-town, his private stowaway, remained hidden below and saw none of this. Today, Graveyard Harbor held an almost poetic beauty. The winds had died down. The Bay shone like a mirror. It seemed frozen in place. A. Bailey, a new arrival, reported over 400 large square-rigged vessels lying at anchor and a large number "hauled in to shore and roofed over like a house having their anchors buried in the ground on shore."

By the time the *Tennessee* anchored at noon and swung to, the Bay was black with creek skiffs, yawls, gigs, launches, all surrounding the mail ship, twenty deep. Folks were eager to board the *Tennessee* and greet friends and get the latest newspapers—as up to date as February 21. The long-haired man and his partner, Jemmy-from-town, were rowed to shore and slipped into the new city. Clandestinely, they took a room at the Jackson Street Wharf with Jack Edwards, an Englishman with flaming red whiskers who shared his quarters with a scarecrow-like man dressed in black. Both men were arsonists. Both men would be instrumental in his plan.

That night, Capt. Coffin awoke before midnight. The tide was glowing red with marine life and depositing a phosphorescent sheen upon the sand. Filled with dread, he could not sleep and went for a stroll along rudimentary and constantly augmented docks. They barely held his weight. In the short time he had been in Graveyard Harbor the piers were much the worse for wear. Such docks were only constructed for the moment. Like dirty shirts, they were discarded and rebuilt. There was the flicker of a lantern on the water. A stooped man was floating his skiff beneath a portion of Long Wharf where there was a storehouse above. Coffin was suspicious. Using augers and saws, thieves sometimes saw away the floor planks beneath safes above and let them drop into boats buttressed with feather beds. Whoever the man was, he had come from the direction of Sydney Town, the haven of the Ducks. It was only one-half mile north of Long Wharf at the base of Telegraph Hill. Another man appeared on the pier above.

Under bright moonlight, Capt. Coffin saw Jesus Christ strolling along San Francisco's Long Wharf as if on a sunny day in Nazareth. A resurrected Messiah was walking along the central pier leading into a floating city of nearly a thousand abandoned ships and ten thousand fugitives. Slender as a stalk of wheat, nearly six-feet tall, the familiar figure walked in a slow, measured stride swinging his arms pendulum-like. Every few steps, he stopped, lowered his head, and peered menacingly out from under the broad brim of his low-crowned hat. Then, his head, sharp-featured and dark-complected, would fly up like a snake about to strike. His beard was twin-pointed as fangs. His rich, dark-brown hair was fine, wavy, and worn long like the traditional portraits of Jesus hanging on every wall. His nose was aquiline and his thick-lidded eyes, black and glistening as anthracite, perpetually brightened under the luminous light. His face had an intellectual and thoughtful cast, a feature belied by the wicked smile that played about his lips.

The same Spanish who had renamed Yerba Buena Cove "Graveyard Harbor" had named him, "Creeping Jesus." There was something mystical about Creeping Jesus. No jail could hold him. He could not die. More than once he had stood beneath the gallows with a rope around his neck, yet still lived. More than once an innocent man, his identical twin, would stand in his place on the gallows. He and his loose-knit gang of eight ruthless apostles—arsonists, robbers, cutthroats, corrupt officials, and inside men (including the man who built the city vault and had been entrusted with its fortune) were planning to rob San Francisco of three million dollars in gold. The innumerable lives lost and a city destroyed multiple times were only collateral damage in carrying out his cunning scheme.

First, more men would have to die.

On Thursday night, April 18, four days after his first sighting of Creeping Jesus, Coffin was back on Long Wharf busily settling his accounts in the light of a lantern. Just then a big quake (two sharp jolts worth) rocked San Francisco. He was so deep in his problems that he scarcely noticed the tremor. When the shaking halted and his cup of chocolate ceased rippling, he continued writing. Disgusted, he threw down his pen, and left his ledger without totaling his figures. He did not have to finish. He knew the answer. He was without a dollar or place to live unless he could find another lodging within the Ghost Fleet. He began exploring the rudimentary piers.

Minutes later, Coffin encountered the man with long, wavy hair to his shoulders again. As he passed into a narrow space between two houses fashioned from ships, he was caught in a pool of light. This time, Coffin observed more detail. He had a small slit over one ear, a one-inch scar over his left eyebrow, and a long scar on his cheek on the right side of his jaw. He couldn't tell how long it was. It disappeared down his collar. The stranger's fingers were constantly in motion like a conjurer.

Coffin tried to focus on them, but they always slipped away. At last, he captured them at rest, but only for a few seconds. It was enough.

The middle finger on his right hand was missing a joint. A ring of India ink, a tattoo, ran around that finger. Similar tattoos ran around all his other fingers. He was marked with more ink between each forefinger and thumb. Coffin watched Creeping Jesus's long hair sway as he walked with a long measured stride. His Christ-like resemblance totally belied the impression that he had all the cunning of the hundreds of ex-convicts unleashed upon San Francisco.

Creeping Jesus slid down a rough ladder into a skiff beneath the central pier. In mid-descent, he stopped, and his head, sharp-featured and fanged with twin beards, shot up and peered in Coffin's direction. Its three occupants greeted Creeping Jesus, and began to work their way beneath the central pier. Storeships were connected by fragile bridges and narrow catwalks and connected to those were small docks and pilings. To those were connected massive wharves which became land streets. Coffin watched the trio, tools in hand, work through the maze, then slip beneath a portion of the dock and reappear on top of Long Wharf.

"Now, what are they up to?" Coffin wondered, not for the first time, not for the last. On the wharf Creeping Jesus and his Apostles conferred in whispers. He tried to overhear their conversation, but he was too far away. He watched as they returned to their boat having reached some sort of decision. Before he could observe more, they rowed into the Ghost Fleet. A shadow fled before the boat as if she carried a torch of darkness into the moonlight. A cloud had moved over the moon, but light enough remained for him to determine their direction—Clark's Point, the farthest northern point of the Ghost Fleet. Coffin's old friend, Capt. Jones, was anchored there onboard the *James Caskie*. All around, the inhabitants of Graveyard Harbor, disturbed by the actions of the tide and weather and their own restless dreams, were awakening to a nightmare.

I*T WAS A DIRTY*, gristly dawn when the Devil came to Graveyard Harbor as Father Taylor had warned. He arrived cloaked in brimstone and wearing a cloak of cunning. His story had not begun then, but four months earlier and far away. Snow was falling in New York City when an officer shone his lantern onto a longhaired man in the shadows. His furtiveness at the sight of the officer's tin badge (all police officers wore plainclothes until the mid-1850s) had provoked his curiosity. As far as he could discern of the stranger beneath his long, English-cut coat, was that he was tall, five-foot, nine-inches or more, but stooping to hide his true height. He was slender, well-proportioned. Certainly, the policeman thought, as he followed the stranger though the gathering drifts, it would be hard to mistake his measured stride and long swinging arms for that of anyone else.

Most unnerving of all was the menacing look he gave the officer from under the wide brim of his low-crowned hat. It was direct and unflinching. His dark-brown, shoulder-length hair was fine like the traditional portraits in the Bible of Jesus Christ whom he uncannily resembled. His chin beard was well-groomed, trimmed with two rounded points. Beneath his felt hat, the man's forehead was low and broad. He was good-looking with a fine straight nose, and a narrow projecting chin. The stranger had good strong teeth, but the wicked smile which played around his thin lips troubled the officer. It hinted at danger. Curious, he drew closer so that his lantern showed the man's face in more detail. Moments before he would have sworn his eyes were light-blue. But, his eyes, blue-black in the midst of a saturnine face, were lit like bright coals. Up close, the stranger's hair was coarser, straighter, and darker than the policeman had assumed. It seemed subject to the weather.

His face, a "peculiar sharp face," had an intellectual cast as if he might be an interesting man to converse with on a long journey. The policeman was close to his quarry now. He saw that the stranger held his head erect. It would not stay down. When lowered, it would snap up and out as if on a spring. His motions were quick—always, unless he was playing a part. He had a one-inch scar over his left eyebrow and a long scar on his right cheek that trailed down his neck and vanished under his collar. How long the scar was, the policeman could only guess. The middle finger on the man's right hand was cudgel-stiff and swollen. Likely, he was missing a joint.

Closer inspection revealed a ring of India ink, a black tattoo, that ran around the deformed finger—not unusual. Many men tattooed wedding rings on that finger. There were similar tattoos encircling his other fingers, one between his thumb and first finger in the shape of a star, and ink marks between each forefinger and thumb. Fastened to his belt was an oiled revolver of fine finish which shown blue in the night. Strapped to his side and far back, was a fourteen-inch-long knife. The policeman caught a glimpse of it and placed his hand on his truncheon. He drew himself up and came as close as he dared.

"I was born in Brighton, England, Sussex County on March 3, 1819, or 1820," the stranger claimed. "When I was sixteen years of age I committed forgery [a crime that calls for great skill and intelligence] and was banished to New South Wales for life. My friends interceded and procured my emancipation."

He spent six years in Adelaide, got his ticket-of-leave in 1842, and sailed to Montreal where he was apprenticed to a tailor. Two and a half years earlier, he had left Montreal for New York City where he became associated with a famous London burglar and sharper named "Bristol Bill" who had escaped from Sydney after serving a fourteen-year sentence. Bristol Bill's real name was never known in the United States, but the London police knew it well as their own. They were forbidden to divulge it to American authorities because Bristol Bill's father had been a member of the British Parliament.

For several years, he and Bristol Bill operated in Boston, New York, and other Eastern cities until the police got too hot on their trail. In search of safer pickings, they traveled to Vermont in the autumn where they prospered. Within a few weeks, they had robbed a half-dozen banks, floated a large quantity of counterfeit money, and swindled a score of merchants. When the police caught his partner Bristol Bill, they convicted him of counterfeiting and burglary, and shipped him to state prison for fourteen years. The stranger escaped back to New York. Whenever he had to explain those pesky missing years he spent with Bristol Bill thieving and bludgeoning, he usually claimed he had been in Peru, not New York City or Boston. "I was on the Coast of South America for two or three years," he lied, [sometimes he said he was in Chile, sometimes in Peru, it depended on his mood and the importance of his prevarication] "and when I heard about the recent discovery of gold I set out for California."

Amidst a flurry of snowflakes, the long-haired man and the policeman chatted pleasantly. Soon, they forgot they were adversaries, and swapped stories. The gun and knife were no longer feared. Ultimately, he was, for all purposes, hardworking William Stephens from Brighton, Sussex, England, a good man to know. He spun another story for the policeman replete with astonishing detail, the mark of a good liar. "I was apprenticed to a tailor in Brighton," he lied. "When I was sixteen in 1935 I left London for Canada in the ship *Sophia*, and went to work at tailoring when I arrived at Montreal. I left there for New York."

"So that brought you here?" the policeman asked.

"Yes," the long-haired man said.

"Where are you bound, m'boy?"

"Tomorrow, I am headed onboard the *Tennessee* for San Francisco," he replied.

"See that you do," the policeman said.

Some truth had inadvertently escaped the stranger's lips, but he felt that it didn't matter because he was only speaking with a dumb "flatfoot."

Recently, William Henry Aspinwall had bought the New York and Savannah Steam Navigation Company's new coastal side-lever steamer, *Tennessee*. It was then running weekly between New York and Savannah. Aspinwall had taken it out of service because he needed a suitable large vessel to augment his Pacific Fleet mail contract with the government. Swiftly, he had the 1000-ton, wooden side-wheel steamer refitted for a Pacific voyage by way of the Straits of Magellan. He had advertised its departure for yesterday, December 1 for San Francisco, only her second voyage to that city.

The policeman felt the winter storm swirling around them, and shook his head. He felt sorry for William Stephens, or whatever his real name was. He wasn't going anywhere for a few weeks. The snow was thick. He studied the filthy neighborhood streets and wanted to get the handsome young man off them to safety. Above, were crowded tenements where pigs were kept, fed swill and garbage, then eaten by the tenants. If their quarters were ever cleaned, the garbage was only moved to the streets. Had the young man forgotten about the local cholera epidemic which was raging? He hurried him on his way and would be glad to be off these streets himself. The policeman watched him plod through the snow. He would make it, he decided. He soon would be on his way. There was a spine of steel in that young man.

The hundred people who had booked passage to San Francisco would wait days for the weather to clear. By then, Capt. Cole of the *Tennessee* would be beside himself as not one, but two storms kept him from loading the rest of his provisions and coal. The Pacific Mail Steamship was due in Panama by March 12, but by the third day of waiting all but fifteen passengers had thrown up their hands and headed home.

On December 6, the weather cleared, and enough space opened up onboard the wooden side-wheeler for the long-haired man to purchase a ticket and sail as passenger, "J. Stewart." By way of Rio de Janeiro, Brazil, Valparaiso, Chile, and Panama City, the *Tennessee* crawled toward San Francisco carrying one of the most dangerous men alive.

"Among the passengers aboard the *Tennessee* on the voyage," marine historian James P. Delgado observed, "were 'twelve or fourteen women of bad character' and 'a little knot of gamblers with their women.' Every night the gamblers opened a faro bank in their cabin." the long-haired man felt right at home, though many wondered what Jesus Christ was doing onboard gambling. The other passengers had been telling him things that he wanted to hear—the law is lax in San Francisco, and the court is corrupt and every juror's vote is for sale. The long-haired man would do well as long as he didn't run into an honest sheriff.

The people were safe as they didn't run into the long-haired man.

"His childhood was instinct with misbehavior," it was later said of Creeping Jesus. "Every wickedness the human is heir to has its redeeming quality. There are magnificent scoundrels and there are mean scoundrels; He belonged to the latter category. His rascality was of the cold and calculating kind. A very mean man is seldom weak; more genius, more strength of character is necessary in order to become a great bad man than a great good man."

What he was was apparent. That much was not hidden.

TWO DAYS AFTER Mrs. Elliot left for Auburn and the diggings, the *Tennessee* reached Panama City after fifty-seven days at sea. When the *Tennessee* left Panama City on March 24, Jemmy-from-town went with her. There were no tickets available then, so the long-haired man stowed his buddy inside his cabin. The coal was so inferior that passage to San Francisco would take twenty-one days. The crying babies and screaming children, the loose women and men playing cards drove Jim to distraction. Off the coast of Southern California, like everyone, he had to bundle up in blankets and layers of coats to keep from freezing. One passenger, John Pierce, called the trip like living in a "crowded cage in which we have been prisoned." The long-haired man knew there were millions in gold lying about in the sieve that passed for the San Francisco Custom House vault. He had his locksmith in Jemmy-from-town. Now, he needed an arsonist, a firebug of the first water. His gang of tough men would set his plan in motion and handle the rest. After all, he reasoned, the city had no real fire department or law enforcement. But, the coal was so inferior passage to San Francisco took twenty days and set him back. He was irritated. He could hardly wait to reach the Land of Golden Promise and begin filling his pockets.

As for his name, you have been warned not to ask. His true name might never be known. But go ahead and question him. He will claim his name was James Stuart, though he was known variously as James Stephens or Stevens (after his cousin), James Campbell, William Stephens, James Carlisle, James Stewart, and Long Jim. Most commonly, though, he was English Jim, an all-purpose name which fit all his aliases and kept him from mixing them up. So let us use that.

"Next time, you can stay at Mrs. Mary Ann Hogan's boarding house for criminals," Edwards suggested to English Jim. Jim thought this was good information to have, though he wished he had had it sooner. He was attracted to Mary Ann. The charming, attractive woman was well-dressed, well-spoken, even genteel, the sort who might safely keep a crib for gangsters without ever being suspected. The thirty-five-year-old proprietor had been born in England and immigrated with her parents to New South Wales at age two. "During my residence in the Colonies I was never charged with a crime," Mary Ann said proudly. In October 1849, she and husband, Michael Hogan, a former convict, sailed with their son from Sydney to San Francisco. Hogan set up as a general merchant, but when he lost all his money speculating in real estate, he rented a property on Sansome Street and began keeping a public house.

At her urging, Mr. Hogan went to work in the mines while she stayed behind in San Francisco and minded the house. While her trusting spouse was absent, Mary Ann traveled the streets in the most elegant carriage in town and in her finest clothes and feathered hats. Brazenly, she carried on with any handsome man who caught her fancy. Hogan's absences also allowed her to secretly let rooms to Australian criminals as hideouts. Recently, she had taken a new lodger, a remarkable man who did fit in with her hardened lodgers, but attracted her. "The new lodger was attractive and unfettered by scruples," historian Mary Floyd Williams writes. "His hostess was equally attractive, equally unscrupulous and they quickly resigned themselves to an intimacy that became notorious." His name was Sam Whittaker, a goateed dandy and lady killer, with a streak of honesty he couldn't stamp out. Whittaker still had a chance at redemption which Mary Ann encouraged. Their relationship became one of common report.

"Hogan went to the mines and asked me to take charge of the house until he returned," Whittaker told anyone who asked so that he would not be taken for an intruder. He also took charge of Mrs. Hogan herself and openly lived as her husband. Hogan later claimed that Whittaker had been a government man, a convict in the penal colonies, who had been assigned to him to serve them faithfully as a butcher for seven years.

English Jim listened carefully to Mr. Hogan's story about Whittaker and believed most of it. Unquestionably, as an engineer, he would be valuable to an experienced criminal like himself in cracking into vaults, opening jail cells and breaking out his gang, designing burglary tools, and copying keys for new burglaries. Jim had other millwrights in his gang who could do the same work, but Whittaker was special. He was the smartest of them all. Yet, his past was as full of as many contradictions and lies as English Jim's own including his true name. Both were rivals for the love Mary Ann Hogan. She wore a daguerreotype around her neck of each, but only when the other was not present. English Jim's jealousy was such that at one point he had threatened to shoot Whittaker.

"My name of 'Samuel Whittaker' is assumed," Whittaker admitted to her, "it is the name under which I was transported. I desire to suppress my real name for family considerations [his parents and two sisters were still alive] and as an act of humanity." A native of Manchester, England, he was an extraordinary, self-confident individual. Thirty years old, five-feet, six-inches tall, dashing, brave, manly in his bearing, exceptionally neat and particular in his fashions. He was, if not the smartest thief in the world (he was not highly motivated in that regard), the smartest thief in San Francisco, and a very clever fellow in all other regards.

Fourteen years earlier, Whittaker had been transported for life for housebreaking to Sydney where he figured as a "gentleman and prince among the convicts." After serving sixteen years, he was freed by the governor under a conditional pardon at Parramatta. He left Sydney on the ship *Louisa* in February 1849, and arrived in San Francisco a month after Capt. Coffin had. His first job in town was as a steward in Cockstein's Public House on Broadway. He bought a horse, cart and boat, got some men to work the team and boat for two months and became a butcher in unhappy Happy Valley for a year.

"While butchering," he said, "I used to ride my horse two or three times a week to the Mission Dolores to purchase cattle."

One day Whittaker went to the mission to buy a horse, but the animal was too high-priced. As he was leaving, James Curry came running after him and offered him a splendid mare he claimed was his. "I bought the mare, saddle and bridle for one hundred dollars," Whittaker said. "I paid him, taking a receipt for the same, then rode the mare around." As he did, he was stopped by a man who said the horse was stolen and really belonged to "Dutch Charley" Duane, the two-fisted and formidable Volunteer Firefighter. Whittaker located Curry in disguise and packing to skip town and dragged him to Dutch Charley who knocked him down and kicked him all the way to the station house where he was arrested. Whittaker was to get his sixty dollars back after Curry's trial, but was bilked by Judge Levi Parsons who let the horse thief off without a trial. The court kept the money.

"It seemed to me," he said, "that a thief had a better chance than an honest man. From that moment on, I decided to take the crooked path."

When Jack Edwards, Old Jack, and Whittaker won a considerable sum at cards, the loser hired a man named Gallagher to kill the three of them. When the assassin tiptoed into Whittaker's room with a dagger to murder him, Mrs. Hogan intercepted him and told him, "Get out, Whittaker is not home!" A day or two after, Gallagher the hired man was found dead in the street by Edwards' house. "I think that Gallagher knew too much about Edwards' business and for that reason Edwards poisoned him."

On another night Whittaker was at the corner of the El Dorado in a crowd, when he saw one of Hetherington's partners kill a man. "The dagger struck so fast that in drawing it out it pulled the man over," he said and added it to the list of murders he had seen. "English Jim Stuart and George Smith told me that they shot a man on the Stockton Road. The man had considerable money. He ran toward the house after he was shot and died nearly as soon as he had entered."

One time Whittaker and Edwards robbed a miner staying at Mary Ann's boarding house by substituting a bag of rocks for a bag of gold. "Another bag, containing eight hundred dollars, I did not divide," Whittaker admitted. "The whole amount I gave to Mrs. Hogan. She knew how I got it. I also gave her about three hundred dollars which I won at gambling. I exchanged watches with her. Mine was the most valuable. I also gave her a diamond ring." They split the gold with Singing Billy whose real name was Belcher Kay, the Warden of the Port, whom they called "an ignorant man who can scarcely read or write." Yet in between bouts of delirium tremens, Singing Billy planned and executed robbery after robbery and assaults for English Jim and did it better than the more clear headed of the gang.

When Michael Hogan returned from the diggings, he was "very much enraged" at finding Whittaker at his house and in his bed. He ordered Mary Ann to immediately send him away. But when Hogan went to Oregon on business, Mary Ann moved to Green and Dupont Streets with Whittaker and for the next four months lived with him as her husband. During that time, she advised him to break off his criminal associations.

"To do Mrs. Hogan justice," Whittaker said, "I must say she has done all in her power to make me lead a different life. I gave her twenty dollars a week for my board. I also gave her many presents. I exchanged watches with her. Mine was the most valuable. I also gave her a diamond ring and about three hundred dollars which I won at gambling, about twenty-five hundred dollars in all [twenty-one ounces in gold]." Twice, she sent Whittaker to the mines to do honest work, but it didn't take. He soon returned to the beautiful Mary Ann and to his criminal life.

Snow had retarded certain sections of the placer to a depth of six-inches, particularly far up on Yuba and Feather rivers, and at

Georgetown was ten-inches deep and so difficult that many miners like Tom Berdue had come down to San Francisco "to wait a little longer." The long-haired man would have to wait until the end of April or the beginning of May to leave for Sacramento on the *Senator* and from there forty miles due north on a river boat to Marysville and after that by foot or horse.

CAPT. COFFIN WAS WAITING for mail from the Pacific mail steamer, *Sarah Sands*, when he saw the *Massachusetts* arriving from around the Horn. The *Sands* might be bringing important news. Though eager as everyone else to discover whether or not California was to be admitted as a State, Coffin could wait no longer to learn the outcome. The Senate vote had been close last time. By morning, he desperately needed to sign a mate, cook and all-hands crew for his sloop. His meager finances forced him to settle for a one-man crew. Coffin had such confidence in Capt. P. Thurlo of Newburyport, whom he had partially trained at sea on the *Ocean Queen*, that he placed his lighters under his charge. That night, he wrote his wife, Sophronia, confidently of his plans to make money.

On the morning of April 19, Coffin loaded his sloop for a cruise to Marysville. Imprudently, he started at midday unaware he should have gotten across the Bay before the daily northwester got to blowing. In summer the Diablo, a local version of the Southern California winds that blow in from the desert through the Santa Ana Pass, is active. It hurries down the back hills and gullies of the Bay Area, blowing like the devil and carrying along clouds of fine dust that infiltrate every store, house, trunk, and drawer in town. In winter the same demon wind beats before it the dense fog, rain and mud that make San Francisco such a hard place to navigate or even find.

It's worse across the Bay where 60-mile-per-hour winds blow all year below the canyons in the East Bay Hills. Coffin got out from under the lee of the high land and into the fast current. As he did, his sloop began to pitch and jump like "a wild colt under a Mexican horse-breaker." Standing in the cuddy hatch, the tiller in one hand, and the main sheet in the other, it took all his skill to steer a straight course. He ordered Thurlo to secure things. "The sea is so rough, high and short," Coffin said, "that it is dangerous to wear the sloop round till I could get under the lee of Angel Island." Coffin endured an arduous trip warping and tying his sloop step-by-step along the narrow Sacramento River. Sacramento city, about one hundred miles from the Golden Gate, lay next to Sutter's Fort at the junction of the Sacramento River and the American River. Coffin was wary. The connecting bays at the northeastern end were filled with sinister shoals and half-submerged islands.

SURROUNDED BY SCOW SCHOONERS and river sloops, Coffin poked his way all the way up to Marysville. That ragged tongue of land at the junction of the two rivers was an important jumping-off point for the mines. Every sheltered recess and hidden inlet along the river had from one to eight vessels anchored in it, all deserted by their crews. As skippers grew increasingly fearful of being trapped inside the Ghost Fleet, they had begun taking their smaller craft up the Sacramento and San Joaquin Rivers to disembark their passengers in the mining country. But gold fever took its toll on those vessels as it had the Ghost Fleet ships. Deserters, driven by a greed for gold that possessed everyone, abandoned one hundred square-riggers at Benicia, Sacramento, Marysville. and Stockton, all entry points to the mines.

At night the Sacramento boat, observed from the low deck of the *Sophronia*, was a floating enchantment of elegance. Brightly lighted saloons, white-jacketed servants, and shimmering colonnades were mirrored in the water. When Coffin reached Sacramento, he discovered the whole city was submerged to a depth of from four to ten feet.

"It was a curious sight," he recalled, "the whole of the low country was inundated and a vast sea of fresh water extended from the Sierra Nevada to the coast range, and the river was only distinguishable by the lines of trees along its banks."

On his return passage, he spent four days drifting down with the current to the outlet of the Sacramento River. For an additional two days he beat and sweated and cursed his way through the Suisun, San Pablo, and San Francisco Bays to arrive back at the Cove on May 21.

"It seemed to me that the number of buildings had doubled," Coffin exclaimed, "and not withstanding that they had a great fire during my absence." He understood how such blazes might start with only candles and oil lamps for light in many homes and flammable tents, but suspected the May 3-4 fire had been purposely set. But for what reason? The joy of seeing your neighbors homes destroyed? He wracked his brain but finally had to admit that he had no idea. Looking shoreward he glimpsed neat-looking cottages he had never seen before perched on the elevated backgrounds. In the midst of decay and quietude, he saw wharves too new to be so dilapidated. Yet, a substantial wharf had been run out one-third of a mile over the flats.

Two streets crowded with warehouses had been built on piles across the front of Montgomery Street, the dividing line separating the solid portion of the city from the floating portion. All to the north of this street offices stood on piles driven into the mud flats. At high water the sea would rise around and under these streets and buildings and make pedestrians and lodgers feel as if they were sailing as they sat at their dinner tables.

When Coffin went to pay a bill at Othello the Blacksmith's shop at the foot of Clay Street by the water's edge, he discovered only a pile of ashes. His heart sank, but he kept looking. He finally located Othello, and hailed him.

"Hello," he said. "So you've moved further up town it seems."

"No," Othello said, throwing up his arms. "Confound the town! It has moved further out." The commercial heart of San Francisco, thrust by indomitable perseverance, was being shifted toward the waterfront.

While they were conversing by a large forge with wood-and-leather bellows, Coffin overheard a voice from one of the tents mentioning his home port. He tugged aside the flap and out sprang a red-faced bald man who seized him by both hands and cried out joyfully, "Why, Coffin, is that you? Where upon earth did you come from?"

"Capt. John Bradbury!" Coffin said.

Bradbury had lived in town with a party of "North-enders" in an old artillery tent until the water came up to his knees during the rains. Captains Coffin and Bradbury went to the Ward House, sat down, and scanned the menu. Ala carte was tantalizing. For $1.50 they had their choice of ox tail soup, baked trout with anchovy sauce, roast stuffed lamb, roast pork with apple sauce, baked mutton with caper sauce, corned beef and cabbage, ham, curried sausages, lamb and green peas, venison in wine sauce, or stewed kidney in champagne sauce. Other dishes sold for between $1.25 and $2.00: Sweet potatoes, brandy peaches, rum omelet, and fresh, young shark which Coffin professed a love of shark as a delicacy.

"What! Eat a shark!" Bradbury exclaimed.

"And why not?" Coffin laughed. "If I should fall overboard, a shark would not hesitate to eat me."

Bradbury told him that during the citywide conflagration the newly elected sheriff, Devil Jack Hays, had distinguished himself by organizing a bucket and water keg line to extinguish the flames.

"The fires had been purposely set," Bradbury said.

"But for what reason," Coffin asked.

"I have no idea."

Bradbury did have some good news. At the beginning of the month, Coffin's old friend Capt. Jones out of Newburyport had arrived with a shipment of lumber. He was in command of one of Cushing's fleet, the English brig, *James Caskie*, 193 days out of Boston.

O NBOARD THE *BALANCE*, lawyer and artist John McCrackan, had been called up by fire alarms three times in one night. Each time the blaze was extinguished before it got fully underway. "If a person should be caught firing a building," McCrackan said grimly as he returned to the elderly *Balance*, "he would be hung without the least ceremony, for we have no preservation here except in preventing at the time the torch is lighted, for after a building is in flames, all we can do is pull down and blow up about it." He felt glum as he watched homeless individuals riding the surf in their "California-style" hats, India-rubber coats, long boots, and gauntlets. Men and women were walking the lonely mud flats at low tide looking for whatever they could find and doing their best. The Ghost Fleet, in spite of severe damage visited by frequent storms and two catastrophic arsons five months apart, had survived unscathed while the land had been ravaged and had to be rebuilt and so did the people emotionally.

After this second citywide blaze, McCrackan was certain there would be a third. Reluctantly, he left the floating city and moved on land where he would be prey to arsonists. He chose "Vermin Place" (aka "Vernon Place," and "Marcy Place"), a knoll large enough for four lots. Behind his house, the land gradually rose about a thousand yards to a summit and northward the terrain ascended to a greater elevation ending in a very high, graceful hill that lost itself in the shore. Looking eastward from this hill, he observed two neatly painted Episcopal churches and several large ships being stripped and hauled upon the mud as new storehouses or homes. He glimpsed neat-looking cottages he had never seen before perched on the elevated backgrounds. In the midst of decay and quietude, there were wharves too new to be so dilapidated, but at least they were there. One substantial wharf had been run out one-third of a mile over the flats. The hills were brown again. The dry season had come. The "Venice built of pine" had grown by over a hundred vessels in the crowded Cove and showed no sign of stopping.

The high rent at Vermin Place gobbled up the scant profits from McCrackan's law practice and his commissioned art work. For financial reasons he frequently dined with the Brooks onboard the creaky old *Balance*. While Ghost Fleet residents unwillingly paid the two dollar charge to be rowed to their floating homes, Mrs. Brooks was not one of them. She had never spent two dollars because she had never gone ashore. Much later, McCrackan saw Mrs. Brooks at last on land gathering flowers and strawberries like a sixteen year old girl. At dinner that night, Mrs. Brooks spent the evening tenderly rocking her little son, Willey, who had fallen ill. McCrackan was transfixed by such pure love.

"We have long been warm and very dear friends," McCrackan said of her, "the most convincing proof of which was the outpouring of her almost bursting heart. She is a young mother, Willey being her first born and with a fresh, beautiful face even in despair." Usually she nursed her son with homeopathic treatment, but had run out of medicine. At McCrackan's urging, for he was certain the boy would die, a doctor was rowed out to the ship. He pronounced the malady "*Choleric infantum.*" After the doctor left, McCrackan stayed far into the night to keep watch over the child. Outside, the sky grew bleaker, the sea began to pick up and the city of ships began to trundle and slide. Shredded flags, still at half-mast for the last victims of a deadly fever whipped in the wind. On shore, new refuse was being carried by rain down into the Cove to breed more illness.

At 4:00 AM, McCrackan was still nervously watching over Willey when the boy's fever broke; he was still not out of danger but this much was a relief. As Sunday dawned, the young lawyer prayed over the restless boy. A few hours later the child became quieter. For the first time since his illness, the boy opened his eyes and recognized him. McCrackan left the ship at dawn just as Mr. and Mrs. Brooks were finally getting some sleep. The next time he visited Little Willey, the boy raised his face. He tried to extend his thin arms so McCrackan could take him up again.

"I did so," McCrackan said, "and with his arms placed about my neck and his little face resting against my cheek he continued in my arms for some time."

By his next visit the boy had almost recovered. Such happy endings were rare in Graveyard Harbor. One day, McCrackan received a package marked: "Not to be opened until I am dead" from his friend Silliman. McCrackan got a doctor and headed for Happy Valley to search for his tent among the thousands. Two days later he was still looking when he found him. He took him to the hospital and paid for his care, but Silliman died a few hours later. Afterward, McCrackan found a miniature of his friend's daughter and wife in his friend's tent.

"May heaven give consolation to the widow and her fatherless children," he said. "It is dreadful to think of his coming out here to suffer so much, and to die at last. Had he lived, this month I could have given him all the writing he could handle [as a legal scrivener] and thus he might have earned sufficient money to take him back to his dear family. Oh! how I regret that mine is the sad duty to open their bleeding hearts."

He resolved not to end up like poor Silliman. He would stay healthy by sleeping in a good dry bed and keeping his feet dry and warm. Because one chronically sick acquaintance of his ate no meat and drank coffee twice a day, McCrackan vowed to do the opposite. He would "drink porter, eat meat three times a day, leave off coffee," drink chocolate once a day and as little water as possible and then only with a lump of sugar in it.

E NGLISH JIM AND GEORGE PRESCOTT reached Sacramento in late April aboard the steamer *Senator*. Disembarking at the Sacramento end, they considered cruising through the mountains tracing the "Mother Lode," the source of all West Coast gold. The fabled giant vein stretched like an earthquake fault from Georgetown to the North, passing down through Sutter's Mill, Coloma, Hangtown,

Jackson, Mokelumne Hill to Murphys and the Natural Bridge at the South. The colorfully named diggings—Rat Trap Slide, Blue-Belly Ravine, Puppytown, Ground Hog's Glory, Delirium Tremens, Chucklehead Diggings and Git-up-and-git, were rich. A prospector at Weber Creek had chipped out $50,000 in a month. Maj. Reading dug $80,000 with his pick in as much time. Another man unearthed a twenty-three pound nugget.

Their destination didn't really matter. Every camp had the same gambling halls and winding streets. Every mining battlefield was strewn with the same scarred flats, pine stumps, water-furrowed banks, leveled knolls and rusting, half-buried engines. Heaps of tailings, ruined flumes, riffle boxes and shattered sluices lay over every site in the same haphazard manner. English Jim and Prescott took the river boat north to Marysville, a blip in the road—just six hotels, six gambling saloons, and twenty stores, but the launching point by foot or horse upward to unbelievable riches. At Foster's Bar on the western bank of the North Yuba River, Jacob Sholet, a resident of Winslow's Bar, became acquainted with English Jim when he employed him and his friend in May.

"George Hunt and I hired him to work for us, at the Rock Mining Co., to cut a race with 104 other men until June and turn the river," Sholet said. "There was one odd thing about him. A finger on one of his hands is bent and he has a ring of India ink on one finger and India ink on the back of his hand." Mr. Stambaugh, who lived at Foster's Bar, knew Stuart too, and remarked on the same tattoos and Jim's ruggedness. At the riverbed, English Jim and Prescott worked amongst the clink and bite of picks, scrapers, spoons, cradles and crowbars. Men panning for gold with bowls in both hands, whirled them violently back and forth through half a circle, and pitched to throw off the water. The heavier gold settled to the bottom. Jim's "long tom," a wooden box lined with riffles, often washed more gravel than gold and he lacked the diligence to stick with it.

On May 20, 1850, halfway between Slate Range and Foster's Bar, English Jim met a small, but powerful American named John Sullivan. "English Jim carried part of my baggage down to Foster's Bar," Sullivan recalled, "and the next morning asked me if I would work for him for $100 a month. I agreed." Henry Hadden remembered English Jim and described him as a rawboned, strongly built man. "He was a pretty good scholar, too," he added. English Jim worked two or three days for Charles James Hughes and often played cards with him, then got into a fight while playing poker and Sholet and Stambaugh had to separate them. D. W. D. Thompson was on Foster's Bar at the same time as English Jim and later recalled noticing how quickly the sun lightened Jim's dark hair and softened his appearance, but not his attitude. Thompson had seen the change come over him. He had no doubt that English Jim was attempting to live an honest life from now on.

English Jim staked a claim, hired George Hunt and Thomas Belt, Francis Delancy, and another Frenchmen, to work the claim with Sullivan. Jim's heart might have been in the right place, but he lacked fortitude. He worked the claim only a few hours, then quit it. He left the next morning and went four miles down river to work alone on some scheme. Then he hired another man to take his place, so he and Sullivan could work together for two weeks at Winslow's Bar and for two weeks at Slate Range. Sullivan was sick for most of the last week and English Jim surprised him by working the claim by himself. "I knew English Jim to have plenty of money," Sullivan recalled, "but I didn't know where he got it. He did nothing at Foster's Bar, but must have done well at Winslow's Bar because he paid me an extra $20 for two days extra work." Mr. Valley did business with English Jim at Foster's Bar. "He would bring a good many clothes and other articles over the six months I knew him which I am convinced he stole," he said. "Anyone would take him to be a rascal. He was very quick in his movements."

English Jim made another attempt at an honest life for some reason that baffled even himself. Perhaps, he had changed. Assured of a steady stream of travelers after the thaw, English Jim bought a flat-bottomed iron lifeboat for four hundred dollars. It was fashioned from the hull of a mini-steamboat, the *Everett Jr.* With this new acquisition, he began a ferry business on the North Yuba River as a boatman, working the raft by overhead cables and large pulleys. Every miner had to take English Jim's flat-bottomed lifeboat across the frigid Yuba to get to Foster's Bar mining camp and so he prospered.

One day, Tom Berdue, who was mining in the region, took the lifeboat ferry for the first time. While Berdue didn't notice his uncanny resemblance to English Jim, who was concealed by a fur cap and large leather coat, English Jim did. Such a lookalike might be useful to him in the future if he needed an alibi, so he said nothing of his likeness to Berdue. This was not the case with Mr. McGilbert who was immediately struck by English Jim's Christ-like appearance. "I have frequently seen him," he said, "and he has often ferried me across the river. I could recognize him if I heard this voice in the darkest hour that ever was."

At Foster's Bar, Berdue staked a claim and boarded with the mining town's German baker. There was an unfair tax on foreign miners and the antagonism of American diggers prejudiced against the English compelled Berdue to relinquish his claim. He left contact information at William Gwynn's store in Auburn because he would be unreachable as he traveled from one mining camp to another. In this manner, he discovered an impressive amount of gold which he blithely kept in his saddlebag. He was determined not to stop mining until he had enough money to send for his wife and kids.

English Jim, glad to be making six dollars a day from his iron ferryboat, concluded to stay for the winter with Sullivan spelling him as boatman. He contemplated a new life as an honest citizen and began building a boarding house, the largest one at Foster's Bar. He opened a store with Bernard Feller and that succeeded. Tiring of the hard work, he leased his iron ferryboat to a mining company for use on half-shares and split another claim with Sullivan eight miles higher up. He worked that particular claim until 2:00 PM, the first day. When it did not pay more than $12, he abandoned it and left it to Sullivan to manage. Out of sorts, he went down river to Winslow's Bar and fell back into his old ways. While there, he had a memorable row with Col. William Prentiss the Englishman over cards, and came back up to Foster's Bar to cultivate his small garden and make a go of his boarding house. He had never felt like this before. He was filled with pride. Then, Fate stepped in.

On June 2, less than fifty miles away from Foster's Bar, someone murdered Auburn Sheriff Echols. At first William Stewart was suspected of committing the murder. Because Echols had been unpopular, the justice of the peace admitted Stewart to bail. When Stewart was re-arrested on orders of the county judge, he was allowed to exercise outside the jail and easily escaped with his brother, Samuel Hobbes Stewart. Some time afterward, English Jim Stuart, possibly because of the similarity of their names, became the leading suspect in the sheriff's homicide.

Bucking the early morning wind, Capt. Coffin fought his way through a damp, cold fog that he feared would grip the Cove all summer. He moored his skiff at Long Wharf, and climbed a fifteen foot ladder onto the pier.

"It was mail day, June 14," he said, "and I had gone to the post office at Washington and Stockton, the former home of the town's first citizen and hide dealer, William Howard, to deposit my letters. I arrived at 7:30 AM, a half-hour before the office officially opened. Even then, I was too late. Two long lines were already waiting."

There were only two delivery windows, one for Navy and Army, French, Chinese, Spanish, clergy, and woman and the second was reserved for "all the rest of mankind." Later, when the post office was moved three blocks to Portsmouth House on the western side of the Square, they cut multiple windows—one for the French, one for the army and navy, one for women and the clergy, one window for those whose names began with A-D, another window for E-H and so on alphabetically. Some of the well-heeled had their own boxes that could be opened from the outside.

To travel the three hundred yards from the rear of the line to the front windows could take as much as five hours, but Coffin had the time. He had only come to deposit his letters. Newsboys, fruit boys, popcorn boys and candy boys made a fortune off the long line of bored, shuffling, restless, and unemployed men.

Father Taylor was there too. "The slow travelers are weary, hungry, have calls of pressing importance and their time more valuable than gold," he said, "but they must not break rank, or they will lose their turn and have to begin again." Men sometimes bought a chance near the window for five dollars and got their letters without much delay.

"Nothing for you sure," the postmaster said to a man.

"Please sir, look again," he asked.

"Nothing."

Turning away, the man said to another, "I came round Cape Horn, and they were to begin writing after I had been out a month, and now it is eight months and I haven't got a letter."

The next man tore open his letter and turned away, trembling.

"Oh, my God," he screamed, "she is dead!"

Coffin saw Sheriff Devil Jack and his deputies threading their way through the line. Because everyone in the city congregated at the Post Office on the first and sixteenth of every month, the new sheriff used the opportunity to search for absconding creditors, deserters, escaped convicts and wanted men like English Bill.

It was a wonderful, colorful day so far. Flags were flying. Buyers in three piece suits and miners in flowered shirts and rough trousers were howling, laughing, shouting, and slapping each other's backs. Sleight-of-hand card sharps plied their trade on drunken sailors. It was a better than average day on the waterfront.

Coffin heard a low gurgling rumble then a piercing, long bellow and hoarse roar interspersed by the high-pitched scream of a steam whistle.

"The steamer's in!"

Bedecked with flags and funnels, a smoky mass of timber, white paint and machinery glided majestically into the Cove laying behind a wide trail of foam. Its decks were alive with men. Gauge cocks were howling with steam. The semaphore on Telegraph Hill announced the imminent arrival of the steamer *California* with its much abbreviated bow.

The *California*, one of the Pacific Mail Steamship Company's side-wheelers, wasn't a twin. No, not her—she was a triplet. As one of three identical side-wheelers (the *Panama* and *Oregon* being the others), the *California* had slid lazily from her moorings and cleared New York harbor with only seven passengers onboard on October 6, 1848. Sixty days later, gold was discovered in California and President James K. Polk invited everyone to join in the greatest mass migration in American history. In sloops, brigs, and barks, thousands of gold seekers completed the voyage to Panama City, the last stop before continuing on to San Francisco. Cramped bunks on the *California* sold for $1,000 apiece—a profit of $365,000, but Capt. Cleaveland Forbes was not satisfied. He complained that his ship was "filled to cramnation" with the scum of creation—gamblers, thieves, blacklegs, runners, and drunkards.

The *California's* first entrance into the Bay on February 28, 1849, had been spectacular. Thirty ships in harbor boomed salutes to welcome the first steamship to voyage between the two coasts.

Thousands of wintering miners cheered from shore. When the ship, belching smoke first rounded William Squire Clark's Point, a battery of guns overlooking the promontory at the base of Telegraph Hill roared a welcome. Passengers fought with crew and officers to reach shore first, leaving onboard only Capt. Forbes, an assistant engineer, and an oiler boy. Because the *California* had been moored without coal, they had been forced to gather wood at Monterey for fuel just to reach Graveyard Harbor. For two months the hardy vessel had been laid up in the Cove. In the meantime, Forbes resigned and took a job onshore. As more deserted windjammers, sloops, and frigates surrounded it the *California* became locked in until the coal-ship *Superior* arrived with a full load and gave her enough coal to escape the Ghost Fleet's embrace.

The *California* Steamship

A wave-like mass of timber, white paint and machinery glided majestically into the Cove, laying a wide trail of foam. Its decks were alive with men like so many ants on a hill. Gauge cocks were howling with steam. The *California* mail slid imposingly toward Long Wharf as Coffin ran alongside. This was the way to see San Francisco, he said. The vessels closest to Long Wharf had been transformed into lucrative ship-warehouses, ship-restaurants, ship-saloons and even a waterborne city hall the Council prayed would preserve some of the city's valuable records from the series of arson fires.

On both sides of the wharf, dock men labored, lugged, scratched, swore, jostled and sweated. A busy lot, they rang bells, carried messages, drove trucks, and worked lighters. Rival barkers touted various steamboats. New street preachers harangued the sinners. Candy-sellers sold sugar plums. Slop sellers trudged past. But no one was as fast as Coffin who flew past fish mongers and poultry and vegetables markets and Chinese porters embracing this new world. He was racing along what comprised a peddler's avenue that led to a floating auction house. Farmers were rowing up to the pier in small craft to sell their produce.

Coffin hailed "Young Eddie," the assistant wharfinger, "Young O'Brien," the gate-clerk, and Harry Isaacs, who had succeeded Capt. G. Laidley as *major domo*. Buyers in three piece suits and miners in flowered shirts and rough trousers were howling, laughing, shouting, and slapping each other's backs. Slight-of-hand card sharps plied their trade on drunken sailors. It was a better than average day on the waterfront. The line was shorter now, but by not much. What counted was that the mail was in.

To his left, a water carrier sold "Pure water—no soap, salt or sulfur" from a little hand wagon and did a little dance. Ships were discharging cargoes as rapidly as fast-talking auctioneers in shanties were accepting bids. On Long Wharf, Coffin rushed faster than the eye could follow or a rapid heart could beat. Near the end of the wharf was Whitehall, home of the lighters—the bay taxies, and hangout of vulturous crimps with their doctored bottles of liquor.

Coffin paused to listen to the Cheap Johns' patter, then continued past shops and gambling dens lining both sides of the wharf. Frame warehouses had been built over the water. Tinderbox buildings had been erected along the former high-tide line. All shook under the thunder of loaded dray wagons and iron-wheeled handcarts. Coffin felt the whole central part sway noticeably. It was built on pilings the size of ship's masts, driven down into the mud by sledgehammers. The land quivered at a cough. He balanced himself.

"From the time of the building of the first eight hundred-foot long portion, Long Wharf became an important feature of the city," William Heath Davis said. He recalled that Mellus and Howard had begun constructing the $180,000 pier last spring and by winter it had been surging with constant activity. Port Collector Collier had gotten hold of Heath Davis who had just built the city's first multilevel brick building at the corner of Montgomery and California Streets, and leased that building from him. Then, he set about lobbying for building a sunken vault inside the red-brick four-story to profit himself.

In just one month a million dollars worth of trade had been transacted on Long Wharf. Big ships paid $200 a day for wharfage. Those that failed to pay for wharfage had their ships confiscated and sold or broken up for timbers to build new docks. Really big deals were done on Long Wharf, but consistent money was earned on every pier from tolls for foot-passengers, wagons, and ships. Where Long Wharf began its nearly half-mile stretch into the Cove an assortment of bathhouses, eating establishments, saloons, and several gambling dens covered its planks and spilled over the edges. And in such a short time. Graveyard Harbor was magic.

Coffin had just gotten back in line, when the Montgomery engine house's alarm bell rang. Three months earlier, the Council had installed a 270-pound fire bell at Monumental Volunteer Fire Engine Co. No. Six at the head of the Square. Since then an incendiary had burned the combustible town to the ground twice. The bell of Big Six rang almost daily with false alarms and attempted firings. Now, the huge bell clanged again, an insistent toll. Other bells rang, but none like the giant bell which sent shivers down everyone's spine.

Downhill, smoke was boiling out of the Sacramento House bakery on the eastern side of the Square. Someone had intentionally stuffed a rag inside the flue of the bakery chimney at the rear of the Merchants Hotel. The alarm drew thousands of—spectators. Men stood silently as if being entertained. When the manual fire engines thundered downhill, sixty of the Fire Volunteers hauling on ropes immediately became entrapped in mud up to their shins.

"Engineers and traders dashed down the hill like an avalanche," Coffin noted and went to assist his friends Mr. Keith and Mr. Bard Plummer.

McCrackan was onboard the *Balance* visiting the Brooks family to see how their boy was when he again heard the alarm of "Fire!" and raced ashore. "The wind was quite strong for morning," he recalled, "and the fire blazed with a perfect fury. In five minutes it was evident the whole block must go, the flames being driven directly upon the United States Hotel in Montgomery Street."

Five minutes more and the fire communicated across the street.

Nothing could save the warehouses between there and the Cove. The heat was so intense that the Volunteers' few fire engines were deserted upon the wharves and damaged. McCrackan feared the block above would go next. Others who had offices in the same building he did were moving their things. He left his law books behind. Many items from the *Balance* stored in California Street were destroyed, a loss of about $500.

It took Coffin fifteen minutes to fight his way through smoke and panicked citizens to his friend Keith's store. Together, they lugged a chest filled with $30,000 in gold dust to the lower end of Howison's pier. At City Hall, an armed company of marines held the crowd back as soldiers carted chests of gold dust to the mud flats and shoveled mud on top. Coffin was worried over his new sloop, *Sophronia*, and the three small lighters he used to ferry goods to Marysville and decided to use that method. He left Keith mounted on top of his gold chest and rushed between the wharf and the pier by a narrow causeway in front of the Pacific Steamship Company and the Army Quartermaster's Warehouse. A posse struggling to save stored goods dropped their merchandise onto the dock where it was certain to burn before the flood tide came in. Coffin, smoked and scorched and breathless, reached the *Sophronia* lying in the low tide mud. What a cruel blow it would be to lose his sloop after having it refitted. He piled buckets of mud onto her until she was only a mound of mud.

A cart man drove down the wharf, dumped a huge military chest full of gunpowder at Coffin's feet, then drove his wagon furiously back the way he had come. With the help of three boatmen, Coffin pitched the smoking crate overboard and buried it in the mud. Returning to his sloop, he cut its sails from the spars and placed them under deck. He leaped onto shore where he dug out buckets of soft mud and spaded piles of it over the *Sophronia's* decks. Having done all he could, Coffin tried to stare down the approaching fire. Would it be enough?

Small craft, then larger vessels began to catch fire all around him. At any moment his sloop might burst into flame. Stored barrels of gunpowder exploded (almost every store had a barrel or two), their detonations quaking the ground. Exploding munitions from the Quartermaster's Warehouse sent burning coals raining down on Long Wharf. Fumes and cinders blanketed Coffin. Five thousand fully loaded muskets were stored inside the Quartermaster's. "If those stands of guns should all go off—" Coffin cried.

At this, three men abandoned two kegs of gunpowder on the burning dock and ran off. Coffin kicked the kegs into the water and dropped flat on the planks just as the guns onshore began to rapidly discharge. The fire's roar suppressed the noise of discharging muskets and only the rapid succession of flashes and smoke puffs showed him the guns were firing. The firearms had been fitted in perpendicular racks so that the shells were thrown directly upward and Coffin had only to dodge dozens of hot, spent musket balls raining down on him.

Twenty large crates stored just beyond the muskets contained the city's full supply of fireworks for the July 4 celebration. The kegs let go. Continuous blasts and pyrotechnics rose above the inferno. A wall of fire cut Coffin and five hundred other citizens off from the city and drove them along Long Wharf into the Ghost Fleet. Lit by colored lights and exploding starbursts, the castaways cowered among their bundles, boxes, and the pathetic little treasures they had been able to save. Absently, they patted out the glowing embers on their clothes, dodged raining debris, and prayed. Another wave of thermal heat rolled sluggishly over them. The maelstrom, having consumed five-hundred buildings on shore, now imperiled Long Wharf. Coffin felt the fire storm, snapping up ship's rigging consuming sails and twisting gun barrels as it moved swiftly toward him and the other castaways and soon was licking at their boots. They were burning. They lay facedown to accept death.

— II —
THE ZENITH OF INCANDESCENCE

The front of the city is expanding rapidly into the sea . . . . *This has left many of the old ships which a year ago beached as storehouses, in a curious position; for the filled in space that surrounds them has been built upon for some distance, and new streets run between them and sea, so that a stranger puzzles himself for some time to ascertain how the Apollo and Niantic became perched in the middle of the street.*

—Francis Marryat, English writer and artist

"WE HAD NOTHING TO DO as we lay on our bellies," Capt. Coffin wrote, "but gaze at the devouring monster whom at every blast of the hurricane came surging down Long Wharf in clouds of smoke and cinders to engulf us." The survivors were covered with sweat. The fire toyed with them, one moment sending blasts of superheated air and hot coals down the pier, and in another doubling back in a great swoop to ignite buildings and the survivors it had missed on its first pass. Soot blanketed Coffin. It turned black beards and white beards alike chalky gray. Dull reverberations—more munitions exploding like great stomping feet marching toward them, drew closer. The night sky was colored copper. It was the end of the world.

At the end of Long Wharf lay the tranquility of the Ghost Fleet, a gentle counterpoint to the shoreline. To calm himself, Coffin listened to the soothing tinkle of bells and studied the rigging and masts illuminated by the approaching flames. The firelight played tricks on his eyes, casting odd shadows over the water and ships in bold relief, making them "look as if an army of giants was advancing on the city."

Not all the Ghost Fleet would escape this time. Some ships, riding at their moorings, were already casualties. Rigging and masts were alight. No bother, Coffin thought. There were enough Ghost Fleet ships to outlast a dozen fires and more coming each hour. The Ghost Fleet was immortal. Ships ran before the wind from Oregon and Alaska—Savannah packets, Russian sealers, Yankee smugglers and whalers who had cut loose their whales, were rushing to join a variegated ever increasing Armada in the harbor of the "greatest go-ahead country in creation." Every ship brought supporting reinforcements of speculators, money men, traders, gamblers, prostitutes, and murderers like English Jim.

Coffin studied the hundreds of wavering lanterns. Who lit and tended them and whose unseen hands held them now. He had learned so little about so many and needed to know so much more and had so little time. Ten thousand outcasts populated the canting wrecks and intact vessels of this floating metropolis called Graveyard Harbor. He knew that much. The smoke of cooking fires and incoming fog mingled with black columns of smoke and ash, some from his own pipe, spiraling over the Cove. Because the ships drifted side-by-side, close enough for the residents to walk from one vessel to another, cook fires sometimes spread from one ship to another. Thus, the risk of fire inside the floating city was now as great as in the land city. Against a backdrop of fire, the water city went on rocking as if soothing itself— the rhythmical bumping of ships, counterpoint to the land explosions. The castaways on burning Long Wharf forgot their peril and even the Ghost Fleet dwellers paused in the abrupt stillness to listen to its lullaby. Abruptly, Coffin realized he was the one being evaluated too. The unseen inhabitants of the Ghost Fleet were peering back at him. He didn't have to turn to see the advancing fire. It was reflected in red pinpoints of light in the eyes of pale, hopeless faces.

Lit by the land fire, curious figures eventually emerged from hatchways and failings. He could see them now. They stood silently in decaying forecastles and mossy quarterdecks, heads bowed in prayer or sorrow. Others climbed onto bowsprits or clung from chain plates to hang over red-tinted water. All Friday night, the land castaways shivered as they lay 1500-feet into the water, nervously measuring the fire's progress and counting the minutes.

"The fire continued burning most of the day in particular points of the City," McCrackan said, "and has made dreadful destruction I assure you."

At dawn, a thick fog kept Coffin from seeing anything of the shore. What of his ship? he wondered. What would he see in another hour or so? He was certain it would be the loss of everything he held dear, and worse, the death of those denizens of Graveyard Harbor that he had come to prize.

"The fire was fast subsiding," English Journalist Frank Marryat observed, "and as the embers died away and the heavy smoke rolled off . . . the town and shipping are almost indistinguishable." Finally, the red curtain dimmed, leaving a heavy canopy of blue-gray smoke hanging in place.

"Fire! Fire! Fire!" Rev. Taylor cried as he took to his pulpit, a tea chest this time. The liquor barrels had exploded long ago. His eyes were bloodshot and full of fury. "A livery stable full of horses in flames," he thundered. "A mother and her infant in the third story of a building enveloped in fire. The returning husband wringing his hands in frenzy. What a dreadful scene!" He raised his fist and brought it down hard. Announcing his text as the fourth and fifth verses of the "140th *Psalm*," he recited. "Keep me, O Lord, from the hands of the wicked, preserve me from the violent man, who have purposed to overthrow my goings."

The conflagration, another arson, had hit the residential section as never before—three hundred major buildings consumed—a four-block square area. Cost—over four million dollars.

"The fire is more extensive even than the one of last month," McCrackan said. "While that fell upon gamblers . . . or merchants of comparatively a smaller class, this fire has destroyed the stores and warehouses of the most extensive merchants, burning quite to the water, good people." Like cholera, the experts felt such horrors fell only on the uneducated and criminal. This fire had dashed that contention. It struck indiscriminately. Dozens of ships crowded at their moorings were damaged. Coffin suddenly remembered his ship and began to run. He had to find out if she had survived. Falling and getting to his feet, helping others on the way, he was making little progress. Slowly, he made headway. He finally reached his sloop, and plumped down in the mud. He put his arms around the perfectly intact bow as if to cradle it. How had his ship fared, he wondered, rubbing his eyes until his face was covered in mud. Then, he figured out why. And that rocked him back on his feet with as much intensity as his vessel's survival.

Williams' warehouse stood at the corner of California Street and the dock, and because the street was very wide and the wind was blowing in another direction, the fire had not crossed.

"Thus," he said, "Happy Valley and my ship were saved." He snorted. Happy Valley! Happy, Happy, Happy! This stretch of dismal shoreline where hundreds had perished of cholera had saved him and now he loved it. Nor did the fire cross to the north of Montgomery Street or west of Long Wharf, although east of the wharf was all cleared off. If the large wooden store of Hussey, Bond & Hale, which formed the western boundary of the wharf, had taken fire, nothing could have halted the blaze. Coffin got down on his knees and thanked merciful Providence that the fire had not exploded the large bluff-bowed *Niantic* storeship. A month earlier, the *Niantic* had taken aboard nearly two thousand tons of combustible merchandise—about two hundred casks of gunpowder. The *Niantic* was a particular favorite because his nephews had re-floated her to her present location and been responsible for its great success.

But, the city had lost its expensive new plank roads and most of its new wharves. Coffin picked his way over lava-like ground, smoking timbers, and pools of melted gold and silver. While the fire was raging those who had just been burned out were signing contracts for new buildings. Before nightfall, the same men were carting construction materials to the blackened ruins. Two days later, they were rebuilding in a landscape of fused metal skeletons, tottering walls, and tilted brick chimneys. As if on cue a powerful and evil wind swept in from the ocean and tumbled a wall into the mud. The men leapt to their tools. Up went the wall again. The gale was drying the living firetrap, making it ready for the next intentional burning. He wondered how people could rebuild so soon after losing all they had. He smiled at the indomitable grit of San Franciscans. It took fortitude. It took firmness. It took resolution.

"Surely," Coffin said, "it is not so easy to raise money in California. The banks will not take these evanescent buildings as security. Of course! The losses had not been their own. Nearly all were commission merchants who had not been prompt in making remittances to their constituents at home. Instead, they had deposited the proceeds of sales, intending to remit the whole at once. Well, the fire affords an excellent opportunity to close accounts and benefit. Books and merchandise are all burnt, but the bankers vaults are safe."

Money and fire went hand in hand—a terrific motive for these city-destroying arsons. He wondered who was behind them. He suspected that there was another motive involved altogether, an insidious plan he could not fathom.

ENGLISH JIM BELIEVED the two objects on the table before him were the most glorious things he had ever seen. Auburn dry miners had found a six-pound lump of gold and a fourteen-pound lump shot through with two pounds of quartz. Another miner, Mr. Netherby, had unearthed a splendid 127-ounce lump of gold. English Jim could see the quartz was of a very dark color, and fine particles of gold were closely and regularly commingled throughout. Mr. Nickerson bought it for $2,500, and got a bargain. "If it is such a curiosity for this land of gold and wonders," he said, "what would it be in the States?" English Jim's head spun with thoughts of gold. He hefted the ore and smiled. He knew there was more like it in the Custom House vault of San Francisco, many millions and he had plans to make it his.

"Auburn is in status quo," one observer cautioned English Jim. "Believe me, the dry diggings have just one more good season left. You better tread carefully." Originally called North Fork Dry Diggings and Wood's Dry Diggings, the town had only two streets, Court and Commercial. "Those who have passed the winter here having pulled up stakes and started off up the Forks."

Several mining companies, including the Bay State and California Mining Company had set up to channel the river to the diggings. Frank Randall had formed his own mining company three months earlier. English Jim had worked for him and invested $300 in the Missouri Company. As predicted, three mining companies at Foster's Bar were three too many. English Jim wished he had heeded the warning. Operators in the mines had been averaging only an ounce a day near the North Fork of the Yuba River.

As predicted, all failed that summer. With this, English Jim decided to go straight. He went back to work on his boarding house, refining and adding new rooms. His garden flourished and became the talk of the neighborhood. Surprisingly, he had become an honest man almost without realizing it. No one was more shocked than himself. Now if only he could stay on this path.

English Jim's attempts at honesty began to fail in sudden, and spectacular ways. After all, he was quite inexperienced in the art and had no idea what to expect. None of his failures were really his fault. They began this way. When Edward Gifford built a toll bridge across the North Yuba at the end of June, he put a damper on English Jim's iron ferry boat business. Disheartened, Jim gave his boat away (though it would be used as a ferry for the next one hundred years). Then, the Missouri Company closed and left without paying him for the use of his iron boat. Nor did they repay the $300 he had loaned them.

"When Daniel Casey sold out," English Jim explained, "I bought all there was in the house."

In searching their abandoned house, he discovered an open trunk full of clothing. The shirts, dyed drab green and brown, fit him well. Because they had come with the house he figured he had a right to them and took the clothes. He wore one the next morning. The shirt was a long, pull-over wool tunic closed by three buttons. The cuff closed with a single button. The shirt was very recognizable and would get him in terrible trouble.

"The night after I took the clothing," English Jim said, "I went to Capt. Ezra Dodge's [public house] and played two hands of [French] Monte, where I lost $200. I felt that I had been cheated and determined I would get even with him." Being cheated gave him the right to reclaim his money. "I watched him closely that night from an adjoining tent and saw him put the money in a wooden chest. Waiting until they were asleep, I entered the tent and carried off the chest." Inside the chest, English Jim discovered more than $200. There were two gold specimens, a piece of gold worth $1,568, another worth $738, $600 in silver, and $1,349 in dust—a total of $4,300. "I took it all home, secreted most of it in my flower bed which had now taken on a dual function, that of beauty and that of a bank. Then, I resumed my honest toil as usual and forgot all about it." As Mark Twain later wrote: "Do the right thing. It will gratify some people and astonish the rest." English Jim liked the feeling of self-respect that now possessed him. He walked a little taller, and looked folks directly in the eye. Yet, the most surprising setback of all came from within himself.

"I realized I had grown bored with the honest, uneventful life and let my garden go to seed." He had had enough and returned to his old ways. Honesty could have been his, but he lacked staying power in any job and had become a garden of weeds. Those who knew him were both disappointed and surprised. There was no going back.

Over time, English Jim committed a string of crimes for which his unsuspecting twin, Tom Berdue, mining elsewhere in the region, was identified as the assailant by witnesses. When Berdue was sighted by Jacob Sholet in September, he mistook him for English Jim, a man he had worked with closely.

"Stuart was a hard and quick worker," Sholet said, "two things English Jim had never been. The juries in the mining camps couldn't be blamed for mistaking the two for each other, rushed as they were to bring in a verdict within the required three hour time limit. Murder was punishable by hanging, but then so was hanging.

Bob Booker, a friend of Charles E. Moore, had known English Jim for about a month.

"I saw him frequently," Booker said. "He went by the name of James Stuart, or more commonly, English Jim. I did not work with him but, played cards with him. I heard of difficulties between Stuart and Moore who was sometimes called 'Sheriff' Moore or the 'Sheriff of Yuba City', though he was in no way a real sheriff. Moore dealt monte and Stuart played at his bank and lost heavily. I know that Moore was afraid to go to Foster's Bar because he was afraid Stuart would kill him."

Eight miles above Foster's Bar, at Slate Range, John Sullivan awakened in his tent to a strange sight. He froze, afraid to move in fear of his life. He remained rigid in his bed and waited until it was safe. "How odd," he thought, sitting up after a few minutes, "to see Jesus Christ creeping out of our tent dressed in a fur cap and large leather coat and armed with a fourteen-inch Bowie knife lashed to one leg and a brace of double-barreled pistols at his belt."

The next day, English Jim returned to camp flush with money again and able to pay $100 to redeem a precious gold watch (he already had four). Sullivan would not see him face to face again until October when he was arrested for robbery and sentenced to be hanged and only by divine intervention was saved.

AFTER COFFIN HAD COMPLETED another round trip to Marysville, he hurried to the waterfront to learn what handsome sum his lighters had earned him during his absence.

"But, I was disappointed," he said. "Two of the tenders had been lost or stolen and one of the scows had been smashed, and it cost me $300 [the same amount stolen from English Jim] to repair her." His one-man crew, Thurlo, had been a poor choice. He had permitted some sailors he had hired to run roughshod over him. Coffin fired the unfortunate young man and put his lighters up at auction. Their sale brought him only a little over $1,000. To outfit them had cost him three times that much. "The parties who fixed up the *Sophronia* had built a fine sloop of twenty-five tons," he said, "well-suited to the river trade, which they urged me to purchase for $4,100, one-third cash, the balance payable in four and six months, and in an evil hour I consented. Oh! That abominable *IF*!"

Beneath the piers, slender boats slid through the dark, carrying limp bodies that had been passed down through the trap doors of saloons. The water was misty and iron-colored. The silhouettes of masts peeked over low rooftops. Canvas tents made gauzy by interior light shimmered in the fog. Long Wharf led into a place unlike any other in the world—a phantom metropolis of nearly a thousand lost ships. Tattered sails flapped in the rising trade wind. Coffin's boots echoed hollowly on the planks. He descended a wooden ladder at the far end of the pier and dropped into the skiff he had tethered there. He itched to remove himself from the land of disappointment and death and get back on the water, the best and only life he had ever known.

From the jumping ships, the rotating masts, the drumbeat of a thousand hulls, he felt a sense of energy. Soon, his heart began to jump and beat to the same rhythm. It was the song of the Ghost Fleet. As he had lain down on Long Wharf with fire approaching Coffin had had time to think. That night he had conceived a history like no other. He had not only decided to write a biography of Graveyard Harbor, but paint its soul and map it. The geography was simple. The vessels sat in the Cove both north and south of Market Street, separated by Long Wharf. The corners of Sansome, Battery, and Sacramento Streets had been put on piles and piers large enough to accommodate the stores and premises forming the junction of the streets. The *Daily Alta California* had shown interest in this strange floating settlement as a place to live. By night, nameless loafers slept against clusters of piles on the central wharf.

"Keeping track is impossible in a city like this, where whole streets are built up in a week and whole squares swept away in an hour," the city directory noted, "where the floating population numbers hundreds, large portions of the fixed inhabitants live in places which cannot be described with any accuracy." Writer John Williamson tried. He noted that the water population included "Swiss, Jews, Turks, Chinese, Kanakas [Hawaiian Islanders], New Zealanders, Malays, and Negroes, Parthians, Medes, and Elamites, Cretes, and Arabians, and the dwellers in Mesopotamia and Cappadocia, in Boston and New Orleans, Chicago and Peoria, Hoboken, and Hackensack." Italians, Spaniards, Norwegians, Russians, Englishmen, Frenchmen, Germans, and Dutchmen lived there. Williamson could think of no more and put down his pen.

Coffin pulled hard along the ship corridors, relying on flickering lights on the docks to guide him as he explored the water city by night. Quite quickly, he discovered how difficult it was to judge direction between high wooden walls against the howl of the sand shore. Acoustics within the Bay were tricky. Mile Rocks at the Gate picked up sounds, amplified them, and dropped them somewhere within the watery canyons of the Ghost Fleet. Yet, that was not the end of them. Noises were magnified between the hulls and funneled through the narrow water roads between ships until they unexpectedly exited somewhere on land fully as loud as they had begun so that you thought a fleet was sailing outside your front door.

Eventually, Coffin peaked his oars to get his bearings and wait for the echoes to die away. He rowed on, keeping all two square miles of the leafless timberland fixed firmly in his mind—two tightly clustered groups of over four hundred vessels each separated only by Howison's Wharf, Long Wharf, and Clay Street Pier. Among the 775 to 900 orphaned Gold Rush ships comprising a rotting, rocking city of secrets, few escaped the crowded Cove. Only men-of-war with their officers' iron discipline onboard ever escaped. The rest were there to stay.

Graveyard Harbor was constantly at the mercy of the rhythms of the receding or filling harbor. The ships arched their sterns toward the Golden Gate or optimistically pointed their bows seaward into the oncoming flow. Some ships pointed inward, precisely in the attitude they had evidenced on the day of their arrival. Frigates and windjammers that could swing round without bumping their neighbor did so with the ebbing current.

Patiently, seaworthy ships waited their chance to escape, but surrounded by half-sunken hulks and linked by rusting anchor chains so much penned-in tonnage could never be moved. On the abandoned armada's outskirts the most recent recruits danced sluggishly with the tide. For them, escape from this Sargasso Sea was still possible, but they would have to act fast to get away. Each day, each hour, ships were coming to surround them and block their exit. Hundreds of ships, dragged about by the currents, swung helplessly on their anchor chains that only tangled into knots with other anchors and fouled cables until all the yards, rigging, chains, and shrouds were wedded to each other. Many vessels were still sail-worthy, if only crews could be found and enticed away from the mines.

"Had there ever been a place as unique as this water metropolis?" Coffin said. Its existence was a book that needed to be written. He was thinking of his *Log*. Each orphaned ship had its own story to tell and he should get them down while he had time and all was swept away or buried. The *Cadmus* had carried Lafayette to America twenty-five years earlier, and another, the *Plover*, had sailed the Arctic in search of Franklin. A heavy fog drifting about two-feet over the surface of the water city made the setting even more mysterious. Dim lanterns glowed inside each ship. Steps led up from the water to doors cut into the planks. What was behind those doors? He drew closer and pressed against the side. From inside, he could make out the buzz-saw snores of lodgers crammed thirty-six per cabin into six-tiered pine bunks.

Coffin rowed on, losing his way and finding it again and growing more confident as he went. The long unraveled ends of hanging stays and shrouds brushed his face, then dropped away with the roll of the ships on both sides. He rowed faster, fearing the huge vessels might swing about on their anchor lines and crush him. The smallest vessels were the *Breeze*, a fourteen-ton yacht, and the *Toccao*, a twenty-eight-ton schooner. The largest was the *Grey Eagle* at over a thousand tons. Coffin passed the *Talca* lying about a cable's length off the foot of Washington Street, had been since late December. He listed the *Golconda, Copiapo, Regulus, Alceste, Thames, Neptune, Mersey, Caroline Augusta, Dianthe, Bay State* and *Genetta de Goito.*

Rushing through one shadowed alley, he heard a rattle of chains behind timbers and a moan that transcended all languages. He halted among the rocking ships and listing hulks and listened. Among the trapped schooners, square-riggers, colliers, brigs, windjammers, steamers, brigantines, and barks he heard only whispering. Graveyard Harbor was speaking to him. Someone was speaking to him. Anchored in the deep fog ahead was a rotting two-masted brig square-rigged on both masts. Sturdy anchors at its stem kept it moored off the Battery Street Wharf, the intersection of Battery and Jackson. When it was moved it lay close to Long Wharf where it intersected Battery and Sacramento. Its sides were lit only by rows of pale lights showing in her lowest deck. A flight of steps led up to a platform about two-thirds up. From the platform a separate, shorter flight continued to the deck. A uniformed man on her uppermost deck suddenly appeared out of the fog and leveled his rifle at Coffin.

"Get on with you, whoever you are."

"What?" Coffin said. "What is this, whoever you are?"

"This is the *Euphemia.*"

"The *Euphemia!*"

The word hung in the air as if the beaten, lashed and mistreated prisoners confined inside had spoken the hated word, "*Euphemia,*" and not the guard.

"Keep your distance if you don't want to end up with these wretches," he said.

Far out to sea approaching ships heard the clanking and groaning of the Ghost Fleet, but not a whimper of the jail's suffering prisoners. The disease-ridden brig's floating dungeon housed twenty-five of the region's most hardened criminals in the lower main hold. When the Town Council asked for a catchall ship to confine drunks, thieves, and deserters, they never expected to get "the most awful and filthy den, perhaps ever beheld by any human being." Formerly, the *Euphemia* had been the *Uphamer,* an English brig (not Spanish as Coffin erroneously believed) that sailed the China trade for Henry Skinner and his bunch. She sailed under the Sandwich Islands (Hawaiian) flag. But not for long. Heath Davis persuaded malleable Commodore Jones, our friend of the missing maps and cannon-powered hangings, to fly an American flag. A slow trader, the *Euphemia* carried more than double her tonnage in freight and on its first voyage to California cleared $30,000. For years it carried lumber and furs between the Islands and San Francisco until Sam Brannan bought the *Euphemia* for a city jail for $3,500, and spent another $8,000 to turn it into "a regular Calcutta hole."

"Damn them anyway!" Brannan said of the prisoners. "They're guests of the town. All we're doing is keeping a hotel for hoodlums and thieves. I think we should make them work. Put a ball and chain on their legs and shovels in their hands and lash them to put in an honest day's labor." Warming to the idea, Brannan spent $520 for new balls and chains and a barrel of handcuffs.

Coffin had no idea handcuffs came in barrels. A line of heavy iron links held by a series of hooks, ran the length of the hold. Any sudden movement by any single prisoner pinned the other men sharing the chain to the wall. Prisoners were flogged for minor transgressions, their heart-rending pleas and screams rising above the thumping and scraping of the waterborne city. Coffin heard them now. In the fall and winter the captives were allowed on deck for sun and exercise, but when the summer haze filled the Cove for weeks at a time they were locked in their cells so they wouldn't run off under the concealment of fog. When cells were full, guards kept the overflow in an after-hold reserved for supplies.

Two months earlier, five convicts had escaped the floating jail. Devil Jack was still looking for them. Because the *Euphemia* was commonly surrounded by frigates and men-of-war and anchored near wharves, an escaping prisoner had only to step over the rail and walk to shore.

"A floating prison," Coffin said, "is inadequate for a city that doubles its population every few months." Eventually, the city would force the prisoners to build a new city prison on Angel Island, then transport them to San Quentin Point to construct California's first land penitentiary. When the hell ship's usefulness as a prison ended it would be towed to North Beach as the town's first "lunatic house." But that was not now. Coffin rowed away shaking his head. "The harbor is choked with abandoned ships that could be used for no cost at all," he said, "and the citizens went ahead and paid for this obscenity."

A frigid wind blew across the mud flats. It sang through an awful rigging of parted shrouds. Coffin climbed aboard a frigate that interested him to study a swirling design inscribed on her deck. "What can it mean," he thought. "Such intricacy—a maze of dark rectangles and intersecting lines like a map. See how the lines turn back upon themselves, and whirl across the hatches." Following the serpentine design, he noticed large wet footprints gleaming on the deck. "They are not footprints at all," he consoled himself, "but only puddles reflecting back the light from shore."

Looking over his shoulder, Coffin returned to his skiff and began to row. The exercise was marvelous and he was in the best shape of his life. All the adversity he had suffered had made him stronger and tougher. As he floated among the forbidding passageways of the *Chateaubriand* of Le Havre, the *Sarah Parker* of Nantucket, the *Carib* of Salem, the *Naumkeag* of Providence, and the *John Allyn* of New Bedford, flocks of seabirds took wing. He followed the dark shape with his eyes until they vanished in the distance. He traveled on. He passed a windjammer rocking unsteadily in the swells leeward. His objective was the low marshlands, rocks, headlands, shoals of mud, and deep water channels which encircled the Cove. He rowed on.

Eventually, he reached the outer fringe of the floating city. Here the Bay was silent except for the wind in the rushes and crash of surf against the black rocks at the Gate. It surprised him that from this spot he could not see the Golden Gate. He wrestled with this riddle until he answered it. As the incoming flow funnels through the narrows between Lime Point and Fort Point it piles up and the water level inside the Bay rises as much as eight-feet. Eight feet! This action rounds the back of a harbor already bent to the curvature of the earth so that a clear view of the vestibule is hidden to a man in a small, low boat. Naturally, any ship twenty miles out to sea would be invisible to Coffin. The Bay, bent like a goose's neck, sends ships sailing uphill for the last two miles. "Perhaps," he thought, "that's why so many exhausted vessels faltered on the last lap and sank with the finish line within sight. They never knew how near they were to their goal and gave up."

Coffin was eager to authenticate the various legends of Graveyard

Harbor. In an article for the *Sacramento Union*, Mark Twain described the creation of a ghost ship in the Ghost Fleet, the first of the Cove's famous legends. "A swift-sailing vessel was built," Twain wrote, "in a single night, in the midst of storm and thunder, and rain, by the ghastly hands of dead men! Tradition says that by the weird glare of the lightning a noiseless multitude of phantoms were seen at their strange labor far out in the midst of a ghost fleet at dead of night—flitting hither and thither and bearing great timbers clasped in their nerveless fingers—appearing and disappearing as the pallid luster fell upon their forms and faded away again. Even to this day locals hold this dread craft in awe and reverence and will not row by it at night."

Coffin had heard that the spirits of the prison ship *Euphemia's* flogged convicts had returned in thunder and rain to construct a ghost ship. Her hull of copper plating was hot to the touch, her prow sharp enough to cut through toughest rock, and her rusting chains unbreakable. Designs on her deck, burned into the wood, were decorated with elaborate bits of shells that could never be dug out. Smoke curled from the rigging. The workers grew transparent and faded away before dawn. Ships approaching the abandoned ship claimed to hear her sloshing against the waves, but she was always gone by the time they reached the spot.

Soon it was morning. He had seen nothing.

Coffin prepared for his trip to Sacramento by loading his new sloop with corn and potatoes. His timing was good. Pork and mutton in San Francisco were selling for seventy-five cents a pound. Butter, lard, and cheese were going for a dollar a pound, and eggs for ten dollars a dozen. His cargo would go for a good profit in Sacramento. As he lay down to sleep onboard his ship, Coffin discovered that he was supremely uncomfortable. His bed was a narrow shelf so close to the deck that once he squeezed in he could not turn over.

"If I wished to 'tack ship' I was obliged to back out and get in afresh t'other side to," he complained. "It came on to rain during the night in true California fashion, and my ear being within six-inches of the deck, the beating of the raindrops kept me awake."

As he tossed in his wooden coffin, he became depressed. He had descended precipitously from command of one of the largest freighting ships to setting out on a voyage of uncertain fortune in a small sloop to sell potatoes.

Coffin turned out by 4:00 AM and fried some salt pork and potatoes on a Portland patent compact miner's stove—energy for a day's work. "I enjoyed it much," he said, rubbing his stomach. "A good appetite kept the dirt out of sight and made the coffee palatable, which at any other time would have seemed like sweetened dishwater, seasoned with tobacco."

By 6:00 AM, he had passed two small islands on the starboard hand called the Brothers off Point San Pablo and two others on the other side off Point San Pedro called the Sisters. The passage between the two, about one-mile wide, connects San Francisco Bay with broad, shallow San Pablo Bay. San Francisco Bay itself extends nearly forty miles southeastward from where the Golden Gate thrusts through the Coast Range and ten miles northeast joins San Pablo Bay and connects with Suisun Bay through the Carquinez (kah-kee'-nes) Strait. The sun was up early and so was he. As the fog burned away, Coffin tried to calculate the growth of the discarded armada filling the Cove behind him. He failed.

"How to describe this amazing spectacle?" he said?

He attempted it: "Ships from every nation and country lay here, idle and worthless, with no prospect of ever leaving—many must go down at their anchor, for there are not enough men to work the twentieth of them. The Bay is literally a sea afloat."

As far as Coffin could tell, the Ghost Fleet had no real beginning or end.

At its inception at the Golden Gate, it was not yet a ship city as it was constantly growing and moving like the Mississippi, not from a trickle of water but from a steady flow of ships. At its end it was no longer the Ghost Fleet but, as it crowded onto shore and its lumber and ships were detached to become new buildings, became part of the land. As San Francisco's cityscape rumbled into the Cove under its own volition and around and over the orphaned ships, the city itself became part of the ships which were its bones.

Life on the water was a tradition in San Francisco Bay. From the earliest days there had been floating homes in Yerba Buena Cove. A dozen years earlier, pioneer Nathan Spear tried to build a home on land while his Boston bark *Kent* was being overhauled. Because Mexican law then forbade anyone building closer than two-hundred yards from shore, he devised an alternate plan. He bought a discarded deck house, floated it near the Cove shore and lived on that. And that was the beginning. As more families moved from their ship homes to land, those who remained aboard began living more spaciously. Onboard the *Balance*, passengers, despite the recent loss by fire of furniture they had stored on shore, remodeled the salon and cabin and hung them with paintings. Coffin began experimenting on the dock and discovered he had a gift for oil painting. San Francisco Bay lies at right angles to the entrance and extends nearly seventy miles north to south. Capt. Coffin wasn't about to set any speed records in either direction, including east to west, on his laborious trip along the Sacramento River. He averaged five-miles-per-hour.

"Warp and tie, warp and tie, warp and tie!" he lamented, gnashing his teeth. "Sun shining down in a blaze of fury, with not a cloud to screen his scorching rays; thermometer one hundred and ten degrees, not a breath to cool our frizzling livers—and mosquitoes! Oh, my conscience!"

Yet, he only prepared for another trip as soon as he could. On July 30, full of hopeful enterprise and ready to try again, he loaded both his sloops for Marysville, hired three young Germans to navigate the *Sophronia*, and ordered them ahead to wait for him at Sacramento. On August 1, he enjoyed a breakfast of fried fish and chocolate onboard the *Adelaide* with his cousin Capt. George Noyes and his friend, Louis Martin, who was living onboard the battered brig. Coffin liked Martin enough to hire him to follow the Germans onboard the sloop *Merlin*. The vessel had a shallow keel and a center board traversing on a pivot to keep the ship from drifting sideways. Coffin and Martin set off early with ten-thousand pounds of potatoes that were currently selling for twenty-five cents a pound.

"I had a fine breeze from the westward," Coffin reported, "and went on swimmingly through the three bays, San Francisco, Pablo, and Suisun, and at night brought up at the New York of the Pacific where there were three buildings and four condemned ships and that was all." The elevation to New York Slough is forty-five-degrees and to Benicia Town thirty-degrees. Gulls were crying across the choppy water, when Coffin unaccountably felt a chill up his spine. Cautiously, he anchored for the night but the feeling persisted. He had to find out why.

On JULY 4, 1850, as flags waved and guns fired, Calhoun "Cal" Gardiner, "a loose fish ready to snap at any bait," had come down to the city that he called "full of impecunious specimens of humanity ready to jump at any means of subsistence." He was one of those very people. Over the last year, he had tried mining on the Tuolumne River, but his claim, the richest on Hawkins Bar, was jumped. Then, he joined the diggings at the southern mines. In the winter, he had fallen ill with dysentery and fever at Sullivan Creek, but was cured by a prescription of brandy and peppermint. He returned to Hawkins Bar where men were being buried daily. "It was raining all but one day a week," he said. Supplies were nearly exhausted and it became necessary for him to get away to avoid actual starvation. Before he left, he witnessed his friend shoot a man in self defense.

Gardiner hurried down to the Cove to see if the *Sylph* which brought him to San Francisco last year was still there. It was, but in far worse condition than he had imagined. She was now only a rotting hulk in the Cove with red-eyed strangers living aboard her. Gardiner had boarded the former Fair Haven whaler at Panama with a friend's $300 ticket, a bucket, a sawdust-filled mattress, and a borrowed copy of *The Three Musketeers* that he read in the rigging. The *Sylph* had drifted northwest in search of trade winds as passengers survived on salt pork and weevil-fouled hardtack. It was said of the ship's butter that, "the sight is sufficient without the smell." He had come to the Gold Rush from the upper crust of Sag Harbor, Long Island and spent a privileged childhood playing on Gardiner's Island and swimming in Gardiner's Bay. What a precipitous drop in fortune, he thought, as bad as the *Sylph's*. These days, he was working in the Square for twelve dollars a day as a carpenter. This was in spite of the fact that he had no carpentry skills). To survive, he went about cadging meals, moving cargoes up and down the waterfront (he had a strong back to go with his raging appetite), selling fruit trees and loading kegs of nails on a storeship. He even charged a man $16 to sit with him at a card table and $200 to escort him home that night through the dangerous streets.

Defeated, like so many around him who were struggling to regain their feet, Gardiner dragged himself down to Long Wharf. A large sailing ship, the *Una* under Capt. Causzer, was at anchor. She had cleared Sydney on April 3 and sailed four days later for San Francisco packed with building supplies. Among its passengers were Joseph and Mary Anne Windred who had emigrated from Windsor, New South Wales, to dig gold. The Windreds, glad to be on firm ground again, went immediately to Happy Valley to locate John and Elicia Gough who had earlier led a party from Windsor which included Thomas Berdue, English Jim's identical twin.

Instead of mining like their friend, Berdue, the Goughs leased a two-story wooden house near First and Mission and turned the ground floor into the Panama House Restaurant and Bar. Several police from the corner station boarded with them and kept them safe. Of the three men in Gough's party who knew the mining region, two were unavailable. Joseph Wright had died, and the whereabouts of the other, James Smith, was unknown.

"And the third man?" Windred asked John Gough.

He described an inoffensive shipmate, casual acquaintance, and luckless young gambler. "Tom Berdue will be able to guide you," Gough told them confidently. Tom Berdue was a name to remember, a very important name in the saga of Graveyard Harbor. "You can find him at a small trading place about six miles from the North Fork of the American River and some forty-five miles from Sacramento. There is some little digging about the place, but the principal digging is from the North Fork."

John copied the contact information down: "Thomas Berdue, city of Auburn, Dry Diggings, to be found at the German baker's there. Write to the care of Mr. Gymas, storekeeper."

The Windreds stocked up with some of Sam Brannan's overpriced mining supplies, then took the steamer up the Sacramento River to Auburn. Berdue was not there, though they learned that he and Bernard Feller were partners in a dry goods store. As the Windreds waited for Tom to come down from the hills, they prospected a little. It seemed as if he would never come, so they learned to fend for themselves. As for Berdue, he was running for his life. Crimes committed by his identical twin, English Jim, had been pinned on him and there was no way out.

P̲ROSPECTOR RICHARD LUNT HALE had endured a chilly

159-day voyage to Graveyard Harbor aboard the *General Worth* of Newburyport. Now, he was paying for it as he recovered from a long illness. As an observer, though, he was in fine fettle. His initial look at Graveyard Harbor brought Capt. Coffin's *Log* up to date. "The Cove is thickly covered with sails and hulks of all descriptions," Hale commented his first day, "every craft of sail, and every shape of spar surrounds us. There must be close to a thousand vessels at anchor in the Bay . . . of every grade and every rig of vessel, representing every nation that has deep water craft."

Southward in a long, high sand-drift lay Rincon Point, scattered with pitched cloth tents, wooden hovels, and broken ships. As the *General Worth* passed Clark's Point, a rocky and windswept headland to the North, the warm sunny day quickly altered. Before Lunt got to shore, strong breezes from the ocean became a gale driving sand before it. In the late afternoon, he got a job pulling down shacks partially destroyed by one of the recent fires. "They were still hot," he said, "the nails burning hot, but we kept at it, working all through the night. In the morning when presenting our bills we were told to go to a place for our pay which was hotter than the fire."

Next day, Hale was ill. He was trembling in his sick bed when things got worse, but not for himself. He heard blasting and limped to the window. Peering down from his hillside, he saw a man and his helper trying to sink a water shaft. Water was more precious than gold and silver in San Francisco. The two men had drilled down ninety-feet through a solid ledge, and one was standing in a big tub secured by a chain to a cranked windlass. As the other man began lowering the first down in a bucket, Hale heard a snap.

"I saw the chain give away three links above his grasp," he recalled. "Then came a sound of thunder as his car struck the walled sides of the well in its rapid course downward."

Hale cried, "Man killed!"

Gear was rigged and the well-sinker was brought to the surface. To their surprise, he had suffered only a bruised knee.

"It was not the fall that hurt," he called up to Hale with a laugh, "but the sudden stop."

The next day, a foggy day, Hale was no better. He threw in the towel and decided to leave the City of Golden Promise to better his fortune in Portland. He had not the fortitude of Capt. Coffin, or the endurance of the battered well-digger who was back in his bucket. Just as Hale departed San Francisco on the *Tarquina*, he passed Capt. Coffin who was sailing back from Sacramento with a lighter heart and a rare success. Absent a fortnight, he had cleared $1200. As Coffin anchored in the Cove, he saw the rapid progress the piers were making. Long Wharves would be needed, the longer the better, he decided. Big men with big dreams in big ships were sailing into the most rambunctious port anywhere and needed depth to anchor. The future "Emperor of the Cove," and consequently of Graveyard Harbor, was at this moment finding his way through the heavy mist at the hidden Cove. He was a Hudson River swashbuckler with tattoos, cutlass, twin flintlocks, and everything one would expect in such a bigger than life character.

On July 11, 1850, one hundred-and-fifty days after boldly stealing a Hudson River paddle wheeler from under a sheriff's nose, a sun-baked pirate with jet black hair and glistening whiskers sailed his prize through the Golden Gate. Burly and big-fisted, the Pirate kept a brace of pistols at his belt and a Bowie knife strapped outside his jacket much as English Jim did. He was so big that he hardly needed weapons. A blue-black streak, the permanent mark of a belaying pin, ran alongside the bridge of his nose. He had the standard set of strong white teeth, though his father had possessed a *double* row of teeth all the way round.

Tattoos inscribed by a sharpened whale's tooth covered his bronzed skin from head to foot. Many told his life story. The names of his wife and children were artfully tattooed on his arms. A colorful Goddess of Liberty unfurling an American flag was leaning nonchalantly against a cannon. This stirring scene was etched on one leg. All the images were crisp except those across his chest. The slashing claw of a Malay tiger had rippled and distorted Liberty holding the American flag, Christ on the Cross, and a sailing ship. They looked as if they had been tattooed on the water. Freshly gilded name boards flanking the pilot house spelled out the steamer's name: *New World*. At the wheel, Capt. Edgar "Ned" Wakeman, brass-buttoned in blue broadcloth, gave one steam-clouded blast of the multi-note chime, a combined whistle and calliope. The Pirate was so versatile he could play songs on it. His white side-wheel, flat-bottomed river paddler was a high-pressure ship, boiling at its average working pressure of fifty pounds-per-square inch. Below a vertical-beam engine, sucking steam from brick backed boilers, turned thundering side-wheels, one on either side of the ship, with unceasing rhythm. The paddlewheel was enclosed in a housing to minimize spray. Trailing a heavy cloud of smoke, Capt. Wakeman swept into a thick bank of fog and added his own smoke to the murk.

The giant gritted his dazzling white teeth as he gave another burst on the whistle—a deep burbling that swelled to a gravelly roar that might have originated from his throat. For a minute the whistle roared like the tiger that had mauled him, then stopped short. Wakeman waited for the answering echo to give him an approximation of their distance from land, but the reply was unsatisfying. The shoreline's odd configuration at the Golden Gate which had so confounded Capt. Coffin deflected sound waves and made fog signals ineffective. Additionally, the shape of the Gate's cliffs created mazes of sound that delivered noises from one section of the harbor and deposited them unscathed elsewhere. In between were bewildering pockets of silence at the spots where the greatest hazards to navigation lay. Ships entering these regions of inaudibility abruptly found themselves deaf to fog bells, whistles, and ships horns. This did not deter the Pirate. He would find San Francisco Bay if he had to put in at every inlet "as big as a half-inch auger hole."

His experience echoed Capt. Coffin's. Sharp-eyed Sir Francis Drake had overlooked well-concealed Yerba Buena Cove. Spanish explorers had flown right by though Capt. Sebastian Cermeno had come the closest. He cast anchor at nearby Point Reyes, but only because he was shipwrecked there. He passed the Cove a second time as he returned south to Mexico in a longboat. Granted he had other things on his mind. As you know, the entrance, a five-mile-long strait running north to east, was dangerous. Its narrowest point was little more than one-mile wide and its widest point two miles wide. A half-mile off the southern head, Point Lobos or Wolves Point, and a mile south of the main ship channel.

Wakeman listened patiently to the slatted paddle boxes above him in the fog, regularly filling and emptying as the racing side wheels made full revolutions. He estimated the tidal stream though the Golden Gate to be running at six knots an hour. He was concluding a five-month, fifteen-thousand-mile sea chase with bullets, cannon shot, disease, peril, and dishonesty (his own) at every port. A British frigate had fired upon him, yet he kept on. He had made Valparaiso, coaled up, somehow acquired three hundred cash customers and boiled in the direction of the Golden Gate where he was now blocked by a wall of fog. He smiled as he remembered the morning creditors attached the *New World* at her launching slip along the East River and how he had talked them into taking a trial run. Undersheriff Willard Cunningham had been suspicious. He thought it unusual for a ship to be launched full steam up, but Wakeman had explained it was to keep the boilers from bursting.

"I want to see that everything is in good order and that the steamer is seaworthy," he said. "Come on, Sheriff, bring your deputies. Let's just cruise a little and enjoy such a fine Sunday."

Turning in a widening sheet, the *New World* headed down harbor.

"Why are you headed this way?" Cunningham asked. Wakeman only smiled and blew his bosun's pipe. His armed crew boiled onto deck. "I am the sheriff of New York City and County," Cunningham said, drawing himself up. "This vessel is in my charge and she shall be taken back to the dock."

"And I am master of the good ship *New World*, afloat upon the high seas," Wakeman replied coolly.

He put the officers over the side onto a Staten Island mud flat and then into a towing rowboat. "You might want to row that way, Sheriff, if you don't want to be late for supper," he said, pointing toward Sandy Hook. "You can catch the Staten Island ferry after wading three miles through mud. Have a good journey."

Boarding up the glass-sided, flat-bottomed paddler's hold and windows, Wakeman stocked it with fuel and charged into an Atlantic storm like a bull. Head down and teeth gritted, he ordered his diminutive engineer Billy Van Wert to sit up in his cushioned chair and hold the steam gauge needle at the pin. When the steam chest cracked, Wakeman bound it with a chain and iron wedges. Then he just kept going. Yes, Wakeman had stolen himself quite a ship. The beautiful balustrades, deck beams, stanchions, knees and braces were all perfection in the art of joinery. In the salon, the detailed moldings were fashioned into decorative trim, the intricate etched glass work was set in hardwood framing. Red silk-covered chairs, fine statues, ornate maps and silver drafting and navigation tools, were all works of art. At the stern, Wakeman flew an oversized American flag onto which he had personally sewn an extra star proclaiming California a state in advance. Such a star was in everyone's dreams.

The Pirate quickly learned the daily weather pattern of Graveyard Harbor. Barring any unforeseen events, the dawn slowly rises low and heavy, takes two leisurely hours to rise above the hills, then generously treats San Franciscans to a scant two hours of sunshine before fierce winds set in from the sea and rock the Gold Rush town into a fog-shrouded afternoon. When the fog does burn off the sunlight is blinding. As Wakeman threaded a mere eyelet of a strait, the fog backpedaling before him, a wide expanse of water and a bold mountainous range abruptly opened up. He stepped back as if struck. He raised his arm across his eyes. Wonder after wonder opened before his eyes. The vista was as broad as his huge frame.

"Our eyes," Wakeman wrote, "were greeted with the sight of one of the most magnificent harbors on the globe. I took a good look at all that I could see, and came to the conclusion that I would finish this roving life I had led by settling in this wonderful spot."

Wakeman ran the *New World* up around Clark's Point at eighteen-miles-per-hour, but the ships were so thick and the alley so narrow he could not anchor. The rocks were so close that he could go no further and found himself in a fix. At high water, he ran out a line and hauled into where the first piles for Cunningham's Dock had been driven. He made fast, then put out the gangplank. Almost immediately a little lawyer rushed up that plank waving a sheaf of papers. It was as if he had been stationed there.

"Are you the captain?" he asked.

"Yes."

"Then give me a $500 retaining fee, or you will be thrown into prison within half an hour. I come from McAllister, the judge of the Marine Court, who knows your owner well and it is our duty to retain us at once by giving me five hundred dollars. If you don't we will go over to the other side and you will be deprived of your liberty."

He did not know the owner, Mr. William H. Brown, and so never spoke his name Wakeman which convinced the captain that it was a shakedown.

"Young man," Wakeman roared; his broad shoulders widened. "I have not got the vessel fast yet. Moreover, I don't have the pleasure of your acquaintance—as far as you going to the other side is concerned you can go to hell if you like. And if you and your friend take any special interest in seeing me deprived of that liberty, you had better come here with some fifty of your friends and make the attempt, and you will have a good chance to find out how long it will take to kill that number of people!"

The shakedown lawyer timidly backed shoreward where a crowd of San Franciscans waited. They broke into cheers as he fell off the pier into the Cove. No one bothered to fish him out.

Wakeman's crew, as had all earlier crews, abandoned ship for the gold fields by flying over the side. Even Capt. Wakeman could not hold them. By noon the *New World* was completely deserted. As Gordon Newell notes, "She was not like the other deserted ships which lay dead and rotting in the harbor's backwash. The *New World* was not dead like these, only dozing in the watery sunlight."

Wakeman wasted no time. He reconstructed, enlarged, and converted the *New World* into a powerful riverboat from engine to elegance. He filled her interior with glittering brass chandeliers, elegant wainscoting with rosewood mahogany, red-plush satin upholstery, marble-topped tables, and a square grand piano which he could play. Immediately, the Pirate began dreaming of setting speed records from San Francisco to Sacramento. And, if Wakeman dreamed it, it would be, or know the reason why.

William Brown, the *New World's* owner, arrived in San Francisco in the morning, and been pleasantly surprised to discover his steamer was not only safe, but improved. Thanks to Ned Wakeman! By God! The old Pirate had refitted it and added hog-frame bracing to the hull and a nodding walking beam. A walking beam engine—cylinder, valve, gears and crank, was an A-shaped gallows frame projecting above the weather deck that actuates the wheel crack and operates the air pump. Brown settled with his creditors that day, and good riddance to them. He put the *New World* on the 125 mile San Francisco-Sacramento run every Monday, Wednesday, and Friday. Bored by one-sided steamboat races with his rivals that he always won, Wakeman the Pirate inaugurated the first rapid inland navigation in the Far West. As he backed the river steamer away from Long Wharf for his first run late in the day, he called down from the pilot house to a stranger.

"How do you get to Sacramento?" he asked.

"Go about two or three hundred miles in that direction," said a noncommittal seaman, who made only a vague pointing gesture which consisted of a nodding of his head in some direction.

The Pirate followed his gesture, vowing to better the best time to Sacramento. Race or not, maniacal speed on the river was essential. Gold seekers were always in a rush; a lost day might mean a lost fortune. Wakeman was sharing his route with the *Wilson G. Hunt*, the *Antelope*, and the *John Bragdon* and seventy-one other steamboats and an equal number of non-steamers, including three barks, two sloops, and three brigs. All were plying the Sacramento and American Rivers, all were eager to be first. It was a lucrative run. The present charge for a boat load of miners, gamblers and gospel preachers or men pretending to be preachers to get a discount, was $30 a head.

The *Sacramento*, a brigantine rigged with a black hull, had completed the first successful run between San Francisco and Sacramento ten months earlier. Soon the *Jack Hays* would be making runs to Redding, far up the Sacramento and forty-three miles from the Trinity diggings. *The Lady Washington*, a flat-bottomed sternwheeler, traveled the Sacramento and American Rivers and looked to Wakeman a potential rival until its captain looked behind him too long and struck a snag and sank.

Having safely passed the straits, Wakeman's course turned at a right angle to the East as he rapidly crossed the twelve miles of San Pablo Bay. On the northern side of this inland lake, several small streams ran up a few miles into the most fertile district of California. Making good time, the *New World* reached the Carquinez Straits, a passage of about two-miles-wide leading to Suisun Bay, and made Benicia Town on the northern side of the straits some thirty miles from San Francisco.

Local men had built dozens of schooners, barks, barkentines, and brigs on the beaches north and south of the wharves as part of the coasting trade to carry cargo and passengers up the Sacramento and San Joaquin Rivers. These smaller vessels ran the broad Bay, skipping over waves and zipping through the Carquinez and past the many small islands of the Delta to where the rivers snaked toward the gold hills. They ventured into the shallows where large deep-sailing ships dared not go.

Over the next thirty years, the Benicia yard would launch more vessels than any other shipbuilder in North America—288 brigantines, and three-and four-masted schooners, barkentines, stern wheel steamboats, tugs, pilot boats, and yachts. In the meantime, the Benicia's Union Iron Works was busily manufacturing mining machinery to be carried on these new vessels.

An hour later the *New World* entered the Sacramento River, a half-mile wide at that point. Night had fallen. Rocketing along in the coolness, bullying other vessels aside, Wakeman listened to passengers singing nostalgic songs on the hurricane deck, joined in, and soon was performing a stamping dance on the walking beams. He grinned. He was in his element. In the grand saloon, he told one of his forecastle tales in a strong, cherry voice, and with dramatic arm movements. "He was soon back in full stride as a spinner of yarns," Gordon Newell writes of Wakeman, "a talent which was to bring him as much fame as did his epic feats of seamanship and he was never without an appreciative audience aboard the *New World*."

The passengers went to sleep to his wonderful tales and when they awoke, thought they were still dreaming. They flocked to the portholes and were amazed that they had arrived at Sacramento. Wakeman had cut the *McKim* steamer's seventeen-hour record from San Francisco to Sacramento to five and a half hours—a virtually unbeatable record the *New World* would hold for ten years. When he returned to San Francisco in seven hours and five minutes, he tied a broom on her jack staff signifying a clean sweep just as San Francisco's Volunteer Firefighters placed on their water wagons to signify the same.

On AUGUST 2, COFFIN STARTED on his river trip again with a fresh breeze. In two hours he came upon the twisting Sacramento River coming short round a marshy point from the Southeast. On the twisting Sacramento River, he watched passenger and express traffic flowing round a marshy point from the Southeast. Soon, he was out from under the trees of the river and the sun had become brassy and the air heavy. "Now the sun is glaring," he wrote. "The air is suffocating, and the mosquitoes are as greedy as sharks." Fearing his potatoes might rot in the heavy heat, Coffin urged his ship to greater speed. To the Northeast extended a number of small reedy islands and a five-mile sheet of water.

The passages between the points all led to the Sacramento. He steered, following a torturous route of dirty water up to Sacramento from a wide mouth that grew progressively narrower, so narrow he began to sweat as the sides of the channel closed in upon the broad-beamed *Merlin*. He did not reach Sacramento until August 11, a full ten days behind Capt. Wakeman.

As he neared the city he thought it was on fire just as San Francisco had been so recently. "Volumes of black smoke were rising from all quarters," he wrote. "The cholera had commenced its havoc and the health police were burning the masses of corruption in the streets . . . Most of the places of business were closed, and three-fourths of the population had run off, in double quick time, to the mountain elevations." One of the first Sacramento cholera victims was Coffin's old friend from the Russia trade, Capt. William Rand of the *Roxbury*. Fate seemed to deal harshly with anyone who was his friend. The speed with which cholera struck was most terrifying. "Rand was taken at nine o'clock in the evening and was a corpse before morning." As Gold Rush cholera expert George Groh explains, "A man might set out in seeming health and vigor and be stricken within hours with diarrhea, spasmodic vomiting, painful cramps, burning thirst, and complete prostration, then die in convulsions. There was something fearful in the mysterious way that the outbreaks struck without apparent cause of reason. What was this evil, unseen thing that brought death among them?" They knew so little about its causes and prevention.

As promised, the *Sophronia* was tethered and waiting for Coffin. First, he brought some of his potatoes ashore to sell at auction before they rotted. During the auction he noticed a young man buying huge lots whose face seemed familiar. He offered his hand to Coffin and asked, "Don't you remember Tom?"

"Tom! What Tom?" Coffin said.

"Why, Tom that came out with you in the *Alhambra*," the boy said.

Coffin recognized him as one of his poorer sailors in all his years of sailing. "He had been to the mines, dug a little, and then commenced trading," he noted, "and now was as large a merchant as any of them." Tom bid off bags of flour, coffee, and sugar by the wagon load and was a customer to be reckoned with by other bidders. Coffin, who could not get a satisfactory price for his potatoes, was crestfallen. He set off again up the dirty river. Eight days from Sacramento he moored alongside Fremont, and received a visit from the same Indian chief who had tried to sell him a bear cub. Instead, Coffin sold him three sacks of flour and some molasses. His good luck was instantly swept away when he returned to the *Merlin*. The water in the hold had risen noticeably.

Twelve days from Sacramento, hard work brought him to the rapids of Yuba City. With a bit more labor he reached Marysville, laid his sloop alongside the landing and began trading. Shop owners were burning sawdust and peat in their tents to smoke away the mosquitoes, but this method was ineffective on fleas. When he returned, every individual onboard both his sloops had been taken down with fever.

"I had them all to nurse for a week," he said. "I had thus my hands too full to think of being sick myself . . . While busy in the rapids I missed my mate, Louis Martin, and found him down in the hold, laying on some bags of rotting potatoes. He had given up sick."

Coffin covered him with an awning and made him comfortable. Amazingly, his fever vanished.

At night Martin asked for bread and milk.

"I gave him a teacup full, and he lay down and went to sleep. I was worn out myself and went to bed early."

About ten o'clock the *Sophronia's* skipper woke Coffin.

"Louis Martin is worse," he said.

Coffin went immediately for the doctor, who came in ten minutes, but in those few minutes, poor Louis had died. Coffin slumped in the corner and thought. He wondered who would be the next to go. It never occurred to him that it might be himself. The next day, he was sitting in Mr. Farish's store and feeling fine. On the counter was a pair of small scales, perfectly adjusted and used for weighing gold dust by the ounce. He played with them awhile and looked around the tidy store. The blanket separating the back of the store from the lodging area began to wave before his eyes. The room spun. He steadied himself. In an instant, Coffin felt like his body had been turned to ice.

He lurched from the store and threw himself into the burning sun to thaw. It only made him colder. He went onboard his ship, covered himself with blankets and shivered and shook uncontrollably for the next two hours. Then, he grew momentarily warmer, then hot and hotter, till he had a raging fever. For the first time in his life, he had gone through a fit of chills and fever.

"My ague returned daily for a week," he said, "which they told me was a good sign, till at length a short fit of shivering left me in a settled fever." Sitting up, Coffin sipped a bottle of Doctor Osgood's "Indian *Chorugogue*," a sovereign remedy that had no effect. He called his friend, Capt. Powers, who took him up to his house. There his wife and daughter nursed him. In ten days the fever left him and he was attacked by an attack of chronic diarrhea that wasted him. On Sunday, September 1, ill and worried, he was lower than ever. His show of strength and invincibility had vanished.

"Oh, my unfortunate career," he lamented, "my unfortunate life." It was rare for him to show such self-pity and he brought himself up short. He prided himself on being self-reliant and without fear, and his thoughts turned swiftly to that of his fellow creatures who lacked his strength. If they wanted strength he would provide it for them. "The world will never know the distresses of this place," he lamented. "Where all is bustle and hurry, and nobody feels any interest in the affairs of another. Many a poor mortal breathes his last alone, without a friend to smooth his pillow or convey his last message to his friends, who will never know when, how or in what place he ceased to struggle with his Fate..."

Coffin's troubles doubled when he went to the *Merlin's* cuddy for a cup of coffee. "I had finished my breakfast and was lighting my segar," Coffin said later, "a dear and costly segar it proved, when I felt the sloop hit a snag." He looked down the cuddy hatch and saw the cabin was full of water. "I staggered and fell, for I saw at once that I was ruined. I had staked my all and twice as much more on this adventure. I resolved to do all I could. I had 5,000 board feet of pine boards on deck, and the first thing to be done was to make a raft of this."

He hailed another boat nearby and two English passengers came to his aid. Working alongside Coffin, they got out the lumber to make a raft. Before they could get any perishable goods on deck, the *Merlin* filled and sank. After pumping and bailing for hours they loaded rafts with 10,000 pounds of corn, 5,000 pounds of rice, and 40,000 cigars, and floated them to a sandy beach to dry.

"While busy at this work," Coffin recalled, "a scream from the boy left on board to cook announced that the sloop was on fire!"

After they got that blaze under control, he loaded the *Sophronia* with the salvaged dried goods. With the lessened weight, he floated the *Merlin*, and made the necessary repairs by working up to his waist in the river. He was freezing. The water had been made icy by the winter snow. He started on his miserable trip again. Tie and warp. The pace was slow and killing.

The sugar and salt dissolved.

The spices spoiled.

The rice and corn mildewed.

The potatoes decayed.

The cigars matted together.

The lumber warped into corkscrew bends.

Result: his entire cargo was completely worthless.

Then, the *Merlin* was threatened with seizure by Sacramento Sheriff Hudson over a lawsuit over four month's back pay he owed crew members. Coffin didn't know what to do. He was legally obligated to deliver the *Merlin* to Marysville in a few months.

"I discharged all the cargo," Coffin wrote, then sent the lads back to San Francisco in the *Sophronia* and *Merlin* under instructions to employ the ships in the freighting business. "I remained myself at Marysville to make the most of my shattered interests," Coffin said. In Plumas, a spot in the road about ten miles above the town of Nicolaus, Coffin met a man from Illinois, Old Robinson, who ran a tavern.

"His whole soul," he commented, "was given to peddling rot-gut liquors from his bar at twenty-five cents a glass. He was deaf as a stone and talked endlessly. I tried not to listen, but his tale was one of tragedy. When he and his wife and four daughters came across the plains, they endured five months of suffering. He led me behind his house where there were four little hillocks, side by side. I noticed them and asked, 'What are those?'"

Without shedding a tear, Robinson replied, "There lie my wife and three of my daughters. The typhus fever carried them all off."

"The girl that was left," Coffin wrote, "was a good looking lass and very industrious. And, I dare say, will make a very good wife. This was probably one of the old man's inducements in coming to California, to find a market for his girls. He has succeeded in regard to three of them. They will never cost him any more."

JUST OFF BENICIA, the *New World* rang off her engines and drifted to the wharf. The men of Benicia put their hands at their sides, some in their pockets, and looked away. They were disinclined to take up her lines because a rival steamer, the *Washoe*, a Benicia favorite, was headed for the same wharf across the bows of the *New World*. Naturally, such impoliteness and inaction produce very real tragedy. The *New World's* bow cut into the side of the *Washoe*. Passengers were caught in the flying wreckage as the ship began to sink. The mob onshore was incensed. Soldiers from the Benicia Arsenal came down to protect the *New World*. This craze for mindless speed and competition between steamboats caused similar tragedies. Another time, the *New World* was rushing at full steam through Steamboat Slough when she suffered a ruptured steam line and scalded seven crewmen and passengers to death. Hundreds of others died while standing by a boiler and egging their captains on to faster speeds. The *American Eagle* was coming down from Stockton to San Francisco when it blew up near Three Sloughs, killing five and wounding several. Ten and half hours later the *Stockton*, bound upriver from San Francisco, exploded killing one and scalding eight. That summer, the *Fawn* blew up and the *Major Tomkins* exploded. When the *R. K. Page*, the ex-*Jack Hays*, was plodding along with the *Governor Dana*, the *Dana*, egged on by cheers from passengers, began to race the *Page*. Her engineer, in attempting to pass the *Dana*, took a cask of oil and sluiced it into the roaring furnace. One of her boilers shot forward like a rocket. Three passengers went with it and were completely obliterated.

Northeast of Capt. Wakeman and the *New World*, a sheriff arrested a very dangerous individual whom he had been warned to look out for—English Jim. Some irony was involved. He jailed English Jim, not for the theft of gold from Dodge, but for the theft of shirts he had lawfully bought from Dan Casey and his brother. English Jim was inflamed. This seemed a great injustice to him, but he paid a $500 bail anyway. Foolishly, he plunked down one of the stolen gold specimens as security and thought nothing more of it.

IN SAN FRANCISCO on September 14, a Sunday, English Jim's double, Tom Berdue, returned from Rich Bar happy to be back in the big city again. Unfortunately, there was no sign of his wife and children in the city yet. This troubled him. When he dined with John and Elicia Gough at their Panama House restaurant that night, there was still no word. On September 17, he dug into his poke and left five pounds of gold for safekeeping until his family reached San Francisco. Via a ship sailing for Sydney, he sent word to his spouse of his arrangements with the Goughs just as another huge arson fire erupted in San Francisco. Citizens were threatening retribution as they rebuilt yet again. Their tempers might be short, but their ropes were long as was their boundless passion for rebuilding. Berdue returned to Auburn.

Mr. Harris, a packer, saw him at Downieville and came down with him and Col. Utting to Goodyear's Bar where they spent the night. Next, all three stayed at the Dobbins Rancho and Goodyear's Bar for over a day so they could rest their mules. At that same moment, G. W. Tompkins, who resided eight miles above Foster's Bar, noticed English Jim riding his black horse when he stopped in Placerville, and at his Slate Ridge House with four others on his way down.

Berdue and English Jim's paths did not cross, not now.

Ten days from the time English Jim was arrested for taking the trunk of clothes at Foster's Bar, the gold specimen he used to pay his bail was traced to him. He was re-arrested for something he *had* done—stealing $4,300 from Dodge. English Jim was committed to Marysville jail. On October 4, he was brought again before Judge Stidger who had fined him so many times in the past that they were practically old friends.

"The mob this night attempted to hang me," English Jim recalled. "The judge swore in about sixty men to protect me and I thank them for that." Judge Stidger's guards frustrated the crowd's first attempt to lynch Jim, but the image of a Christlike figure with a noose around his neck was unforgettable. On the mob's second attempt, English Jim narrowly escaped when the rope broke. He was taken into protective custody by Sheriff Ed Burr.

"Well, how about that!" English Jim thought. "What luck! What undeserved luck!" But, he knew the mob would try again that night or the night after until they got him. Somehow, he had to escape Sheriff Burr's custody. To raise money, he had his belongings sold at auction, except for the iron boat which he had given away to a friend. Then, he deposited the proceeds, $1750 (minus $110 he claimed he had lost), with Burr as a very blatant bribe. Burr needed more, wanted more, had to have more or he would do nothing. What else did he have? Of course, he had what remained of Dodge's stolen ore. With this as a bargaining chip, a deal was struck. Jim told the sheriff where he had buried the loot—in the wonderful flowerbed behind his house that he had let go to seed. The garden was a symbol of his attempt at an honest life which had also gone to weed. The sheriff had no sooner raced out the door into the night, shovel in hand, eyes aglitter, than the jailhouse cook approached English Jim.

"If I were in your place," he said through the bars, "I'd leave while he's busy."

"I can't go without my money."

"You damn well better go without it!"

"What?"

"I tell you, you can't trust him."

English Jim started at once, walking three miles in the dark. "I had no money to buy a horse," he said, "so I stole one and rode the rest of the way in style." He headed toward Sacramento where he sold the horse.

In the meantime Sheriff Burr dug up two huge lumps of gold from under English Jim's flower bed. More honest than his jailhouse cook had indicated, Burr returned the ore to Dodge & Co's office. John Sullivan was there then, and was impressed with the size of the specimens. He was more impressed when he heard who had stolen the gold nuggets.

"I stopped at Moore's house in Sacramento at L Street," English Jim continued. "I was using the alias of James Campbell then. I paid $70 rent and did nothing but play cards and won a deal of money." He winked. The first two weeks that English Jim was there, he worked with a gang of horse thieves led by a Sydney man, Dab the Horse-Thief, whose real name was James Peate. Jim added Dab to his own gang. Bill Brown and Johnny Griffiths sold the gang's stolen horses for Dab. On his own, English Jim stole a horse or two and robbed homes to raise working capital to pay his men. Another gang member, "Big Brummy," aka Mat Hopword, a Sydney mate, robbed a house with him. They got about $900 worth of property—not bad. But English Jim needed much more. He began looking around the gang. He had worked with one of them in the past.

Fifty-year-old John Morris Morgan, "Old Jack," was one of Mrs. Moore's borders with whom Jim had earlier worked. He was the fattest man Jim had met so far in California. Built like a fireplug, Old Jack had a thick mustache and huge whiskers, and was extremely short. What intrigued English Jim was that he was not only a seasoned stone mason with an extensive criminal past, but Port Collector Collier's ill-considered choice to build a vault for the Casa Grande Custom House. Old Jack still possessed the plans and combination to the safe. Of course, English Jim added him to his gang of experts. With Old Jack as an inside man, he would be one step ahead all the way.

English Jim was sick of small robberies that were advertised to contain so much, but amounted to so little. When a boy who boarded at Moore's house, told him of a brig in the Sacramento River with $20,000 onboard, Jim's eyes lit up. He could barely contain himself. As soon as he could, Jim led three of his men onboard in a daring robbery. "We got all the money which turned out to be only $170," he said. "The next day we all agreed to go back to San Francisco with Jemmy-from-town and lay our plans for the really big robbery. This time, we would gather our own information and be certain of what we would get."

Back in San Francisco two days later, English Jim and Sam Whittaker were strolling over the mud flats deciding on their next job. Whittaker reached into his coat, and, with a flourish, produced a list of potential targets on a neatly folded sheet of paper. Young's Bank and the El Dorado were at the top. Underneath were ample reasons not to rob them. Whittaker crossed them out.

English Jim's attention wavered. Nearby, workers dressed in warm clothes—oil skins and insulated boots, and other workers attired not so warm, were laying a framework of two-by-fours on intersecting walks and pilings. He walked over to the open pit and peered below. Just how were such tunnels shored up? Air pockets, of course, were plentiful in the subterranean world of the Ghost Fleet and would provide any tunneler a head start. The workmen dug down to stones, planks, and bone as more pockets of honeycombed mud broke down. Beams, masts, pilings and entire ships were locked into place so the city could build out over the listing decks, quaint figureheads, and lacy catwalks until land and sea were indistinguishable from each other. There was a buried city beneath their feet. They used boulders and timbers—

anything, including garbage, to push back the water and tame Graveyard Harbor once and for all. With rigid iron rods, they marked buried ships and prows thrusting out of the mud. The sinking sun cast their long shadows across the shore.

Freezing, the shirtsleeve workers hung their lanterns on pilings and went to warm themselves. English Jim and Whittaker moved to the edge and dropped down. Jim studied the work done so far. In all respects, it was poorly executed. Abandoned cargo, rock, sand, and garbage had been dumped into loosely packed areas that were certain to collapse. Networks of fossilized roots, abandoned cargo, rotted timbers and rusted chains were visible. The many layers of the Cove were like an archeological dig.

The mud flats had long been a quicksand region to be avoided. Now, the exhaled breath of man-made marshes filled their lungs. The howl of wind passing over the excavation filled Whittaker and English Jim's ears. They listened to the creak of expanding wood, the drip of water, the gasp of mud creeping slowly over weathered masts ensnarled with ropes. English Jim looked to the side and held up his lamp. Yellowing bones and white bones were stuck firmly in mud walls.

"Are those the bones of human beings or animals?" he asked.

"Both," Whittaker said. He knew his anatomy. "Those are the bones of horses lost in mud pits *and* passengers who perished in the explosion of the *Sagamore*, and unfortunate hunters dragged below under along Mission Creek."

"How can you tell?" Jim asked.

"The Creek skeletons are brown as mud. Those of passengers are yellow as corn."

Mud waterfalls spilled all around them as the pits collapsed under their own weight. The high curbed rib of a ship alongside a running stream created a waterfall that doused Whittaker and English Jim as they dashed beneath it and climbed out. Whittaker wondered why English Jim had insisted that they come here. It had to be important, but why. He suddenly felt chilled as if someone had walked over his grave. His throat was tight. So was English Jim's. The underworld was a dangerous place.

In search of a Sydney Town bar to soothe their throats, they climbed a series of slimy steps leading up from the water at the foot of the Pacific

Street landing and passed through a notorious area of haunts filled with the city's riffraff—cutthroats, swindlers, prostitutes, muggers, crimps, murderers and burglars, in other words: people like English Jim. Whittaker held himself a cut above English Jim and the other members of the gang, if only in his fine dress, physical appearance, and a shred of morality as yet not entirely deadened—thanks to Mary Ann. They felt their way along the dark alleys, stumbling over stones and pigs. Light glowed ahead. The two rivals for Mary Ann's affections slowed to a stealthy walk as they passed gambling halls, low dives, concert-saloons and grog shops. They went on until they came to the Boar's Head, a lewd dancehall. Inside, they moved to the bar but were careful what they drank. Seamen were sometimes slipped drugged whisky and recruited for outbound vessels. Crimps who delivered live bodies to ships were rewarded with the sailor's first three months pay and any money left in their pockets. Even if a Crimp delivered a corpse, he still got paid. They mixed the dead among the living shanghaied men, sewing the sleeves of corpses shut with live rats inside so the squirming made them appear as living men. They had made the dead come alive.

THREE DAYS LATER, Tom Berdue reached San Francisco. He saw his friends, John and Elicia Gough at their Panama House Restaurant and left them with five pounds of gold for safekeeping until his wife and children joined him. Via a ship sailing for Sydney, he dispatched word of the arrangements he had made with the Goughs, and returned to Auburn just as another huge arson fire, the fourth, erupted in San Francisco. He told himself he would probably be blamed for that too.

IT WAS 1:00 AM a week later, when Capt. Briet onboard his French brig, *Gruges*, was awakened by the sound of splashing in the water below. He got his gun, crept on deck, and saw his own crewmen, luggage in hand, jumping over the rail. He ordered them to stop. When they refused, he fired at a small lighter alongside and fatally wounded Capt. Pierre Delion whom he had seen trying to lure sailors away from his ship. The court ruled that Briet's act was completely justified. Angry shipmasters and shipowners protesting conditions such as the shooting of another captain at the Port of San Francisco attended a meeting conducted by the outgoing Collector of Customs Collier. Though he was widely disliked, no one disputed that Collier's reports would be instrumental in the passage of federal and state legislation to better administer the port and establish a US Admiralty court.

Five days later, Collier formally lost his job at the Old Custom's House and with him Old Jack's access to the building. President Millard Fillmore had nominated Collier for Collector of the San Francisco District, but his confirmation foundered in the Senate. Thomas Butler King of Georgia supplanted him in the post. Collier was not particularly sorry. The Ghost Fleet had worked its dishonest magic on him. He had been finagling sweet deals for himself for some time and word had gotten around. He had a three-percent commission on all duties collected, a $400 annual expense account, and $1000 a month in salary. As early as April, he had accumulated $130,000 in his personal bank account on five percent on all deposits the government made to his office. The real prize had been the *new* Custom House on California and Montgomery Streets. When Collier moved out of the Old Adobe, he had been canny enough to lease the building in his own name for three years. The man who took over his job would have to pay him $9,000 per year for its use. Next, Collier arranged for his son, John, to collect rents on Clark's Point and claim them as part of his fee. What a profitable ride it had been for Collier, but the job was grueling and would be for whomever performed it. In just three years San Francisco's population would surge from 800 to more than 50,000 desperate citizens at odds with each other, and looking to the Port Collector for guidance.

IN MARYSVILLE, CAPT. HAIGHT offered Coffin steamer passage back to San Francisco. He gladly accepted. Health unrestored and suffering huge financial losses, he limped back into the Cove on his old friend's ship. He was wrung out, but not too weary to take in the beauty of flocks of geese blackening the sky over Suisun Bay. Haight explained that they were commencing their southern migration. Approaching the Straits of Carquinez, Coffin observed flocks alighting on the banks opposite Benicia where men were busily capturing them by hand and clubbing them to death. The wild birds had not yet developed a fear of man. Coffin's own fear of man had been fully developed during his sojourn in Graveyard Harbor.

As Haight's ship turned a bend, the wide sweep of San Francisco

Bay opened up before Coffin's eyes. It took his breath away. In the short time he had been gone, the city had grown broader, deeper, and more substantial, though, he had to admit, it was no safer. It wasn't until Coffin passed Alcatraz Island and saw a ship solemnly riding out an unspecified period of quarantine, that he realized San Francisco had suffered a cholera outbreak at the end of September similar to the scourge that had ravaged Sacramento.

In his absence, the *Morrison*, built entirely of live oak, had become a storeship near the California St. Wharf. Dozens of other ships lay off the waterfront. They had been hauled in close and housed over for thriving businesses. By year's end, it would be common to convert abandoned vessels into lodging houses and set up floating warehouses of multiple stories between two buildings. Merchants acquired as many cheap vessels as they could for storeship use. Shipping competition in the outer Bay was fierce. Now a hundred side-wheelers beat the water, and small steamers were rushed into the river freighting trade. Coffin counted his dwindling funds. There was no way he could pay the $200 per day for wharfage for the *Sophronia*. Those who accepted this service, but did not pay, suffered grave consequences. They had their ships confiscated, sold, or broken up for timbers. But, Coffin had worried needlessly. There was no space to accommodate his ship or any others at any price on either side of the pier ends. On the mud flats, sailing craft were lying all about in attitudes of death and lassitude. Sadly, he would have to lay the *Sophronia* up among them for sale to pay any back wages he owed. Debts came first. He was an honest man.

"The lad who had remained with me in the *Merlin* had a claim of $120 for wages," Coffin said, "and I was obligated to pay that. The result was that I had to sell the *Sophronia* at auction." She had cost him nearly $3,000 to rehabilitate, but had gone for a mere $300. A pittance!

Tuesday afternoon, October 15, Coffin found himself sitting on the blunt top of a wooden piling on Long Wharf, dangling his legs, tallying his latest losses, and gazing down on his skiff below. It was one of his few remaining possessions. At least he had his pipe. The *Sophronia* had made two trips to Stockton, but instead of earning him a cent, had run him into a debt of one hundred dollars. All that work. He was worse off than before.

"The harassing trials I had undergone made me sick again," he said, "first, with fever, and afterwards again with weakening diarrhea." He had no place to live unless he could find lodging within the Ghost Fleet. Aching and sick, he had landed without a dollar back on Long Wharf only a month after a fourth city-destroying fire. The good news was that the wharf had been repaired. The pier now stretched two thousand feet into deep water, enough to reach large freighters. He turned his eyes toward the Ghost Fleet where many in need of a home had found free lodging and a place to recover. As Coffin waited for inspiration, he heard his name called. The water was flat now and sound carried easily. Capt. Stephen Haskel, his former mate in the ship *Arragon,* was hailing him from the Clay St. Wharf. "Here now was I, the veriest wretch . . . in all California," Coffin noted in his *Log*. "I have no means, no employment, no energy, but I was not wholly forsaken. What was life without good and kind friends? Thank God, I have so many."

First, he considered his old friend out of Newburyport, Capt. Jones, who had lived in the Cove since May onboard one of Cushing's fleet, the English brig *James Caskie.* There was plenty of room onboard the 268-ton English brig. There were just Jones, his wife, their baby, a cabin boy, five passengers who came and went as their fortunes changed and went, and a large cargo of lumber which wasn't going anywhere. Coffin knew Jones anchored his ship off Clark's Point and decided to visit him. Zephyrs and a few blue-black clouds were crawling over the city of ships. Fog, its lesser brother, trailed meekly behind. Both darkened the early afternoon. "If it is winter, it will rain—and if it is summer, it won't rain, and you cannot help it," Mark Twain wrote in the local press. "You never need a lightning rod," he added, "because it never thunders and it never lightens. And after you have listened for six or eight weeks, every night, to the dismal monotony of those quiet rains, you will wish in your heart the thunder would leap and crash and roar along those drowsy skies, once, and make everything alive."

Coffin studied the sky. Halos around lanterns made misty circles. Waves washed over decks. Harbor waters began to roll. Rain stung Coffin's face as he climbed down a ladder from Long Wharf and dropped into his rowboat. Shielding his eyes, he plunged through the choppy inlet. As he passed the *Lenore,* he turned up his collar. He considered her an abject lesson. A fast sailer, she had flown from Boston Harbor to the Cove in a record 149 days. Such a speedy performance had not guaranteed her future, not by any measure. Her creditors had cast her off, sold the expensive unassembled little river steamboat in her belly, and marooned her as just another storeship in the Cove.

Beneath soft peals of thunder, castaways slunk below decks. The wind was singing the dirge of Graveyard Harbor. On better-heeled ships, hearths were lit, and comfortable chairs occupied to ride out the storm in comfort as grandfathers told stories. Coffin continued to work the watery maze between ships. The tempest stalled above, singling some ships out for punishment. A few with lightning rods attracted bolts to their yardarms. Sails glowed with phosphorescence. One mast was left burning like a candle. Coffin observed seaweed patches swirling in its light. A climbing figure on a nearby mast was a blur in the sheeting rain which had begun so abruptly. Further out pinpoints of illumination sparkled like diamonds. He was passing a cluster of trapped ships when he saw a skiff exactly like his at the far end of a corridor between ships. A shapeless figure was rowing. Flickering cooking fires on surrounding ships lit patches of water, but not him. He had stopped at the edge of a slice of light. Coffin called out so that they might not collide in the narrow passage.

"Another boat here," he said.

Silence.

Coffin called again.

Silence.

Only rolling swells gave the stranger any degree of animation.

The pale light of returning daylight, cut neatly into vertical sections by the masts above, slid in his direction as if climbing stairs. *Click, click, click*—until finally a shaft caught and held the man. Coffin had seen that face before. Abruptly, the skiff vanished into the next corridor and the man was gone. Curious, Coffin followed along the sinister alley. The storm had tired him and he was still not back to his former robustness. He gave up the chase and napped upon the waves for a while. At four o'clock, the red tide was depositing new phosphoresce along the distant mud flats when he saw the man again. He was floating his boat beneath a wharf.

Coffin watched him climb onto the pier. His long hair swayed as he walked. Every few steps he would peer out from under the broad brim of his black hat, then, his head would fly up defiantly. In minutes another skiff approached the wharf from the direction of Clark's Point, and tied up next to the first man's boat. The three occupants scrambled out onto a narrow catwalk, and slipped beneath a portion of the dock only to reappear on top of the wharf. Now what are they up to? Coffin wondered.

On the pier, English Jim was speaking in whispers to Jack Edwards the arsonist, George W. Smith, a dark-haired, dark-complected Englishman, and an American, Bill Brown. Jim reached beneath his English-cut coat, made certain his oiled revolvers and long knife were securely fastened to his belt and smiled. The very image of Jesus Christ, he listened to the calls of police in their boats and imagined they were drawing closer. Perhaps they were men from Foster's Bar, Marysville, or Sacramento. But the boats passed uneventfully, and English Jim began conferring again with his men. Plans made, they returned to their boats. Enough light remained for Coffin to see them row in the direction of Sydney Town, the waterfront haven of the Australian gangs only a half-mile north of Long Wharf. This "Devil's Acre" at the southern edge of Telegraph Hill was bounded by Pacific and Montgomery. Under another name, the Barbary Coast, it would flourish for years. The *Call* described Sydney Town as:

> "That sink of moral pollution, whose reefs are strewn with human wrecks, and into whose vortex are constantly drifting barks of moral life, while swiftly down the whirlpool of death go the sinking hulks of the murderer and suicide! Here the favored instrument of execution was the sandbag which jars the brain to utter and eternal oblivion and leaves no outward marks."

Coffin continued to Clark's Point. His hunch had been right. The *Caskie* was there and so was Capt. Jones.

"I wonder if I might stay a few days with you?" Coffin called up to him. "I know this is not much warning."

"Of course, George my friend, anything you like," Jones said, hurrying down the gangplank and clapping him on the back. "We have plenty of room, and plenty of food. Come aboard. Let's drink to that." Jones went to fetch a bottle while his spouse cooked them dinner.

"There's enough for all," she assured him.

Dinner smelled delicious. Coffin felt his appetite returning. After a tasty *caldo de pescado*, the two captains found comfortable chairs, settled back, and smoked. Between puffs, they speculated about the motive behind the series of violent crimes and arson fires afflicting Graveyard Harbor, and all San Francisco. Neither man came to any conclusion. Nothing was to be gained from such random looting and loss of life as everyone was experiencing. And the fires themselves? Incomprehensible! The indomitable city would only rapidly and foolishly rebuild itself again with the same shoddy materials, and with the same shoddy results. Then, the populace would settle back until another blaze galvanized them into action.

The two skippers could only agree that the arsons would continue and that Coffin could stay on the *Caskie* whenever he wanted. One captain helping another. First Capt. Haight, now Capt. Jones—Coffin was lucky to have such good friends and belong to such a fine brotherhood of the sea as captains.

A fine dinner and companionship were just what Coffin had needed after all his tribulations. As he watched Mrs. Jones. He was moved by how loving she was of her husband and what a fine home she had made for them and their passengers. It was exactly what Coffin had intended on the *Alhambra* for his passengers. Alone, and so far from his family, Coffin feared he might never see them again. Filled with nervous energy, he couldn't sleep onboard tonight. He thanked Mr. and Mrs. Jones, promised to return on Thursday, and went to his boat. He rowed south to Long Wharf where he moored his boat and walked to Montgomery. As he studied the crowds on the uneven mud road, he hoped a friend he had glimpsed in passing might amble back and accompany him. He didn't like to walk alone in the dark. He didn't carry a gun or a knife, never did. He had his fists and he had his temper.

His shadow blended into other shadows, some in the water, some on the land. The sound of his own deep breathing filled his ears. That was all. Parted halyards swung to the slight roll of the ships at the foot of Sacramento Street where the *Apollo* sat between two piers. He sat down on Howison's Pier, arranged a series of candles around the brim of his wide hat. He lit them one by one. By their light, he worked on his *Log* and his visit to this strange and raw land. Circling gulls above followed the shape of his flaming circular crown. As he watched traceries of fog scud across the water, he thought of his wife, his home back east, and his new friends in Sacramento and Marysville, some now deceased, or lost to Cholera. Then, he wondered what to do with his sojourn in Graveyard Harbor no matter how much longer it lasted. When he remembered what had brought him to Graveyard Harbor, it made him laugh. His pesky obligation to keep his word and do the right thing—had brought him here.

"Capt. Henry Shoof at New Orleans," he wrote in his *Log*, "had come to relieve me, he being part owner of the ships and my term of service having expired. I was free of service now and under no obligation to stay. I had to get back to my family. As I was leaving for home at last, I received an application to take command of a ship about to sail for California with freight and passengers. Shoof was too busy to make the long trip. At first, I peremptorily declined, but on reflection I considered it my duty to accept the situation, and I was placed in charge of the old ship *Alhambra* with *carte blanche* to put her in condition for the voyage and to fit her for two hundred passengers which I did." In Coffin's case, *carte blanche* meant "use your own money."

Coffin admired a Japanese pearl-diving ship shrouded with nets over her masts and hull. Her orange sail was brilliant against the purple-gray sky and last blaze of sinking sun. Yawning, he felt the cold waters stretch their broad shoulders and the wind freshen. Rain was coming. Coffin breathed in the water city's perfume—tar, rusting iron, mildew, rotting canvas, grease, decaying wood, the odor of burned timber, and incense from a nearby Chinese Pirate ship. Rain stung his face. He shielded his eyes. The fragrance of the Ghost Fleet altered to that of a meadow. On better-heeled vessels, hearths were lit and windows glowed. Cosy chairs that had come Round the Horn were drawn close and people sang songs and told stories.

Out of the rain, Coffin relit his "candle hat." The storm is vengeful tonight, he thought, singling out some ships for punishment and pardoning others. He read by the light of his hat until he fell asleep.

ENGLISH JIM GAVE A SHAKE of his long hair. Thankfully, he had gotten out of Sacramento with a whole hide. Now he was on the verge of activating his plan to rob San Francisco of millions in gold and could brook no delays.

"We came to San Francisco," he said later, filling in the gaps of his story. "Jemmy-from-town came down with us. He robbed a Spaniard of about 30 ounces when we were coming down from Sacramento City. We divided the money between us." Now that he was back in the Cove, English Jim swiftly consolidated his gang, known in the underworld as "Mrs. Hogan's Boarders."

Joseph Hetherington was one of the gang's chief members, along with Singing Billy, Tommy Roundhead, Old Jack Morgan, Earl Briggs, Dab the Horse-Thief, and Sam Whittaker whom, according to Hetherington, was probably the smartest man in Jim's gang and still had an opportunity for rehabilitation if he ever wanted it. Whittaker, was about thirty and exceptionally manly in bearing. He began living at Mrs. Mary Ann Hogan's rooming house for thieves while the unsuspecting Mr. Hogan was away at the mines. Earlier, English Jim, Tommy Roundhead, Jim Briggs, and Jack Edwards had met at Edwards' house in Sydney Valley north of Broadway and Pacific Streets. They were there to plan several robberies. One soared right to the top of the list.

"John Edwards said there was a vessel here with considerable money on board," English Jim said.

"How much?"

"$15,000 or $16,000," English Jim replied. "Jemmy-from-town is going to come down with us tonight to go on board the *James Caskie* and rob her."

In disguise, Jim Brown, Edwards, Smith, and English Jim, who was without a mask, boldly swarmed aboard Capt. Jones's brig at Clarke's Point. They kicked in the doors and smashed precious furniture brought all the way to San Francisco. The captain and his wife and a cabin boy were the only ones aboard. The others were away.

"We had some hard fighting to do," English Jim said afterward. "Capt. Jones and a cabin boy put up a fight. The captain became desperate. We left him nearly dead. There was blood everywhere." He smiled wolfishly. "In the fight the captain's wife rushed out with a cutlass in her hand and began to fight us. I finally took it from her. What spirit!"

"Are there any arms aboard?" he asked, shifting his eyes around the room.

Mrs. Jones began to cry.

The baby was crying too. Jim raised his pistol.

"Yes there are," Mrs. Jones said suddenly. "I'll get them."

"And the money too."

Presently, Mrs. Jones brought out all the money and weapons onboard, including an Allen sixshooter. She piled them at English Jim's feet. Bleeding, she begged him to spare her husband's life. He was moaning in pain and slipping in and out of consciousness and creating considerable noise.

"I'll be glad to do as you say," English Jim told her, "if the captain will remain quiet. I don't want to take his life, but I will if I have to." His voice was soft, threatening, seductive. She could feel its contained energy. "Only be quiet."

It was then she saw the face of Jesus Christ before her and paled. It was, she said later, "as if he had stepped out of the Bible." English Jim reached down, plucked a gold watch from the pile at his feet, and dropped it into his pocket. It had caught his fancy. Mrs. Jones begged him to allow her to keep the chronometer.

"It was a gift from my mother," she said.

Surprisingly, Jim fished it out without another thought and handed it back to her.

"The others kicked up a row for not taking it," he said later, "but I told them I was master, that they had made me so, and I would do as I liked. They backed away. We searched the cabin to be sure we had obtained from the wife all the money that was onboard." English Jim had to be sure.

"Is this all?" he asked. It was a shockingly small amount.

"You have got it all," she said. She was down on her knees now. A stream of blood was running from her eye and onto her cheek. "But you're too late, you see. We sent nearly all of our money home on an earlier packet. Otherwise, you would have got it all without a doubt."

"Before leaving the vessel," English Jim recalled, "I tied the captain's hands behind him and the hands of the cabin boy, and shut him up in the cabin. Then I ordered his wife not to speak for two hours. 'If you raise a cry within that time, we'll be back with worse, as I should not leave the ship.' We made shore within that time and went to Edwards' house to split our meager spoils—less than $200. Discouraged, we returned to Mary Ann's to plan. We decided to go right out again that night to get our hands on more money. I broke into Smith's lumber yard at 8:00

PM. At 8:15 PM, Jemmy-from-town stole a safe from A. J. Ellis's house, then he robbed Dow's safe and blew it up with gunpowder."

English Jim, his anger rising, spent the rest of that night in Grayson and Guild's trying to lift a safe containing the store's gold. He was a powerful man, but it was too heavy to move, a common problem for the gang. He left it where it was. As the sun came up, he returned to Mary Ann's.

In the morning, Wednesday, October 16, waterfront lumberyard proprietor George Gordon, infuriated by the robbery rate, painted a sign in bold letters: "Notice to Timber Thieves & Wharf Rats. The gentlemen who are in the habit of casting about piles and timber and stealing from wharves during the night are respectfully informed that if they meddle with the timber moored behind my office or remove lumber from the wharf after dark they will be shot."

Discouraged by their meager haul, English Jim's gang realized they had to stay in San Francisco for the next five or six days. They had to get their hands on enough money to fund Jim's plan. His men could feel the rage within him. There was an excellent chance he would take his anger out on them. Next morning, the storm had cleared. The smell of the Cove was fresh. A torrential rain had washed the runoff and refuse out to sea. The air was pleasant. Swift breezes would keep it that way over the next few days. The water was safe for a swim, but drinking water still had to be carted in from Marin in bottles or sold door to door by the water cart man. Along the shoreline the smell of fish and abandoned garbage were barely discernible. Soon, they were gone altogether. Now, the dominant odors were wood, coal fires, hemp, salt, bilge water, roasting meat, bacon, and baking bread. English Jim managed a smile. His confidence had returned along with a pleasant day.

COFFIN SMILED CONTENTLY. After a rain shower, he found the Ghost Fleet quite a serviceable and pleasant place to reside. He could row ashore for fresh water or food or visit a floating store for delicacies prepared by cooks. The stunning landscape of the Golden Gate was food for his spirit and mind, a valuable thing because he was prone to depression and irritability. He dropped his canvas bag of river-stained shirts and bloodied pants into a skiff, and rowed to a floating laundry which was doing a brisk business. Some miners sent their shirts all the way to the Sandwich Islands to be cleaned or relied on a consortium of women to wash them at a local lagoon. Coffin preferred to utilize the Ghost Fleet laundry.

He circled the *Canton* and climbed to her main deck. The nearly 200-ton bark also contained a book bindery, pistol and knife factory, and a harness and belt shop. While the *Canton* had carried her forty-eight passengers of the Island City Company out of New York to San Francisco in record time, it had been a gastronomically unpleasing voyage for all except the captain who loved briny dishes. After Chatham Island, the *Canton's* deck had become so crowded with sixty Galapagos turtles that passengers got salty turtle for breakfast, extra-salty turtle for lunch, and over-salted turtle for supper. Passenger Joseph Kendall hated the "tubfuls of filthy and rotten codfish," that the steward passed out as treats. "We receive half a pint of the stinking, rusty, brackish fluid twice a day and each man disposes of it as he sees fit," he recalled. "The thoughtless gulp it down at once and a few hours later are seen with parched tongues and burning throats cursing the ship, its captain, and the day they departed their comfortable homes." Coffin delighted in such stories of gastronomic horrors.

After he left his laundry for later pickup, he explored the Cove for more wonders. He encountered one immediately right under his nose—a Ghost Fleet railroad. How could this be? It ran the length of narrow Howison's Wharf where there was a strip just wide enough to permit an ingenious "hand-car tramway" to pass with room on each side for pedestrians to walk. Coffin watched the train unload in a cloud of steam at a storeship moored on the southern side of the pier. With pleasure, he watched it chug back for more freight and then go again. What a morning. Now to soothe his growling stomach. He bought provisions for the first time in a while at a restaurant on Montgomery. The sea breeze was so refreshing that he stayed at a little table to eat a piece of crisp bacon and drink a cup of strong coffee. He pushed back his chair. As he was leaving, he heard a boy hawking the news. He had nearly passed by when he heard terrible news.

"Give me that," he snapped, snatching a copy of the paper. It read:

> "A party of four went on board the brig *James Caskie* in the night, attacked Capt. Jones in his cabin and left him for dead shut up in a

stateroom, plundered his desk of what money he had on board, and retired unmolested. Capt. Jones owes his recovery to his wife who was fortunately with him. Mrs. Jones had been injured too, though less severely."

Coffin flung down the paper. Pages blew out across the water. He leaped into his boat and headed for Clark's Point, flying by Long Wharf—Clay St. Wharf—Washington St. Wharf—faster than he had ever rowed. He bent his back into the oars. Jackson St. Wharf—past Pacific Street Wharf—Clark's Point was ahead! He tied up by the *James Caskie*, climbed to the deck, and hurried to Capt. Jones' bedside. Jones's face was ashen and bruised. He was bandaged and hardly recognizable. A monster had done this. Coffin heard voices in another cabin. Mrs. Jones and the cabin boy were describing the leader of the robbery and attempted murder to Sheriff Devil Jack and pointing out his resemblance to Jesus of Nazareth. Dr. Sam Merritt, another witness, had seen English Jim on the street last night. He too described the attacker as looking like the painted images of Jesus Christ which adorned the frontispiece of Bibles.

Capt. Stephen Haskel off the *Talma* arrived. Together, he and Coffin nursed Capt. Jones with warm compresses and bowls of hot soup. Doctors determined Capt. Jones would mend, though slowly and painfully. So would his wife, but what a terrible experience for her and how brave she had been. As the day waned, Coffin had to leave Jones' bedside. Two of the passengers, C. H. Hale and George Currier, assumed charge of the ministrations of Capt. Jones and his wife and cabin boy. Dr. Merritt was to join them.

As Coffin stood unsteadily at the bow, he felt a wall of oppressive air roll over him. It was warm as the Devil's breath. He berated himself. He should have trusted his instincts last night when he saw the four men in two boats. He had seen what only could have been English Jim and three of his men reconnoitering the area where the *Caskie* was moored. He was not a vengeful man, but he vowed to find English Jim. Capt. Haskel joined him, and agreed to hunt him throughout the city. They quit the *James Caskie*.

"The city has very much altered," Coffin told Haskel as they walked the streets. "When I first came here there were no thieves or assassins," he said, "or, if there were, they could get their living so much easier in an honest way that it was not worth their while to run the risk of detection and punishment by lynch law. Now, robberies, assaults and murders were everyday occurrences. England's convicts doomed to exile in Van Dieman's land have been set loose from Botany Bay and have come here in droves. If a robber or even a murderer is by chance arrested, he is never brought to punishment. He either escapes from the rat trap jail, or if brought to trial, he goes clear with some flaw in the indictment or he bribes the police with his ill-gotten gains. 'By hook or by crook,' he escapes. This laxity on the part of the magistrates has at last aroused the indignation of the community, and induced a large portion of the respectable classes to form themselves into an association for the detection and prompt punishment of crime—the Vigilantes."

Coffin remained a firm opponent of the Vigilantes. As an ethical man, he believed in the rule of law. Haskell went his way and Coffin continued looking for English Jim. Rival gangs continued to set fires and loot, making the city unsafe to store any valuables. In this atmosphere an irrational mob looking for criminals might, on a whim, string up an innocent man like Coffin. All the men he passed carried weapons. The stranger that appeared next to him carried a new Colt 36-caliber percussion revolver strapped to his side. He persisted in showing it off. Though Coffin appreciated the precision craftsmanship of the Colt, he had never been one for guns. Instead, he chose to use his fists. He had only to channel the righteous anger seething inside him.

"Murdering and stabbing are the order of the day," a local *Yreka Union* journalist, R. H. Taylor, wrote. "Scarcely a day but someone was shot or stabbed. Often have I heard the cry, 'Don't shoot this way!' and immediately afterwards the report of a pistol. On one occasion a ball passed so close to my arm that my coat was marked by it."

In a city populated mostly by men, the effect of so much artillery had an opposite effect than one would expect. It kept the young bucks cool and polite. Men measured their words, each knowing that quarreling over a simple misspoken remark resulted in certain gunplay. Anyone who claimed not to be armed was always searched—in disbelief. Public temper had grown so short, that roughnecks and bullies got short shrift, a long rope waxed to perfection, and the commencement of a search for the perfect tree, flag pole, or overhang.

Coffin had often passed the epicenter of all Graveyard Harbor's lawlessness, the Port Phillip House and Bar, a low grog shop in Jackson Street opposite Stuart and Raines' store. But, that had been in daylight. When night fell, it was to be avoided by all men of honest intent. It was the Duck's favorite meeting place, and a rendezvous for thieves, racketeers, fugitives, and murderers. The Port Phillip was owned by English Jim's Australian henchman, Teddy McCormac, and by the beautiful Mrs. Mary Ann Hogan's consort, handsome Sam Whittaker. Whittaker, an English engineer, had been given a second chance last year, and was, according to Mrs. Hogan, squandering it. Transported to Australia for housebreaking under a life sentence, he had received a conditional pardon and immigrated to San Francisco. Once there, Whittaker fell into his old ways, and began designing burglary tools for English Jim and copying keys for other robbers. Mary Ann believed that Sam was meant for better things. For that matter, so was she. She was going to do something about that.

Coffin dared to enter the pub. He saw no sign of English Jim. The night passed as Coffin waited and scanned the crowd until he could keep his eyes open no longer. He returned to the Ghost Fleet which now numbered over eight hundred vessels, and where he had glimpsed the Jesus Christ lookalike earlier. When asked to name the moment when his story intertwined with that of English Jim. He enumerated his first two sightings of "Creeping Jesus," and the attempted murder of one of his best friends. It was difficult to choose which was more important, but he was part of English Jim's legacy for certain. He arranged boards on a piling for a makeshift catwalk to a ship, then crossed a series of swaying bridges, and leaped awkwardly for the safety of a deck where he intended to remain on watch all night. Last night's assault had put him in mind of Heaven. His heavy losses had put him in mind of Hell. English Jim had put him in mind of Justice.

Thursday morning, Coffin dressed, retrieved his skiff, and rowed around the busy Cove. Wind was whistling over the diminishing dunes of the city and whipping down the mud streets. Most of the sand, Coffin complained, was getting in his eyes. So often one terrible event is followed by a grand event that makes all the suffering worth it. It was October 17—Coffin had almost forgotten about impending statehood for California. It could be any hour now. The date put him in mind of the celebratory day onboard the *Alhambra* at 3:00 AM on July 4,

1849. That day, he had also been roused to high spirits by a patriotic celebration on deck. An attorney selected to deliver the day's address was speaking from the top of the capstan. His voice rang over the waves. He could still hear his words.

"Fellow citizens," the barrister began, "this is by God, is the greatest day, by God, that ever dawned, by God, since the creation. We, by God, are the greatest American people, by God!" The congregation sounded back, "Good, by God! By God. By God." Would California ever become a state, wondered Coffin. He hoped it would. By God! San Francisco needed the United States and the US needed San Francisco. And she would have it, By God!

That memorable day, Ghost Fleet ships *Edward Everett* and *William Ivy* had been two days away from San Francisco. The *Duxbury* was not far from the Equator off Peru. The *Henry Lee* was just north of Juan Fernandez Island, and society miner Cal Gardiner had been 600 miles west of Baja onboard the *Sylph* celebrating a patriotic Fourth. Gardiner especially, had been enjoying a banquet of "handsomely sliced" beef and pork cake, "excellent pickles, a large, whole pie for each man, plum duff, boiled rice, bean soup, and twenty-one doughnuts each." All the vessels were firing volleys of gunfire and shouting the Declaration of Independence at the top of their lungs.

Coffin climbed to the summit of Signal or Semaphore Hill overlooking San Francisco. In two years the introduction of the telegraph would cause the name of the peak be changed to Telegraph Hill. Coffin calmed himself and worked himself into a drawing mood. He would lay in wait as he had for English Jim. He dropped down in the grass, moistened his watercolors, pointed his brush between his lips, and began painting a "Birdseye View of San Francisco." First, he depicted the Square, Broadway Street and its wharf, and Pacific Street and its wharf. Then, he painted in the piers of California, Mission, Market, Rincon Point and its Observatory, and Front and Montgomery streets and drew in the road to North Beach and the Presidio. His hands flew. The wash underpainting was clear as day. Coffin could see Yerba Buena Island and the distant peaks of the Sierra Nevada and with deft, transparent strokes laid them in.

"At my feet lay the city of wonders," he would write in his completed book, *A Pioneer Voyage*, "every street and building distinctly traceable in this birds-eye view, while in front expands the noble Bay, capable of containing all the navies of the world and beyond, another and still another beautiful inland Bay." The wharf projects in the Cove were reaching to their final lengths. Any further out and they would have to construct a sea wall to protect the piers from being smashed to bits by the sea. Cunningham's $75,000 Wharf, a "T"-shaped pier between Vallejo and Green streets and just north of Clarke's Point was 375-feet long. Its right-angle extension was nearly as long, 330 feet by 30-feet.

Starboard off Cunningham's Wharf lay the *Resoluta*. Pilot agent James Nelson and California Steam Navigation Company manager Ben Hartshorne lived aboard. Nelson was jovial. Hartshorne was morose, yet this odd couple got along. The *Resoluta* would end its days as a coal ship.

Standing in the high winds of Signal Hill, Coffin shaded his eyes and peered out to sea looking for the single steamship that was to bring the news to San Francisco of statehood. Tension was high. From his high vantage point, he would be one of the first in the city to know the answer. The steamer would indicate "yea" or "nay" by which flags it ran up on its deck. Coffin kept watch, painted, and reflected upon the glorious career of his young country and of the great and good men who had achieved her independence and of the bad men who inspired them to keep it. From his boyhood on, Coffin had never been able to think of George Washington without finding his eyes moistening "with a tribute of veneration such as no other mortal of ancient and modern times has ever been able to call forth."

He thought he saw a white speck in the distance slightly below the horizon. It could have been a disorder of the eye, a crumb or speck. It probably was. He went back to work. Or it could have been the tip of a mast. So, Coffin waited and waited. Every muscle in his body was tight. His heart began to thump; his senses to reel. Yes, it was the *Oregon*. It had to be. In minutes, he saw the ship steaming between Alcatraz Island and San Francisco. With his naked eye he could make out a deck alive with men firing small cannons and raising a large banner in her rigging. Coffin lifted his spyglass and adjusted it so he could read the writing. He grinned.

"We're the thirty-first state!" he cried.
"We're in! Oh, God, thank Ye!"

California had been admitted to the Union on September 9. Only now was San Francisco learning the good news. Statehood! The intensely patriotic Coffin felt tears well up in his eyes. It was as if George Washington had personally given him the good news. A thrill went through him. Though he was alone, he got to his feet and danced and clapped his hands. Now larger cannons were roaring from men-of-war, splitting the morning air. Men in boats firing their revolvers made smaller puffs of white on blue water. Gulls scattered into clouds.

Thousands of people converged on the waterfront waving their arms.

The city came alive with joy.

Atop his crate, Father Taylor on the Square was preaching. "Full as the moon, clear as the sun, and terrible as an army with banners," he said, "and from all these streets, and our beautiful valleys, and from hilltop to hilltop, nay, from the coast range to the snowcapped summits of the Sierra Nevada Mountains, one universal California shout shall arise, 'Hallelujah!' Let the infant Church of Jesus in this wicked land, 'stand in the ways, and see and ask for the old paths, where is the good way, and walk therein,' obeying God rather than man. 'Arise, shine, thy light is come, and the Glory of the Lord is risen upon thee.'"

Aboard an anchored ship in the Bay, star-crossed Dr. Stillman heard shouts ashore and guns blasting from the fort and misunderstood them.

"Another fire," he moaned. Over the last fourteen months, he had been delayed at every sailing by illness and fire, and more fire. He was eager beyond words to finally leave San Francisco. "It is man here that passes into sere and yellow leaf and not trees," Stillman said. Another booming cannonade shook the Cove. Stillman covered his ears. And looked for smoke and fire and crawled below.

Coffin descended the summit faster than was prudent, stumbling and fumbling here and there and almost falling and kicking small rocks before him. Once down on what flatness there was, he ran to Law's Wharf near Union Street. Then, he dashed to Buckelew's Wharf at the base of Green Street. Waving his arms, he came to Long Wharf which had been seriously damaged by the June 14 fire. Once more, it stretched into the Cove and its very foot was packed with cheering citizens. The Council proposed a future celebration, but impatient citizens demanded an "American Ball" be held "Now!" this very night and put Devil Jack in charge, a sheriff who got things done.

The only man in town unhappy about statehood was merchant Sam Brannan. "There's that damn rag, again," he had uttered after traveling from New York onboard the *Brooklyn* and seen the stars and stripes waving over San Francisco. That banner had dashed his plans to set up a colony on the Stanislaus River with two hundred Mormons. He had never forgiven that slight.

OVER AT RIDDLE'S WATERFRONT STORE in the Cove, Coffin waved to good old Charley Schofield. Good old Charley had been a fixture since Riddle's establishment first opened. Folks joked that Riddle dusted Schofield along with the gold-washing machines on display out front. As usual, Charley Schofield was providing unintended comic relief. Dressed in an old-fashioned full suit of navy blue, he affected a "nautical, bluff style." Eventually, such old timers would no longer be seen at their old haunts. Or was it that their old haunts would no longer be there? In the relentless progress around Graveyard Harbor everything familiar was being swept away.

As for English Jim, he had obviously have hightailed it for other parts. Coffin doubted he would return to Sacramento. That town was too hot for him, but then so was San Francisco. It didn't matter. Coffin had given up the chase and gone back to admiring Graveyard Harbor. He wondered how much longer it would exist. As the wharves stalked eastward over the distant flats they extended from the tips of the existing main roads—Market, California, Sacramento, Clay, Washington, Jackson, Pacific, and Broadway streets and raced down to where eight hundred deserted ships waited to be absorbed into the growing city.

The six thousand feet of piers cost a million dollars and to extend two miles of boardwalks into deep water would cost a million and one half dollars. Collector of Customs Collier had kept careful notes and these were updated and supplied to his replacement. The piers now extended to these distances into the Cove: Market Street Wharf, 600-feet, California Street Wharf, 400-feet, Stevenson & Parker's Sacramento Street Wharf, 800-feet, Clay Street Wharf, nearly 1,000-feet, Washington Street Wharf, 275-feet, and the Jackson Street Wharf, 552-feet (though it ended at Front Street in thirteen-feet of water). The

Broadway Wharf, 250 feet long, was designated the landing place of the Sacramento steamers. The solid Pacific Street Wharf, at a cost of $60,000, stretched southward for over 500-feet of its proposed 1800-foot total length.

"Within another year," The San Francisco *Courier* predicted, "one half of the city will stand on soil wrested from the sea. Thus, were overcome difficulties not unlike those encountered in placing Saint Petersburg upon her delta, Amsterdam upon her marshes, and Venice upon her island cluster." A week earlier the *Evening Picayune* had noted the "numerous floating depots for storage of merchandise." Merchants, seeing the low prices for Ghost Fleet ships, bought as many as they could to profit though large volumes of storage. The *Tuhmaroo* at Agnews Point was the latest to offer storage of "merchandise of all kinds" at the lowest rates yet.

By Saturday, October 29, San Francisco was still celebrating statehood. Who could blame her citizens? Everyone had a hangover, especially aboard the new river steamer *Sagamore* bound for Stockton and Sacramento. Coffin was watching it and enjoying the experience. The *Sagamore* was gently blowing off steam and preparing to cast off from Long Wharf. The day was autumn-like (though there were really no seasons in California). Breezes were gently ruffling the surface along the mud flats and stirring patches of red algae in the Cove. A fog cloud, its ragged edges softened by a traveling shower, dropped over the Bay. Coffin saw a trace of the moon still hung in the sky. Against that faint sliver, black cormorants hung on the wind. In single file, they flew low over the *Sagamore* as if to escort her to another world, a better place. Vessels at the Ghost Fleet's furthest edge swung round and arched their bows as if in expectation of something to see. Even the breezes stopped and clouds seemed to freeze in place.

The *Sagamore* was a work of art with white wooden filigree work, gilded acorns and deer horns, chandeliers and stateroom doors with paintings such as Audubon or Catlin might have done. Belching blue-black smoke from its stack, the steamer continued to fire up. In the pilot house, the skipper reached for the bell pulls. Gongs clanged against the hiss of steam. The six-foot-long throttle lever quivered. Towering columns of steam billowed from its escape pipes. A hissing and roaring gurgle filled the air. The long side-wheeler had mounted three sails that served as backup against engine failure and assisted her powerful engines. It also carried $6,000 in gold aboard. In contrast to the chilly conditions outside, the atmosphere below deck was hellish, sweltering as the Coastal Miwok sweat house on Goat Island. In the furnace room gauge cocks hissed, dials spun, and deck valves shook spasmodically. The steamer's engine, a side-lever type, frantically pumped. Rapidly the piston's eight-foot stroke developed over two hundred horsepower. Sweating men fired the boiler, shoveling coal like devils. Soon the paddlewheel was beating the Bay mightily. The engineer was ready to run the steam gauge right up against the pin, the way the skipper liked it. He had records to set and an itchy palm.

At a steam pressure of one hundred and twenty-two, the paddlewheel was scooping out water a mile a minute. The people on Long Wharf and on Howison's Wharf knew the steamer was preparing to race another ship or break another captain's existing record. Such ships as the *R. K. Page*, later a casualty of an exploding boiler, commonly used tar, oil, and pitch as quick starting fuel to give added speed.

"It is a tacit agreement that if the passengers will travel on his boat," wrote the *Alta* of steamer commanders, "he shall blow them into eternity sooner than see his boat left behind . . . in accordance with the implied contract, he ties down the safety valve and they all go into eternity together." Thus, what happened next might have been foreseen.

In his cool pilothouse, the captain, a Mississippi-type, one of the gold-leaf, kid-glove and diamond-breast pin types, was unconcerned. He went on calmly clanging his bell and listening to the jangle of smaller silver bells. As he spun the wheel, keeping one eye on his watch, the ship began to moan. Merchants who shipped freight and passengers demanded speed and demanded he give it to them. At a steam pressure of 127, the boiler began threatening and complaining. At a steam pressure of 144 on the gauge, the ship began to shiver. Below decks the shaking was even more violent. The stokers' eyes grew wide. Steam continued to swell its heart. The steamship had yet to clear the Cove, but straining, the massive boiler already carried every pound of steam available because the engine room boys had tied down the safety valve and were busy piling on coal. The boiler screamed, howled and tried to attract someone's attention. No one was listening. Daggers of steam burst out through metal seams. Bolts shot off like bullets. The big wheel churned. Sparks spun around with every revolution and plowed coal fires beneath the surface of the cold harbor.

Patches of dead water near the Ghost Fleet thrashed into life as fish and rats swam for their lives. The water around the *Sagamore* boiled. The whistling of scalding steam magnified. Passengers on the deck above heard it. They saw steam merge with black funnel smoke in a storm of cinders, clinkers and sparks that rained down upon them. Valves howled and metal heated to red. The captain jangled his bell in a fury for more steam as the ship bucked and plunged. It was now too late to save them. To halt such a powerful engine with a full head of live steam on was madness. Steam had to be let off gradually to relieve pressure and allow the engines to be shut down. If this was not done, fantastic forces could rip through the cylinders while they were still running.

At that moment a man came running down the pier—James Kirker, Colonel Doniphaus's former guide who had just spent five years trapping furs in the Rockies, fighting grizzly bears, and battling hostile Apaches. Kirker reached the *Sagamore* and leapt aboard.

"I had just got onboard," he said later, "and was going aft to pay my passage... I should think that there were as many as one hundred thirty persons on the upper deck." Abruptly the boilers shattered. Scalding water sprayed over every man in the engine room, peeled the skin from bare-chested stokers, and roared up through the splintered deck as live steam. With a rumble, then a barrage, the boiler kicked loose from her foundations and ripped up through the crowd, lifting Kirker (among others) off his feet. The air around Kirker quivered with live steam as stanchions were blown away. "I was thrown some ten to fifteen-feet into the air and lit on the bodies of two persons, dead."

The boiler demolished the upper works, tore out the forward superstructure that disintegrated into flying splinters. The upper sheet of the steam chimney detonated. Men were pinned to the deck under broiling steam. Shrieks preceded each shock wave. Abruptly, every person and every ship within the phantom fleet was made visible with amazing distinctness. Supercharged light froze men in high contrast at their oars in mid-stroke. The sustained brilliance, cast inky shadows behind the passengers in an explosion of light from zenith to horizon. The dazzling whiteness was appalling. There was no color now, only white and shadows of white and black, like a negative. A boom like thunder reechoed across the Bay as a shower of wooden and human debris showered over a vast area of the Ghost Fleet. People on the docks were stunned. Tears started in their eyes. Their chests heaved. Breath caught in their throats. Others were sickened by the odor of seared flesh and scattered body parts.

"When I recovered my presence of mind," Kirker said, "and the steam had cleared away, I saw as many as twenty-five persons on deck who were apparently not hurt and a great many who were either killed or badly wounded. I saw two hanging on the side of the wreck and calling for help. I caught hold and pulled them in ... Being blown sky-high by a little hot water ... is more than I've been accustomed to."

Crews hacking with axes freed some passengers, but multiple coats of oil-based paint covering the steamer ignited, catching the wheelhouse afire. The hull of the steamboat went into death throes, then gradually settled beneath the waves as men and women dove over the side, flames trailing after them.

Many good Samaritans were scorched rescuing the *Sagamore* passengers, but the steamboat sank completely and a canopy of ashes drifted down and shrouded the corpses of fifty women and men. "By this time," Kirker said, "several boats were alongside and were busy picking up those who were thrown in the water." The *Lawrence*, always in readiness on the Bay, responded. The marine ship plucked survivors from the water and took them ashore to hospital. Water firefighters were already there. Land firefighters from shore arrived shortly after. More searchers in boats reached the scene.

When the *Sagamore* blew up Sophia Eastman, a former "Lady of the Lake," was working at Dr. Smith's City Hospital and prepared to accept the wounded. "This was the most melancholy accident which ever occurred," she said, "for among the eighty-five persons on board not one escaped uninjured. I have not had time to give you a full description of the awful scene which offered so much gloom and sadness over those who witnessed the scene." She now placed the dead at seventy-five.

"State Senator David C. Broderick, the man who had created and organized San Francisco's first Volunteer Fire Company, had been on the dock and been thrown into the water. He was taken along to Dr. Smith's hospital along with a few who had escaped with their lives, but were dying. Multitudes crowded in to learn the fate of their friends.

Father Taylor was there giving comfort to the injured. "A number of patients," he said, "were men who had been blown up in the explosion of the steamer *Sagamore*. Some had broken limbs, and others were badly scalded."

Coffin helped beat the fires down to make certain the flames did not spread, and was still there when the *Lawrence* returned to gather up valuable papers floating on the water and left to deliver them to the consignee of the *Sagamore*. "What had become of the gold on board?" he wondered. Curious, he stood watch all night. By morning that only oily ash rode the swells. Still no one had searched for the ore that conceivably lay on the shallow floor of the Cove. "Well," he thought, "someone's going to get mighty wealthy out of this tragedy someday."

Coffin saw smoke wreathing skyward. The billows were dark, but not as dark as the unmoving silhouettes gazing impassively at the carnage. The rigid heads were bowed as if in mourning. When Coffin looked away and then back, the figures were gone. That was the case with the Dark Watchers. No one knew who they were or where they lived, but it was wise to never show interest in them because they never bothered anyone who minded his own business. From Gold Rush days to modern times, miners, mountain men, and washerwomen have seen giant figures framed against the sky, silently watching. In 1700, the Spanish called them "los Vigilantes Oscuros," the Dark Watchers. Writer John Steinbeck wrote of them in 1938. It is hard to discount the existence of giant beings whose only vice is shyness and who give such zest to life. The Ghost Fleet's deserters, drunks, pirates, whores, put-upon-men, and comfortable families claimed to have seen the inexplicable Dark Watchers—if they existed at all. Coffin needed the unspeaking shadows to be real; they filled his heart with romance, his artist's eye with images and his *Log* with unforgettable pictures.

The *Sagamore's* engines were removed and installed on the *Secretary*, but tragedy came with them. The *Secretary* exploded later at Brothers and Sister's Island in the North Bay while racing a rival to Benicia. The engineer had been holding down the safety valve on the boiler with an oar, as he had been warned not to do. That blast killed sixteen, scalded thirty-one, and sent one passenger riding a flying mattress a hundred feet to a nearby wharf where he landed surprised and unhurt, and was able to walk away.

Calamities continued on the Bay. Port Collector Thomas Butler King, the much-maligned James Collier's replacement, surveyed his watery kingdom. What to make of this string of bad luck? he wondered. The day before the *Sagamore* exploded, the *Mariposa* had been rammed and sunk just past Suisun Bay at New York of the Pacific. King walked to the new Custom House, a four-story red brick building on the northwestern corner of Montgomery and California that his predecessor, Collier, had leased from William Heath Davis after the May fire. He was making a tidy profit from it each month.

The old adobe Custom House in the Square was being repaired and fitted out for offices. There was a vault there too in case it should be needed which King hoped would not be. He entered the new Custom House by the Montgomery Street entrance. He climbed the dual wooden staircase to an upper floor, his footsteps echoing on the stairs, entered his office, and hung up his coat. He sat down at his desk and began rereading his impressive list of steamboats sunk in the Cove in 1850:

> A side-wheeler, the *Colonel Cross*, had been wrecked on January 29 and on June 25, the *McKim*, a 327-ton side-wheeler out of New Orleans, collided with the steamship *Gold Hunter* in the Straits. Steamers like the *Belle*, *Helen Hensley*, and *Pearl* soon littered the bottom of the Bay and its nearby rivers. In July, the *Utica*, a Havre packet ship, burned as it reached a wharf and was towed to Goat Island to sink. Shoals and rocks took many vessels as they arrived in the Cove. Others were wrecked within sight of the Cove, among them: the *Carrier Pigeon*, *Dashing Wave*, the *Flying Dragon* and the *Noonday*. The *Carlotta* wrecked at Tonquin Shoalf and the *Crown Princess* hit Blossom Rock. On November 19, the *Thomas Burnett* sank at Alcatraz and the *Gloucester*, a British barque, capsized in the Bay. The *New England*, a barque, wrecked at Angel Island four days later.

The wrecked ships were sold, abandoned, or left to rot among hundreds of other decaying hulls in the Ghost Fleet. Ah, thought Collector King, as he put down his pen, and rubbed his back, so many ships had batted their way thousands of miles to Graveyard Harbor only to wreck without ever lowering an anchor. He completed his report on the "Port of Lost Ships," considered it well done, and sat back to eagerly await the praise of his superiors. He put the report in his file cabinet and slammed it shut. He stood for a moment considering the oddity the study had revealed to him. Although the Cove offered hundreds of menaces to navigation and during the year over fifteen hundred ships had entered, there was no record of any ship striking a sunken hull and being distressed. King scratched his head.

That was downright impossible.

IN SACRAMENTO ON NOVEMBER 1, 1850, George Mason, who had worked with English Jim on Foster's Bar at the Yuba River, passed him on L Street. Yes, it was the wanted man. It had to be and no one else. He knew him too well. Mason wheeled about and ran after him. "I spoke to him and asked him what he was doing here," Mason said. "He pretended he didn't know me and told me he was James Campbell. I wasn't fooled. At Foster's Bar, he had worn a cap to cover his thinning crown. In Sacramento he was wearing a hat, but that was the only difference. The constable, Mr. Burr, who had arrested English Jim at Foster's Bar, agreed and told me he was the same man. By any name, the man did not bear a good character in Sacramento. He had money and gambled a good deal."

It was worse than that. English Jim had committed a murder under the alias, "Mason," and unlike his other murders which he had covered up, this one could be attributed to him. He escaped into the crowd. After a number of easy burglaries with his cohort Big Brummy—they had gotten $800 worth of property from a house on the corner of Front and K Street, English Jim had become overconfident. On November 25, he was arrested for housebreaking by Officer Charles Tureman. The next day he was brought before Recorder Benjamin Franklin Washington on a charge of petty larceny and gave his name as "James Campbell." A recorder is a part-time judicial appointment given to practicing lawyers, a record keeper acting as a court of justice. English Jim wasn't too worried about Washington, who usually issued warrants, after he employed young Frank Pixley to defend him. Pixley was a mere babe, but smart as a tree full of owls. "He got me out of the scrape for $20 but afterwards told me I must give him $50 more, which I did," English Jim said. "Old Jack swore false, and I gave him twenty dollars."

"English Jim was at Winslow's Bar when the murder was committed," said John Longmaker, who had known English Jim in

June at Winslow's Bar. "I saw English Jim on the opposite side of the river above the Bar." A posse was formed to go after the three killers, but they had too great a lead and could not be found. Mr. Broadwater, though, had not given up. On arriving in Sacramento he learned that three men answering the description of Moore's killers had arrived in that city.

Officer Stivers, a new man on the force, had been going through Second Street when he heard someone cry, "Stop, thief!" and caught a robber who "answered to the name of James Campbell or James Stuart."

"I was arrested again in Sacramento on Monday, December 9," English Jim recalled, "this time for breaking into Smith's lumber yard—I was very nearly shot there. A bullet went through my hat." He showed the hole in his hat. "I got taken and committed for trial the next day by the City Recorder, Washington."

"On December 10, upon going into my office," Washington recalled, "I saw 'James Campbell' sitting there yet again and recognized him. The prisoner had been before me three times before. This time, the fourth, he was charged with breaking into a lumber yard office of a lumber merchant and stealing $4000." Washington, whose patience had run out, jailed English Jim aboard the de-masted *La Grange* prison brig.

"I hired Pixley again," English Jim said, "and admitted I had broken into a house." He spoke easily of minor infractions with his young lawyer, but behind his beatific smile concealed a multitude of violent assaults and three coldblooded murders whom, if Pixley had known, might have refused to defend him. While English Jim was confined in the brig he was recognized by the dogged Mr. Broadwater and some visiting Marysville citizens as the killer of Charles Moore. When a posse was formed to go after the three murderers, they had too great a lead and could not be found. Broadwater, though, had not given up. On arriving in Sacramento, he learned that three men answering the description of Moore's killers had arrived in that city. The Marysville citizens were so certain English Jim was their man that they set about procuring the necessary papers for his removal to their jail and subsequent trial.

"Two days after I had been on board the prison brig," English Jim added, "a constable came down from Auburn and identified me as the murderer of Sheriff Echols of Auburn on June 2. Because of my last name I had been confused with Hobbes and William Stewart who were now the prime suspects in the murder of Auburn Sheriff Echols. Two or three hours afterward, two more constables came on board, one from Foster's Bar and one from Marysville and identified me as having murdered Charles Moore. One had a warrant. They went to Judge Sackett who gave them an order to bring me ashore and taken to his office on J Street. Frank Pixley appeared for me and would not allow the judge to examine me. I was then sent on board the brig again. The next morning the sheriff came for me."

English Jim was terrified. For the first time, he began to doubt that his wonderful luck would allow him to escape hanging yet another time, and all because of a coincidence of names and a murder that he hadn't committed. That vexed him most of all. He was fortunate that he had Pixley who knew exactly what to do. The young lawyer boldly headed off the Marysville sheriff, told him his warrant to take English Jim was not legal, and sent him scurrying home after a new writ.

"I then gave Mr. Pixley my bag of gold dust," English Jim said, "to weigh out $600 and an order [under the name of James Campbell] for $130 which he told me he had got and would pay me next day. That night I made my escape from the brig where I had spent three days since sentencing. A deputy snuck me a key to my shackles and the cell door. The brig was tied up to a jetty on the Sacramento waterfront, so I only had to shake off my chains, open my cell from the inside, and stroll onto the darkened shore at the river end of H Street. Good old Pixley! I walked the next day to Dry Creek, halfway to Stockton and got into Stockton the next day."

English Jim was recognized again, and arrested by Dr. Ash, Sheriff of the County who delivered him to Stockton Deputy Sheriff Emil Goenge.

"I took charge of him," Goenge said, "but being obliged to leave for Sacramento for the 'Squatter Riot,' I left him in custody of a deputy. That slippery rascal escaped from my vessel, the *Susanna*. I do not recollect the name he went by at the time, but I do remember the charge was murder."

After English Jim escaped, he hired a horse to go to San Jose to meet George Smith the gambler. He had known the clean-shaven

Englishman for eight or nine months and had kept a monte bank with him in Stockton. In San Jose, Smith and English Jim made devout attendance at mass at all the churches. The visits had nothing to do with religion. They were robbing them of gold and silver images. English Jim was seeking one particular ten pound golden statue that he had heard was enshrined in one sanctuary. He could not find it. That same night he won $160 gambling at San Jose and left for San Francisco the next morning at the end of January. Smith went on to Monterey to refine English Jim's master plan which he was refining.

"I disguised myself," English Jim said, "and Jemmy-from-town and I came down on the *New Star* from the Embarcadero of Alviso, a San Jose town. I was using the name, 'James Stevens.'" They had left at 9:00 AM, but the steamship ran aground on a sand bar and was stuck overnight.

"This is no way to start the New Year," Jim thought.

Monday after breakfast, passenger Robert Pollock was walking the deck with English Jim when Capt. Sampson, the *New Star* skipper, asked them to seat themselves in front of his office and wait. After a while a bell was rung for all sixteen passengers to go into Sampson's cabin where they were told there had been a robbery.

"Between 3:00 AM, and daylight," he told them, "a thousand dollar bag of gold dust was stolen from a passenger's valise."

A committee was chosen to look for the dust and when English Jim was searched, they found gold dust in a leather bag and a large lump of quartz rock and gold which the committee confiscated. One other passenger besides English Jim, an engineer, had dust on him, about $200 dollars more than was taken from the stolen $1,000 bag. The owner of the dust spoke with English Jim who had been showing a Spaniard sitting next to him several pieces of coin. He claimed that he had but twelve dollars on him of which he intended to give the stage driver two dollars and the balance to go to Capt. Sampson for bringing him down on the steamer.

One of the crew felt in a water cask and discovered a bag containing $600 of gold dust.

"That's my bag," said the man who had been robbed, "but some gold has been taken out." That was then compared with the dust of about $400 taken from English Jim that compared favorably with the stolen dust and made up the amount lost. Capt. Sampson called him into his cabin and accused him of robbing a passenger of one thousand dollars of gold dust.

"And why is that?" he asked.

"It's because you have an India rubber coat that is unlike the other passengers. One of the passengers felt some person feeling about in his pocket in the dark and reached out his hand and felt the India rubber coat."

"But I did not commit the robbery nor know anything about it," English Jim said. "You took my gold dust amounting to about $600 and that of another passenger."

The passenger who had lost the money couldn't wait and went directly to the steamer for Panama without coming on shore. He left the $400 of fine dust taken from English Jim behind in Capt. Sampson's hands to give him an opportunity to prove where he got the money.

"Before leaving the *New Star*," English Jim said, "I threatened the captain that I would report him if he did not give me back my money."

On Tuesday, January 29, Thomas Cunningham was onboard when English Jim came for his money and demanded it from Capt. Sampson.

"What do you think I should do?" Sampson asked Cunningham.

"You should see some of the Committee [the Vigilantes]," he replied.

"What the hell do you have to do with it," English Jim snapped at Cunningham. "I will hold you accountable for anything you say in regard to me. I want my money!" English Jim had his hand on his pistol. Sampson's eyes were wide with fear.

"Don't irritate him," Sampson told Cunningham. He raised both hands. "I'm afraid if I detain the money, this man or his associates will injure the ship."

"I can establish a good name at San Jose and Santa Clara," English Jim said in a milder tone. "Give me my money, Captain. If you do not give me my money I'll attach your boat. I'm very anxious to go to Monterey on horseback and want my money. I have got to be there Monday night. I promise to return by the boat next trip to show where I got the money."

Capt. Sampson noticed a friend, Capt. Baker, passing.

"I'll step out and speak to him and see what he thinks," he said. "The ship is already behind in her schedule."

After Sampson left the cabin, Cunningham noticed English Jim had become very nervous and, quick as he was in his movements, was even quicker now.

"I'll be damned if I'll be troubled more about this business," English Jim said. "I'll have the money and prosecute the boat the first thing in the morning."

After walking up and down the cabin several times, English Jim went down on the wharf and was leaving when Sampson called him back. The sight of an angry Jesus Christ threatening to call the police must have shaken the captain and his hold on reality. "As the owner of the one thousand dollars has left in the *Panama*," Sampson said, "we have concluded to give you the money."

"'Tis' best for you to do so before the Committeemen come along," English Jim said.

"He does not seem like an innocent person," Cunningham told Sampson, "and I would bring this man before the Recorder." At this English Jim seemed eager to leave. Wadsworth the engineer and the crew were now watching and he could not handle them all at once. He and Capt. Sampson went into the office. Sampson took the sealed bag which contained about $390, wrote a receipt for the money that English Jim signed and watched as English Jim left.

"I then went to Mr. Miles and exchanged my dust for coin," Jim said. Afterward, he walked to the Square, jingling the coins in his pocket. Later, he would be identified by several passengers of stealing gold dust while a passenger on the *New Star*. But it was Jemmy-from-town who had actually stolen the money and divided it equally. Still fuming about being accused of stealing the gold, he decided to even the score with Cunningham and the quavering Sampson. On the *New Star's* next arrival in San Francisco two days later, English Jim was waiting.

"I met Teddy McCormac and John Edwards," he said, "and went down to the steamboat. I went on board, cut open the window and broke into the desk and took about $250."

Shrouded under a Mexican serape and sombrero, English Jim returned to Sydney Valley, and boarded again at Jack Edwards' house. With the Moore murder hanging over his head, he went out only at night to the Port Phillip House that Whittaker and McCormac, kept on the corner of Jackson and Gold Streets. As English Jim drank, Whittaker told him there were eight or nine thousand dollars in a heavy safe in a meat shop in Broadway.

"Whittaker and I," English Jim said, "with Edwards and Jack Dandy took the window out of Flet's Butcher's shop. We got the safe into the street, but once more it was so heavy we could get it no further."

When Capt. Wakeman publicly expressed concern about Charley Minturn who kept thousands in gold in flimsy strongboxes in the steamship *Senator* offices, English Jim took his comments to heart and decided to rob Minturn's next following his unintended instructions. If Wakeman the Pirate said so, then who was he to doubt his word.

"We got this information from Wakeman and from Singing Billy," English Jim said. "It's there. Billy went several times during the last three days to inquire about the money." They went over the details. English Jim, Billy, Edwards, Whittaker, McCormac, and Robb McKenzie stole a boat and set out that night. They were well-armed and carrying handmade shears, augers, saws, a kit of expensive tools belonging to Jack Dandy, and a featherbed in the bottom of their boat. They nosed silently along the piling until they came to a mooring directly under the deserted building. McKenzie, a brawny, towering and fastidious twenty-six year old from Cumberland, England, was the lookout.

"Three or four of us got inside the building, shoved some desks aside, and moved the safe a little," English Jim said. "We got it in the right position and made a few auger holes in the floor. We were cutting away the floor and preparing to drop the safe onto the mattress in the boat, when someone came to the door. It was a clerk who had forgotten a paper. McKenzie, who had gotten his signals wrong, gave a false alarm, and dashed up the pier."

At this, the windows were suddenly thrown open. Five robbers hurtled into the water and swam away empty-handed. When they met up with Dandy at the Port Phillip House, he was furious that he had not only been denied a generous share of the plunder, but the gang had left his expensive burglar tools behind. He hoped English Jim wasn't losing his edge. This was twice he had failed. From what he knew, Jim's plan could net them millions. They were wasting time. Dandy, an Englishman from Sydney, was a seasoned criminal. English Jim had chosen him because he was an engineer like Whittaker, and a millwright who could design tools and keys for them. He could construct bank vaults like Old Jack the brick mason, too. Always a fugitive, Dandy was a slippery pig whenever he was captured. Police were usually hard-pressed to authenticate his identity, but whenever he was identified, he slipped out of jail as if greased. He had just made his fourth escape in as many months from the station house.

Their next target was a jewelry shop that Singing Billy claimed held $20,000 to $30,000 in diamonds.

"He better be right this time," English Jim said. He had to get money soon. It was just one delay after another. He had a big payroll to meet, real estate to buy and men to bribe. His gang now amounted to twenty-five principal participants and inside men including two crooked San Francisco cops, R. C. McIntire and A. J. McCarty, who kept them from arrest. Ultimately, there would be a total of eighty-six gang members and only twenty of them highly respected citizens and lawmen. "Edwards and I went at night and looked at the place," English Jim recalled. "There were four or five men inside and too much of a risk. We gave it up as another bad job." His eyes flared. His fury rose and whenever that happened people died.

Tonight, the core members of English Jim's gang gathered at Mary Ann Hogan's House to lay out the biggest heist of all—English Jim arrived first, then Jemmy-from-town, worn out from engineering several recent jailbreaks at Devil Jack's jail, and on the prison ship, *Euphemia*. Edwards arrived, accompanied by a grim, oil-stained, scarecrow of a man in black, Ben Lewis, who was ninth in importance in the gang only because of his special skills. Whittaker, McKenzie, and Jack Dandy entered next. Old Jack was with Singing Billy whom Whittaker called "an ignorant man who can scarcely read or write." Yet, in between bouts of delirium tremens, Singing Billy planned and executed many successful robberies for the gang.

Whittaker considered him the most untrustworthy member of the gang. Billy would turn on a pal or foil a robbery for no reason except spite. An expert boxer and, according to the *Call*, "An all-around good fellow and boon companion," he had also served time in Van Diemen's Land before sailing to San Francisco on the *Hobart Town*. Secretly, Singing Billy led a dual life as a public official by day and ruthless criminal by night. Appointed Warden of the Port by Port Collector of Customs James Collier last January, Billy had recommended that he hire Old Jack to build the vault in the Old Adobe Custom House which they intended to rob. Naturally, Old Jack's plans gave the gang a tremendous advantage.

English Jim evaluated the men who were absent: Joseph Turner, Richard Osman, Jim Briggs, and Kitchen the Boatman [aka William Kitchen]. Kitchen, thirty, heavyset, very dirty, and a former convict from Van Dieman's Land, provided transportation. Jim made a check mark by several names—Dab the Horse-Thief, Big Brummy, and George Arthur the master burglar. They had their faults but their combined knowledge might enable English Jim to pull off the greatest robbery in history.

Each and everyone agreed that English Jim's multimillion dollar robbery had every chance of success. After last May's fire destroyed San Francisco for a second time, English Jim had drawn a diagram of his plan to rob the Custom House on the northwestern corner of Kearney and Washington Streets. The map was so valuable, English Jim kept it on his person, along with maps to rob Macondray and Co, Dewitt & Harrison (which he said he claimed he could "rob at any time"), and a diagram of Young's next to the El Dorado in the Square. English Jim was after San Francisco's gold reserves, upwards of three million dollars in gold when gold was worth only $19 an ounce.

"In the meantime, I must have some money," English Jim told Old Jack. "When I went to have my likeness made today," he said, "I saw $300 in a box at the Coombs Gallery."

That night, he, Old Jack, and Singing Billy went to rob Coombs. When they reached the second pair of stairs that night, they encountered someone sleeping on the landing.

"There is a man here," English Jim said.

"What the hell are you doing there?" Singing Billy asked. He hauled off and gave him a good kick.

"Oh! I am a watchman," the man replied, rubbing his thigh.

"So you are. Lay still, old fellow. I won't disturb you tonight. Tell Mr. Coombs we will come back in the morning."

Just before dawn English Jim and Sam Whittaker visited Jack Edwards and his partner, Ben Lewis. Lewis lived in various lodging houses along the waterfront awaiting orders from English Jim to commit acts that were to fetch them the city's gold. After they had rowed to Long Wharf, Whittaker dropped down onto the sand. He and Lewis helped pull the skiff ashore on a mud flat. A gray light tinted the Cove's glassy surface. A black cormorant landed on the stump of a partially burned piling, stretched its huge wings, cocked its head, and looked dispassionately at them as if it understood what was coming next. Inexplicably, the men were chilled by the sight of the bird's wings swaying from side to side.

The land city of San Francisco was slowly absorbing the Ghost Fleet. Montgomery Street, the former shore, with its new fireproof brick buildings, iron shutters, and unexposed woodwork was edging seaward. Wharf projects and buildings ringed the outside rim of the Cove as San Francisco pushed and bullied its way into the Cove headed westward.

Battery Street and Front and Davis streets were built up. Buildings rose to flank ships berthed at every angle. Wharves, mini-piers and catwalks anchored to the saw-toothed waterfront linked the nearly one-thousand deserted ships into a taut web spanning two square miles. As the piers edged into the water, each was crisscrossed with a series of transverse docks that had to be filled with dirt and gravel. Merchants, confident that dry land would completely overtake the Cove in two years, three at most, laid planks on top of the piles to facilitate movement between the quays. Then, they linked the planks with more crosswalks and the spaces between these began to be plugged.

Along the mud flats enterprising storekeepers pulled deserted hulks onto the beach. As the flats filled in with sand from the adjacent hills, land began to surround these ships. Soon it became commonplace to drag floating warehouses onto land, set them up between two buildings and convert them into multiple-story buildings.

TODAY, COFFIN STUDIED the white-painted *Alida* on Davis Street, the *Almandralina* lying on the corner of Pacific Front, and three unknown hulks and a storeship at California and Battery. He did a few sketches. He also went to see the Bay Hotel. Peter Le Guervel had advertised it as such after he built a house on its deck and moored it at the southeastern corner of Battery and Green streets. In his *Log*, Coffin correctly placed the *Brilliant* at Davis and Pacific streets next to the *Magnolia*, and *Globe*.

He hadn't forgotten John McCrackan's home ship, the aged *Balance*, either. Later the *Balance* would become a storeship on the corner of Front and Jackson streets, then be moved next to the Pacific and Broadway Wharves near the bark *Cordova* and eventually be buried in mid-Gold Street at Balance Alley. In time, the *Cordova* became Goodall and Nelson's Sausalito water ship as did its companion ships, *Emma* and *Clara*. "The *Garnet* floats alongside the *Cordova*," Coffin wrote. "The *Elizabeth* is an office and bonded storehouse run by the Collector of Customs and, along with the *Bethel*, lies on the Embarcadero. The *Georgean*, a popular storeship, is between Sansome and Battery. The Chinese warehouse floating at Long Wharf lies beside the new Steamboat Hotel."

The twilight faded, Coffin dozed. When he awoke, the police cutters were out again, winding their way in and out of the deep shadows and shining their dark lanterns in the search for English Jim and his men who had made the Ghost Fleet a hunting ground. Since the city was so volatile, everyone feared the hanging men who were congregating on every corner. Coffin listened to the creak of mat sails as stars rose over a red-tinted moon. The days passed slowly.

Coffin completed his arrangements with Captain William Le Craw for another arduous river trip to Marysville to deliver a load of lumber. He also had to deliver the *Merlin* to the sheriff there. With his crew, two lads and an Irishman, he steeled himself to fight the high river, raised to its ultimate by the rainiest season on record. "At last, a breeze came along with the wet, which allowed me to complete my irksome task," he said. "I gave the sloop up to the sheriff and she was sold at auction for $400 to the same party I had bought her eight months before for upwards of $4,000."

"The result was that owing to my long passage and its injured state from being wet, warped and split, together with the expense of cartage," he said, "I had made nothing. Having wound up my affairs, I bid adieu to Marysville. Captain Haight offered me a passage down in his steamer, and I landed on Long Wharf... The harassing trials I had undergone made me sick again, first, with fever, and afterwards with weakening diarrhea... sick and without a dollar and no place to lay my head." Coffin turned his eyes toward the Ghost Fleet where many in the same fix had arranged temporary lodging. Bone-tired, Coffin tethered his skiff at the Market Street Wharf to grab a bite and watch the Cove grow steadily brighter. It was a gold-like dawn on the midst of so much destruction. The Chinese call gold the "Elixir of Life." Drinking a potion of it supposedly grants the drinker immortality. Yet real gold had brought San Francisco so much loss of life. As he walked along the mud flats, he sank up to his knees. No one was stronger and more resolute than he was, but he had to fight to keep from crying. He had reached bottom. Because he had remained at Marysville until late February to dispose of his lumber he was left in debt to Capt. Le Craw. He would have rather been in debt to the Devil.

OVER AT THE JAILHOUSE, Sheriff Devil Jack, in his firm, compulsively polite manner, was doing many things at once—stirring a pot of beans cooking on the stove, turning the bacon frying in the pan next to it, waiting for a wanted picture of English Jim, trying to find five escaped prisoners, and lobbying the Council for funds to build a more secure lockup. The number of men escaping his jail was enough to give a person a cold from the rush.

"It is astonishing," wrote a city editor of the jail, "that the Sheriff and his deputies have been able to hold the prisoners put under their charge as long as they have." The first time "Oregon Pete" escaped from the city jail, he showed up at Alcalde [Mayor] Leavenworth's house carrying the jail front door on his back as his way of protesting the awful jail food. Watkins, a veteran burglar, had escaped three times and boasted that no jail could hold him. Devil Jack had him incarcerated now, but for how much longer? He was sick of Rattlesnake Dick Barter slipping in and out of San Francisco whenever he pleased, and tired of using one-third of his officers as jailhouse guards. He was fed up with buying food for the prisoners out of his own pocket. The saddest prisoner was Brier who was serving five years for receiving stolen goods. When he was locking Brier in his cell after his last escape, he asked, "Do you hope to escape again?"

"I'll escape in some way!" Brier said.

"Perhaps you may," Devil Jack said.

"You may keep my dead body," Brier said, "but that's all. If I could hope to escape, I could endure a life in prison, but in this prison hope is dead, so why should I live?"

Touched, Devil Jack decided not to wait on the Council to pay for upgrading the jail. On December 14, he installed new double-acting cam and lever locks on the doors to halt the frequent escapes, hired two builders expert in jail construction, and paid them out of his meager savings. He estimated that his savings would be gone by spring and he would have to lay the workers off. Devil Jack continued making improvements on the Swiss-cheese jail, though it was a useless endeavor. What he really needed was a new jail centrally located on Broadway between the two hotbeds of criminal activity—the Square with its crooked gamblers and Sydney Town, with its Australian gangs.

Gen. Joe Lane said the way to put down outrages in the mining country was to put Devil Jack Hays at the head of a regiment divided into companies and have these companies stationed at different parts of the mines under command of suitable officers. "Let Jack Hays be everywhere," the General roared. "Old Hays would have a regiment that no three thousand men on earth could whip."

Palmer, Cook and Company in the Square were among the owners of the Mariposa Mining Company which was robbed more often than all the others. General Joe suggested, "What if Devil Jack was hired to guard your gold bullion from Mariposa to San Francisco?"

"How would you manage its safe conduct?" Palmer and Cook asked when Devil Jack came to their offices, and put his boots up on the desk.

"With twenty-five men I might enlist from my Texas Rangers scattered over the State, I could guarantee the safe delivery in San Francisco of any amount of gold bullion that might be enlisted to me." Devil Jack paused. "I would undertake my responsibility for $25,000 payable monthly."

Devil Jack would only spend the money to keep the jail afloat. It was agreed. It was announced that a new custom house all of iron had been contracted for by the government on the condition that the city donate an eligible site for its erection.

On Steamer Day, Devil Jack was at Long Wharf early to welcome Susan, his wife of three years. During his term the city had provided him with a house on Powell Street between Pacific and Broadway streets, though for a time he slept at the city hospital and paid fifty dollars a month to have a little privacy. As soon as Susan had disembarked, Devil Jack took her into his wagon and whipped his team all the way to Mountain Home Estates down the peninsula. He couldn't wait to show her the new ranch he had bought. On the two-thousand-acre spread stood a fine house he had improved, and a third of the Hawes Steam Sawmill. On his new ranch, as in his office in town, Devil Jack retained his Texas habits. He still rode horseback to San Francisco each day, a thirty-mile trip, and kept a simmering pot of Mexican frijoles on the grate, and grilled a slab of venison over the coals. "As he sits yonder by the fire, cooking a rabbit," J. Ross Browne wrote of him, "you would never take him as a hero. He is the very plainest and most unsophisticated of mortals—unconscious of the difference between a great man and a common man, treats us with equal simplicity and is constantly trying to do somebody a service." Devil Jack's genial simplicity was evident even as he slept. He curled up in a poncho before the embers of his fireplace as if he were on the prairie. Devil Jack's detractors joked that his reports were written in an illiterate script and said things such as the fugitives had "runnen quite a spell eastwise, then up a holler" or "crossed a right smart flood and on past a big-size tree." In truth, Devil Jack wrote in a beautiful, flowing script.

As COFFIN PASSED THE PACIFIC WHARF, he came level with the *Henry Lee*, a small bark of great antiquity which had been abandoned. He paused to study the *Lee's* rotten bottom. Bobbing with the current, he decided it had been "a miserable sailor," and its 15,000-mile voyage from the East River to California as protracted as his ill-fated Sacramento River trip.

For his *Log*, Coffin classified the *Lee* as one of the three floating churches of forthright men in the Cove. Before sailing, her passengers, healthy, upright young silversmiths, upholsterers, navigators, manufacturers, machinists, potters, farmers, paper makers, tailors, shoemakers joiners, brick makers, professors, tanners, curers, lawyers, stage drivers and printers, signed a declaration of temperance at Gilman's Saloon. For "medicinal purposes only," they did store twenty-five gallons of whisky in their dispensary. This floating New England village had been packed with mining equipment, carpenters tools, lightning rods, brass cannon to fend off pirates, a small steam-operated launch, four steam engines, wagons, spades, picks, wheelbarrows, bricks, and the frames of two houses that would serve as Hq. The *Lee's* 122 passengers kept a police force that was hardly needed.

The only time they paused from working was to pray and eat. On the first leg of their voyage, fanned by summer breezes, passengers moved about in light clothing, straw hats, and bare feet. Over ten days, summer became winter. Around Cape Horn they huddled together, shivering and blue-lipped in unheated below-deck quarters. Like moles in a swamp, they crept out, blinking, onto the snow-covered deck to see where they were. When the *Lee* reached San Francisco, the well-stocked professionals realized, like every captain before them, that having lighters ferry goods from ship to shore was ruinously expensive. Because they had so many items to sell in the hold: boots, apparel, hardware, clocks, seeds and stoneware, they opened a general store in the Ghost Fleet. Eventually, they abandoned the floating factory beyond the Pacific Street Wharf in the site that would become Selby's store.

John Linville Hall, one of the *Lee's* passengers, had used his hand-press to print a weekly paper, *The Barometer* and completed an eighty-eight page book. In San Francisco, Hall provided the Ghost Fleet with its own newspaper. This was not unusual. Many Gold Rush ships had their own shipboard publications. Onboard the *Duxbury*, an old three-master so unwieldy it needed all of Massachusetts Bay in which to turn, the weeklies *Petrel*, and *Shark* were published by twenty-five Harvard students.

The second righteous ship was the 700-ton Boston ship *Edward Everett* which, trailing just behind the *Lee*, passed through the Golden Gate with no less than six captains onboard. It had a social hall, a spacious dormitory with triple rows of berths, "picknicks" of cheese, plum pudding, potpie, and applesauce and a full two years of provisions in its hold next to a small, flat-bottomed, steam-operated mini-steamer, the *Edward Everett, Jr.* There were also four steam engines, and the frames of two houses to be used as company Hq. "You are going to a strange, immoral country," the President of Harvard College Edward Everett cautioned the 150 young passengers. "Take the Bible in one hand and your New England civilization in the other and make your mark on the people and the country." Later, Everett was crestfallen to discover one of their members had sold a Bible for the price of a drink. Scandalized by San Francisco's fleshpots and saloons the *Everett's* moral passengers fled Graveyard Harbor for Benicia and Sacramento, leaving behind their one hundred volume collection of great books and providing Graveyard Harbor with its own library to go with its floating city hall. The burning conditions of the Mokelumne River diggings, blazing summer heat and hard work finished off the pampered Bostonians. They disbanded in nine months and sold their ship for a dividend of $160 each. The min-steamer, *Everett Jr.*, was landed at Benicia, but made only three inland trips before being wrecked in the Sacramento River before they sold her hull to miners to be used as a flat-bottomed ferry.

The third, the psalm-singing *Sweden*, did much better. The Sunday before sailing for San Francisco, the *Sweden's* passengers had gathered at Boston's Seaman's Bethel to pray and present Capt. Cutter with a Bible and a gold fringed, white satin flag that optimistically depicted the vessel already lying off the California coast. "Unfurl it as you leave your native shore," they said, "and bear it over the broad ocean as a passport to a distant land. Let it be to you a cloud by day and a pillar of fire at night." That they did.

THE PIRATE NED WAKEMAN, the popular, though inefficient head of the Citizen's Water Police and fan of the Vigilantes, was no friend of the sheriff's. He got in Devil Jack's craw because he did whatever he pleased. He commanded a large fleet of sloops, Whitehall skiffs, and open boats that carried several men and stout lines for towing law breakers.

"At this time," Wakeman said. "I was sometimes called the 'Emperor of the Port,' as all vessels coming and going out were under my orders and subject to my inspection, the revenue cutter *Polk* being especially under my orders." He made special expeditions aboard the *Polk* to Contra Costa, the Bay Islands, and the faraway Farallones in search of opium smugglers who kept their hideouts in these remote locations. He and his officers were charged with reducing Shanghaiing, patrolling the Cove storeships and enforcing mooring and quarantine regulations, though their main duty was meeting all incoming ships and detaining their personnel until they made certain they were not wanted for crimes anywhere.

Wakeman patted his coat pocket and smiled. He had an edge—

copies of special passenger lists that would identify any Australian ex-convicts being smuggled into the US. Today, he had targeted the British bark *Chief* in from Australia, anchored and awaiting the assistance of a steam towboat for docking. It was a chill morning and a salty wind was rising, as Wakeman stalked along Long Wharf flanked by six of his men. When the wind swept out his blue broadcloth, it revealed a brace of pistols jammed in his belt. He reached the pier head, stepped into a Whitehall boat, and was rowed out to the *Chief*.

"How many passengers do you have aboard, captain?" Wakeman asked as he climbed aboard.

The skipper answered truthfully.

"Very well. Now I'll thank you to show me their passports and other papers authorizing them to enter the US."

"Here, all printed up proper," the skipper said, handing the Pirate a stack of banknotes.

Wakeman held the notes lightly in his tattooed fist, then opened his fingers slowly, and let the money blow out into the Cove. When the skipper bent to retrieve one bill that had not blown away, Wakeman gave him a fierce kick in the ass suitable enough to be heard back on the dock.

"That!" Wakeman cried, "Is for trying to bribe the Captain of the Citizen's Harbor Police. The monetary price for hauling undesirable aliens into the Port of San Francisco is going to be considerably higher." Only one passenger had proper papers for legal entry. Wakeman lodged the other fourteen in jail until the *Chief* was cleared to sail again and take them with her. In a few months San Francisco lost its charm as a dumping ground for criminals.

"A certain amount of hanging is necessary to make this a decent place to live," Wakeman believed. Sam Brannan pumped his fist in agreement. As historian H. H. Bancroft observes, the Vigilantes knew when "a vagabond deserved banishment or hanging." They knew how to banish and they knew how to hang. Wakeman's Water Patrol swept the Embarcadero, keeping storeships and warehouses safe and watching out for thieves who robbed dockside merchants. For all his effort, Wakeman's Water Police accomplished little. Many blamed Wakeman. who filed few reports and allowed many vessels from Sydney into Graveyard Harbor without a port clearance. His piratical, vaguely illegal talents, and thirst for Biblical vengeance suited him more than rules.

Moorhead, Whitehead and Waddington were in the market for "good strong vessels for storeships" for the Cove. S. A. and J. G. Thayer put their storeship *Calumet* up for sale, but no water lot where they could support it with pilings could be found. The storeship *Thames*, moored off Central Wharf since May, had a similar problem. Finally, they found a water lot for her at the northeastern corner of Jackson and Front streets. This opened up the area a little. The Russian-built *Roma*, run aground and beached on the waterfront, was converted into stores that brought in $3,000 a month. Eventually the *Roma* was used for a coal ship, then sunk at the southwestern corner of East Street, its bow just touching the edge of Market Street. Thirsty San Francisco erected the *Ensign* Saloon over it. Coffin had some wise words for them. "The prudent must guard their remaining supply of the warm, obnoxious liquid with the utmost care, and woe to anyone who thoughtlessly approaches so close as to run the risk of upsetting their precious cups of nectar."

DURING THEIR WALK on the flats, Sam Whittaker suggested a lucrative target to English Jim.

"I live next door to Charles J. Jansen," he said. Jansen was a popular dry goods merchant and senior member of Jansen, Bond and Company in Montgomery St. One evening Whittaker and Old Jack went to Jansen's home to buy some sovereigns and confirm that he had a large amount of them he was about to move.

"Many persons from the colonies frequent my house," Whittaker told English Jim. "On learning that the country generally wasted English sovereigns, Jansen told me that he would usually take them and safe keep them for homeward-bound Australians. A fortune in sovereigns is to be carted inside a trunk by Jansen's head clerk."

"Just when is this?" English Jim asked. His eyes were wolfish. Here he was quibbling over thousands when he was after millions. Whittaker's promising scheme led English Jim to use trickery instead of his usual strong arm tactics, though that was subject to change depending on his mood. On the appointed moving night, Whittaker sat down on Jansen's trunk and pretended to rest. Secretly, he was removing a linchpin from the cart axle. English Jim's plan was to strike along the clerk's path when the wheel broke and the trunk and clerk were dumped onto the road. During the trip, the head clerk perched on the trunk with a candle in his hand and kept watch as he was pulled slowly along. Because the cart's joints were stiff, the wheel stubbornly remained in place even with the linchpin pulled out. The gold coins were safely deposited. The gang, glowering in the shadows, gave up—for the time being. He would have to think of another way to rob Jansen and use that money for the vault heist.

Joseph Hetherington, cofounder with Teddy McCormac of the Port Royal House, lived at Mary Ann Hogan's lodging house for criminals with Whittaker. Hetherington, who had been accused by the authorities of sheltering incendiaries last year, claimed to be an American by birth who had moved to Liverpool in childhood, and then to Australia when he was thirty. It was at Mary Ann's that he saw English Jim for the first time. "This was a few days before the 'Jansen affair,' and it came to be called," he said. "Mrs. Hogan told me his name was Jim Stuart or English Jim, his constant companions were Jim Briggs, and Whittaker, all of whom used to hang around the house." Hetherington failed to mention Singing Billy the corrupt official, who for a month had been shadowing Macondray's store fronting the Cove east of Clay Street and observing the daytime movements of the staff. "He told me there were three safes and one vault filled with money," English Jim said, "lots of money, more than enough to fill a boat."

On February 17, English Jim and his men stole a boat of the correct size to hold all that money.

"We came up in the night to Macondray's to do it," English Jim said. But, Macondray's bookkeeper had suspected Singing Billy from the first and doubled the guards at the store. When the gang discovered numerous watchmen on duty in all the buildings, they backed out.

"Considering there were eleven guards," English Jim said, "I realized the job was hopeless and gave it up." Yes, English Jim thought, he had fallen into a rut with one failure after another. Later that night, a wary San Franciscan saw Creeping Jesus walking along the Central Wharf. His shirt beard was pointed, his rich brown hair was fine and wavy and worn long in the style of the traditional portraits and statuary of Jesus Christ whom he uncannily resembled. His nose was straight and his eyes were dark blue-gray. The citizen watched as this apparently unique man vanished and realized that this had to be the notorious English Jim Stuart. It had to be. He ran to find Devil Jack.

Amazingly, the man was *not* English Jim, but the unfortunate gambler and miner Thomas Berdue. Shaken by his narrow escapes from punishment in the mines, Berdue had come down into San Francisco with the Windreds to see if his wife Elen and their children, Mary Ann, Catherine, Thomas Jr., and an infant son had arrived in California yet. When he had enough gold, he hoped to open a little store or operate a pushcart in San Francisco to make a home for them. Dark-bearded and lean from hard work, Berdue, normally fair-complected, had been bronzed by the summer sun until he was a perfect twin to the dark-complected English Jim.

Berdue was about two-inches shorter than Jim who was about five-foot-ten and stockier, thicker through and through. English Jim walked in a graceful, long-measured stride, while Berdue, still recovering from the sickness he had contracted in the gold towns around the Yuba River, moved stiffly and painfully. English Jim moved fluidly and had a habit of swinging his exceptionally long arms, "rubber arms." Routinely, he halted every few steps and, lowering his head, and peered out from beneath the broad brim of his low-crowned hat. As always, English Jim's head would not stay down. Berdue, fair-complected, with a full face, never exhibited such body language, and kept his head on his chest as if he lacked confidence.

Like English Jim, Berdue had an India ink tattoo around his finger and a facial scar that trailed along his cheek and down his neck. Like English Jim, he had a light-brown beard with twin points and a deformed finger. Like English Jim, Berdue had been convicted and exiled for life to Australia, served six or seven years, been given a ticket of leave, and come to the United States. Both were identical to the traditional church statuary, egg tempera frescoes, and oil portraits of Jesus Christ.

Mistaken for English Jim, Berdue had been tried, convicted, and narrowly escaped hanging not once, but twice for crimes in the mining camps that English Jim had committed. "This uncanny resemblance," historian Mary Floyd Williams wrote, "had imperiled his life and liberty in three successive trials for the crimes done by another man." The semi-respectable British subject, miner, and itinerant gambler's only crime, besides some minor con games, was his uncanny resemblance to English Jim Stuart.

"I never saw before or since such a resemblance!" rugged newspaper reporter, Edward Gould Buffum swore. His eyes were wide. His mouth was open. He was still in disbelief. "Stuart was, perhaps, a trifle stouter, but having seen either one, I think I should have unhesitatingly, at any time thereafter, been willing to swear to the other as that one. It scarcely seems possible that the men could have so perfectly resembled each other."

By the time Devil Jack learned this salient fact it would be too late and the Yuba County district court would be fitting Tom Berdue's neck for a hemp necktie. At sunset, the unfortunate Berdue, having lost at the gambling tables again, slogged to the Dime House on the waterfront where he consumed pork chops, sausages, pickles, and grease, his favorite dish. The food was hot. It was cheap. It filled him.

"Cigar?" asked the barkeep.

Berdue declined. He knew all about "Shanghai cigars"—tobacco impregnated with opium, smoke acting like chloroform. Four puffs of that, he thought, and the next time I wake up I'll be somewhere past the Farallones.

He realized now that he hadn't enjoyed his snack. It had upset his long-empty belly. Ah, well, he would eat better tomorrow when he and the Windreds were to have dinner with his friends, John and Elicia. They laid a splendid table, Berdue could see it now, none better. In the blaze of light from a gambling saloon and whale-oil lanterns storeowners had hung outside their shops, passerby were visible, but outside those random circles of illumination, the streets were dark as a moonless night. A man could see shapes, but not the features of men standing in front of him. That was dangerous, too dangerous for Berdue. He returned to his room on the Central Wharf and went to bed. Where was his wife? he wondered. He tossed and turned all night.

On February 19, a Wednesday, Berdue took care of his empty stomach in a more traditional way. He had a lunch of meat pie and damper bush bread cooked in hot coals—a staple of Australian cowboys, and cooked just the way it should be. It was so good that he shared his bounty with his friends at the Panama House. When sunset fell at 5:52 PM, Berdue, eager to gamble a little, headed northwest from

First and Mission Streets. He crossed Market, looking both ways, and headed north on Battery until it intersected Clay. February is decidedly a dry month, but it was drizzling tonight and gloomy, but it fitted his mood. He picked up his pace and followed Clay to the Central Wharf Exchange. For the next two-and-a-half-hours, he and twelve others, all perfectly good witnesses, played cards, and drank claret wine together.

William Stokes had known Berdue for two months prior. He recalled a number of Australian guests at his table. Among them were George Turner, Capt. Robert Patterson, Mr. McDonald and Bungarribee Jack, one of English Jim's men. There was no other explanation for Bungarribee's presence outside of his love of gambling, while there remained the remote chance he might have been keeping an eye on his English Jim's lookalike. James Ewbanks, who kept a house on Long Wharf where Berdue and Windred were lodging, played cards with Berdue until well after 9:00 PM.

Finally, Ewbanks threw down his cards and said, "Let's go to bed," and went out the front door. Horatio Utting, keeper of the Exchange, saw Berdue there until 10:00 PM. Berdue had finished drinking and playing cards when he heard a fog bell moan on Alcatraz. On such days as this, when rain and fog roll in, and the night becomes mysterious, lightkeepers are compelled to ring their bell continuously for as long as twenty-four hours, a task that takes amazing stamina. Yawning and content after a sumptuous meal, Berdue entered his lodging house, and climbed upstairs to sleep. His wife and child had still not arrived, but he decided he would wait for them for one more day, then return with the Windreds to Auburn on the Friday afternoon steamer and wait there while looking for gold.

IT HAD BEEN two and a half hours since Whittaker told English Jim that Charlie Jansen had a bag filled with ten or fifteen thousand dollars. Jim was still short of funds to put his master plan into operation. He and Whittaker, seated inside the Port Phillip House, needed to decide when to move. Jim knew he should wait, Whittaker even cautioned him to do so, but he was impatient and greedy, and did not like to wait. After all, his plan was surefire. "We agreed to go and get it from his store that night," English Jim recalled, rubbing his palms together briskly. There was a gleam in his eye that always came when he was on the prowl.

A half-hour later, after he had briefed his men, he and Whittaker left the Port Phillip House and walked two doors down to the front of Jansen's new dry goods store. It was forty-eight degrees out. The moon had not yet risen. The unpaved streets at the intersection of Washington and Montgomery were nearly deserted. Lit only by the gambling saloons' bright chandeliers, shallow puddles reflected English Jim's men in twos and threes as they arrived to join Jim. Eventually, eight robbers were huddled on both sides of Montgomery in various positions—Briggs, McCormick, Edwards, Singing Billy, Billy Hughes, Morgan, Whittaker, and English Jim.

Robert Reed was passing Jansen's store when he saw four of the men a few feet further on, engaged in close conversation. "I thought then that they were upon no honest business," he said. "One of the men had on a gray coat, another had on a cloak and was well muffled up."

Whittaker was to be the lookout. He had no taste for bloodshed. English Jim and Old Jack were perfectly willing to spill blood and would commit the actual robbery. Old Jack slipped into the store first, but pulled the brim of his hat down over his forehead. It was essential that Jansen not recognize Jack from an earlier visit and identify him later. The store was a single room with a narrow frontage extending fifty-feet back and lit by an odorless, solid fat, stearine candle. Jansen, a slight, friendly man, was alone and reclining on a bench after a hard day's work. He heard footsteps and became aware of someone moving about his store. He roused himself, leaned forward, and saw the backlit silhouette of a stocky man halfway up the passage. He was staggering about in an exaggerated manner as if intoxicated.

"He was of low stature, stout built" Jansen later said, "and had on an overcoat, a wide-brimmed hat, and black whiskers, and a mustache."

"I need a dozen pair of blankets," the stranger muttered. His words were slurred and Jansen had to ask him to repeat them.

"Why, yes," Jansen said, and handed him a colored blanket from the counter.

"Not blue," he said, "white."

"There are more in back," Jansen said. He rose and moved his candle along the countertop as he walked toward the rear of the store. Outside, English Jim and Whittaker were waiting impatiently with their coats held over their heads though the rain had ceased. Through the window they saw a dim light inside, probably a candle, moving slowly toward the back. That was according to plan.

"Old Jack's taking too long," English Jim fumed. "If I do not go in there we are not going to get any money." He pulled down his hat, pointed in the crown, muffled his face in his long wool and silk cloak, a "camlet," and entered as quietly as he could. His plan was to sneak up on Jansen, but the storekeeper heard the loud rustle of his camlet, and looked up before English Jim had walked many feet into the store. Jansen later described the stranger as tall, and dressed in a Spanish cloak. "He had whiskers and a mustache and was not as heavy as the first."

"What's the price of canvas?" English Jim asked.

Jansen again pointed to the rear and all three men walked single file toward the back. When Jansen had gone two yards, he put his candle down on the counter and bent to retrieve some blankets from a lower shelf. The second man was within three feet of the candle when Jansen heard a single word.

"Now!"

"I hit Jansen on the head with a slung-shot [a monkey's fist used to cast line from one location to another]," English Jim said, "and knocked him down."

His eyes grew bright at the recollection. He had put all his power behind the blow. Jim was proud of how remarkably accurate he was with this ingenious weapon that silently rendered a man suddenly unconscious. He often carried a lump of printer's lead inside his pocket handkerchief that he fastened to a line tied to his wrist and then swung. At the approach of the law he untied the line, dropped the lead from the handkerchief, ground it into the mud, and stuffed the handkerchief into his back pocket. Thus, he would survive any weapons search by Sheriff Devil Jack and his deputies.

Tonight, he was using a different type of slung-shot—a short stick with an egg-sized, two-pound piece of lead on one end that could crush a skull with moderate effort. He struck Jansen hard on the right temple, but failed on two counts. First, Jansen wasn't silent—he let out a wail as he dropped. It was loud that Singing Billy, Edwards, Hughes, and McCormac plainly heard. Second, Jansen wasn't dead. He fell to the floor spouting blood, a spray that made tracks on the wall, on the floor, on a pile of canvas and on his writing desk. English Jim put his foot on

Jansen's chest and struck him two more times. Then, Old Jack rushed forward and struck him. Together, they repeatedly beat Jansen and stomped his chest until they believed him to be dead.

Winded from the rush of murder and urge for more violence, English Jim calmed himself. He had to hold Old Jack at this point. His blood was up. Jim moved Jansen three or four feet from where he fell, snatched his gold watch and chain, then walked back to the front. Old Jack broke open the desk. Inside was a canvas bag of gold dust, $338 in gold coin, and a shot bag of cash. They ransacked the store for more, then left. Now, there were people in the street who had grown suspicious of them. They began to run, calling more attention to themselves.

"I carried the money home to Sydney Valley," English Jim said, "and counted it all. There was $1,568 in gold coin—eagles, Washingtons, California coin, and even a few sovereigns. We divided it among we eight, making it $196 apiece. We went downtown and spent a few hours celebrating our night's work at Mrs. Mary Ann Hogan's barroom on Sansome Street. This was just east of Jansen's. Her house [at the corner of an alley leading from Gold Street into Jackson Street above Sansome Street] was a crib for stolen property. She knows all about our motions."

English Jim admired Jansen's gold watch in his palm. He turned it this way and that in the light of the bar. There was an inscription on the back. English Jim realized the distinctive timepiece might incriminate him, so he gave it to Jack Edwards' brother. But he was no fool, either. Walking down to the dock, he took the watch by its chain and, swinging it over his head, flung it far into the Cove. There was the faintest ripple.

Theodore Payne, who had a prosperous real estate agency across the street from Jansen's, was pacing the floor. He consulted his watch. He had a dinner engagement with Jansen that night at a little after eight. He was getting worried when he didn't show. At 8:20 PM, a friend across the way rushed into Payne's store, gesticulating wildly. "There's some trouble across the way," he said. "I think it's bad. You better come." Payne leapt to his feet and for the first time saw the crowd gathering in front of Jansen's open door. It was as if someone had rushed out and left the door open. Payne dashed across the road, burst inside, and discovered Jansen covered in blood and sitting on a bale of goods. He was only slightly conscious which in itself was astonishing. Payne ran to fetch Dr. Temple. He hoped that Charlie Jansen would recover and name his attackers so they could get after them as soon as possible. Temple, shocked that the blows had not killed Jansen, was working over the shopkeeper when he suddenly lapsed into a coma.

"What Jansen might say, if he ever wakes," Dr. Temple said, "is anyone's guess."

By now the trail was growing icy.

Early Thursday morning, February 20, Jansen regained consciousness long enough to mumble something.

"What is it?" Payne asked.

"Two robbers took $2,000 from my desk," Jansen gasped.

The shopkeeper was unique among the merchant class. He only exaggerated the amount stolen by $94. Devil Jack at first suspected Jansen't two clerks. He arrested them. Subsequently, he discharged them when Jansen was able to give a description of one of his attackers as looking like Jesus Christ.

The call went up: "Find English Jim!"

In a frenzy, the mob began to scour the waterfront where "Creeping Jesus" had months earlier been glimpsed skulking about the Broadway Wharf off Clark's Point. Down the street the *Courier* editor, rolling black ink onto beds of movable metal type, was making certain everyone knew what had happened. Feverishly, he cranked out a new edition with a screaming headline railing against the growing boldness of the gangs.

"Is it worthwhile, if caught, to offer the criminals a trial in our courts?" the *Courier* asked, "Is it not better to make examples of them, if found, by hanging them at once."

The attack on a storekeeper had been a commonplace occurrence, but Jansen was so beloved by his fellow merchants, a powerful class, and his injuries so severe, that the crime took on epic proportions.

On Long Wharf, Father Taylor, no friend of criminals, was doing his part. He was haranguing the crowd like a *Courier* editorial, as fiery and as impossible to ignore as a burning city. A man in the crowd listened awhile and then, looking upon the lawlessness all around him, shouted that they needed considerably more preaching than Father Taylor was providing. Next, sixty-three policemen were stationed at the wharves, scanning the faces of any men foolish enough to try to leave San Francisco by steamer. No one would dare, except Tom Berdue, and his friend, Joe Windred, who needed to get to Auburn by Friday afternoon and were seemingly unaware of the attack.

A LITTLE AFTER 4:30 PM, Friday, February 21, Dutch Charley Duane noticed a tremendous commotion. The two fisted fire warden and first assistant engineer of the Volunteer Fire Companies was returning from a ride with his friends. As they passed City Hall on the corner of Pacific and Kearny Streets, he saw an excited mob shoving his way. He leaped onto the road and demanded to know what was happening.

"They had surrounded two men accused of assaulting Charlie Jansen," Dutch Charley explained later, "and were preparing to hang them from the most convenient projection."

The two suspects were identified as an Australian ex-convict named Joe Windred, and the Sydney criminal, English Jim Stuart, who had been seen emerging from the maze of ships and then walking on Market Street earlier in the day. The two hapless men had been identified by visiting Sacramento policeman Charles Tureman who had arrived in San Francisco only a day earlier and was on his way back to Sacramento. When English Jim was jailed for looting a lumber yard in Sacramento, Officer Tureman had been the one to take him into custody. Now, as Tureman was passing up Long Wharf, he saw English Jim again, but with a companion he did not recognize. The pair were waiting for the Sacramento steamer *McKim* and playing "strap," a popular bunco game with some suckers crowded around. Tureman alerted officers Casserly and Hill by the gangway that English Jim was escaping the city by steamer and he better be quick about it. The officers seized the two men and were stagger-walking them toward the Jail. On the way, a mob gathered around them and began surging forward.

"As soon as I learned the state of affairs," said Dutch Charley, who was famous as a brawny shoulder-striker for the David Broderick political faction, "I rushed into the mob and with the assistance of my friends succeeded in rescuing the intended victims of lynch law and conveyed them and the two officers safely the rest of the short way to the city prison where they were locked up to await trial in a legal court."

Sheriff Devil Jack shared office quarters in the City Hall, a wooden building originally erected for a hotel, with the Town Council and a courtroom on the second floor. No one used the lower floor because it was filled with two manual 2,000-pound fire wagons used to fight the terrible arson fires which kept afflicting the Gold Rush city. The basement was taken up with a police station and dank prison. This unsanitary hoosegow, intended for twenty prisoners, held more than sixty in each of the thirteen eight-by-twelve foot cells. The former army building had "the distinction of being able to hold prisoners before trial, but was inadequate to hold them there after they were convicted." From the first days when a schoolhouse had served as the city jail, escapes had been as common as arrests.

By 10:00 AM, Saturday, Charlie Jansen's condition had worsened. Dr. Taylor feared he would die and sent word to the court that if they wanted to speak with him they better hightail it over to him. "And bring along the two suspects," Taylor said. An hour later, authorities hurried Joseph Windred and Berdue by carriage to Jansen's apartment and hauled them up to his second floor bedside for a death bed identification. Weaving in and out of consciousness, Jansen lifted his head, then fell back on his pillow. With some help, he got his head erect. His eyes darted about. The room was still. No one dared speak. For seconds, he studied the features of the two men, then pointed at the shorter, bearded man, Berdue, and identified him as English Jim Stuart.

"That is the man, of this I have no doubt," Jansen said. He let his head drop back. "He wore the same clothes he wore when he struck me." Oddly, Jansen remembered the clothes more distinctly than he did the man, but even had some doubt about them. "I do not exactly recollect the color of his coat. I think this is the coat. It has the general appearance. I distinguish him from his general appearance and his clothes. I have not the slightest doubt as to the resemblance between this man and the man who struck me. It is my firm belief this is the man. There is a most perfect resemblance. I have no doubt in my mind of the identity of this man. It is English Jim."

Just as fervently, Berdue denied he was English Jim, and said he was a miner named Thomas Berdue. When they placed Berdue's hat upon his head, Jansen identified him more distinctly. "The resemblance is still greater," he said. "I cannot swear that *is* the man, but I cannot conjure up a resemblance more striking."

When Berdue was searched, authorities discovered two bags of gold dust, $390 in gold coin, and a gold watch and chain.

"Jansen's missing watch!" they cried. The real watch was resting at the bottom of the Bay.

When they discovered a certificate of deposit upon B. Davidson and Co. for $1,720 on Berdue, they gave the entire amount to Jansen to compensate him for his losses and injuries. Further damning evidence was a mark on the right sleeve of his coat, near the elbow, that looked like a clot of dried blood, but could have been anything. One of Jansen's clerks testified that there was blood on a piece of goods on a writing desk near the door at just such a height that a man might have gotten it on his coat as he escaped.

In the Recorders room a spirited discussion began. Theodore Payne, Jansen's friend, who had just been elected secretary by the Committee, was speaking. "It is proper that something should be done," he shouted, "The police and courts are feeble when compared to the populace. That population will act tomorrow morning and they expect some investigation on our part. The people demand it." Merchant Sam Brannan had been chosen to preside in this people's court. A hard man with great power, he moved that the Committee proceed at once to the investigation.

"When we questioned the prisoners," Brannan said, "both men cried like children, and protested their innocence."

"Our only duty is to keep the prisoners safe," F. W. Macondray said.

Brannan said the Committee should be the ones to guard them and everyone agreed. He didn't trust the legal courts. "The prisoners are here and they ought to be tried now." The words "And hung," did not have to be spoken. They were written across Brannan's face. He was ruled out of order.

"The Committee is not a jury," he was told.

"I'm very much surprised to hear people talk about grand juries or recorders or mayors," Brannan said. "I'm very much tired of such talk. They are murderers as well as thieves, and I know it, and I will die or see them hung by the neck. I'm opposed to any farce in this business. We are the mayor and the recorder, the hangman, and the laws! Resolved, we the Committee recommend to the people to choose a judge and a jury of twelve men to obtain whatever evidence may exist against the accused and let their decision be final as to the guilt or innocence of the accused and if found guilty be hung in fifteen minutes."

The Vigilance Committee's unlawful court had been organized as the result of these frequent robberies, and the inefficiency of the legal courts. They executed some and banished others to parts unknown. Macondray was shocked and his expression showed it. The resolution was withdrawn.

Sometime after 2:00 PM, a furious mob encircling the building crashed through the door, and spilled inside the Recorder's office. Several hundred men rushed into the room where the police were questioning the prisoners and attempted to drag them into the street and an eighth-mile to the Square where there was a convenient projection on the Old Adobe to hang them from.

The Recorder thought fast.

He sprang up and flung open the door communicating to another room where members of Sen Dave Broderick's Washington Guard, a volunteer military organization, were drilling. In an instant, fifty good men with fixed bayonets hurried into the crowd and, leaping onto desks and benches, drove the intruders out and bloodied the courtroom floor.

Outside, the mob hissed, catcalled, and cried, "Hang 'em!"

"Lynch 'em!"

"Bring 'em out."

A handbill was circulated. "Fie upon your laws," it said, "they have no force. All those who would rid our city of its robbers and murderers will assemble on Sunday at 2:00 PM, on the Plaza, and we will do some business."

The prisoners were hustled into the more secure basement and locked up for their safety. The crowd melted away in the late afternoon, but vowed to hang the pair on Monday. As darkness fell, Judge Tilford said that one of the men had not been positively identified by Jansen and there is great doubt of his participation in the crime. Twenty guards were stationed outside Windred and Berdue's cells to protect them throughout the night.

"Two men by the name of Windred and Stuart were arrested on Sunday morning," Father Taylor preached, "and lodged in jail as the supposed perpetrators of the deed. It was requested by Windred's wife to visit him, as it was believed that the prisoners would be hung before night. I had great difficulty getting through the crowd, but finally succeeded in having an interview with both men." Cries of, "Have them out! Hang them!" filled the air. It was with great difficulty that the public's indignation would be suppressed, so as to give time for an examination and trial of any kind. A doubt as to the guilt of the parties arrested, prevailed and calmed the mob's excitement.

"I preached on the Plaza that day to about fifteen hundred persons," Father Taylor said, "on the value and indispensable necessity of the Bible, indispensable to our safety and happiness."

It was a cool, clear afternoon and Rev. Taylor's strong voice could be heard for a block. His square beard and glaring eyes were mesmerizing. His text today was, "Let the wicked forsake his way. The way of the wicked is exceedingly offensive to God and most hideous and hateful in itself."

The preacher's words gave the wicked who had really committed the crime pause, but only momentarily. They had more crimes to commit.

AT MARY ANN'S GROG HOUSE, English Jim scratched his head and asked, "How could he have survived?" He was honestly puzzled. Until now, he had believed Jansen dead. He had done his best to achieve that result. Now, to avoid being identified, he had to change his appearance. How bothersome. He decided to shave his beard. It worked. All day, in plain sight, Jim and Old Jack, Dab the Horse-Thief, Hetherington, and Whittaker had been drinking and closely following events at City Hall. The criminals felt some measure of pride in the crime they had committed and that others were going to pay for with their lives, all except Whittaker who was deeply troubled by the outcome. It showed in his handsome face. He had not expected this.

English Jim had always looked after his criminal offspring by breaking them out of jail, suborning perjury, bribing jurors, and collecting bail money for them. Abruptly, he decided to do it again. Something had come over him. It might have been regret. "I will shoot fifty men rather than see Berdue and Windred hung!" he vowed. "There is quite a fuss about town made over Jansen's assault and robbery. We will not commit any more robberies while the trial of the men arrested for striking Jansen is going on, as we do not wish them hung." They agreed that if the two innocent men were hanged, as they expected they would be, they would "fire the town on Sunday night in four or five different places."

There was still a shred of decency in the man, Mary Ann thought.

Singing Billy dropped by in a buoyant mood. Governor McDougal had appointed him as State Harbor Master of the Port of San Francisco, a popular choice in spite of his close association with Sydney men like English Jim. This appointment gave Singing Billy access to all shipping schedules, cargo manifests, and custom house entries, including the biggest custom house in Monterey.

Early the next day, nearly six thousand citizens gathered around the courthouse to demand an immediate trial of Winfred and Berdue. Because of Jansen's positive identification, no one among the thousands doubted their guilt or that they would probably escape punishment through the connivance of crooked politicians and officials or bribery. "Now's the time!" arose from the lips of men on the outskirts of the crowd, "Hang them! Hang them! Hang them!"

At 9:00 AM, a hearing of evidence began in the Recorder's Courtroom before a judge, but without the prisoners in the court. Such an administrative hearing may take place outside the judicial process before officials who have been granted judicial authority expressly for the purpose of conducting such hearings. The conclusions of a court that has no legal authority and disregards all rights normally afforded to persons, are not legally binding.

Judge D. O. Shattuck agreed to act as counsel for the defendants and inquired for the charges. Vigilante William Tell Coleman for the prosecution, said the judge should proceed to arraign "James Stuart, alias English Jim Stuart, charged with an assault and attempt to kill, burglary, and larceny." The Committee recommended that citizens appoint a committee of thirteen citizens to serve as judge and jury and to proceed with the trial of the suspected criminals today at 2:00 PM, and act in conjunction with the courts. Judge Shattuck volunteered to act as defense counsel, but was uncomfortable with this rush to justice and said that the matter should be postponed until Monday morning. "In a matter of so great a responsibility as the spilling of blood," he said, "I hope the jury will not act in haste. The prisoner should have an opportunity to show his identity, or to bring testimony to counteract the suspicions that have attached to him." All judges but Judge Townes had declined to serve as judge, so he was selected. Hall McAllister represented Windred.

Theodore Payne, testified first. "I have seen the prisoner James Stuart," he said. "I was present when the prisoner was examined before Justice of the Peace Phillip W. Shepard. I know by Mr. Jansen's testimony that Stuart was identified as being connected with the transaction." Payne paused, then proceeded. "I was in Mr. Jansen's room yesterday when he identified the prisoners, Windred and Stuart. The tall man, Windred, was brought into Mr. Jansen's room. James Stuart was next brought in and handled roughly. Mr. Jansen had described the hat worn by one of the men who assaulted him. Stuart's hat corresponds with the description. He said the tall man had on a cloak, and had whiskers and a mustache."

At the same hearing, Officer Tureman swore positively that Berdue was the same man charged with murder on the Yuba River. On his evidence, Shepherd was about to release Stuart to Sacramento authorities when he was positively implicated in the Jansen robbery and retained.

"Mr. Jansen is very feeble, and I think he is unable to attend court. His injuries are altogether upon the head but they have affected his balance and ability to walk. When giving his testimony he remarked that he was perfectly sensible, that his mind was not impaired by injuries received. I have watched the prisoner carefully. On his examination yesterday, I saw upon the right shoulder of his coat a spot of blood, and I thought I saw marks of blood upon his elbow. The spot of blood upon Stuart's coat, in my opinion, was made by the slung shot in raising it to give a second blow. The slung shot was broken in giving the blows, and it was left in the store of Mr. Jansen."

Judge Shattuck objected to the kind of such testimony. "Mr. Jansen should be present to identify the parties as connected with the outrage upon the person of Mr. Jansen," he argued.

The jury signified they were willing to receive such testimony as could be obtained, whether hearsay or otherwise. Court clerk W. H. Jones, a self-proclaimed "professional chemist," asserted that the stain upon Stuart's coat was blood. "It has the appearance of being made by rubbing against the blankets in Jansen's store which are saturated with blood. I was in this city eighteen months ago, at the time the Hounds were out. I was called into service then, and I would hang a man who committed murder as quick as I would hang a dog."

"You would find out first whether they were guilty, I suppose," Shattuck asked.

"That would depend upon circumstances."

"On Wednesday evening," Robert Reed testified, "in passing Mr. Jansen's store, I saw four men near Mr. Jansen's store in close conversation, but I could not hear any words. One of the men had on a gray coat; another had on a cloak well muffled up. I have seen the prisoners Stuart and Windred. Stuart resembles the man in the gray coat and Windred resembles the man in the cloak."

"One of these men I knew in the mines," William Gambert, testified, "and went by the name Thomas. He is the small man." He indicated Berdue. "Thomas had the reputation of being a quiet man. He is not the man who shot the sheriff at Auburn. The man who shot Eccles was named Hobbes Stewart. There were, though, a number of things proved against the defendant. Among other things he stole a watch which was found upon his person." The gold watch and chain had been identified as the property of Mr. Noyes who resided at the *Niantic* warehouse.

"I knew James Stuart, the person charged with the crimes mentioned," Mr. McGilbert witnessed. "The prisoner is the same James Stuart. I have frequently seen him, and he has often ferried me across the river to Foster's Bar. I am positive he is the man. I could recognize him if I heard his voice in the darkest hour that ever was."

"I know the man Stuart who was tried at Foster's Bar for the murder of Capt. Moore," Charles J. Hughes declared. "The man in the station house is not the Stuart I knew at Foster's Bar and I should know. Stuart was in my employ for two or three days."

Judge Shattuck was troubled. He went downstairs and spoke with Berdue in his cell, then, as promised, went outside and addressed the crowd.

"I have been to see the prisoner, Stuart," Shattuck said, "and conversed with him. The prisoner has given me the names of two persons who could prove his whereabouts on Wednesday evening and he has sent to Long Wharf for them."

"How much did he pay you, Judge?" asked someone in the crowd. There was a loud hiss like the crashing of waves.
"I mean to perform the duty assigned to me," Judge Shattuck said. "We'll give you twenty minutes to bring in the testimony."
Twenty minutes passed and still no witnesses.
"Half an hour longer," some in the crowd pleaded.
"An hour," others cried.
"No more time!" the majority roared.
The jury came in and reported that they had agreed they should proceed.
"The prisoner is in his cell," Judge Shattuck told them. "He is not confronted with you and he looks to me to plead his case. And here, there is a desire that I should give him up to your rage —that I should give him without saying a word. I have seen but few things like it in my life. I have seen men arraigned in this same manner, before an enraged populace, and I have seen life taken by that populace, and I have seen the men engaged in that transaction live to regret that day as one of the bitterest of their lives. They would give their life to blot out the record of that day's history." He decried their "hot haste." "Every opportunity should be allowed for the accused to send far and near for witnesses—to give the prisoner a fair trial. And now, is a man's life of so little importance that you are willing to shed human blood upon the uncertain testimony which had been adduced? There is doubt to his identity. The upriver cases, the murders and robberies on the Yuba, were the cause of the suspicions against Stuart as connected with Jansen affair. We are all here in a land of strangers and it is not impossible that some of us may fall under suspicion, and I be of you as you would in such an hour that men would do to you, so do towards this wretch."

"We are now overriding the law," Coleman, an extraordinarily handsome man, addressed the jury, "and making ourselves the judges and jury of a miscreant to whom we have appointed a certain form of trial. We have all agreed to submit to your decision gentlemen of the jury. If you say hang him, you must take the responsibility, and so be it."

"So be it!"

About 3:00 PM, the prisoners were escorted into court. Jansen, a bloodstained bandage wrapped around his head, was weak. He had to be aided to walk. His face was swollen and in places blackened.

Reporter Edward Buffum noted that Jansen gave his testimony, "clearly, distinctly, and with evident conviction of its truth." Though he swore positively that Berdue was English Jim, he again expressed slight doubt that Windred was the other man."

Mr. Osgood rose.

"I can, if a short time be allowed," he said, "to produce a man, the keeper of a public house on Long Wharf, who could testify that he was in Stuart's company on Wednesday evening in his own house from seven to one o'clock."

The jury began deliberating. By an unanimous vote, the mob relieved the jury from the responsibility of assigning the punishment. It found the defendant guilty and refused to hear any more testimony. When the jury had not reached a verdict, a rough-looking man entered the jury room. "We will wait for the verdict but five minutes longer," he said, "when, if not given, we will break into the station house and get the prisoners."

Between ten o'clock and midnight the jury retired to an adjoining room while the defendants remained standing, quivering, and swaying on their feet from fright and sheer exhaustion. A little before midnight, the jury sent a message: "It is impossible for us to agree." Nine jurors stood for conviction and three were unwilling to convict.

Outside the disappointed crowd roared, "Hang them anyhow! The majority rules!"

The prisoners had been spared and would be tried legally.

"It takes every man of a jury to find a prisoner guilty," the *Alta* editorialized. "Eleven cannot do it. To be consistent, then, with their previous acts, they must not harm a hair of the prisoner's head. To hang him with three of the jury chosen by themselves, declaring him not guilty, would be in the eye of all law, except mob law, totally inexcusable."

Throughout the night floating bands of bloodthirsty men tried to storm the jail, but 250 policemen repulsed them each time. All Berdue could think about was that they had lynched a young man at Martinez accused of stealing a pair of boots. Boots! Death for boots. He was accused of far worse. His true crime was looking like another man.

Monday night was clear and calm.

Tuesday morning was pouring rain, a regular deluge.

ON FEBRUARY 27, Coffin returned from another grueling trip to Marysville, his most difficult yet, and least productive. The river had grown shallower. In the Sierra foothills, forces were at work that would affect his river trade. Gold hunters using high pressure hoses were directing huge volumes of water at cliff sides, washing the soil and gravel into the rivers. Their unceasing hydraulic mining swept massive amounts of silt down as liquid mud to raise the waterline around the Cove. Deep water vessels were still able to scud the Sacramento and San Joaquin rivers not yet silted by debris washed into the waterways. Those days, though, were ending. The increasing size of ships, such as the revolutionary new clippers that flew like eagles, coupled with the increased deposits of sediment would soon close the inland ports to all but the smallest local boats.

Wharf projects and buildings ringed the outside rim of the Cove as San Francisco pushed and bullied its way further seaward rushing over everything in its path and filling in behind. Battery Street and Front and Davis streets were built up. Buildings rose to flank ships berthed at every angle. Wharves, mini-piers and catwalks anchored to the saw-toothed waterfront linked the hundreds of deserted ships into a taut web spanning two square miles. As the piers edged into the water, each crisscrossed with a series of transverse docks that had to be filled. Merchants, confident that dry land would completely overtake the Cove in two years, three at most, laid planks on top of the piles to facilitate movement between the quays. They linked the planks with more crosswalks and the spaces between these began to be plugged. As mud flats around the wharves filled in, the Ghost Fleet ships anchored at the sides of these thoroughfare-piers were incorporated as part of the land.

Along the mud flats enterprising storekeepers had pulled more deserted Ghost Fleet hulks onto the beach to serve every purpose imaginable. As the flats filled in with sand of the adjacent hills and diminishing dunes, land began to surround these ships. Soon it became common to drag floating warehouses onto land, set them up between two buildings and convert them into multiple-story buildings from the deck skyward. Coffin knew a list of the hundreds and hundreds of abandoned ships could probably never be complete but must include the following: he consulted his *Log*: The white-painted *Alida* on Davis

Street, the *Almandralina* lying on the corner of Pacific Front, and three unknown hulks including a store ship at California and Battery and another known only as the Bay Hotel as Peter Le Guervel advertised it after he built a house on its deck and moored it at the southeastern corner of Battery and Green. The *Brilliant* lay at Davis and Pacific next to the *Magnolia*, and *Globe*. McCrackan's home ship, the aged *Balance*, became a store ship on the corner of Front and Jackson, then moved next to the Pacific and Broadway Wharves. Eventually, she was buried in mid-Gold Street at Balance Alley. A Chinese warehouse floated at Long Wharf at Battery and Sacramento beside a new *Steamboat Hotel*. The bark *Cordova* became Goodall and Nelson's Sausalito water ship as did its companions, *Emma* and *Clara*. The *Cordova* and *Garnet* sat on Davis between Pacific and Broadway near the Pacific Wharf. The *Elizabeth* was an office and bonded storehouse run by the Collector of Customs and, along with the *Bethel*, lay on the Embarcadero. The *Georgean*, a popular store ship, was between Sansome and Battery. Coffin closed his book. He had gotten all their names down. He studied his firm, strong handwriting. He had regained his confidence if not his health. "Never give way to despondency under misfortune," he said. Whenever he encountered misfortune, he remained honest, firm and resolute, the family motto. "Hope now, hope always," he said, "reflect that all things are under the direction of a Supreme Being, who doeth all things well, and in the darkest hour seek consolation in that reflection."

CAPT. COFFIN WENT TO see Capt. Haskel to catch up on the latest news.

"English Jim has been captured," Haskel began, stating the most important first, "and is being held for trial."

"Well," Coffin replied. He gave an exhalation of breath. "If that isn't the best thing I've heard in ages. English Jim is about to pay for his vicious attack on Capt. Jones and his wife onboard the *James Caskie*." He pictured his friend's battered face. The corners of his mouth turned down. His teeth were set. He filled his pipe and lit it. When Capt. Haskel told him another bit of information, Coffin was elated, then doubtful, and at last puzzled though it was a secondhand report. It seems that shortly after the Jansen attack, the captain of a British ship had been passing quietly along Montgomery St. when someone cried out, "There goes Stuart!" The man was immediately seized by an infuriated mob, and only escaped being torn to pieces when recognized and rescued by the consignee of his ship.

"The community is in such a state of excitement that no one is safe," Haskel said to Coffin with a shake of his head.

Now that was odd, Coffin thought. Here was an unfortunate individual who closely resembled the culprit, Stuart. What if he had been arrested and undergone a trial like the suspect in the city jail? The man being tried was English Jim, wasn't he? He must be. Mr. Jansen had positively identified him as one of the men who attacked him in his store. Not only that, but a Sacramento police officer swore positively that he was the real English Jim Stuart. Yet, the defendant continually declared his name was not Stuart, but Thomas Berdue, whom witnesses said was elsewhere at the time of the attack.

Earlier that morning, Recorder Washington had ridden from Sacramento to add to the confusion by the shovel-full. He visited Berdue's cell in the Station House to see if he was the same man who was examined four times before him under the name "Campbell," and had been confined in the prison brig of Sacramento.

"This is not Stuart," Washington said firmly. He was breathless, but firm. "He is *not* the man."

In the afternoon, lawyer Frank Pixley swore before Justice Shepherd that he was counsel for Stuart when he was charged with burglary in Sacramento and in Marysville before Justice Sackett. Berdue was *not* that man. Coffin did not know what to think. That night, he noticed Vigilantes on every corner awaiting the rallying sound—the solemn clanging of the Monumental Fire House bell—three taps at one-minute intervals.

Men lifted their lanterns and scanned passing faces. It was odd to see so many stand so still and stare so intently at strangers and for those strangers to stare back as intently. The Vigilance Committee held the waterfront as their turf and hung any man without thought or remorse. Crooked politicians, frightened by the temper of the people, had hidden the two suspects in the Jansen robbery away instead of releasing them on bail. They decided to wait until the furor died down and the two could be tried on charges of assault to murder to robbery without interference. The more Coffin watched, the more uncertain he became that they had caught the right English Jim. Everyone was in too much of a rush. He decided they should keep looking for English Jim until there was better evidence than the testimony of unreliable and traumatized eyewitnesses.

The next morning, Coffin was awakened by the *rasp* of saws and *bang* of hammers. Stacks of building materials were massed on every street corner. Large substantial warehouses with numerous floating depots were being erected. One four-story warehouse on Pacific Street fronting Battery Street was supported by three-ton columns and solid iron flooring. There had even been changes within the shallow depths of Graveyard Harbor. Only a year earlier the *Kangaroo*, the first propeller-driven ferryboat to ever ply the Bay, had replaced Don Victor Castro's oar and sail-propelled schooner run.

Capt. Thomas Gray had today abandoned the *Kangaroo*. It broke Coffin's heart to see such a hardy pioneer wrecked, smokestack lowered, and left lying north near a partially submerged ferryboat where the water depth plunged to almost six fathoms. He heard the *toot* of horns and saw the darting *Hector* and *Boston*, two small steamboats, that had assumed the *Kangaroo's* twice-weekly, round-trip run between San Francisco and the East Shore at San Antonio Creek where Rev. Taylor had singlehandedly hewed the timber for his church with his huge hands.

Shelter was still scarce; that much had not changed in his absence. Whenever torrents of rain washed miners down from the hills along with the gold, San Francisco could offer few lodgings other than overpriced ramshackle buildings, crude, uninhabitable wooden sheds, or leaky canvas tents that were worthless. The only places that remained were exorbitantly expensive waterfront dives or overpriced lodging houses. With so few places to live on land, the water colony swelled in the Cove until it was alive with thousands of living human beings roving the dead wood and rusting iron wrapped in rotting canvas sails. The lucky few reposed on fine furniture in splendid drawing rooms on abandoned ships. Studying the stained and superannuated hulls sliding by as he rowed, Coffin sketched vivid mental pictures of their inhabitants. There were ex-convicts and fugitives waiting out the roving bands of Vigilantes who were filled with blood lust and trial in illegal courts. There were homeless men trying to sleep. He drew a mental picture of them stacked upon each other like cordwood. There were prostitutes with hearts of lead yearning for the miner's gold and bone-tired gold hunters happy to lay their heads down next to them. Then, there were respectable gentlemen and officers like himself who needed a place to stay until the fires on shore ceased and they could decide what to do next.

"Who could fault those who chose life on the water?" Coffin asked himself. He looked to the shore where there was so much anger, danger, and greed and shook his head. For him, life on the water was a far better choice.

Beyond the Pacific Street Wharf, he spotted two tall black smokestacks peeking just above the waterline. All but the upper curve of an abandoned side wheeler was submerged. He fancied that if he got bilge pumps going the main hall with its submerged marble bar and floating tables, could be cleared to allow a view of the sandy Cove floor though the glass portholes? Then, he would have his own Ghost Fleet aquarium. Half-sunken ships such as this offered homes for many unusual plants, tide pool creatures, and fish. He was very interested in such things. He pulled himself onto the hurricane deck which offered a splendid view of the adjacent vessels connected by planks and passageways. The day passed with not another thought about Windred and Stuart though something more about the arrest still bothered Coffin. He just couldn't put his finger on what.

He stretched when evening fell and watched night guards patrolling the storeships where the city safeguarded its goods. In the distance "Emperor" Wakeman and his new water police were patrolling, a rare sight. Wakeman only patrolled when it suited him or provided a good battle which he always loved or a chance to flex his authoritarian muscle through his leadership and iron rule in the Vigilance Committee. A book had been started about Wakeman's adventures with the Water Police (it would never be finished). Coffin vowed that his book about Graveyard Harbor would be published.

Tonight, the denizens of the water city, those thousands whose names will never be known unless Coffin got them down on paper, were eating late suppers. As the smoke of their cooking stoves and tantalizing smells mingled with the fog, he realized he was hungry too. Taking some sea biscuits from his pocket, he chewed one absently and watched the fires go out one by one. Lanterns aboard ship-hotels and ship-stores began to sparkle and dance in the waves. Beneath those waves an underwater city went about its business, filled with otherworldly creatures.

AT THE CITY JAIL, Tom Berdue was not sleeping. It was now March 1. His only touch of fortune was that volunteer firefighter Dutch Charley and his friend John Brady visited him each day to keep up his spirits. Berdue admired the man. Dutch Charley, blond and cold-eyed, filled the cell so there was scarcely any room for Brady and the prisoners. This ex-gunfighter and bare-knuckle boxer was always dressed in the latest fashions, one of the things his dozens of girlfriends liked best about him. Each time Dutch Charley visited, Berdue earnestly protested he was innocent. Dutch Charley believed him.

"He had been mistaken for English Jim who looks like him," he told Brady, "but the circumstantial evidence against him is so strong that even his friends would be forced to believe him Not Guilty." As he scrutinized Berdue each day, Dutch Charley found no consistent similarity between the two men. To his eye, Berdue was fair-complected, with a full face, and auburn hair, while English Jim was darker. Berdue was short while English Jim had to be two or three inches taller. And they did possess undeniable similarities. Berdue had a small slit over one ear. So did English Jim. Both had a one-inch scar over their left eyebrows and "a rather long scar on his right cheek." Both had been injured or lost a joint from a finger. English Jim had a stiff middle finger on his right hand; Berdue's slightly stiff forefinger was on his left hand. English Jim was tattooed with rings of Indian ink around his fingers and was marked with ink between each forefinger and thumb. Berdue had a single tattoo around his ring finger like a wedding ring. No two men could look so much alike, and yet Dutch Charley saw the subtle differences.

After Washington and Pixley stated that Berdue was not Stuart, The *Alta* wrote, "It is certainly a very peculiar case and there appears to us to be some deep-rooted mystery in the whole affair. We have heard that Stuart is one of the most successful disguisers in the world, but the man now in jail here has a peculiar voice which, once heard, we should never forget."

Windred and Berdue's trial for the Jansen assault and robbery continued. Though Jansen and many others had been positive in their eyewitness identification of English Jim, others had been equally certain he was Thomas Berdue. On March 12, the first witnesses for the defense were called.

William Stokes had known the defendant for two months and seen him daily for several days prior. He testified that on the night of February 19, Berdue was drinking wine with him from 6:30 until 9:00 PM. Stokes also gave the names of several other witnesses, but his eyesight was called into question—one eye was askance and looked to the left.

Mr. Horatio Utting, keeper of the Central Wharf Exchange testified he saw the prisoner there until 10:00. Mr. McDonald and Mr. James Ewbanks were also positive that Berdue remained playing cards with them until after 9:00. Ewbanks had gone into the house about sundown and was in the room with Berdue for two hours.

The *Daily Alta California* called Tom Berdue "a man who rejoices in two names," and deemed his defense imperfect because his alibis were provided by his fellow countrymen. The DA summoned officers Casserly and Hill to prove that the coat produced in court was the actual coat taken from the prisoner at the time of his arrest. The defense objected to introduction of the testimony. The objection was sustained.

Coffin rose at dawn to enjoy a light breakfast at the Dime House on Long Wharf where every meal cost a dime. He sipped hot tea with molasses and counted himself lucky in spite of his many losses and dashed hopes. His eyes followed the blunt tops of wooden piles marking the port's future course. They led like steps into the coveted deep water channels farther out where the black skeletons of deepwater draft ships traced the rim of the Cove. In the brilliant light, Coffin observed a sidewheeler bursting with sparks approaching Long Wharf. Beautiful, he thought. He took a deep breath. Life upon the water was life itself.

The morning *Alta* newspaper of March 5, 1851, brought Coffin up to date, not about the two misjudged men on trial, but about Graveyard Harbor and the wonderful changes at work beneath his feet. "The US Assay Office is now in full blast," he read with growing pleasure. "Messrs Moffat & Co, who have the contract, opened their new office on Montgomery St. this week, and within two or three hours received about a hundred thousand dollars in dust, deposited to be converted into coin. One effect of this office will be to give honest men a chance to obtain the worth of their gold, and put a check upon the process of adulteration which has been carried on here to a very great extent. We refer the reader to the very interesting table which we publish today, giving the names, routes, etc of the steamers now upon our waters. This illustration of our progress must astonish our friends on the other side of the continent, as well as in Europe. It has astonished ourselves although living at the very center of their operations.

"San Francisco is still constantly enlarging her borders, and spreading on all sides up the hills, filling the valleys, walking out toward and beyond North Beach, towards the Presidio, to the south away towards and at the Mission, and especially into the harbor, fast filling up the whole shallow part of the harbor in nearly a straight line from Rincon Point on the south to Clark's Point on the east side of the city. Hope beckons on Industry, buoyant and jubilant."

Today, Coffin was filled with that same hope. A cloud drifted over his pleasant morning as he sipped his tea, filled his pipe, and watched a gull circling overhead. He put his cup down when he overheard loud voices speaking of vengeance against suspected arsonists and murderers. "Hang any evidence," one said. English Jim's brutal assault on Jansen had inflamed the populace as never before. Coffin sighed and took up his newspaper again. The *Alta* newspaper raged against the frequent murders and robberies:

> "And who has been hung or punished for the crime? Nobody! How many shot and stabbed, knocked down and bruised; and who has been punished for it? Nobody! How many thefts and arsons, robberies, and crimes ... and where are the perpetrators?" All along the waterfront, bloodthirsty men waited for the whisper of the Vigilante's secret code word, '33 Secretary,' the Committee position by which twenty-two year old Isaac Bluxome was known. At this, the hanging men stood poised and listening for the two ominous taps of the great Monumental Fire House bell to call them to action and to death without trial."

Coffin pushed back his cup. Enough! It was time to stretch his muscles and map a few of the marvels of the Ghost Fleet. On the water, always on the water, he would forget all this foolishness about trials and who was who. This exciting pastime would provide him with some grist for the *Log* he was writing as an heirloom for his family. He smiled as he visualized his descriptions of the horrible prison ship, *Euphemia*. It hardly needed exaggeration or embellishment. His family would claim he had made up such a nightmare while he had not. He would not even attempt to disabuse their minds of that.

The Ghost Fleet was aptly named. The earliest ships to arrive in Graveyard Harbor had been derelicts dragged out of ship's graveyards and hastily refitted to transport gold hunters to California. The resurrected ships, mere specters, from converted whalers from New Bedford, to traders, packets, and brigs like the *Belfast*, the first square-rigger to discharge cargo at the Broadway Wharf. Early on, two unnamed lorchas, coastal craft of the Orient, had joined the Ghost Fleet. Coffin added their names. He came to the *Hope*, *Aurora*, *Dolores*, and *Bonne Adela*—optimistic craft with cheery names. Few ships ever "shook free of the Cove." Coffin searched his memory. Yes, there had been one, the *Eliza* of Salem, a crisp little ship altered to a bark in 1838. The most acclaimed, she had inspired the most celebrated song of the Gold Rush.

After three whaling voyages, and years engaged in the Zanzibar trade, the *Eliza* sailed from Derby Wharf with six passengers and a cargo of pork, sugar, dried apples, cheese, rice, sweet figs, and sour pickles. In the hold were stoves, materials for building a scow to dredge sand bars, and a small steam engine. The *Eliza* became the *"Liza* ship" of the miner's song. Coffin knew the words—"I came to California with a washboard on my knee ... It rained all night the day I left ... the sun so hot I froze to death." The *Eliza* reached San Francisco in June 1849 and sailed up river to Sacramento just in time to prevent a famine. She filled Coffin's heart with joy. He tapped his pipe against the rail, filled it with fresh tobacco, and repeated the process. He had the smoke easily now, and rowed on singing under the blazing sun. "The sun so hot ..."

The *General Harrison*, a "fine and commodious storage facility," was secured with pilings as a floating warehouse owned by E. Mickle and Company. Her neighbor, the *Niantic*, looked perfectly natural nestled among the more conventional land buildings crowding the water-locked vessels. As Coffin rowed, he kept an eye out for the seaweed-like vegetation that had a life of its own—undulating, snaring vessels in their place. They were reaching out to him. The water around these patches held whirlpools that in seconds became gentle eddies which disappeared to reawaken in another spot. Further out, by the *Piedmont*, a biological phosphorescence glowed beneath the water in layers. It had an explanation. The glow was emanating from discarded goods undergoing a chemical change. Beautiful and mysterious, the city of trapped ships held so many secrets, so much romance and mystery, that had Coffin the time he would have documented its life below the surface, too. He measured his chances of ever leaving the Cove. It just might just come to that.

ON MARCH 15, JANSEN testified as the last witness. It was troubling to Coffin that he had begun to pad his part. He now claimed that after the three blows on the head he "jumped up and ran out to call for assistance." There was a mark of blood upon the right elbow and shoulder on the prisoner's coat. When Jansen was cross-examined he admitted that, "I can't swear positively that those spots are blood."

The court adjourned at 10:00 AM.

In the afternoon, George Platt for the prosecution commented at length on the positive identification of the accused by Mr. Jansen and the failure of the defense to establish an alibi inasmuch one of the witnesses for the defense had sworn that the prisoner had left the house on the pretense of going to bed about the time of the robbery. Calhoun Benham for the defense said an alibi had been established, and argued that point effectively.

Judge Levi Parsons delivered a brief charge and the jury retired. This was it. The time had come. The jury deliberated only thirty minutes before returning to a nearly deserted courtroom with a verdict of guilty. Windred was sentenced to ten years in prison, but Berdue got the worst of it: fourteen years imprisonment in the overcrowded county jail which was temporarily serving as the state prison. Trembling and white-faced, he dropped from his seat to his knees and moved his lips as if in prayer. What would his wife and kids say? Tears rolling down his cheeks, Berdue cried, "I am innocent, I am innocent," then stood and addressed the court. "After having been wrongfully apprehended," he said, "and sworn to for 'James Stuart' by a Sacramento policeman named Tureman—insulted and dragged through the streets, nearly to scaffold, for crimes I was totally ignorant and innocent of, and but for the kind intervention of Almighty God, I should have suffered an ignominious death; after having spent upwards of $3000 for defense in trials, where witnesses against me swore erroneously, and those on my side dare not speak in my favor for fear of being assaulted..."

It took him a minute to choose his words. His knees showed oblongs of dust where he had dropped to the courtroom floor. Berdue choked up, then regained his voice. "After having been deprived of all my clothes which were taken away by Andrew McCarty and deposited with the Marysville authorities, what redress do I have? Men should be more particular when they swear away a fellow creature's life. How could anyone swear away a fellow creature's life without another thought? And yet that is what you have done."

Berdue went limp. He was removed to the station house. In the mining country he had been tried and narrowly escaped hanging twice for crimes he was innocent of committing—impossible to believe and yet it was true. He knew he would not escape hanging a third time in Marysville where he was now to stand trial for the murder of Charles Moore. He had ceased to hope. A noose would be a relief from all this pain. Yes, his life had been sworn away.

On March 17, the *Alta* issued a warning to the police. "The prisoner Stuart, convicted on Saturday, of robbery and assault, with intent to kill, is almost certainly known to belong to a regularly organized gang of Australian thieves, robbers and murderers. The Police, therefore, should be upon their guard against any attempt on their part to effect a diversion in his favor, or to rescue him by force. The world cannot produce a more desperate set of unhung cutthroats than are to be found among us, and they stop at nothing to effect the escape of so prominent a member of their fraternity."

An upcountry sheriff called at the city prison and identified Berdue as English Jim Stuart who was wanted in his county for murder. Berdue was given over to the custody of the sheriff and taken to Marysville where he was certain to be misidentified for a second time and be tried for the infamous English Jim's crimes and this time be hanged for murder.

IN SAN FRANCISCO AT 4:00 AM, there was another cry of fire. Two steamboats at Central Wharf between Clay Street Wharf and Howison's Wharf burst into flame, threatening other vessels at anchor. The *Santa Clara* burned to the water's edge and three lives were lost. The arsonist was at work again. Six hours later, English Jim, still beardless and in disguise, sailed for Gold Bluff aboard the schooner *B. F. Allen* to meet up with Robb McKenzie, Peet, and Dab the Horse-thief who had come in from Oregon where they had just sold the sixty horses they had stolen in Sacramento.

They made the long trip to Trinidad Bay where English Jim won all of Dab the Horse-Thief and Peet's money at cards. In Trinidad Bay he called himself "James Campbell." One night while playing cards with a New Orleans policeman, Joseph Wall, McKenzie blurted out English Jim's real name.

"You don't know me, sir," English Jim replied coolly. Outside, he warned McKenzie to keep his mouth shut. "Trinidad is a bad place for me," he explained, but laughed when he easily escaped detection. "My luck is up," he said gleefully, even if he had to pay Dab and Peet's passage back to San Francisco. Now, he felt ready to rob an entire city of its gold. He had worked over his multimillion plan until it was perfect. Had English Jim possessed any self control, he would have lingered at Trinidad Bay playing cards until his unlucky twin was hanged.

When he disembarked from the *H. L. Allen* on April 27, he had become "James Carlisle." Kitchen the Boatman was in rare spirits as he rowed Jim to his house by the rocks of Clark's Point. English Jim said nothing. He was awed by the immense growth of vessels from all parts of the globe anchored in the Bay. More were east of the City, between Clark's Point and the Rincon. All night, he dreamed fitfully of the city's gold and his plan to get three millions of it moved from the new, nearly impregnable Custom House on Montgomery Street back to more accessible Old Adobe in the Square.

English Jim was counting on the fact that the adobe had survived every burning so far because of its construction. Adobe bricks of sand, clay, horse manure, and straw can weather any fire. To get the gold moved from the sunken steel vault in the new Custom House would require another fire, one so huge it would not survive, and the gold would have to be moved to the less-impregnable building and stored in the vault Old Jack had built and the combination to. In between, they needed another smaller blaze to establish a launching site for the robbery and at the same time find a way to place the blame on someone else. For his team this time, Jim would need only four of his men. They were Singing Billy, Jack Dandy, a seasoned locksmith, Sam Whittaker, an engineer, and Old Jack, especially Old Jack, builder of vaults and keeper of keys, to complete his plan. Yes, they would be enough.

English Jim awoke suddenly. A false alarm had sounded in the dead of night. He relaxed. He knew what it was. He was responsible for the alarm. Tonight's fire alarm was only another of his diversions to allow a number of prisoners to escape the City Prison.

On Monday, he went to Mrs. Hogan's boarding house. There, he received a rude surprise. She cautioned him that there was a warrant out for Whittaker, Teddy McCormac, Robb McKenzie, and Old Jack, the very men he needed. They had earlier robbed $900 from a bear hunter named Vyse. Then, Old Jack had robbed his fellow thieves of $600 on the way to town. The $1,500 really belonged to Vyse's friend, James "the fighting man" Kelly, a fearsome and well-named juggernaut who roared down from Sacramento, shook McKenzie by the throat, threatened legal action, and snatched his money back. Impressed with Kelly's boldness, Whittaker and McCormac, copartners in the profitable Port Phillip House, developed an intimate business relationship with Kelly that would come back to bite them.

English Jim was not surprised that Whittaker had overestimated himself in the robbery. He usually blundered in his crimes. His heart was not in them, and he was only going through the motions. It was not about the money for Whittaker. More often than not he gave his spoils to Mary Ann Hogan. As English Jim was on the way from her house, Dab the Horse-Thief, who was not to be trusted, and a policeman stopped him on the street.

"The policeman wanted me to go to the Recorders with him," English Jim said, "but I drew my pistol to shoot him, and he stood off. There were many people around and I gave the policeman $100 to quiet him." Then, English Jim went to Kitchen's and stopped for the night. He went to see Mary Ann and then returned to Kitchen's. "She advised me to leave town again," English Jim told Kitchen, "and I agreed." Another setback, Kitchen thought. He was eager to get started on the big gold robbery. On May 1, the first and least of four quakes that month, rattled the city, and shook English Jim out of bed. He was getting little sleep these days.

Port Collector James Collier, whose flawed judgment had selected a safe cracker, Old Jack, to install the new vault and locks in the Old Custom House, had committed another error. This time, he placed Dr. Andrew Randall, an elderly, sedate, self-appointed medic to be in charge of the Monterey Custom House. Dr. Randall unwisely kept the accumulated money flowing through his office in an unguarded strongbox sitting on his desk. As to be expected, $14,000 of gold dust and silver dollars was stolen from him on December 8. Later, it was estimated that only $8,000 had been taken. Port Warden Singing Billy had been absent from San Francisco for a few days before the theft "for a visit to San Jose." Suffering from delirium tremens, he had ridden to Monterey to confer with Dr. Randall, who agreed to make himself absent when Old Jack, Richard Osman, Mike Ryan, and Jim Briggs robbed the Custom House and got away clean. They were jailed when a like amount of money was found on them. Briggs put up considerable bail and returned to San Francisco the day after the robbery. So did Singing Billy who was perceptibly worn and sober. His horse was lathered from hard riding. But, Singing Billy was not needed now. It was Old Jack whom English Jim needed if his master plan was to succeed. Jim hired a horse and galloped to Monterey at top speed in order to spring him.

COFFIN WAS ON THE WATER working in his *Log*. "Let the archeologists of the future divine the depths of Graveyard Harbor," he decided. He put the book under his jacket and put his strong back and arms to the oars. The day passed into dusk. He sat and smoked until night and thought about all the things he had seen and done in the time he had been in this strange harbor. He calmed. Past the active water lay leaden water where another group of abandoned vessels floated. Tide lines on their hulls demonstrated that while other ships were sinking, others had risen and sunken many times. Gases from decaying cargoes and water-absorbent loads created this action. He threaded his way through the rocking, creaking maze. Tiny fish leapt ahead of his skiff and left little potholes of sparkling light in his path as if leading him somewhere. Dousing his light, he glided silently northward counting on the brilliance of the rising moon to light his way. A shipboard light cast a square patch on the water in the perfect shape of a doorway. It looked flat, gold, and three-dimensional enough to open. The slow, steady tread of footsteps sounded on deck above. He yearned to climb up and look around. Discarded goods bobbing in the current blocked his way and kept him from investigating further. A gusting hot wind whistled down the alley. He cupped his pipe and lit it, tamped down the tobacco with his pipe cleaner, waited a quarter minute, tamped it down again, and then relit his pipe. He took a deep drag. The smoke flowed smoothly.

In the tide, the vessel swung about, her fixed support, a fulcrum anchor at her bow. Coffin felt the side of another ship closing upon him like a vise. He rowed heartily for the end of the corridor where an underwater sun was blazing. This Light Ship blazed as if daring the heavens to outshine her. Men onboard the whaler were feeding the tryworks with the copious stores of abandoned whale oil. Coffin looked up. Sea birds were circling the illuminated frigate. Fog stayed back, warned off by its heat. Across the water, light flickered from another ship's bow—a signal to gangs onshore or to searching Vigilantes? A signal from the real English Jim to his men?

Coffin passed through a bank of fog like gray cotton, one of several patches spotting the water that were nearly tangible. Graveyard Harbor was alive with turbulent water and life flowing underneath. As the moon climbed to its highest, stars filled the sky. Tides running high on black rocks raised the lost ships at their moorings. He touched the side of a listing frigate that he came to. Some tentative salvage efforts to pump her out had been made—in vain. Every hour she was slipping deeper. Water-swelled cargo onboard was splitting the planking and allowing water to flood the holds. The high cost of lighters, four dollars a ton for moving merchandise a matter of feet, was prohibitive to emptying their ships of cargo that had become a glut on the market. Exorbitant harbor fees made it more expedient to store unsold items in ship warehouses until the goods were profitable again to sell.

From the leeward side, Coffin scaled a hanging rope, and dropped onto the slanting deck amidships. Tangled cables and fouled rigging littered his path. He dodged them all. The muddy shore had made him surprisingly agile. Peering upward, he saw high masts carved from white pine heartwood stretching skyward. He climbed to the spar deck where halyards ran like webbing to the fife rails. Forward of the mizzenmast, he discovered the ship's compass still in its binnacle at the side of the wheel, just as it should be. Two capstans, enormous spools of oak designed to be turned independently on the same axis, were in working order too. One spool weighed the anchor and the other worked the rigging. This was still a worthy vessel. In the first hold, he discovered a lake of mud. Crabs scurried away from his light. He pried open the second hatch cover. The biological phosphorescence of decay covered the surface of the water below. Swelled barrels, crates and kegs bobbed in a brackish lake and threatened to burst through the side. With each movement of the ship more water rushed in. Coffin glimpsed a swift movement—a slick ripple in the flat gray surface. Patiently, he waited, watching the spot intently. Abruptly, a form drenched in mucilage stirred the muck again near submerged beams and looked up at him. It was one of the magical creatures of Graveyard Harbor.

IN MONTEREY, A DISGUISED English Jim secretly attended the trial of his four men. From his seat against the rear wall, he could barely hide a smirk. Dick Osman, the first of his men put before the jury, was defended by Lawyer Parburt who had come down from San Francisco to do the job. English Jim testified in Osman's favor under his alias, "James Carlisle." After he had committed perjury on the stand, he successfully bribed a number of police officers and jurors. In one case he offered one $700 and a gold watch. One juror, though, held out. He had already been bribed by the prosecution and held to his honor over a deal well made. He had his ethics, even when he was being bribed.

In San Francisco, Mary Ann Hogan had decided never to go back to her honest, hardworking husband. She was in love with Sam Whittaker and proved this by hiding him from the police inside the Mission. In the morning, she called Whittaker aside. "You are to take this thirteen thousand dollars to the men at Monterey, and deliver this letter," she told Whittaker. She placed her arm around him and tucked the envelope inside his pocket. The letter was from Judge Bowie and contained certificates of money that the four captured gang members had in the San Francisco banks. Well-dressed, and eloquent, Whittaker reached Monterey. Inside the courthouse, he testified for Osman. At the end of his testimony, he looked up and was shaken to see English Jim glowering at him from the rear of the courtroom.

"I knew all about the robbery [of the Custom House] at

Monterey,]" Whittaker said. "and I think he came down to shoot me either for the money or for jealousy over Mary Ann."

While Whittaker was in Monterey committing perjury in a very artful way, Kelly the fighting man sold the Port Phillip House out from under him and Mary Ann. When he returned to San Francisco, he found himself dispossessed. He moved in with Mary Ann, a not unpleasant side effect of being swindled. Meanwhile, Briggs had arrived in Monterey. English Jim laughed when he saw him take the stand. Briggs, had no intention of losing the considerable money he had put up for bail. It was comical that he had escaped jail for the sole purpose of appearing at his own trial in Monterey.

When the jury remanded the prisoners, English Jim, realized that perjury and bribery wouldn't free his gang. In that case, he would use a stronger and more murderous method. Securing nitrated explosives and black powder, he blasted open the cell wall. In a cloud of smoke and pistol fire, Jim led his men to waiting horses. In a flash they galloped away. English stayed behind to resolve the ownership of the stolen money. Though Singing Billy, he reached a lucrative compromise with Dr. Randall. A thousand dollars went to the judge for court costs, and the remaining money was split equally between the gang and Dr. Randall.

"Then, I started on foot from Monterey for the southern mines," English Jim said. "I now had no horse—mine had been stolen my second night in Monterey. When I reached San Jose I stole another horse, saddle, and bridle. "On horseback, I got in row with eleven Mexicans who took my gun and said I had stolen their horse. They took me back to Livermore Pass. I gave them my watch and chain to release me and I started on foot for Sonora."

English Jim worked at John Sullivan's claim mining for a week, but fled when he saw someone watching him. He sent word to Jack Edwards to be ready—"The time to act is soon." They just needed a little more money to bankroll his plan.

A BONELESS, FEATURELESS FACE cracked the surface of the water, then slid beneath followed by a rubber body, which vanished through a rent in the side of the ship. Coffin held his breath and waited. Oily water curled beneath the beams. Bright bubbles exploded on the surface. As the wind turned, the weather-beaten hold creaked. Coffin heard something swimming away. Gliding in his skiff between rows of abandoned ships, Coffin reached a half-submerged vessel. Inside, he heard an odd squealing, braying sound. The creature had followed him. As the mist parted, a powerful animal clamored up from a hold, rested on the shattered wood, and challenged him with a thunderous bray. Swelling cargo had ripped a hole in the ship's side. The dark form swam out the other side. Abruptly, a featureless face with a pointed snout broke the surface a few feet from Coffin's boat, a safe distance. A seemingly boneless, black body began to roll as if on a spit. The sea animal applauded with its short flippers and somersaulted. Puzzled, Coffin watched a sea lion swim away. Every type of creature lived in Graveyard Harbor.

ALONG WITH BILLY MULLIGAN and "Yankee" Sullivan, firefighter Dutch Charley Duane believed in Berdue's innocence. He was a good judge of human nature and had decided that within seconds after they met. At this time, Dutch Charley was part of a web of informants and political enforcers maintained by Sen David Broderick. Sensing the mood of the community, Dutch Charley decided to locate the real English Jim Stuart, put his little army on his trail, and in this way prevent a miscarriage of Justice that woud stain the soul of the city. Broderick's agents, including boy firefighter Tom Sawyer, fanned out to search the waterfront. The hunt would be treacherous. Ida Pfieffer, a new arrival in town, saw it with fresh eyes. "I was disgusted with the frightful disrepair of the wooded quays," she said. "For the sea beneath them has not been filled up, and the boards are so worn and rotten that they often break under your weight. Even in the daytime, caution is requisite on account of the frequent holes; and at night it is no uncommon incident for passengers to fall in, and never be seen again. When we hear of the floating corpses of unfortunates who daily fished out of the waters of the Bay."

John Purkitt agreed. "When we hear of passengers arriving, passing safely over all the dangers of the ocean . . . only to perish like drowned dogs, strangled in filth and slime," he said, "when we read of citizens who live in the vicinity of these pitfalls hearing every night the splash of heavy bodies in the water, and the heart-stirring cry for succor. It is a sin."

As gold hunters became homemakers, they set about making San Francisco more substantial. Ragged tents gave way to frame houses and sturdier buildings erected on conglomerate layers of garbage, surplus merchandise, barrels of brandy, mud, and the commonplace corpse. A new house or warehouse went on top of the undulating surface. The first structures on this foundation of trash and unwanted merchandise sank as water seeped in and undermined their foundations. One dramatic theater, tossed together atop a patch of settling fill and garbage, sank under the weight of its first capacity audience. They fled as the tide flowed down the aisles and up to their boot tops.

Driving piles on water for support was almost impossible, and comical to watch. With the first blow of a driver, eighty-foot-long piles disappeared into the mud below. Another pile, driven on top, still did not reach bottom, nor did the next. Finally, the builders drove bundles of piles, spaced every ten feet, into the water, capped the piles, and laid building frameworks on top. "A ship master anchored in a legally assigned berth," Amelia Ransome Neville recalled, "might wake up to find a pile driver noisily surrounding his vessel with structural timbers at the behest of a supposed water lot owner. The sale of water lots, plots of the Cove water sold for future development, provided endless troubles, for purchasers wanted to fill them in despite wharf owners' opposition—Sunday night pile driving and extracting, sinking of sand-filled hulks by sea-borne squatters and even armed clashes."

Bullets began to fly—and all over little squares of water.

On MARCH 27, SNOW in the mountains fell at Placerville to a depth of ten-inches. To the northwest of Placerville, Marysville was as cold as a well-digger's toes. In his Yuba County Jail cell, Berdue was freezing. He opened the *Marysville Herald* and read, "Another Man Hung." He put the paper down and stared at the wall. When he had regained his composure, he began to read again. When two men in Shasta City had a dispute, it said, one seized a gun and shot the other. When the murderer started to run, he was easily captured. His tribunal was eerily similar to Berdue's. On Sunday, a people's court was formed and witnesses examined. The jury was out for only a few minutes before they returned with a verdict of guilty. The man was sentenced to be hung at 4:00 PM, *that day*. He acknowledged his guilt, sat down to dinner, ate a hearty meal, even called for desert. His stomach full, he was led to a raised platform that had just been constructed. The rope was placed around his neck. He was called on to address the crowd as Berdue had been.

"The murder was the result of drinking," he admitted. "My only regret is that I did not have time to write to my wife." He did not wait for the platform to be knocked from under him. He suddenly leaped and broke his neck. He had been his own executioner.

Berdue folded the paper and sat back on his cot and stared out the little window. When he was found guilty, and he was certain to be found guilty, he might consider going out that way. As for notifying his wife who was on the way from Sydney to join him, Berdue was so universally reviled, he doubted anyone would write informing her of his ill fate, much less honor his request that his father in England be told of his death. Even if the real English Jim were to step forward and confess now, the dark cloud of suspicion over Berdue would never lift.

Now, all he could do was wait and pray for a miracle.

SAM WHITTAKER, ENGLISH JIM'S dapper romantic rival for Mary Ann Hogan's heart, faced a dilemma of his own. Not all of a conscience had been stamped out of him. He was still redeemable and much of this was due to Mary Ann's love for him and her guiding words.

"Windred and Berdue were tried for having robbed Jansen and convicted," Whittaker said, "but they had nothing to do with it. I knew that very well and that knowledge kept me awake nights. I exerted myself very much to save them. I said they were innocent, but did not say who was guilty." As a last resort, he might have to confess who was really guilty—English Jim.

Mary Ann Hogan knew her lover was facing a crisis and encouraged him to do the right thing. Whittaker reached a decision. He resolved not only to right the injustice, but facilitate Windred's escape from the city prison cell where he was confined and see him safely out of the country and back to Australia. Now, for the first time, Whittaker realized, his criminal skills would be used to save a life. One of the reasons that English Jim had chosen Whittaker as a co-leader of his gang, was that he was valuable designing burglary tools, and copying keys for new burglaries. That's what he decided to do next.

"I went to the new jail with Windred's wife and Mrs. Hogan and sent a key I had fashioned [for a fee of $400 to procure the master key] in with them," he said. Officials later reported that Windred had tunneled out of his cell. That was not true. He had used the provided key.

The minute Whittaker learned Windred had escaped thanks to his efforts, he acted. He hid Windred out at the Mission, then hurried to the Pacific Street Wharf. "Jack Dandy and Windred were there," Whittaker said. "I took Windred to a stable, got horses, and took him to Dr. [Arthur] Lambert's at 248 Montgomery St. where he stayed for two weeks, or until a safe passage could be engaged for him to Australia. I paid his board and got him fed and cared for. Dr. Lambert is a man from the colonies. At the end of that time I engaged passage for Windred and appointed a night to put him onboard the ship. The vessel in which he was placed remained in port a fortnight and everyday I waited I feared he would be apprehended again."

Though English Jim had pledged not to commit any more crimes before Berdue was hanged, he needed money. Whittaker agreed to join him. He claimed his share would go to Windred. "After a few nights," he said, "we agreed to rob a bank kept by Beebee, Ludlow, and Co., on Montgomery St. In this we were to be assisted by Bob McIntyre and Andy McCarty, the two crooked cops in English Jim's employ. They told us that whenever we were ready they would take the watch off. These police officers knew all we were about in those days. We tried two nights and finally opened the outside door to the bank by false keys that Old Jack had made. There was not enough money to pay for attempting the robbery, but we did observe the porter of Young's Bank come each morning from Argenti's with heavy bags of money.

"The next night we went to Young's Bank next to the El Dorado, in Washington Street to look it over." The job was considered problematic. English Jim decided to get more input so he attempted it. Jack Arentrue, a former street commissioner, stopped Whittaker on the street. They went into a bar where he discussed several places to rob that English Jim had mentioned. He took him to see a convicted bigamist named David Earl, a dandy at the use of calipers. Earl showed Whittaker how he robbed a sleeping man in the next room without him being aware of it. It was an amazing performance. Earl and Arentrue's visits to Mary

Ann's hotel to dine and play cards with Whittaker confirmed to her that her lover was still involved in robbery.

"We drank together and then went down to the Custom House [on Montgomery]," Whittaker recalled. "Arentrue said there was $800 of sifted gold dust there in the drain. Then, we went to the other Custom House [at Dupont and Washington]. He took me inside. Earl proposed renting space next door to the Custom House and opening an architect's office in it, and we could rob the building from this office. This was practicable. We could do that." It was close to English Jim's master plan.

Next, the two corrupt policemen, McIntyre and McCarty, proposed to Whittaker that they rob the El Dorado gambling house, a substantial brick building with iron window frames, shutters, and doors. It took up the southeastern corner of Kearney and Washington Streets.

"We had an understanding with McIntyre and McCarty for a long time," English Jim explained, "they were concerned with us in the robbery of Young's Bank next to the El Dorado. Singing Billy was an accomplice. There were eight in the gang. Kay was usually outside watching."

Hetherington accompanied English Jim inside to case the El Dorado to see if they could work the robbery from there. "We went down the El Dorado steps, opened the door with false keys, entered and found two beds," English Jim said. "I discovered there were too many people sleeping down there. I considered the job too dangerous and gave it up."

English Jim's problem was how to empty out the El Dorado so they could work uninterrupted. He remembered how he had handled the Monterey jail situation. It might work here, again.

He and Hetherington walked across Washington Street to the two-story brick Verandah Saloon directly across from the El Dorado on the southwestern corner of Kearney and Washington. The hastily refitted Custom House was on the other side of Kearney on the northeastern corner. Yes, there were possibilities here, and they fit in with English Jim's original plan. But how to get three million dollars in gold out of the new Custom House and into the older, more vulnerable to theft, adobe Custom House on the Square?

Next, he and Briggs stole a small safe from the Emerson and Dunbar Auction House on Washington Street and blew it open. The next night, they lifted a huge safe from Gladwin and Whitmore's on California Street and took it up into the sand hills to break open. It was so tough to crack they were discovered and lost $500 worth of burglar tools as they fled. Old Jack lost his watch as he ran, but police caught him and Jemmy-from-town and arrested them both. The loss of the tools was a disaster, but the capture of two of Jim's most important men, was a tragedy.

"I went to Mrs. Hogan's house," English Jim said, "to plan how to help my two men escape. I wanted to go to the police station and take them back by force, but the rest of the gang refused." Instead, they employed Mr. Parburt the lawyer, and the next day Old Jack was acquitted and Briggs committed to jail.

With Berdue, his lookalike about to go on a second trial in Marysville, English Jim had to be careful. He moved about only at night by horseback, and always in disguise with a sombrero and serape. When he was in a more reasonable frame of mind, English Jim realized it might just be a matter of time before the authorities realized their mistake. English Jim should get out of town until the trial was completed and Berdue hung. He needed a diversion, and went to see his accomplice, Jack Edwards.

FOR FOUR LONG MONTHS Coffin had been in despair. He had no hope of getting another ship. "I had no means, no employment, no energy," he lamented. "No man had worked harder than I had. I had at first prospered . . . A constitutional melancholy which has afflicted me through life at intervals, now seized upon me with tenfold force . . . I wandered about this busy town without an object."

There was some escape. He had his writing and his art.

"As I was strolling along Montgomery Street, carefully picking my way through the bogs, I was accosted by a person in corduroy trousers, a fustian coat, hickory shirt, and a Mexican sombrero. He was calling me by name. I saw him dashing along through the mud in boots that reached to his thighs and as soon as he drew closer, I saw it was Mr. Bard Plummer, Esquire from Newburyport and he was excited to see me."

"Come on down to my store, Capt.," he said. "I have a proposal for you."

Coffin followed him. Plummer's store was a rough-boarded frame building, a modest fifteen-by-twenty-five feet structure "situated in a mud puddle" near the foot of Sacramento St. One corner, the lodging and counting room, was partitioned off with lumber and contained three bunks and shelves.

"Rent for this miserable place is a thousand a month—in advance," Plummer said. "Can you believe that? Everett's sheet-iron store opposite is two stories high and twice as big. It costs $60,000 a year." Plummer pulled out a stool for Coffin and they sat down over drinks. After more complaints, he sprung his surprise.

"[Plummer] voluntarily offered to buy a vessel for me," Coffin said later, "whenever I could find one to suit me, and let me take her and find my way home in the best way I could. And while I live I shall never cease to be grateful to that man. It will probably never be in my power to reciprocate his kindness."

A heavy load had been lifted from his shoulders, but he still had to pay for desk space at $100 a month. Joy had made Coffin hungry. He hugged his friend goodbye, and rushed away to a beached Italian frigate at Davis and Pacific where Giuseppe Bazzuro served his native Genoa cuisine. Coffin ate the first pasta he ever had there and enjoyed a fish stew, very likely the original *cioppino*, the local version of bouillabaisse. Stomach full, mind at ease, future guaranteed, full of energy, he made his way to the foot of Second Street where the city's first dry dock had just been completed. He took a deep breath of the night air. "So many changes," he thought, and retired early aboard his friend's ship, the *Talma*.

He awoke to flames much fiercer than before. It was May 4, 1851, the anniversary of the third city-destroying arson fire.

Coffin should have expected such a calamity. He heard the Monumental Fire bell clang at Brenham Place. A fire had been kindled in a Clay Street upholstery. The heat reawakened the howling nor'wester that had died away at sunset and sent it rushing down the gully between Signal Hill and the Heights like a tidal wave. The entire northeastern side of the Square was on fire. The wind drove the flames over the part that had burned in June, then swept them over two hundred Ghost Fleet ships close to shore. Coffin beat out flaming coals raining from the sky and burning holes in the *Talma's* sails, but couldn't rescue his charts, nautical instruments, books, and clothing. They were in Jackson St.

Volunteer fire companies, working with crowbars and axes, disconnected the new eleven million dollar wooden wharves, and cut them in half to keep fire from the waterfront and dozens of ships crowded at their moorings. Nearby, the *General Harrison*, at the northwestern corner of Sacramento and Battery, met her demise. She burned to the water line, and lost most of her copper and brass filings. Two blocks away the *Apollo* was damaged and would have to be refitted. The Beach family, the *Apollo's* owners, had counted on the ship store to lift them out of debt. Perhaps, after the refitting, they would struggle back on their feet. Five large storeships full of merchandise were burning. The *Georgian* warehouse, connected to the city by catwalks and wharves, was flickering with flames. The *Callao, Byron, Galen, Autumn,* and *Roma* were fully ignited. The *Niantic*, so miraculously saved in the fire last June 14 and enclosed in a wall of sheet iron, was afire. Had her time come?

Pitiful men, pitiful women, and pitiful children huddled on Long Wharf for a second time. A sheet of fast-moving fire extended a half-mile in length over San Francisco. As it swept the city, stored barrels of gunpowder detonated. Severely burned men clawed their way to safety and rolled to extinguish their burning clothing. Timbers crashed in cascades. The thirsty town's generous provisions of whisky sent blue fire spiraling skyward. Frightened horses charged from burning liveries. Their heavy wagons overturned in the mud. The stiff northeast wind quickly gained strength. The fire jumped Kearny St, flew southeast, then whipped north again with a resounding crack. It marched along Commercial, Sacramento, and Montgomery streets, and raced along Washington, Sansome, and Bush. It battled against the wind to Stockton St. to Powell, then ran in a southeasterly direction crossing Sacramento and California to Market.

"All the rest of those brick buildings in Montgomery Street which had been thought to be fireproof," Coffin said, "were but tinder boxes." Thirty-six of the new "fireproof" iron homes and warehouses failed, their double-layered iron shutters expanding; their double sheets of bolted metal growing white hot and sliding into glowing slag and trapping the inhabitants inside. "In the morning, their burnt and mangled bodies were found among the ruins near the door. They had endeavored to escape, but the intense heat had so warped the iron doors and windows that they could not be opened. Mr. Wells, too, the Boston banker, and three or four of his friends remained in his fireproof building too long and did but just escape. Wells got dreadfully burned and will carry the marks to his grave."

The blaze leaped Jackson and Pacific streets to Broadway. It ate hungrily to Clarke's Point. A strangling noose of fire tightened around the entire city. In two hours eighteen square blocks were ablaze. Planked roads and wooden sidewalks burned and shriveled all the new frame houses on both sides of Clay. In minutes every structure between that street and California Street had ignited. The first house to go was the Dramatic Museum with its roof that was covered with highly flammable pitched-felt. The flames communicated from the roof to the new Custom House next door. The Cooke Brothers store directly across the street from the Custom House caught too and fueled the flames. Davis's glorious red brick four-story at the northwestern corner of Montgomery and California Streets erupted in fire.

Capt. Hante of the Revenue cutter, *Polk*, got to the Custom House faster than English Jim and his gang had expected. To deter any robbery, Hante had swiftly stationed thirty armed guards around the burning building and saved a million dollars of specie by tossing it down a well. The $3 million of gold melt inside the sunken vault was safe, but $300,000 in goods were lost. Hante, a very practical hero, preserved all the new Naval department papers. Any records older than two years were still at the old Custom House which, because of its fire-baked adobe construction, shrugged off flames like a Spring rain. By now, the maelstrom had consumed five hundred buildings. Flames chased citizens east along Commercial Street between Dupont and Montgomery. The city's copious amounts of liquor colored the night sky in uncanny brilliance.

"A space of a hundred acres," Coffin wrote, "which at sunset stood thickly studded with buildings—by 4:00 AM, was cleared away (except for three buildings in Montgomery)." The fire had consumed everything east of Sansome Street except for two forlorn buildings on the corner of Vallejo St. Poor Colonel Poore's new building, built out over the Bay, marked the northernmost limit of the conflagration. Ten thousand piles stood in the mud, their tops burnt to the water's edge. "From Clark's Point to Happy Valley," he said, "there was nothing to be seen except for the foundations of that portion of the city which had stood over the water."

At 7:00 AM, the fire ran up against a fragmentary brick structure and died out. First light gave the shell-shocked survivors their first good look at the devastation caused by the deadliest arson in US history. This time three-quarters of San Francisco had burned—eighteen square blocks. The total number of structures destroyed over the last year now totaled over three thousand. Coffin estimated the cost at twenty-million dollars.

Coffin rushed to the *Niantic*. He expected little as he picked his way through the charred landscape. That portion of the Ghost Fleet's flagship that had been above water had burned. What had been submerged, and that was a considerable amount, had survived. No wonder San Francisco would adopt that eternal creature, the Phoenix, rising from its own ashes as its emblem. The unofficial city slogan became, "Go ahead, Young California! Who the hell cares for a fire!" Only in the magical city of lost ships could such a vessel as the *Niantic* rise again from a second fire and be as great as ever and spawn a dozen legends.

As Sheriff Devil Jack's launch was rowed along dark corridors formed by abandoned ships the fire had not reached, he saw a heavily laden sampan slide noiselessly northward toward the *Kangaroo's* remains. The Texas Ranger and his men trailed it, then steadied their boat on the rolling tide. He was now certain that the devastating series of arson fires over the last year had been set by Australian protection racketeers. He placed at their head English Jim, Sam Whittaker, Jack Edwards, and Ben Lewis the oily smelling man in black who reeked of burned timber. Devil Jack suspected that the blaze had been kindled as a diversion to allow the gang to loot the large quantities of gold dust miners had put in safe keeping while awaiting transportation back east. He continued tracking the missing gold which led him to one of the islands in the Bay, but from there he lost the criminals when they escaped on a frigate and outpaced him. His personal belief was that he had so surprised them that they had left a fortune behind.

According to then-Mayor Geary, a towering thirty-one-year old, sometime during the fire the Hounds, a ragtag battalion of demobilized New York military turned rogue, had reportedly stolen $150,000 to $200,000 in gold and hidden it somewhere inside the Ghost Fleet. Several caches of gold were reportedly cached there and at least one hidden inside an unidentified vessel that was turned into a storeship or hotel and dragged onshore as a building. This fifth big arson increased the fury of its citizens against their "brazen chaos" and "society-cankering rapacity."

WHITTAKER'S CONSCIENCE had been bothering him for two weeks and now relief was here. Predawn light colored the crest of each wave as he stood on the shore, hands on his hips. He scanned the horizon. It was obvious he was troubled. In the midst of such beauty, he slowly relaxed. The lines of his face softened. There was still danger, but his redemption was almost here. He had to be cautious, but he had earned enough money as his share of English Jim's robberies to pay for Windred and his wife's passage back to Australia. He took one horse with him and rode to Dr. Lambert's. Now he could spirit Joseph Windred away from the city and see that right was done and a worthwhile life was saved.

"I gave Windred my old cap," he said, and bought a new one for myself. We passed through Sansome Street to Broadway, down Broadway to Battery Street, and directly onto Clark's Point. Then I put Windred down a passageway at Clark's Point and told him, 'Stand there until I come for you,—the watchword is '*Ferguson*.'" As Windred waited in the alley, money changed hands to ensure that the two policemen patrolling the street would be blind to Mrs. Hogan and Mrs. Windred who were concealed close at hand. The two women in disguise stepped out and boldly waited in the open to say goodbye. The police who are patrolling the street were, as arranged, equally oblivious of Windred and of the two other fugitives, Adams and Jim Biggs, who were enjoying themselves in the neighborhood. Kitchen the Boatman was there too, waiting in his boat, ear cocked for the password to spring to the oars and spirit Windred away. All were well paid.

"When the coast was clear," Whittaker said later, "the password was spoken. With a wave of my arm, I summoned Windred from concealment. Mrs. Windred was in men's clothes," Whittaker said. He had provided her his old cap. Her disguise as a man recalled Shakespere's gender-switching comedies.

"In that disguise," Whittaker said, "I had taken her frequently in a carriage to see her husband, Joe. Windred snatched a moment with his wife and took some slick steps down to the water, slipped into Kitchen's boat, and was rowed away to the anchored ship.

But this was not the end as they had expected. More waiting lay ahead for Whittaker and Mary Ann and for the Windreds. They all suffered together. With this delay, a positive side suggested itself to Whittaker. With this unexpected delay, Mrs. Windred might be able to escape to Australia with her husband. Whittaker was only glad that Mary Ann had been instrumental in his escape, and been there to see Windred go. Best of all, she had been there to see Whittaker at his best. There was good in her too if only he could reach it as she had reached into him. As with himself, any goodness was buried deep but was not beyond recovery.

It was now May 4.

One more day, Whittaker thought.

AT FIRST LIGHT, Coffin got to Stuart and Raines' lot to look after his nautical equipment. He needn't have bothered. As he had feared, he was too late. "Not a piece is left large enough to make a clothespin," the owner of the lot told him as he searched the charred timbers and came up with scorched fingers. Full of spirit, the owner turned back to a contractor he had hauled in off the street and ordered him to have a new store ready for occupancy in one week.

"Agreed," said the builder, who could have done it in less time. He got right to work just as everyone around him was doing.

And so the city went about rebuilding once more, swifter than before, and shoddily as before. Maybe this time they had learned their lesson. When the hammering and sawing, and lifting and cursing ended, the Cove suddenly became silent except for the creak of the flotilla and the song of the wind whistling through the dunes. A small skiff perched atop the waves slid silently into the heart of the Ghost Fleet. A shapeless figure with a large bundle was rowing. His movements were quick and otherworldly, his back was hunched, and his coat was blowing out behind. He left a wake lifeless as the shrouded sky. Coffin suspected it was English Jim on some mission or other, but soon lost him in the maze and a fog bank considerably higher than the canopy of smoke shrouding the Cove and hiding its secrets.

English Jim had gone to Mariposa to meet with Joseph Hetherington and go over his ingenious plan for a multimillion dollar heist. English Jim laid out a map he had drawn and began to explain what the gang had been building up to with their series of arsons. The city vault with three millions in gold inside had been their target from the beginning. Hetherington whistled under his breath and sat back as he absorbed the genius of English Jim's scheme which would place the blame on others and not themselves. This is what the fires had been leading up to. Each of the arsons had necessitated the city's treasury be moved. In transit the gold was vulnerable and subject to attack from along its route. He knew English Jim's men had already stolen $14,000, although he had heard it was really $30,000, from the Monterey Custom House. This new scheme would net them a fortune. Singing Billy was earning his pay. In his position as Port Warden he had access to all the information English Jim would need.

That afternoon, Jack Edwards sailed his black yawl with its green top for Angel Island. Jack Dandy and Singing Billy had been there committing some mischief and needed transportation to their next crime. Jack Dandy robbed a Mr. Wilder of $190 and was arrested. Now, English Jim's locksmith would not be available when he needed him. Though there had been fires on both sides of the El Dorado, its iron shutters and iron doors had saved it. Young's Bank, the Verandah, and the Old Adobe had also survived the Anniversary fire. Now, the city would have to move three millions in gold from the melted underground vault though the city streets in broad daylight to what was now the only available vault in San Francisco.

Singing Billy provided a paper to English Jim. There were just three words on it —"Thursday, May 28." He had already arranged for Old Jack to get busy on a new vault. Jack Dandy's magic fingers would be needed once the gold was transferred. English Jim would have to break him out. For English Jim and his gang to work unobserved would require another, but smaller arson. The purpose of this blaze was to empty the Verandah so they could rent it and work from inside unobserved.

"There were anxious days ahead," Whittaker wrote. "Mrs. Windred disguised as a man called regularly on me to learn if her husband's vessel had sailed. I was touched, and for no money at all, I smuggled her onboard her husband's vessel." Still the departure was delayed. "Every day, I feared the couple might be detected, arrested, and taken from the ship. Then, came the great fire of May 4—a godsend as it turned out in spite of all the devastation."

On May 5, the ship's owners, gazing upon a city still flickering with flame, decided it was high time to get the hell out of Graveyard Harbor. Within minutes, they set sail for Australia. At the stern, his arms wrapped tightly around his wife, Windred studied the smoldering city." His features were agonized. He was painfully aware that he was abandoning his innocent friend, Tom Berdue, to certain death and his family would be there to see the hanging.

"The ship cleared away," it was written of this adventure, "bearing two happy passengers who invoked blessing upon each other, and bestowed even more kisses upon the head of Samuel Whittaker."

On May 15, at 12:45 am, nine days after the anniversary of the conflagration and thirteen days before English Jim's robbery was slated to take place, Ben Lewis, the ninth most important member of Jim's gang and its chief arsonist, set a fire at the rear of the Verandah bar. The dark man was clever. He kindled the blaze between a chest and a door to a small storeroom. First, he had soaked part of the door with oil, the *modus operandi* of the incendiary who had razed the city many times before. The fire had burned through the upper half of the door before a night watchman unexpectedly discovered the blaze at 1:00 am. Making countless trips alone with a leather bucket, the trustworthy guard wore himself out putting the blaze out before it ate its way to the second floor. English Jim had achieved his purpose. Now the building would be temporarily uninhabitable. The saloon was empty, and they could tunnel from there without being seen. They would have to be careful. With the city calling for blood, police patrols were increased in the Cove. Capt. Douglass Ottinger, the revenue marine commanding the *Lawrence*, kept several boats patrolling the waterfront twenty-four hours a day and had two 32-pound loaded cannon onboard his brig ready to fire.

IN HIS DANK, WINDOWLESS cell, Tom Berdue imagined the minutes of his life ticking away.

He heard other prisoners coughing and made out gentle footsteps in the adjacent corridor. The heat was suffocating. He could hardly breathe, He felt the noose tightening around his neck, and began involuntarily choking.

He was going to die and his wife and children would be there. And they would see his execution in an ocean of emotionless faces who viewed it as entertainment.

III
THE COVENANT OF PROMISE

Skeletons of ships, wharf projects and buildings fringed the outer rim of old Yerba Buena Cove, as San Francisco pushed farther seaward through the early fifties [creeping across the murk at an annual rate of two and half miles]. This fast growing Venice was typical of a careless impatient West. The blunt tops of wooden piles marked the port's unplanned course; mud and sea water oozed through uneven planking; houses of all sizes and shapes rose in clusters to flank the lofty masts of ships. Like a crouching, ruffled porcupine that inhabited debris lay, as confused as the drawing of an imaginative child, its outlines as vague as its purpose.

—Felix Riesenberg, Jr.

A peculiar feature of the harbor and one that struck me forcibly on our first approach, was the great number of dismantled ships that lay thickly scattered about it...

—J. Lamson on the *James W. Paige*

N EAR EVENING, THE CRY of gulls awakened Coffin from his afternoon nap. He stretched, washed his face in a pail of brackish water, and climbed on deck. He stretched. He must be getting old, he thought. He had never needed naps before. He felt the wind in his beard and the cold fog nipping at his cheeks. Naturally, he lit his pipe first thing and watched the smoke intermingle with the mist. He spent some time rereading a letter from his wife. Before he knew it, he found himself thinking about Tom Berdue for some reason, and whether he was guilty or not. He had watched him in court because he wanted to get a look at the English Jim in the flesh. Of course, he was innocent! The thought struck him suddenly as a lightning bolt, though he had been thinking about the problem for some time. It would be a horrible miscarriage of justice if the young man was hanged for another man's crimes, especially if the other man was the real English Jim Stuart who would escape scot free, without paying the price.

Grabbing up his *Log* and pen, he placed them in his pocket in a waterproof pouch, went over the side, and dropped into his skiff. He laughed when he thought about where he was going. The same place as always. Once more, he had landed back on Long Wharf without a cent in his pocket. He was still paying off his debts because he was an honest man. A friend bought him supper and placed it before him. His friends were his true wealth, Coffin thought. He had never doubted that. The fog was thicker by the time he finished eating. He wiped his chin, thanked his friend, and dropped back into his small boat. Minutes later, after a bout of spirited rowing, he stopped alongside a charred boat. The recent blaze had been so hot it had consumed part of a neighboring ship's hull. The tear amidships was bigger than the one the sea lion he had encountered had swum through.

Coffin peered inside. In the light of his lantern, he glimpsed ceramic bowls and unopened crates with oriental writing swirling. About sixty feet away, he saw a tall figure silhouetted by the sunset surveying him. Coffin instantly looked away. He came to a deserted whaler close to the Clay Street Wharf that was lit up with candles. The frigate was a stage to minstrels and touring actor companies. Scattered applause skittered across the waters from a small audience in circling boats. A clown in black and white makeup was holding a large hoop through which a small dog was jumping tirelessly back and forth.

When it was too dark to see, Coffin rowed to the Washington St. Wharf, tethered his skiff, and went ashore. Halfway down a passage between land-ships, he saw a woman smiling at him from the second story. She was shaking out a blanket as she went about her household duties. She did this as if a home that was also a ship was the most natural thing in the world. Dust was showering down on his head. He brushed it off, and nodded to her. "Sorry," she said. He continued feeling his way in the dark until he saw lights glowing ahead on Clay Street on the waterside of the Union Saloon. The long silhouettes of anchored vessels stood out against the hearth-like glimmer of homes across the Bay. On ships further out, Coffin glimpsed twinkling green and red lights. He had heard Sam Brannan planned to erect a stone building an unbelievable four stories high on Montgomery Street between California and Sacramento. He might be a greedy man, but Old Sam was a forward looking individual with dreams of the future.

Coffin knew that the Anniversary Fire had destroyed most of the *Niantic*, at least all that wasn't submerged in the water and thick mud. He quickened his pace. He was eager to see the burned hull of his old favorite again. It was sure to be a disappointment. At length, he came out into a clearing where the wind was whipping a gigantic flag so fiercely that the stars and bars stood out straight.

Not only did the *Niantic* still exist, but she was whole again, and sailing on dry land. Behind and all around the *Niantic*, loomed the shadows of tall buildings. Multistory buildings, so uncommon before, were becoming common. Two doors down, another storeship, the *Garnet*, sailed as imposingly as the land based *Niantic* in the midst of normal buildings and homes.

Coffin encountered Mr. L. H. Roby, who was in an expansive mood. His arms were revolving like the semaphore on Signal Hill. He had just leased the ship and was to sign the final papers in two weeks.

"I'm going to use the entire ship in an amazing way," Roby shouted, so excited he seemed about to levitate above the deck. "I'm going to make the *Niantic* the foundation of the strangest hotel anywhere and raise a three or four-story building on her decks." He caught his breath. "The ground floor will be occupied with offices and little shops, but all of the upper floors will be made up of the *Niantic* Hotel. It will be the first block of its kind and guaranteed to attract attention all over California." What had been little more than a burned hull would now be a hotel.

Glad-handing and backslapping Coffin, Roby spread out a large blueprint he had rolled up beneath his arm. He held it flat with his hand and one foot.

What a pedigree to have, thought Coffin. He had never seen a more enthusiastic man. He could hardly stay still.

"Someday," Roby said, "the *Niantic* Hotel will be one of the most romantic sites in all of old San Francisco. Imagine the hull of a stranded Ghost Ship built right into a block of rugged tenements. It will be bigger, more inventive. and more unusual than all the rest. Think of the contrast."

Coffin said he would.

Later, Roby committed suicide in one of the rooms in his new hotel.

"IT'S A TUNNEL JOB," English Jim explained to Mary Ann. He had pumped himself up with pride so he could impress her. "But more than that, much more," he said. His entire gang was gathered about her rooms and paying close attention to his every word. They imagined the millions in gold, so much that transporting and spending it would be their biggest problem.

"My plan," English Jim said, "is to cut a trench underneath the street from the Verandah building to the old adobe Custom House on the northwestern corner of the two streets for the purpose of robbery and in whose vaults are three millions of gold. Then we will carry another trench from the old Custom House across to the El Dorado. After the robbery has been accomplished, the first trench is to be closed up and the other kept open to avoid suspicion falling on us. In this way authorities will think that the men of the El Dorado, who sleep there, had dug the tunnel and robbed the vault. They would get the blame."

It was a brilliant plan. Jim had drawn a simple map for them, a few rectangles and arrows, but it was enough for his men to see the plan would work.

English Jim's first step, gaining access to a base of operations very close to the new repository so they could work unobserved, had been accomplished. All he had to do now was await the completion of the two tunnels, one to lead the blame elsewhere. Singing Billy had provided English Jim with the date that the three millions in gold would be removed from the melted vault on Montgomery and California Streets. On May 28, it would be transported to the vault of the Old Adobe Custom House. Old Jack Morgan, the brick mason who had constructed that vault, had kept the plans, and could open it quickly. Meanwhile, English Jim and his men began to dig in the basement of the Verandah, emptying buckets and bracing the tunnels with two by fours as they went. Much of the soft ground was fill or mud. Each night they hid the opening to their tunnel and went about other robberies to fund the expenses of the dig. English Jim never went out without being disguised because his unusual, snake-like body language was a dead give-away.

Outside the Verandah, the gigantic fire bell at the Square rarely ceased clanging. It was unnerving to the arsonists behind the fires who were working so close to the bell, or rather below it. Each time it rang, the hollow tolling emptied every theatre and church, and set folks to quivering in their beds. It shook the bones of English Jim's men who scurried for their lives. "So many whirlwinds of destruction had swept over the devoted city at short intervals," pioneer Ralph Andrews said, "and with such fearful strides, that the whole community was as excitable as if they had stood on the brink of a crater."

"The entire city could burn down in a single night," Rev. Sam Wiley added. "And yet, every man was acquiring with such rapidity that all hoped to complete a fortune ere such a disaster should occur."

IN THE COVE, COFFIN contemplated the water city around him. Like the sea lion, he too was a sea animal. So ensnarled by a thousand anchor chains, so penned-in were the two hundred ships still able to sail, that Coffin had come to accept that so much tonnage could never be moved and would become part of the land for all time. The deserted ships, though floating, were landlocked and ossified and married to each as much as he was married to the water and to art and writing. The Ghost Fleet could only be absorbed by the expanding city as its spine. Late that afternoon, he saw an angry crowd congregating on fire-damaged Long Wharf and sidled over to listen.

It was bad news. Australian scalawags Barney Ray and Tom Edwards, who had already murdered three men, were at large again. Two days later, Coffin heard that five more convicts had escaped from the station house. Three days later, another dozen had taken "leg bail." On May 12, two prisoners had swum away from the *Euphemia*, which was the final straw for the Council. They intended to do something about that. Then came the unexpected.

The first shock of a quake lifted the Ghost Fleet and sent swells rolling over the decks. The quake collapsed part of the tunnel English Jim had dug inside the El Dorado. A second tremor hit harder than the first. A mini-tidal wave swept around the pilings and rolled over the mud flats. A portion of damaged Long Wharf collapsed, and three dock shacks and a few auctioneers were thrown into the shallow water. No one was hurt, but another convict escaped from the *Euphemia*. When the jailers returned after an unsuccessful search for the escapee, they discovered a quake had opened a rent in the prison ship's side. Inside, a beam weighing several hundred pounds had broken loose. Guards lifted the timber to free two prisoners penned under it, but the other prisoners were chained in rows and would drown if the brig sank. The jailers, who were used to mistreating the imprisoned men, now had a long night's work ahead saving their lives. Their hands grew raw and red as they went about chaining and unchaining, bracing and re-bracing, and lifting and lowering.

Eight days after creditors repossessed the prison brig, one of the escaped prisoners was found floating off Rincon Point with a chain tied around his neck. His skull and jaw had been smashed by an Australian slung shot, English Jim's weapon of choice. Perhaps the victim had stumbled across some underground secret operation in progress.

THE BIG DAY ARRIVED. On Wednesday, May 28, Thomas Butler King assembled thirty rugged employees and armed them with cutlasses, and carbines. Holding a bludgeon in one hand and a huge Colt in the other, King got to the corner of Montgomery and California Streets and prepared to move the melted gold from the sunken vault. He cut a romantic figure with his long face, mutton chops, glaring eyes, and high forehead as he strode dramatically over puddles from last week's rain. The twisted wreckage of the melted vault containing millions of dollars was slowly lifted to the surface. English Jim in disguise was among the crowd, but he had no intention of stealing the heavy gold. There would have been no possibility of escape.

Burly guards filled the first truck with specie and, hauling the carload of gold and surviving city treasures, began the first of several three-block trips to the Custom House at Kearney and Washington Streets. King puffed himself up with importance during the creeping march to the Square, unaware the vault he was trusting to protect the city treasure had been constructed by Old Jack the brick mason, one of English Jim's top men.

"We looked at the vault that Old Jack had built," Singing Billy said, "and were pleased." He had made the repository and its locks susceptible to his knowledge and to the skills of master locksmith, Jack Dandy. The three millions in gold would have been safer if King had left them lying in the mud of Montgomery Street for people to stumble over.

Sadly, King's March also suggested that San Francisco was so lawless that it needed an army to move treasure in bright daylight along the city's most populous streets. En route, some jokers in the crowd charged the convoy with butter knives and forks. All the guards ran away except King who, in courage born of desperation and with the fighting heart of a failed banker, held his ground. With determination, he raised his cutlass to defend the gold with his life. By the end of the day, the gold had been transferred to the refitted old adobe without further incidence. Now that the gold was in, English Jim's tunnel was progressing through the soft earth drawing closer every day.

Mr. Hall, Superintendent of Public Buildings for California, arrived to select a site for a third and more secure custom house. But where was that to be? The block on the western side of the Square was most suitable, Hall believed, but the merchants had fixed upon the northern side as the best location and he was forced to go along with them. English Jim liked the Custom House just where it was. Unfortunately, the earthquake had done more damage to his tunnel than he had anticipated and he had to endure this unexpected setback.

On June 2, early risers were drinking coffee and eating biscuits and plates of beans at the New York Bakery on the eastern side of Kearny Street. One floating diner was selling coffee and doughnuts for $1.00, even offered a square meal for $1.50 and, if one were in the mood, a regular gorge for $2.50. On a corner of Long Wharf, Albert Benard, wearing a broad-brimmed felt hat pulled down over his eyes, was selling "carefully tested" watches from "the Royal Watch Company. They were guaranteed to keep perfect time for five years." Some of his watches ran for ten minutes, some for half a day, but those were the record setters.

On the southeastern corner, a hawker was selling the *Alta*, and crying "Mornin' Pa-p-u-z! Another jail break from City Prison last night." Though Sheriff Devil Jack had two officers stationed outside the prisoners' cell and three more officers on guard inside the jail, the prisoners had somehow gotten a key. Devil Jack suspected a corrupt guard had given it to them. Altogether, eight prisoners had escaped— four larceners, two robbers, and two of English Jim's gang, Jemmy-from-town and Jack Dandy who was making his fourth escape in as many months. The truth was that their spouses had smuggled in augurs and other tools to enable them to dig a passage through the thin brick wall forming the City Hall foundation. One disgusted prisoner sent Devil Jack a formal notice that if he did not repair the jail he would "vacate the premises."

The prison was still better than the Council's first attempt. They had once hauled a de-masted frigate onto a mud flat to make a temporary town jail, but as the flats about the abandoned ships slowly filled-in houses sprang up on them, and the jail became impractical. Fourteen more prisoners broke out of the wretched cellar. Security was so lax that Trustees were allowed to take an occasional night out on the town and most often did not return.

COFFIN, DRAWN BY THE SMOKE of a freshly burning ship, observed waterfront men using plentiful garbage as landfill—food scraps that attracted vermin and household wastes that bred disease. Rains carried this offensive filth down the east-west thoroughfares and sent it flowing into the Cove.

"When the tide is out," Coffin complained, "the effluvia from the mud, growing worse every day from the deposit of filth and offal, is most abominable." Then, there were the good days, he admitted, when the vigorous action of powerful tides kept the area livable. Without those strong currents the Bay would have quickly become a stagnant lagoon. During dry summer months the garbage stayed where it was thrown and formed a crusty patina over the ground as heat dried it. The Cove was very pleasant then.

Coffin tucked his *Log* under his coat and began to row about the Ghost Fleet to settle his mind. He noted the *Hardie, Trescott, Noble, Palmyra, Phillip Hone, Elmira, Francis Ann, Garnet,* and *Fame*—all storeships, and the *Fortuna,* a ship-hotel. He added considerably to his inventory with important vessels—the *Byron* (on the Mission Street Wharf), and the *Falcon, Callao, Galen, Autumn, Casilada, Piedmont, Inez, Louisa,* a Boston bark and the former yacht of the King of the Hawaiian Islands, had all been ditched at Washington and Battery. Past them was an interesting wooden ship. It was so interesting that Coffin stopped and gave her all his attention.

The ship projected an ominous shadow that extended far below the copper-sheathing which protected hulls from wood-eating worms and decay. From Coffin's point of view, the shadow appeared as a wriggling black mass that was alive. Steps from the water led up the side to the blank side of the ship which concealed a door. It was closed now. As Coffin lost himself in the maze between ships, he felt other eyes watching him—those of the outcasts, the mendicants, the burglars, and the dissolute—self-imprisoned by their own past deeds.

In his *Log*, Coffin entered a new topic: "Knockdown Boats," which were small sail and steam craft stored in the bellies of larger vessels. The first and tiniest, only thirty-seven feet long, was a steam side-wheeler. *Little Sitka*. She had arrived in Graveyard Harbor in the hold of the Russian bark *Naslednich* and been reassembled on Yerba Buena Island. Too small for the Bay she was perfect for transporting furs along the 120-mile Sacramento River run up to John Sutter's unofficial capitol, New Helvetica, and deliver supplies to the Russian Fur Company.

The *Little Sitka* chattered and clattered to Sacramento at a dismally slow pace—six hours and seven minutes. She was so slow people joked that an ox team once beat her into Benicia Town by four days. When a "norther" roared across the Bay, the *Sitka*, moored far out, sank. They salvaged what they could. They installed her engine in the schooner *Rainbow* and hauled her wreckage onto the flats as a reminder of the need for piers where ships might safely tie up. The day passed. On the mud flats, workers were beaching a bark, but it was too dark for Coffin to see further. At 7:00 PM, he had a meal of fish on the rail of the *Canton*, chatted with his friends onboard, then ambled over to Selim and Fred Woodworth's store at the water's edge on Clay Street. The Clay Street Wharf held the office of the Sacramento Steamer, Ogden and Haynes offices, and commission merchants on ships from China.

Coffin returned to his temporary berth and immediately fell into a restful sleep where he dreamed optimistic dreams. Thus, passed one of his best and most interesting days inside the strangest city in the world, but one filled with unanswered questions and an overtone of terrible tragedy to come.

"BLAST YOU FOR A penny-pinching mud shark!" Wakeman bellowed as he barged into Charlie Minturn's office at the foot of Geary. Owner William Brown had sold the *New World* out from under the Pirate's feet and retired from the river business. Minturn, a former pilot of the Stockton riverboat steamer *Erastus Corning*, was the new owner. Wakeman rocked his desk with one huge fist and kicked over a chair.

"Find yourself a swivel-eyed bay scow captain for the dad-blasted wages you pay!"

At that, he stormed out, taking the door off in his exit. "By God, I would commit mayhem before I would ever work for Charlie Minturn!"

"Now what set the Pirate off?" Minturn asked. All he had done was ask Wakeman to stay on as the paddlewheel skipper at a substantially reduced salary.

Now what a tattooed Pirate to do with himself? From the pilot house Wakeman had only to turn his head to see hundreds of intact or de-masted ships, full or empty of cargo, all quit by their crews and deserted in the Cove or hauled up on land to become buildings. The sight of so many orphans shook Wakeman. For nearly a full year he had remained loyal to the *New World* steamer and won all the one-sided races he desired on the Sacramento River. Now, he had been left on the trash heap of Graveyard Harbor.

ON MONDAY, JUNE 9, two hundred leading merchants gathered at Sam Brannan's building on the corner of Battery and Pine. Brannan, publicist for the Gold Rush and for himself, was a veritable Paul Revere for greed. He had called the wealthiest men in town together to offer them a way to eradicate those preying on them without due process. In a few hours, fireman George Oakes, James Neall, and Brannan himself had formed a committee to "watch, pursue, and bring to justice the outlaws infesting the city, through the regularly constituted courts, if possible, through more summary process, if necessary." This meant hanging. The merchants were up for hanging anybody, guilty or innocent, without legal trial. He drew up a constitution giving them far-ranging powers:

> "WHEREAS it has become apparent to the citizens of San Francisco that there is no security for life and property . . . the citizens whose names are hereunto attached, do unite themselves into an association for the maintenance of the peace and good order of society, and . . . do bind themselves, each unto the other to do and perform every lawful act for the maintenance of law and order, and to sustain the laws when faithfully and properly administered; but we are determined that no thief, burglar, incendiary, or assassin, shall escape punishment, either by the quibbles of the law, the insecurity of prisons, the carelessness or corruption of the police, or a laxity of those who administer justice. The committee may enter any persons' premises where we have good reason to believe that we shall find evidence to substantiate and carry out the object of this body."

At twilight on June 10, a hulking man with a thick red beard and tangled hair, rowed out of the Ghost Fleet, and tethered his skiff beneath Long Wharf. The bright moon rose. In his full black suit "the Miscreant," as he was known, was invisible among the charred timbers and to all eyes appeared to be one of them. A convicted arsonist and owner of the Uncle Sam on Dupont Street, he was English Jim's man, as many were, and dyed in the wool to his obedience. At 8:00 PM, shipper George Virgin descended the second-floor stairs to double check that his ship had sailed on the tide. He looked all about, and behind things. He saw no one. Satisfied, he entered the ground floor tavern and deposited some money from his strongbox with the bartender. The bulk of his wealth for that day, $1500, was inside a small iron safe in his office. Without warning, the Miscreant separated himself from the shadows, raced up the outside stairs, barged into Virgin's office, put the safe in a sack, hoisted it over his shoulder, and ran back down. At the foot of the stairs, were several bystanders. He shoved them aside, and raced for his rowboat. Some volunteer firefighters, hearing the commotion, were alerted and began chasing him along Long Wharf.

"Put down that safe, thief!" they yelled.

Staggering under the weight of the safe, the Miscreant jumped into his boat. As he rowed across the Cove, his pursuers tumbled into a dozen four-and-five-oared boats, cast off painters, shipped oars, and pulled after him. The Miscreant was confident that they would not be able to catch him before he reached the Sydney Town landing where he would be safe.

John Sullivan, English Jim's boatman at Foster's Bar, had just taken a fare out to a ship in his Whitehall taxi and was returning to Long Wharf when he saw the pursuing boats and understood the situation at once. Sullivan angled the thief off, raised an oar and threatened to knock him into the shallows. He held him that way until the other boats caught up to him. Cornered, the Miscreant let his oars trail.

"Put down that safe," they called.

"What safe?" he smirked. At that, he flung the safe into the water.

The firefighters answered by giving him a beating. Sullivan and two men dredged up the safe with long handled tongs and called volunteer police officer David Arrowsmith to the head of the pier. Arrowsmith recognized Sullivan as #269 of the Vigilance Committee and escorted them toward the station house. The Miscreant, still denying he had stolen anything, was unconcerned. The local courts were reliably corrupt and juries were easily bought. A number of dishonest judges, shyster lawyers, and unscrupulous officials were in the Ducks' employ. Hadn't they just set their chief arsonist, Ben Lewis, free? Unfortunately for the thief, David Arrowsmith was also a member of the Vigilance Committee. On the way, they met another Committee member, George Schneck, who had a better idea.

"It will be more expedient to take him right to the Committee rooms," he said.

"If you say so, I will," Arrowsmith said.

"Let me have hold of him, and we will go right along."

They dragged Simpton to a large storeroom in Sam Brannan's building at Bush Street near Market. Just before 10:00 PM, George Oakes rang the great bell with a billet of wood—a single stroke then a pause—three taps of the bell. Two centrally located firehouses a half-mile apart, California Four and Big Six, repeated the message at intervals of one minute. The taps were picked up by a third company at the head of the Square. Their combined chiming summoned the new Vigilantes to action.

Coffin heard the tolling of bells coming from all directions on shore and rushed on deck expecting to see the town again in flames. He stood watching for three or four minutes, saw nothing, and returned below. Only later did he learn it was "the death knell of the wretched culprit Jenkins, the Miscreant." The secret password today was "Lewis," the name of the arsonist. The name hissed among the Vigilantes. "Lewis... Lewis... Lewis..."

That hated name summoned men to shed the blood of the wicked without the burden of seeing themselves as equally wicked. The Vigilance Committee had begun its unlawful work in earnest. Lewis, one of the key members of English Jim's gang, had been caught in the act of stealing a trunk from a room on Long Wharf and his room was found to be on fire. He had used a delayed mechanism to ignite the blaze and was to be handed over to the Vigilance Committee as the long sought arsonist who had burned down the city multiple times. Twice Lewis was brought before the district court for trial and twice his counsel unearthed judicial flaws in the indictment which quashed the proceedings. Each time Lewis's lawyer used loopholes which allowed the ex-con to slip out of town.

George Schneck's trial notes said that it was Lewis's trial which had led immediately to the organization of the Vigilantes: "The committee took great pains to secure a complete transcript of the record in anticipation of the District Court trial in July." A mob of one hundred hanging men convened a kangaroo court. William Tell Coleman got to Committee Headquarters within half an hour. At that time there were only forty men inside. He stopped at the head of the stairway, gave his number, and entered a door opening directly into a large room. The Vigilance Committee's huge blue and white flag covered one brick wall. To his left, a door opened from the main room to the cells and a separate chamber where the Executive Committee met. Simpton was standing defiantly inside a large holding cell. Above him were two stout beams the Committee could use to support hangman's ropes if needed. William Howard the ship master rushed in behind Coleman and placed his pistol on the long table to signify they meant business.

"As I understand it we are here to hang someone," he said.

Coleman nodded toward Simpton's cell. "He is well-known as a desperate character," he said, "The Miscreant" John Jenkins, who has frequently evaded justice."

Simpton's bearing throughout his "trial" had been so defiant and insulting it suggested another motive to Coleman—he had the expectation of momentarily being rescued by his fellow Ducks. The threat of an impending rescue called for prompt action. Not only were Simpton's criminal pals gathering to save him, but so were the city's most respected citizens including Fire Chief Broderick and Sheriff Devil Jack. The Committee convened its unlawful court, a mock court, often called a Kangaroo Court because the defendant was an Australian. No matter the designation, they convicted the Miscreant within an hour and set about their business.

At midnight, Sam Brannan ruled that the prisoner would be hung at 2:00 AM in the Square in front of hundreds.

Coleman protested.

"Hang Simpton in daylight as a lesson for everyone," he said.

"No," Brannan said.

The Reverend Flavel Mines prayed with the condemned man for

so long that a member of the Executive Committee, fifty-three year old former printer Garrett Ryckman, intervened.

"Reverend Mines," he said through the closed door, "you have taken three-quarters of an hour and I want you to bring this prayer business to a rapid close. I am going to hang this man in half an hour!"

The Vigilantes ripped Simpton from his ministry so swiftly that, of all the men they hanged, he was the only one not to have signed a confession. They had not given him enough time. By torchlight, they dragged him the half-mile from Committee Headquarters to the West side of the Square. While they were still forty-feet from a 110-foot fir flagpole, they gave him a glass of brandy and lit him a cigar which he smoked with enjoyment. Then, they gave him a plug of tobacco which he chewed with pleasure.

"Do you wish to be provided a minister for spiritual consolation," Wakeman asked.

When a minister of the gospel offered Simpton spiritual consolation,—while the rope was around his neck, he "repulsed him in the most rude and insolent manner."

"This hastens your doom," said Coleman.

"Do your worst," said the prisoner.

At the South end of the old adobe was a jutting beam that might serve as a gibbet. They chose that. They threw one end of the rope over a joist projecting from the banking house of Palmer, Cook & Co. and made ready to hoist him up.

In preparing to hang Simpton, they discovered $200 in gold in his pocket.

"Do you have any friends to whom it might be given?"

"No, scatter it among the mob."

Simpton's arms were already pinioned. The Pirate Wakeman insisted on fitting the noose around the prisoner's neck himself, and hoisted him like a flag.

While Simpton was dangling from the banking house joist, a fellow in the crowd, cried "Served him right, by God!" and was instantly floored by a Sydney Duck.

The Pirate Wakeman felt for Simpton's gold and couldn't find it. Someone in the crowd of crooks and good men had picked his pocket.

For the next five hours Brannan's men stood guard over Simpton's corpse, then laid the crumpled body on the floor of the Monumental Engine House, and left it there for all to see.

"Criminals had little to fear in merciful, gentle, careless California," Frank Soule commented. "Jurors, eager to be at moneymaking again, are apt to take hasty charges from the bench."

If caught, the Ducks shielded each other from arrest, conviction and punishment. They not only intimidated incapable prosecutors, bribed police and juries, but elected criminals who controlled judges who were ignorant of the law, or too timid to mete out just punishment. They hired unscrupulous shysters and two-bit politicians to make payoffs for them and were responsible for most of the vice, murder, crimping, extortion, and arson in San Francisco.

"THE VIGILANCE COMMITTEE HAS begun their work in earnest," Coffin said to Capt. Haskel in the morning. "It was the clang of the well-known signal bell which awakened me. It has a sound different from all other bells in the city. It was the death knell of the wretched Miscreant." He considered Sam Brannan, who directed the movement of two or three hundred merchants, mechanics and others, to be the "*primum mobile*" behind the hanging. I am very glad I had no concern with that Committee."

Haskel knew his friend was not done speaking. He waited. Coffin had another name to add to his list of villains concerned with the Miscreant's hanging.

"The man who was the most active at the execution," he said, "he who fixed the rope about the victim's neck and acted the part of the boatswain and cried, 'Yo heave ho,' was himself a runaway from justice in another state, a man whose object it is to court the applause of the vulgar populace ... a rowdy, who is at any moment liable to a requisition from the Governor of New York for a state prison offense. I mean Capt. Wakeman, he who ran away from New York with the steamer *New World* while she was in custody of the sheriff."

Wakeman had never denied the charge and, in fact, was proud of all the illegalities he had committed. "Of course I joined the Vigilance Committee, and acted as sheriff at the hangings. I have stood many and many a night in the streets of San Francisco looking for malfeasance."

After the cowardly and illegal hanging, the Vigilantes arranged a spontaneous rally in the Square of over 10,000 bloodthirsty citizens to authenticate the hanging men as the only real law and the new government of San Francisco.

San Francisco was no place for English Jim.

THE NEXT DAY, THE REAL English Jim was hiding out in the mines in the Sierras, and reading Whittaker's second note to him. "Old Fellow," it said, "look out. The Hawks are abroad and after you, both here and down below. You had better keep in the upper Country at present, I can say no more at present, Yours S. W."

Though Whittaker had cautioned him to stay in the mountains until the end of the month, Jim did not trust him. Nor did he believe anything Whittaker said or wrote. He was squandering valuable time. He needed to complete his Custom House tunnel, and then attend Berdue's hanging in disguise. He had to be there. His Christlike resemblance totally belied the fact that he had all the cunning and none of the mercy of the hundreds of Sydney ticket-of-leave men unleashed upon San Francisco. Most had settled at the base of Telegraph Hill, and along the waterfront. That the law should hang Thomas Berdue in his place, English Jim could understand; it was just what he would have done.

He had fully intended to wait until Berdue's execution to return to San Francisco, but each day he risked the removal of city gold from the temporary vault or its safety strengthened. English Jim began to imagine Whittaker finishing the tunnel on his own and robbing the vault before he returned. He had never fully trusted his dapper rival for Mary Anne's affections, and as he had often said, wished him dead. English Jim was jumpy, and kept careful watch. When he suspected two Americans in Marysville had recognized him, his fear at being exposed overcame his innate sense of caution.

Against his better judgment he returned to San Francisco to conceal himself at Mrs. Mary Ann Hogan's Rooming House, or at Kitchen the Boatman's home. As he trudged along, a lonely traveler, he estimated Berdue would be convicted and hanged any day now. Unfortunately, English Jim didn't realize how much his beard had grown during the time he had been gone. He and Berdue were once again twins. Vigilante Jacob L. Van Bokkelen observed Singing Billy on Powell Street speaking with a suspicious-looking man who was pretending to be drunk. When Singing Billy realized he was under surveillance he became so agitated that Van Bokkelen reported him to the Vigilance Committee. Their investigation revealed that Billy was a secret member of English Jim's gang. Because of this he was compelled to resign his position as Port Warden and flee San Francisco. But the Committee was a bunch and tracked him to Sacramento where the police arrested him. He gave the police his word that if they let him remain at large, he would let them arrest him again the next day. They agreed. Of course, Singing Billy broke his parole, and escaped back to San Francisco by steamer disguised as an elderly woman. At Long Wharf, twenty well-armed escorts were waiting for him and marched him to Committee Hq where he was questioned about his complicity in the Monterey Custom house robbery. He was released, rearrested, then released again, and, of course, vanished again.

Singing Billy was a very slippery individual.

ON JUNE 19, WAKEMAN and ten members of the Committee sailed to Angel Island, and the Farallones outside the Golden Gate, They were looking for Jack Dandy who had been seen on Edwards' yawl just after the May Anniversary fire. They had no luck.

Four days later, Devil Jack spent $1500 of his own money to buy materials and pay builders to erect a new Broadway jail. He was sick of the escapes. Through his deputy, John Caperton, he asked the Vigilance Committee to repay him and invited them over to inspect the new jail. In a letter addressed to the "High Sheriff for the City and County," the Committee enclosed a three dollar donation from each member toward the Broadway jail bill.

"We regret much that you personally should have suffered any pecuniary inconvenience in the prosecution of [the jail's] financial affairs," they wrote, "and earnestly hope that the pittance raised by us may serve to carry out your sanguine expectations and subserve the public safety. We thank you for your perseverance and skill."

"Three dollars each!" Devil Jack snapped. "If that don't beat all."

COFFIN HAD ALMOST COMPLETED his *Log*. He headed south past the *Swallow*, the *Cherie*, several more feluccas from the

Mediterranean, and a bobbing galliot. Just then, Devil Jack gestured to him from a nearby pier.

Coffin rowed over to him.

"Might I join you," Devil Jack asked.

"Sure, come aboard," Coffin replied.

Devil Jack dropped into the skiff. "I need to learn more about the Cove as a hiding place for fugitives," he said. "And I have something to ask you."

"Sure," Coffin said.

"I understand you saw English Jim one night on the docks."

"Yes, I did. It was the night he robbed the *Caskie* and attacked my friend, Capt. Jones."

"I saw English Jim at trial and wanted to compare notes with you to make certain it was really him and not Tom Berdue."

Coffin explained that he knew English Jim by his body language.

"He walks in a fluid, long-measured stride," he said, " and has a habit of swinging his long arms. He walks with his head lowered, but halts every few steps to peer out from beneath his hat. Then, his head snaps up as if he has elastic in his neck and can't keep his head down."

"I see," said Devil Jack. He was silent for a moment. He had heard that the real English Jim was uncommonly quick in his motions, and now Capt. Coffin had confirmed it. "Berdue never exhibited such body language. He moves stiffly and painfully, though I hear he is still recovering from the sickness he contracted in the gold towns around the Yuba River. His head is almost down upon his chest. It never flies up. More and more I am beginning to think that he is not English Jim, but someone named Thomas Berdue as he claims."

Coffin suggested they get on with hiding places for criminals within the Cove. "The Ghost Fleet is not only a region of criminals and gentle families," he said, "but of pirates—if this century old junk is any example. The *Whang Ho* and the *Balance* must have been born the same year."

Coffin brought his skiff northeast of Long Wharf where there was an exotic Chinese junk draped with nets and roofed over with mats and bamboos. They studied it in wonder.

Stiff breezes sent the junk's colorful flags flying. Two large kites were being sailed from the sampan's deck. Each evening, they reeled in the kites and lit ten-foot tall lanterns covered with painted silk and six leering faces. The junk of teak, and ironwood was a hundred-feet long. Her underwater sections were carved with flush strakes and its upper section with overlapping strakes. Dragons had been incised into the wood. A painted crimson sea dragon guarded her quarter.

Devil Jack, more used to forests of Tennessee than the orient, asked about the huge pieces of timber projecting over each bow. "They seem to have no purpose," he said. "What are they?"

"Anchors loaded with stones," Coffin replied.

Next to anchors were two great glaring eyes painted on the bows. These were a traditional Chinese symbol of *oculi* to guide the ship.

"Without those eyes," Coffin explained, "this great, uncouth-looking ship could not see which way to go."

Long bamboo poles projected over bows from which hung a large drip-net. Four Chinese pirates were laying a new net with bone-netting needles. They were clad in broad-brimmed hats of split bamboo, baggy breeches, and cotton blouses. Below them, a rower was wrapping pieces of net around glass fishing floats. On the lofty stern poop, a pigtailed sailor was twanging a gong. Coffin and Devil Jack were intrigued by carved wooden stairs leading from the waterline to a side door. The sweet odor of incense, spices, and roasting ground nuts wafted to their nostrils. Inside, a horse-faced man in a persimmon-colored robe was sitting with crossed legs. His shaven skull gleamed in the Cove light.

"With his hands folded behind his back," Coffin wrote later, "his *chapeau de bras* in silent dignity, he looked the prince of pilots." With a wire, the man speared a ball of black semi-liquid paste from a horn box and held it to a flame. Smoking, he put the ball into a thimble-sized bowl screwed to a long stemmed pipe and deeply drew in the smoke. "He's dreaming of Ma Chu, the Goddess of Sailors, and her two assistants "Thousand Mile Eye" and "Favorable-Wind Ear," Coffin told Devil Jack. These Bone Trade men worked for the Five Companies, five benevolent men who held a rigid obligation to the deceased to bury them in the earth of their ancestors. The Five tracked deceased Chinese all over California and arranged for the charter of ships like the French vessel, *Asia*, to ship home thousands of polished bones dipped in brandy.

Coffin left Devil Jack off at Long Wharf to wrestle with his own problems, and returned to the *Talma*. He too had a lot to think about. He began climbing to where the air was fresh. From the mainmast, he studied over Graveyard Harbor's listing and sinking ships. He listened to the whisper of wind through shredded canvas and cries of shorebirds. From his perch he filled his lungs with the salt breeze off the Pacific. He cupped his chin, and studied over the Cove with its trapped, listing, sinking, and creaking ships. The Ghost Fleet was not only jammed and turned in upon itself, but changing into something else.

Capt. Coffin had no idea exactly what.

All these wondrous vessels from every deep water port, all abandoned and still filled with cargo, people, and treasure. Then, there were the wonderful stories which would go into his book if ever finished it. A rain washed away the smell and debris that had run down from the muddy streets into the Cove and it was like spring to him. Northward, fingers of fog threaded their way around pines on the slope of the Sleeping Lady as the great Mountain Tamalpais was called. Exhausted, he went below to sleep and dream about English Jim and where he really was. He might be on one of the vessels floating around him.

ON JUNE 21, THE CISTERNS were almost dry, lower than a month earlier and they had been bone dry then. The incendiary set his sixth city-destroying fire in an empty house on the northern side of Pacific Street. The fire could have easily been extinguished if a supply of water had been at hand, but none was nearer than the Bay. "It was about eleven o'clock Sunday morning," Coffin recalled, "and Capt. Haskel and I had left the *Talma*, intending to go to church. We called onboard the *James Caskie* for Capt. Jones and his wife to accompany us." Jones was healing slowly from English Jim's horrible attack and was unable to go with them. Visible scars still covered his face and arms and he limped badly. Coffin saw no such scars on his wife though she had hefted a sword to fight English Jim to save her husband and been bloodied in the attempt. Coffin felt such rage at the Jesus-look-alike that he had to remind himself it was the Sabbath and he shouldn't curse and shouldn't think such terrible things.

While he was sitting in Jones' cabin, bells began to ring and clang. Men were blowing cow-horns, and banging on tin pans. He supposed they were for the morning service. "At the same instant," Coffin said, "the whole broadside of the street burst into flames and began raging furiously down Jackson Street." Thick smoke and flames rose far up the hill in the western section. He hurried down to Stuart and Raines where Capt. Raines gave him a trunk to protect. As usual, he was thinking more of others than himself.

"I took the trunk on a wheelbarrow and trundled it away down Front Street," Coffin said. His legs were moving so fast they looked like many legs in a blur. "I had not been there long before the fire came careening down Broadway and Pacific streets, and I was in danger of being enclosed between two fires, and I wheeled my barrow down to the lower end of Pacific Wharf, where for three hours I remained guarding the treasure of a firm in whose store all I had on earth to lose was burnt up six weeks previously."

Flames devoured the fifteen blocks of the city bounded by Sansome and Mason and Washington and Broadway streets, and destroyed every building in the ten blocks between Clay, Broadway, Powell and Sansome streets. The continuous range of wooden buildings houses on the western side of Powell Street changed color from yellow to brown to umber and began to smoke. Winds whipped up tornados of fire and smoke. As fire sucks in oxygen to fuel itself and the heat rises to hundreds of feet, they create spinning tornados of flame, "firenados". The inferno burned the last traces of Colonial San Francisco. Now the only examples of the city's pioneer days existed inside the Ghost Fleet—the ships which had transported hoards of Forty-niners here. The entire district between Pacific and Cunningham's Wharf between Green and Vallejo burned. Many Ghost Fleet hulks serving as buildings were burned to the keels, their piled goods making impressive bonfires.

Only an alteration of the wind's course saved San Francisco. The blaze burnt itself out against a barren hillside. Clouds of steam drifted over acres of blackened shells—the previously untouched northwestern quarter. Twenty-five million dollars' of property had been lost in eighteen months through the fires which The *Annals* called "unquestionably incendiary." Soot-blackened crowds swelled the smoking streets as the populace called for vengeance.

"English Jim! English Jim! English Jim!"

They had had enough. English Jim's life was not worth a farthing.

IN THE COVE, COFFIN was up early on the *Talma*. He stretched, pulled his coat on, and went on deck. He took a deep breath of the air which still harbored a trace of smoke. Things were getting back to normal. Over the foggy water, he heard singing, a concertina playing, a whistle on shore and fog bells producing a cacophony. He followed the music and came to the noisiest craft in Graveyard Harbor. Certainly, other ships in the Cove moaned, groaned, and creaked and bumped and wheezed, but this vessel clanked and whistled louder than all the others combined. Empty drums rolled in its hold. Chains rattled. Bells dangling from its spars stirred with the wind. In storms those dancing bells and fog horns chimed and howled to earsplitting levels.

As he pulled alongside the noisy vessel, he saw a group of bright-clad Chileans on its deck. After a gang of Hounds drove them out of their homes at the base of Telegraph Hill, they found refuge on this ship. To buck themselves up, they sang rousing songs from their homeland. In the distance some US sailors singing chanties on their own vessel picked up the Chilean melody. Soon their combined harmony became beautiful, blending and melding until Coffin turned back to the *Talma*, refreshed and humming the same melody to himself and grateful he had a ship to live on. Others had no home at all.

On land, rent was $3,000 a month for a quickly thrown together, one-story shack of rough boards. Two years earlier, a small, second-story room on the shore had gone for $1,800 a month, payable in advance, and a fifteen-by-twenty-five foot gambling tent in Portsmouth Square had cost its owners $40,000 a year in rent. Little wonder the abandoned ships had attracted so many seeking shelter. Canny landlords not only collected rent on the abandoned vessels, but made tents from their sails and charged rent on those canvas shanties too.

"During the winter of 1850-51," H. H. Bancroft wrote, "over one thousand people dwelt upon the water in buildings resting upon piers and in hulks of vessels."

Coffin spent an uncomfortable night ashore at Allsopp's Clay Street Hotel. He arose early to arrange passage for a friend and watched the Ghost Fleet grow steadily brighter in another golden dawn. Desire for food and fresh water drove him to the pier late that afternoon. Now the sky was threatening and the sea began to kick up. Black clouds swept in. Coffin knew what was coming. With nothing else to do, he thumbed to his list of "Starving Ships," one of the last entries in his *Log* and amplified it. It told of those who had sailed for San Francisco with parsimonious skippers and few rations. The *Pacific's* Capt. Tibbits was the most tightfisted keeper of provisions. Though the hold carried cheese, butter and flour, he dished out salt pork and beef so wormy there were two bugs for every bean. One passenger vomited for twenty-seven days in a row.

Tibbits intended to sell the leftover foodstuff when they reached San Francisco. When passengers complained, he threatened to fire the powder magazine and explode the ship and kill them all if they did not be quiet. After the *Pacific* dropped anchor in the cove, a passenger, relieved to still be alive, exclaimed, "What hills! What an entrance! What a Bay spread out!"

Then, there was the Newburyport brig, *General Worth*, where hard baked biscuit, beef salty as salt itself, and an occasional dish of beans, together with tea and coffee, constituted the bill of fare. When the brigantine *Laura Ann*, an old fashioned tub, lost half its water on the way to San Francisco and was becalmed in tropical summer heat, the crew and passengers survived on rancid meat, wormy biscuits, hard beans, and weevil-infested rice.

"The smell would sicken all but a California emigrant," wrote Roger Baldwin, a passenger.

The *Laura Ann* crept up the Baja coast, the surf so violent they could not put in for water. A Peruvian brig sold them flour, sugar, cheese and lard, but a nearby valley on the nearby shore was so rich in food that the officers and crew deserted and left the passengers to sail the ship the rest of the way. The *Laura Ann* had reached San Francisco just a week before Capt. Coffin's *Alhambra*. A voyage estimated at sixty days had taken her eight months! Baldwin had lost everything by the delay.

"Sharpers, swindlers, speculators, gamblers and rouges of every nation, clime, color, language and costume under the sun," Coffin wrote. "No account you have ever read can give you half an idea. Double everything, and believe that then you know not half."

He knew the true gold of San Francisco and its greatness, was that of its people.

ON FRIDAY, JUNE 27, R. H. Taylor, the senior editor of the *Herald*, was in the District Court of Yuba County during the empaneling of Tom Berdue's jury. "We can safely say," Taylor complained of the trial, "that it was a greater farce than ever was enacted in any circus in the state of California. We were perfectly amazed to hear men, intelligent men, state publicly to the Court, that they were so biased and prejudiced that they could not give the defendant a fair trial. Hosts of men said they had formed an opinion, merely, as I believe, to get themselves excused."

The jury pool was quickly exhausted. Twenty-nine potential jurors in a row, out of thirty-six, were excused for expressing an opinion as to guilt. Finally, Taylor himself was drafted to serve.

"We are caged on the jury in the case of James Stuart alias Thomas Berdue," he apologized to his readers. "We ask for your indulgence as it will occupy nearly all our time for a few days." At last, twelve professed openminded men were chosen and sworn by the clerk who then read the indictment charging Berdue with the murder of Charles E. Moore.

Taylor's eyes strayed to the bench. The highly religious, reed-thin Judge Gordon N. Mott, one of the first judges in the early days of Yuba County, took his seat. For the defense were Francis L. Aud, and R. S. Mesick. For the prosecution were Charles H. Bryan, counsel for the state, and DA Jesse O. Goodwin. Goodwin, a huge landowner in Sutter County, had narrowly escaped death on the Feather River bridge when a runaway team entered the bridge from the opposite end and collided with him.

Berdue sat stock still, stroking his beard. To the jury he appeared "calm and collected," but inside was all in roiling pain and despair. All his savings had been given to Jansen as restitution, leaving him destitute. Whatever property and money he had left had gone to the lawyers.

The first witness called was Colonel Prentiss of Winslow Bar. He looked toward Berdue and inclined his head in his direction. "I feel pretty certain that the prisoner is the same man I saw at Winslow's Bar," he said. "I brought the prisoner to this county on an order from the District Judge of San Francisco. Mr. Broadwater and myself arrived at Dobbins Rancho and he informed me that Moore had not been there."

"You need not state what Mr. or Mrs. Dobbins may have told you," Francis Aud said. "Confine yourself to what you know of your own knowledge."

"I have not spoken of Mrs. Dobbins," Prentiss snapped. "It will be time enough for you to make your objections when women have been brought into question."

"Go on, sir, I only wished to admonish you."

"Hearing that James Stuart had been arrested at San Francisco," Prentiss continued. "I went there for him, believing he was the murderer of Moore. I recognized him among a number of prisoners as being James Stuart. I had seen Stuart before at Winslow Bar and threatened to hang him provided he interfered with a Kanaka I had there. I feel pretty certain the prisoner is the same man I saw at Winslow's bar. I cannot possibly be mistaken. He even moved like English Jim. At the least motion of anyone present, his eyes, head, or body would move with rapidity." Colonel Prentiss attempted to discredit Stokes who had provided Berdue with an alibi the night Jansen was beaten and robbed. "He had an imperfection of sight," he said of Stokes.

"Was the eye a cockeye?" Francis Aud asked.

"Can't say I understand the term," Colonel Prentiss said haughtily. "One eye was more askant than the other."

"I never saw the prisoner till sometime last January," W. W. Dobbins, the ranch owner declared. "He came to my house with a man named Colonel [Utting] and a man by the name of Harris, a packer. They came in the evening and on account of the straying of some mules, stayed at my house two nights and one day." Dobbins had not seen English Jim, but he had seen Tom Berdue. "About the fifth or sixth of December, three men came riding up to my house on sorrel, gray, and black horses. Two of them got off their horses and came into the house to inquire for shot provisions and some other things. 'Are you going into the mountains?' I asked. 'No, we're looking for mules.' They bought a double-barreled fowling piece, some bread, and a bottle of brandy. I saw Moore a short time before the murder. I was at my house when the body was brought there."

Francis Aud elicited nothing material in cross-examination.

Berdue was more worried than ever.

Capt. Wilson corroborated Dobbins' testimony, adding that he had encountered the same three men while searching for Moore. "I recognized them as the men who had been at our house," he said. "They came from the direction of the encampment near where Moore's body was found."

"I believe the prisoner is the one that rode the black mare," asserted Levi Rowley, a resident of Dobbins' Rancho. He pointed to Berdue. When Francis Aud cross-examined Rowley, he added that when he had seen the prisoner at Dobbins' Rancho in January, he thought he had seen him before. "He appeared to recognize me. I was satisfied when the investigation was held before Judge Stidger that he was the same man I had seen at the woodpile at Dobbins Rancho with the two men and coming out of the mountains."

"I am a packer who lives in Marysville and on the road," Mr. Malcomson testified. He did not give his first name and was not asked. He went on. "I was encamped near where Moore was murdered. I saw three men camped nearby and saw the prisoner at that camp and later saw him on the prison ship at Sacramento. I recognized him as the same man."

Mr. Broadwater also swore as to the prisoner's identity and did so at great length. Court adjourned until nine o'clock Saturday morning when Broadwater could complete his testimony.

On June 28, Broadwater was recalled. On cross, he told Francis Aud, "I heard of difficulty between Moore and Stuart, heard Moore say he was afraid to go to Foster's Bar. He was afraid Stuart would kill him." Dr. B. S. Olds, a former deputy sheriff of Yuba County, testified that when he and Mr. Buchanan came to take Berdue to jail, he told him, "If it had not been for false swearing at Sacramento I would not have been in the scrape here."

"I knew the prisoner at the bar at Winslow's Bar in May or June 1850," Jacob Sholet witnessed. "I am sure this is the man. He has a bent finger on one of his hands."

"Would you please examine the defendant's finger?"

Sholet got up, went over and looked at Berdue's finger. He turned and proclaimed that it was the same one. Under Francis Aud's cross-examination, Sholet elaborated.

"He has a ring of India ink on one finger," he said, "and India ink on the back of his hand." He was asked to examine the back of Berdue's hand and testified that the marks there were the same. The jury then examined Berdue's hands. The Marysville court made Berdue stand up several times so the witnesses could see him better. "His voice and accent are the same," they agreed as if one, "as are the color of his eyes and hair." Direct examination resumed and Charles Bryan asked Sholet why English Jim Stuart left Winslow's Bar. "He left on account of stealing money."

On cross, Berdue's attorney Francis Aud asked, "What money was that?"

"It was stolen from Mr. Dodge of Foster's Bar, the amount was $3,000 or $4,000 and he was arrested for stealing the money."

Judge Mott asked him to elaborate further about Winslow's Bar.

"Stuart worked with a pick. George Hunt worked with him, and also Thomas Belt and two or three Frenchmen."

Francis Delaney, one of the Frenchman was called but was absent. The clerk called the next witness, Mr. Chambers.

"I knew English Jim in Sacramento," he said. "The prisoner is the man. Bob Booker knew Jim at Foster's Bar."

Bob Booker testified, "This is the man."

Booker studied Berdue's hands and found a ring of India ink on one of his fingers. His right middle finger was not stiff, but the broad, thick nail of the finger, bent inward over the end of the finger and gave it a short stubby appearance. "Stuart has a rather long scar on his right cheek," Booker said. This could not be authenticated right now because of Berdue's thick beard.

"I know the defendant," Harris the packer said. "I saw him first at Downieville and came down with him and Colonel Utting. I am sure this is the same man. We stopped at Goodyear's Bar one night and at Dobbins, laid by there a day and a half to rest mules."

Aud asked what name he used.

"The prisoner went by the name of Thomas Berdue."

John Longmaker from Winslow's Bar, testified. "I knew him in June or July at Winslow's Bar and talked to him everyday for a week," he said. "I understood James Stuart was in the jail. I went to the jail with Colonel Prentiss and recognized him before the colonel pointed him out."

Mr. Stambaugh was called to the stand next.

"I know James Stuart and last saw him about four months ago."

"Look around," asked the DA. Do you see him here?"

Stambaugh looked around.

"There he is," he said. He went over by himself and picked him out. "I think I cannot be mistaken in his identity."

Francis Delaney finally arrived. The judge glared as he took the stand. Walker acted as his interpreter.

"I know the prisoner as the man who came to employ me to work for Mr. Chalot," he said in a heavy French accent, "and I am sure this is the man. He went by the name of Jim."

Court adjourned for lunch at 11:30 AM.

At 3:00 PM, Officer Charles Stivers was sworn in and gave evidence.

"I was in Sacramento on the 9th of December," Stivers said, "and walking my beat when I arrested James Stuart. He was going under the name James Campbell. Later, I saw the prisoner in San Francisco." Stivers paused, and turned to look toward the jury. He was eager to give them some information. "He is *not* the man. Stuart is a taller man and has a lower forehead. His nose, though, resembles Stuart's."

Sacramento City Recorder Benjamin Franklin Washington was called to the stand. He knew English Jim from multiple appearances before his bench. "On the 27th of November," Washington said, "a man was brought before me for petty larceny and gave his name as James Campbell. I did not commit him. On the 10th day of December I saw him in my office again. He was this time charged with breaking into a lumber yard office. I committed him to the prison brig from which he escaped. I was in San Francisco in February and went to the jail as a matter of curiosity. This man was shown to me and I said then it was not Campbell. Campbell is a taller man and has straight hair. While there is some resemblance, they are two different men."

Capt. Ezra Dodge testified that James Stuart was at Foster's Bar in May and left about the latter part of September. "I knew James Stuart at Foster's Bar," Dodge said, "and I think I could recognize him. This is *not* the man. I think Stuart is older by ten years than the prisoner."

"James Stuart was not one of the mining company then," Frank Randall testified. He had formed a company to mine on April 19, 1850. "In May, he worked for a man who had more than one share. I do not think the prisoner is the same person. Stuart has a higher and broader forehead and was taller."

"I saw James Stuart there," G. W. Tomkins said. He lived eight miles above Foster's Bar and kept the Slate Range House. The prisoner was asked to stand, Tomkins shook his head. "I think he was a taller man. I saw this man on New Year's Day when he stopped at my house with four others. He went by the name 'Tom.'"

"I know Stuart," Henry Hadden declared. "He was a rawboned, stronger-built man and two or three inches taller than the prisoner. I admit that the prisoner somewhat resembles him."

George Prescott had more to say.

"I have resided at Foster's Bar during the last year and was extensively acquainted with him upon Foster and Winslow bars. I have known Jim Stuart first in Panama in the middle of February of last year. I came in the steamer *Senator* to Sacramento. I started on the boat for Marysville early in the morning with Stuart and from there to Foster's Bar. I was employed with him in a company at Foster's Bar and knew him up to the time he was arrested for robbing Dodge. His hair was coarse, straight and black. I think I would know Stuart again. He was five feet nine and a half-inches high. I was measured with him."

On cross-examination, Aud asked Prescott how Stuart got to Panama.

"I don't know how he came," Prescott replied. "I saw the prisoner in jail two weeks ago and I said at the time I could not swear whether this was Stuart or not. Stuart's hair was thin on top. He was slightly bald on the crown of his head."

So was Berdue.

Mrs. Elliot had come to San Francisco on the same ship as Tom Berdue. "I have resided in Auburn, Sutter County, since March 2, of last year," she said. "I came from Sydney, New South Wales, to this country in the ship *Victoria*. I arrived in San Francisco on February 22 of last year. I went on a Monday to the jail to identify the man. I recollected him perfectly as a fellow passenger of the voyage to my mind."

"Would you elaborate?" Francis Aud asked.

"I left Sydney on November 12," she said. "I did not see this man after my arrival in San Francisco."

Now it was Mr. Valley's turn to be questioned. He was sworn. "I worked with Stuart and ate with him from last April to the end of September," he said. "He was a taller and stouter man than the prisoner. I saw this man at Dobbins."

At 5:45 PM, the court adjourned until Monday. Then, the prisoner would be measured exactly and that question answered.

That afternoon, a woman was hanged at Downieville. Her fate gave Berdue the shakes. The night before, a man named Cannan had entered her house and created a disturbance which so outraged her that when he came to apologize the next morning she met him with a large Bowie knife which she plunged into his heart. She was immediately arrested, tried, sentenced, and hanged by 4:00 in the afternoon of the same day. She did not exhibit the least fear, walking up a small ladder to the scaffold and placing the rope around her neck with her own hands, first gracefully removing two plaits of raven black hair to make room for the noose.

"Do you have anything to say?" she was asked.

"Nothing, but I would do the same again if I was so provoked."

On Monday, June 30, at 9:00 AM, Judge Oliver Perry Stidger of Foster's Bar was called. His testimony would be important to the defense. He had tried Stuart a number of different times on several different charges and should know him well. "As I recall I first saw him in May of last year," Judge Stidger said. He thought a moment and looked Berdue over. "The two men are similar," he said, "but English Jim was two-inches taller than the prisoner." He estimated that Stuart was about five feet, nine inches tall. The prisoner was measured by a juryman with a tape. In a moment he was ascertained to be exactly five feet, six and three-quarter inches in height.

"He stood straighter," Stidger continued thoughtfully, "and held his head erect and himself differently." He mentioned Stuart's coarse black straight hair, light blue eyes, low forehead, and large flat nose and something more that went to the core of his personality. "He was a very excitable man. Jim Stuart was much quicker in his motions than the prisoner. His motions were very uncommon. His are quick as a wildcat. And he has a different, darker complexion. I can swear positively that the prisoner is *not* Jim Stuart."

Mr. Falley testified that he knew English Jim at Foster's Bar in July. "The prisoner does not appear to be as strong or tall a man as Stuart," he said. Prescott had testified that English Jim had a scar on the right side of his face and to determine if Berdue had a similar scar, the court ordered the defendant to be shaved before being brought into trial the next morning. Today's testimony was leaning in Berdue's favor. Next, the court was to determine if Berdue had the same scars as English Jim.

On Tuesday, July 1, Berdue came into court with his face completely shaven. A scar of the length of English Jim's was revealed, beginning on the edge of Berdue's jaw on the right side and running down his neck. English Jim had a one-inch scar over his left eyebrow and a one-inch slit over one ear. Berdue had a small slit cut by a knife in his left ear too." Because of his uncanny resemblance to English Jim, historian Herbert Asbury notes, "Berdue had been tried, convicted, and narrowly escaped hanging not once, but twice for crimes in the gold fields that English Jim had actually committed."

There was a logical explanation for identical wounds in the ear. In the mining camps there were only four punishments for a man suspected of stealing: banishment, flogging, hanging (if it was a sturdy rope, the convicted man might be jerked up and down as many times as it took to break his neck), and *ear cropping*—cutting.

D. W. D. Thompson, a Marysville resident, was on Foster's Bar during the time English Jim was there. "The prisoner resembles Stuart," he said but found fault with his memory. "As I think of it," he decided, "Stuart's head was thicker through, measuring from one side to the other near the ear. I think Stuart's hair was lighter. The prisoner's eyes look very much like Stuart's. He sought an explanation. Fear might have changed the expression of countenance."

Henry Carroll had known the prisoner in Sydney, but he had never seen Stuart. He brightened. "But I can comment on the prisoner's real name. "He went by the name of Berdue," he said, "but I never had any acquaintance with him. I saw Berdue in San Francisco September last. I met him in a gambling house." Later he thought of the trial. "Justice and humanity both seem to require it, and in God's name, let justice be done. Let it not be said that Berdue shall suffer the extreme penalty of the law if he be innocent."

Sheriff Malachi Fallon, the sharp-eyed and former marshal of San Francisco, put in his two cents worth. "I am positive that at the time Moore was murdered near Dobbins' Ranch," he said. "Berdue was in San Francisco involved as a 'capper' for a game of French monte and working the shell and ball game."

"I have been in California since a year ago last April," William Casserly said. "I came in the steamer *Tennessee* from Panama. The prisoner resembles a man on board, but I cannot say it is him." He shrugged.

Court was adjourned until 2:00 PM.

In the afternoon Thomas Jones, a prisoner, testified. "I am acquainted with James Campbell, alias English James Stuart, and I've known him seven or eight months. He is taller than me. He has a large nose, and dark straight hair. I last saw him in Sacramento about the end of November or beginning of December. I have not seen him since. I saw him with two men, one with a cock eye. I saw Stuart on a black horse. They said they were going to Foster's Bar." During cross-examination Aud asked Campbell how long he has been in the country.

"About thirteen or fourteen months," he answered. "I stayed in San Francisco for three weeks, went from there to Long's Bar, stayed there one week, and returned to San Francisco in the ship *Gloster*. This man is *not* James Stuart. I saw this man," he motioned toward Berdue, "playing the string and strap game near the post office in Sacramento."

On direct examination, Jesse Goodwin asked Jones why and how long he had been in prison.

"I was imprisoned on accusation of winning money from a party," he said. "I have not been tried and have been in prison for seven or eight weeks."

Court was adjourned until 10:00 AM.

WHEN ENGLISH JIM REACHED San Francisco, his worst fears were realized. He walked over the area twice to convince himself what had happened had happened. The old adobe Custom House had not survived the last fire. He had thought it was indestructible. After a moment of rage and pounding his fist into his palm, he calmed down. He sat on the charcoaled step where Father Taylor gave his sermons on Sunday, and began to think rationally. The gold was still there, only melted. It was still gold. It wasn't going anywhere. They could dig for it at their leisure until a new Custom House was built on Battery Street but who knows how long that would take.

"I saw Kitchen in the El Dorado and went to his house where he used to live," English Jim recalled. "I left all his things at Kitchen's and went to bed." He was exhausted. His dreams were of gold.

COFFIN ADMIRED the range of buildings fronting the town. He noticed that they were connected with the main lands by means of narrow wooden bridges like the catwalks linking the Ghost Fleet ships. New brick warehouses sat on the sandy fill between indestructible Telegraph Hill. The expanding waterfront trembled at a cough. Two brick walls of the United States Bonded warehouse on the corner of Battery and Union tottered and collapsed under the unsettled ground. Coffin had allowed his pipe to go out. He relit it and gazed over the ruins. Along the fragile finger, crosswalks linked the waterfront piers. Shipping companies had constructed warehouses and erected shops on piles. Simple plank thoroughfares linking the wharves rapidly were becoming the cross streets of the lower business district—Drumm, Davis, Front, Battery, and Sansome.

For some time speculators had collected rent on the abandoned hulks in the Cove from the thousands who lived there, and now were looking for more sources of income. Selling parcels of the Cove to land-poor San Franciscans intrigued real estate promoters. Plots of water! General Stephen Watts Kearny, San Francisco's military governor during the colonial period, had invented "water lots." Coffin laughed, sending out clouds of white smoke. "Lots of water! Ha! What a concept!"

Water Lots had come about in this way. One summer in 1847, Gen. Kearney decided to grant the town over four hundred beachfront lots submerged to a depth of twelve-feet. Then he had the city architect, Jasper O'Farrell, survey them. The first 250 lots, measuring roughly 40-by-144-feet were sold for $16 each in a wholesale transfer of land. Underwater lots south of Market Street were a better size—140-feet square. Coffin thought those were something he might purchase, had he a dollar. While doubt existed about the right of the first town council to sell the water lots at auction, the State Legislature confirmed all sales legal. Last November, the city had sold 150 water lots at auction and the following month another 200 went for as low as $200 each.

Coffin consulted a map the newspapers had printed. He estimated that most of the available real estate lay east of Sansome Street, and nearly all of it in those days was a sucking mud flat which was submerged at low tide. This did not shake the passion nor limit the sales of the promoters and swindlers. With the same get-up-and-go energy that had rebuilt the city so many times, greedy political insiders and land speculators intended to build over all 336-acres of Graveyard Harbor. There was no stopping them. They staked out lots in neat rectangular fences in the shallows. At low tide, they showed about three feet above the water.

The sight of such optimistic property lines made Coffin shake his head. Capt. James Folsom, who had purchased so many of the sand lots on the Cove, had been the first to fill in a water lot. Capt. Selim Woodworth, who bought Red Rock, the high Farallone, filled in his lot with crates of sand. As expected, the most voracious speculator of all was Sam Brannan. Early on, he began gobbling up water properties as future lots. He had somehow convinced LDS miners working at Mormon Bar to give their tithe to him to hold in trust. Though he owned fifty-percent of the city, even lent money to the needy Mexican government, he used the tithings of the Church of Latter Day Saints to buy property for himself. When Brigham Young's strongest young men, polite and fastidiously dressed in black, visited to collect the Church's money, Brannan told them, "You go back and tell Brigham Young that I'll give up the Lord's money when he sends me a receipt signed by the Lord and no sooner!"

When Brannan was cast out, he lost their reliable financial base. Undaunted, he opened an office to rent and sell water lots in Graveyard Harbor. His first ad read, "For sale: water lots, with and without improvements." He sold one lot for $40,000 and another for $16,000. In all he profited $160,000 in rentals. Tom Larkin sold eight water lots for over $330,000. San Franciscans would soon pay almost $2 million for one hundred and twenty small lots *under eight-feet-of-water*.

Only after the city sold ninety-six more water lots to satisfy a judgment against Dr. Peter Smith of the City Hospital did the Council ask a salient question:

"How do we build on water?"

No one knew.

Clay and Montgomery streets, the city trash dump, provided the solution. Developers could use the plentiful garbage usually tossed onto the tidal mud flats to fill in grids between the catwalks. They could then add unsold merchandise—rice, tea, nails, pianos, flour, and two shiploads of Spanish brandy. Mixed into the fill were corpses (one or two a day) supplied by the murderers on the Barbary Coast, flesh for the great sprawling skeleton of Graveyard Harbor.

Atop this, they spaded cubic yards of even more plentiful mud. Obviously, the city intended to roll out and over the Ghost Fleet and grow above it. Hearing this, the sight of staked water lots no longer amused Coffin, only made him fearful that his remarkable floating world was about to be buried and lost forever. San Francisco was constantly enlarging its borders, spreading on all sides up the hills, filling in valleys, walking out beyond North Beach, towards the Presidio, to south away towards the Mission, and into the harbor over the water lots, fast filling up the whole shallow part of the Cove in a straight line from Rincon Point on the South to Clark's Point on the East side.

What city can ever arise on the western coast of North America to rival its poetry and mysterious labyrinths and treasures? There is not a point from Puget's Sound to Cape St. Lucas which possesses the possibility of ever becoming a rival to San Francisco. A Chilean gold seeker echoed him. "The Ghost Fleet is a Venice built of pine instead of marble," he said It is a city of ships, piers, and tides. Large ships a good distance from the beach serve as lodgings, stores and restaurants ... The whole central part of the city sways noticeably because it is built on pilings the size of ship's masts, driven down into the mud."

ON WEDNESDAY MORNING, JULY 2, Francis Aud asked Judge Mott for more time for deputy sheriffs dispatched to Downieville and Onion Valley to bring back additional witnesses.

"You've had ample time for the officers to make their return," Judge Mott replied. "It is ordered that unless said return be made by this afternoon, the cause must proceed." He pounded his desk with his gavel. "Court adjourned to 3:00 PM." Everyone hunkered down to wait except Berdue to whom the time seemed to fly when he wanted it to stop.

ENGLISH JIM LEFT KITCHEN'S place and walked out to the Mission to visit an acquaintance who lived at the bakery there. "This acquaintance wished me to rob a Spaniard's house at the Mission," English Jim said. "I went into the Mansion House, saw the safe, and said I would see him again about it. I took the hills on the way back from the Mission to avoid being seen. I headed back toward North Beach to work out the robbery details and think about the gold inside the Custom House, and how it would soon be mine. I might even cut out my partners if I can find a way."

He walked out to Powell and California streets some distance from the Mission Road along an exceptionally hilly and sandy road. The streets had not yet been laid out and California Street encroached upon the city from the West. From this vantage point looking eastward, English Jim saw a panoramic view of the Ghost Fleet and the distant Contra Costa hills. It was blazing hot. He had hurried away so quickly, he had left empty handed. He needed money and a hat and coat. All he had left was his glib tongue.

At 9:00 AM, James Adair left his small house at the head of steep California Street. Between 10:00 and 11:00 AM, someone had stolen a small carpet bag and a China-blue trunk bound with brass from his home. John Brady's house was about a hundred feet from Adair's, and he told Adair that about 10:00 AM, he had been working on his woodpile when he saw a man at his door.

"He had on white pants and a light coat or shirt sleeves," Brady explained. "My reason for looking at him so particularly was that he looked so much like the pictures of English Jim Stuart. When I saw him, he was within two feet of your house, and seemed to be skulking along. About one hour later, I heard a commotion. Wes Dwiggins had returned and discovered someone had broken into his home, and stolen a trunk containing valuables and clothing including shirts. At first, he thought it might have been an inside job. The robber had known where to find the trunk key inside his vest pocket and where to find forty dollars in cash in the carpet bag."

Tappan Kilburn was working on his house 150 feet away. "I was going up to the house with some cooking utensils for Mr. Perry," he said, "and I met the owner of the trunk, Wes Dwiggins. The piece of iron used to smash the door lay on the path right where I could see it.

"There was another man with me," Kilburn said, who first saw this man standing on a knoll gazing upon the city and he called me to him and told me to go speak with the stranger. After going through the valleys and hills I met the man and thought that he looked suspicious. He was bearded and wearing a linen shirt over a gray woolen shirt, a light-colored English-cut coat, well-fitting pantaloons tucked inside his boot tops, and a narrow-brimmed round-top hat. A Bowie knife and Colt revolver of fine finish was fastened to his belt. He continued walking. I suggested that Dwiggins watch where he went so we could find him if need be. I then ran down to my woodyard and called to some men working there to go with me and look through the bushes for the burglar." The woodworkers told him about a suspicious stranger "of symmetrical build with bright burning eyes, hissing speech and biting smile."

"I immediately started for the places where I thought most likely the things he had stolen would be concealed." Four of the men began searching for the thief uphill and poking into the chaparral where vagrants sometimes hid under blankets to sleep away the summer. The district was filled with sand hills and hollows and matted with dwarf oaks and there were plenty of places to stash loot. As they pawed the underbrush, they surprised a flock of quail in the undergrowth. They flew up in their faces. The going was tough, and the searchers were soon sweating.

English Jim, catching their gaze, hurried away in the opposite direction. He was understandably wary of any attention and crouched down in some tall bushes until it was safe to go ahead, meet with Kitchen to work out the final details for the Custom House robbery and assemble the men to dig from inside the Veranda. Jim was retiring stealthily, when he spied a group of four strangers approaching in the middle of the block. He was caught between them two teams of searchers. He slipped furtively behind a bit of scrub oak in the sand hills near Powell and Stockton and waited. Surprisingly, for such an unflappable man, English Jim was having trouble catching his breath. Was this what fear was like? he wondered.

Dwiggins and the searchers began beating the bushes and pawing through clumps of milkweed and brush. They had arrived at midpoint between Powell and Stockton streets when they caught a bit of a man hunched down in the overgrowth of bushes.

"Come out of there," they ordered.

The searchers observed that he had a bundle by his side and that his jacket, white shirt and light brown pants were still creased and had folds in them as if they had just been taken from a trunk minutes earlier. This led them to suspect he was the thief and had discarded his own suit and replaced it for clothes from the missing chest. "I called him to stop," Dwiggins said, "and he turned and stood still until I came up to him a quarter-mile to a half-mile from the Adair house. My suspicions were aroused because the man's breath was very short. We called to him and requested that he come toward us and give an account of himself."

He did.

"Good day, stranger."

"Good day," English Jim replied.

"Have you seen anyone in your travels?"

"I saw two or three."

"Did they have anything with them?"

"One had a handkerchief with something in it."

"Do you live about here?"

"No."

"What are you doing in this neighborhood?"

English Jim explained that he was only walking back to San Francisco from Mission Dolores after seeing John Stephens, a cousin who baked at the Mission and lived there. He claimed he was walking toward North Beach where he lived, but refused to give the address.

"Well, you've chosen a damned pretty way to come from the Mission," snapped one man. "This is not the road. Two houses have been robbed nearby this morning. Where did you get the clothes you have on?"

"What! The devil! Who are you to question me?" English Jim said.

His hands shot toward the fourteen-inch long Bowie knife at his side. His motions were "quick as a wildcat," but instantly two cocked pistols were at his head. In Gold Rush San Francisco everyone was armed. He removed his hands from the blade. Now the expressions were reversed. Now it was English Jim who looked frightened and confused.

"I am on my way from the Mission to North Beach to meet my friend Kitchen and his wife," he said. English Jim relaxed as he began to lie, lying was his natural state of being, fear was not. He denied he had stolen a trunk, which was true, and insisted he had not changed clothes for some days, which was not true. "I know nothing of your robbery," he said. "These clothes I have worn ever since I left Sonora." That was one hundred miles away. "I saw someone with a bundle but a moment since disappeared over that hill. I tell you I am not the one you are looking for."

"Listen to me, my friend," one of the men, a painter, said. "You say you have worn these clothes from Sonora and that you have walked some distance this morning. That is not true. The weather is warm. The roads are dusty." He pointed to English Jim's shiny patent-leather boots. "Your boots are not sufficiently travel-stained with dust, your linen shirt is clean, and the woolen overshirt you wear carries yet the creases of its original folding and storage in a trunk."

They studied English Jim's high forehead, well-groomed beard and mustache and long, curving hair and erect bearing. His features had an intellectual cast. His mouth was compressed and his chin was narrow and pointed. His motions were so confident that the men began to doubt this was their thief. They were moving on when they saw John Brady approaching. He had just located the empty blue China trunk in some thick bushes when he saw his neighbors walking up the unruly and overgrown California Street hill.

Brady hurried after them to alert them. He stopped running when he saw they had stopped ahead and were holding a slender man with an auburn mustache and beard and long hair like the traditional portraits of Jesus. He had a high forehead and aquiline nose and stood very erect. As Brady drew up to them, he immediately took the man for Berdue whom he knew and who had recently been convicted of murder in an interior county and was being held for trial and almost certain execution there.

"Why, Berdue," Brady cried, astonished to see him, "how did you get out?"

"My name is not Berdue," English Jim replied sullenly.

In a flash it dawned on Brady that this well-proportioned, thirty-one year must be the real English Jim Stuart. He had disguised himself by growing a mustache and beard, but his features had the same compressed mouth and slightly outward-jutting chin as English Jim's. The growth of beard was the same.

"Then, is your name not Stuart?"

"No."

"Well, I think your name is Stuart, and I'll bet that you will not dare to accompany us to the rooms of the Vigilance Committee. If you are an honest man you have nothing to fear."

"I will take that bet," English Jim said confidently. "Sure, I'll go there with pleasure. I'm anxious to get a look at that far-famed institution." He piled the compliments.

His captors agreed and they headed to the western side of Battery Street between California and Pine. Stuart walked confidently, chatting as they walked. He acted as if he would not be identified. After all, he knew Berdue would be convicted of the crimes that he himself had committed, and would be executed in a few days. He just had to run the clock out.

Upon arriving at Battery Street, English Jim saw the *Tecumseh* storeship ahead and then the Hq of the hanging men. He studied the two heavy beams projecting ominously outward above its windows into the street and felt a few qualms which he effectively suppressed. He and the men climbed the narrow steps to the illegal Vigilance Committee rooms. The Committee's newly modified second story rooms were more secure than Devil Jack's jail, and more spacious, measuring sixty-feet by eight. Two smaller rooms had been partitioned off, one as a jail and the other for a meeting room for the five hundred Vigilantes.

English Jim had favorably impressed Vigilante James Dow by his apparent frankness, intelligence, fine language, coolness, and attractive personality. After all, Dow thought, the man's features did suggest the traditional pictures of Christ and that was a face to be believed. Another member of the Committee described their captive as exceedingly handsome. He had enthralled them.

It was now 1:00 PM. Earlier that morning, President Sam Brannan of the Vigilance Committee had written the Marysville Vigilance Committee. "We are very desirous to receive the person of Stuart," he said, "the assassin of Jansen, and if you can render any assistance by securing him there, we'll send a committee up to receive him from you."

Brannan wanted to be the one who hung English Jim who was closer than he knew.

On the hill, English Jim smiled at the gathered men and gave his name as William Stephens. Vigilante George E. Schenck, a commission merchant, noted that the suspect's answers were so prompt, his manner so open, and his emotions so cool, even courageous that he thought they should release him at once and said so. Schenck was a reliable, respected man from an old Dutch family of Amsterdam. He had been one of the two holdout jurors for acquittal during Berdue and Windred's San

Francisco trial. Vigilante Fred Woodworth also suggested that they let the suspect go.

The members were so impressed by Jim's beautifully crafted alibi that they wrote it into the official Vigilante records: "When interrogated he gave his name as William Stephens or Stevens, denied his connection with the theft for which he was arrested, and again tried to establish an alibi by stating that he had that morning walked back from San Francisco to the Mission Dolores and back again."

Such a story may be true. They had no reason to doubt it because the Marysville authorities had English Jim in jail and were sure to execute him in a few days if Sam Brannan didn't get his hands on him first. Logically, this man could not be English Jim. What a foolish mistake they had made.

"Either let him go," demanded Woodworth, "or lock him up overnight." Everyone now agreed that the man who called himself Stephens should be freed. English Jim smiled. He could always talk his way out of anything. At his most charming he picked up his bundle and started toward the door. He had a robbery to commit and a tunnel or two to complete and men to frame. No one would catch him now. The gears of his master plan began to turn as if oiled. It was all coming together. Soon his lookalike would be dead and he would have all the city's gold in his hands. He had committed murder and more and was about to go free. English Jim started for the door. He took the first step, then the second, and then . . .

IN MARYSVILLE, THE TRIAL was coming to an end. Before night, all the jurors except one had turned over to the side of the people. Two or three times the jury asked for instruction from the Judge. They hung fire on reasonable doubt which, if they entertained it, they were to find for the defendant according to the common law and the statute law of California. The jury was locked up for twenty-four hours and would remain in court all night.

It was now Thursday. The jury was split four for acquittal and eight for conviction. The cry went up to lynch Berdue anyway. After more deliberations, they reached a verdict of guilty and the prisoner was sentenced to be hanged. Francis Aud asked that the jury be polled. The clerk went over the list of the jurors, calling each name and each juror if guilty was his verdict, all answering in the affirmative—Locke, Taylor the reporter, Lester, Pixley, Bean, Tompkins, Carey—till the name of J. D. Arthur was called. When he arose, he remarked that he had doubt whether the defendant was English Jim Stuart or not. He stated that the entire jury doubted, but he did not believe he had a reasonable doubt. Therefore, he would agree to the verdict. The balance of the names were then called, and they all answered guilty. And that was that. The verdict was ordered by the court to be immediately recorded, which was done.

The defendant was sentenced to be hanged on Monday.

Berdue only looked serene now that the worst had happened. "We could not notice the least change of a muscle in his face," Tayor wrote, "and we must that the appearance was far from being that of a hardened villain listening to the fiat deciding his fate. Not a word was spoken by the defendant or his counsel."

Berdue was ordered to be remanded to jail. His lawyer, Aud. called at the jail. Berdue offered his hand to him, and then to Mr. Mesick. With tears in his eyes, Berdue thanked them both kindly for having defended him, then clenched his hands in prayer, dropped to the floor, and looked to Heaven. As he did, he protested his innocence.

"If I was given one million dollars and sent out of the country free," he said, "I could not say where Mr. Jansen's store was in San Francisco. I am innocent of the murder charged against me."

He remarked that death had no terrors for him any longer and he was perfectly ready to die and wished to be executed right then and there. He said he had been seized in San Francisco as Jim Stuart and came near to being hung there for a thing he knew nothing of. He had been cursed, hated, and madly abused till his friends had abandoned him. His friends feared retaliation by the Sydney Ducks, the powerful Australian gang of deported ex-convicts. His enemies were afraid not to convict him because they feared reprisal by the deadly Vigilantes who never let truth stand in their way. They were afraid to ask him to render him any little assistance for fear of being insulted, mistreated, and suspected of being "Sydneyites."

"All I want done for me is a letter written to my poor wife," he said, "informing her of my ill fate, and that she inform my father in England."

ENGLISH JIM WAS ON HIS WAY downstairs when one of the Vigilantes stopped him on the thirteenth step. He looked Jim over and pointed out his fourteen-inch long Bowie knife and his pistol under his coat and a few other things that had been bothering him. Now that he thought about it, the prisoner's clean clothes belied his assertion that he had worn them during a long, dusty walk from Sonora. This aroused fresh suspicion. There was no way to get around it. To come down on the side of caution, the hanging men decided to hold Jim overnight. They turned and all went back upstairs. English Jim was still smiling. As Wednesday night fell he put his feet up and chatted amicably with them, claiming to be William Stephens from Brighton, Sussex, England. Like a great spider he spun a story replete with astonishing detail, the mark of a great liar.

"Left London in 1835 for Canada in the ship *Sophia*," he reeled off, "was sixteen years old when I left England, was apprenticed to a tailor in Brighton and went to work at tailoring when I arrived at Montreal, left Montreal two and a half years ago for Charges, arrived here in the American bark, *J. W. Coffin*, from Panama, had ninety passengers, arrived here in November or December, 1849, went to Southern mines, has worked the last five months at Sullivan's Creek; two months on the Tuolumne, four months at Savage's Creek on the Mariposa [River]."

Now, he added some new material.

"I arrived in this city last night," he said, "and walked here via Livermore's Ranch, where I have a horse and mule; they have been there this past six months. I slept last night on North Beach. A man by the name of Kitchen showed me the house; [he said he had known Kitchen, a boatman, since last November] do not know the occupants; I know of nothing detrimental to the character of Kitchen. He named people who could vouch for him: Capt. Henry Ravenon, and two Canadian brothers by the name of Wilson cutting wood on the other side of the Bay.

"Went to the above named place with Kitchen a little after, about nine o'clock. Went to bed about ten o'clock and did not go outside during the night and got up this morning soon after daylight, near about five o'clock, went over to the Mission, arrived about six and remained until ten. Left the Mission and took the road over the hills, thinking it was the nearest road; saw two men with only one bundle, was questioned by four men whether I had seen any parties carrying a trunk. Told them I saw two men with a bundle. They told me there had been a house robbery and pointed the house out to me. I know nothing further of the charge of robbery or of any person connected with it."

W. A. Thorp, who had seen English Jim when he was confined at the station house under the name of James Briggs and some other name for stealing a safe and hightailing it out the backdoor, believed he also went by the name Briggs.

"He looks a little like Berdue," Thorp said, thoughtfully. He stroked his chin. "I think Stephens is an inch or so taller than Berdue, hair about the same color. Stephens wears his hair and whiskers longer than when I first knew him. At the time I took persons into the prison to see Berdue, I saw the prisoner Stephens there."

Soon English Jim drifted off into blameless sleep in his cell. The watching men, looking through the bars, could plainly see there was obviously nothing on the prisoner's conscience and began to doubt themselves more than they doubted the prisoner.

ON THURSDAY JULY 3, at the exact moment the Marysville jury was entering the courtroom to render their verdict as to Berdue's guilt, John Sullivan, the small Whitehall taxi boatman who had captured Simpton the Miscreant, rose to go on guard duty at Vigilante Headquarters. After he had taken down the burly Simpton, he had joined Wakeman's Water Police.

He was tired after a long shift when he arrived at the Committee rooms. He stopped at the desk. Sergeant at Arms Jackson McDuffee checked his badge. "V. C. NO. 269, yep," he said and patted him down before stationing him as a door guard. Sullivan wasn't offended. He knew the Vigilantes didn't trust him even though many of them didn't know him. Truly a part of the Ghost Fleet, Sullivan had a wide acquaintance with the rough element on the waterfront.

Van Bokkelen's memorandum said of him: "Knows too many men of bad character—would recommend that he be not trusted too much." Sullivan, as the Committee's official boatman, had also run up a bill of "appalling magnitude." Now he made up for that. The first thing Sullivan did upon arriving was to open the door into the next room and peek in to see who they were detaining in the cells since he would be guarding him. Crouching in a corner of the room was a man with a familiar face.

"Halloo, Jim!" Sullivan said. "How come you here?"

"I don't know you," English Jim said, and turned away.

"You needn't pretend not to know me," Sullivan said. "I know who you are. I worked for you at Foster's Bar."

Sullivan closed the door, sauntered into the next room, and went up to Schenck.

"Do you know who you've got in here, boys?" Sullivan said loudly. "No, who?"

"Why you have got English Jim, he who murdered the sheriff of Auburn and I was present when he was about to be lynched at Marysville, when the rope broke and he escaped. I knew him well as I worked for him six months and there's no mistake about it!"

A cheer went up from the other men in the room at the unexpected capture of one of the great villains of California. Then, one of the Vigilantes thought suddenly of poor Berdue and looked to the clock. How much time did the mistaken man have left? All of them realized the truth. They had condemned an innocent man to death. It might already be too late. G. E. Schenck rushed down the stairs into the street to locate Watson, one of the three dissenting jurors in the Jansen case who had voted for acquittal. Ironically, Schenck had been partially responsible for the arrest of John Simpton "the Miscreant," and was present at his disastrous hanging in the Square. That had bothered him. Now, he could set things right and this time save an innocent man from hanging, but only if he hurried. Fortunately there were five or six others in town who could also identify English Jim. Even if he reached Marysville in time, he still had to convince the authorities there of the truth.

A T 3:00 PM, THAT SAME DAY, the Marysville court officially set Monday, July 7, as the date for the execution of "James Stuart, alias Thomas Berdue," guilty of killing Charles Moore by shotgun."

Berdue had three days to live.

In San Francisco, Stephen Payran, the Committee's most skillful inquisitor, began to probe English Jim about the Jansen robbery, and the Foster's Bar murder and any other crime he could think of. Payran had replaced Sam Brannan as general president of the Executive Committee and was "painstaking, cautious," and indefatigable in preparing precise reports. He was the antithesis of Sam Brannan who would hang first and think afterwards. He found Jim's conversation intelligent, logical and interesting.

"I don't see how any of this applies to me," English Jim said unconcernedly, "my name is Stephens."

English Jim then changed the subject and, showing emotion for the first time, railed against another group that he considered far worse than the much-maligned Sydney men.

"The Pike County people," he said, "that is to say emigrants from the Missourian frontier are as bad a lot as any from Australia. In intelligence they are little above the beasts. Why, I have seen their skin-cracked, tangle-haired, barefooted, bag-breasted and alkali-seasoned women take from a store a whole barrel of salt port, just as if they had bought it and carry it to their camp and open and eat it before the very eyes of the trader. They are blockheaded and base bunglers like these that bring discredit on a country."

As he continued speaking, full of venom, he persistently separated himself from that "criminal English Jim Stuart," claiming he had been mining and trading and was going to stock a ranch he owned in San Luis Obispo County and should really get on that and not be bothered with this English Jim business.

Finally, Payran had enough of the sneers, and condescending manner. His tone changed from conversational to severe questioner. He fixed his eyes directly on English Jim and leaned into him. He was shaking with rage. Enough!

"Stuart, I am perfectly well aware that every word you have told me is false," he said, "but I shall get the truth from you before I am through. By God, I will."

Momentarily a glare flashed from Jim's eye, then dimmed, as he began to inch toward the loaded revolver on the table. English Jim's aristocratic hand had the same energy and quickness as its owner. As if he had not noticed, Payran inched out as carefully with his own hand, and casually slipped the pistol into the table drawer and slid it closed.

"Do I understand you to affirm you are not the man called James Stuart," he continued as if he noticed nothing, "and that you are not guilty of the crimes of robbery and murder?"

"Most emphatically I do!"

Payran signaled the sergeant-at-arms to bring in the witnesses from the other room.

Stuart looked up and saw George Mason from Foster's Bar and Charles Hughes who was present at Stuart's trial for the robbery of Dodge, and even George Hunt who knew his voice.

"Stuart, do you know any of these men or any one of them?"

"I do not," English Jim said, but his voice was thicker now.

"Did you ever see this gentleman before, or this man," Payran asked. Jim admitted he knew the man. "State where and under what circumstances you have seen him."

"I saw him at Sacramento while undergoing trial for housebreaking," he hissed. Then another witness was brought in and another. Now English Jim refused to speak at all.

Schenck had been busy all afternoon raising funds to send an express messenger thundering almost 150 miles north to the Marysville court to prevent Berdue's hanging on Monday. The rider carried a note from the San Francisco Vigilance Committee asking the Marysville authorities to send their important witnesses to San Francisco to examine the "Prisoner Stephens." The Vigilantes waited impatiently. They might have a big fish to hang, the biggest of all, or they might not.

BY THE NEXT DAY Friday, July 4, Berdue had lost all hope. He had stopped pacing his cell and lay on his bed watching a square of bright blue outside his window. Now that he was to be executed on Monday, and no doubt about that, he asked that writing paper be brought to him so that he could write a last despairing letter to a friend, John Goff. With a shaking hand he signed it, "Yours truly but very unfortunate, Thomas Berdue."

"Why would no one believe him?" he lamented and began to sob.

Unaware of the secret drama inside a lonely Marysville cell, San Francisco was wildly celebrating the Fourth of July. Coffin felt like enjoying the day alone. He left the intoxicated revelers, and climbed to the top of Telegraph Hill where, in the high wind, he opened his watercolor box and painted his second birds-eye view of the city and, of course, the Ghost Fleet. When he was done, he listed the street names across the bottom and descended to join the patriotic celebrations on the piers. On Long Wharf he ran into Maj. Braman whom he had met in Marysville during one of his river trips.

"I propose to buy you a ship," he said, "and lay her on for Panama for passengers. If you will look round and find a suitable ship and would take charge of her, I will find the means. You may take what interest you choose. I will meet you at 10:00 AM tomorrow at our friend's store."

Coffin was not as enthusiastic about the proposition as he should be, but it would provide him some work and might drive away the blues which his favorite holiday had not. It would also allow his escape from Graveyard Harbor. He quickly found a suitable ship that could be had cheap. The next morning, Saturday, July 5, he showed up for the meeting, but there was no sign of the Major, only a stranger who handed Coffin a note:

> "DEAR SIR:—By the advice of friends I have concluded not to engage in the enterprise we talked of yesterday, and I leave in the steamer at noon. Hoping that you will, etc., I am, dear sir, Yours Truly, CHAS BRAMAN."

"I have been trained in the school of disappointment," Coffin wrote, "but coming upon this as I did at a time of unusual depression, I was but poorly able to bear it." An hour later, he decided it had been for the best. His hope had been crushed before he could become fully engaged in an unpleasant business.

The mood was brighter over at Vigilance Committee Headquarters. Witnesses had been arriving from Marysville all morning. One by one they confronted the prisoner and each identified him as English Jim Stuart without exception.

"My name is Stephens," the prisoner replied each time, cool, confident, and apparently frank. "I don't know any of these people." Now doubt was in the air. The Vigilantes suspected that English Jim expected to be rescued by his gang. They posted more guards.

AT 9:00 AM, SHERIFF DEVIL JACK rowed out to the *Euphemia* which was being repaired for repossession by her creditors. The carved figure of Justice on her prow held her scales in the direction of a dockside saloon as if making a toast. "Here's to Injustice," she said. Devil Jack pushed back his hat and visualized escaping convicts slipping over the side into the cold waters and swimming away. How would icy water feel on open wounds made by fists and whips for the guards there were the cruelest anywhere ? How many runaways had survived and how many still-manacled bodies would he find floating between ship corridors or lodged under the docks?

An hour later, the sheriff heard a shot echo over the water and headed north where a family was cooking over a small fire on the deck of a houseboat. Astern, he glimpsed an escapee just losing himself in the fog, the Cove's greatest asset to concealment. Devil Jack had had enough. At 1:00 PM, he transferred the remaining sixty-eight *Euphemia* prisoners to his overcrowded station house lockup. After the public subscription had fallen short, the City had ceased to upgrade the jail. Thus, it was only partially complete when Devil Jack moved in the *Euphemia* convicts. For some time, he had been contributing his own money to feed the convicts, but now was compelled to raise the last $15,000 from his savings and from private sources.

That afternoon the city towed the *Euphemia* around to North Beach as the town's floating "lunatic house and receptacle for the insane" to confine "any suspicious, insane or forlorn persons found strolling about the city at night." The odious prison ship would float for years at Battery and Sacramento, an odd place for a ship that used to sail the China Trade for Henry Skinner and his rambunctious crowd. The *Euphemia* would never outlive her reputation as a "Calcutta Hole." Eventually she would be sold for a mere $70 to pay for one creditor's judgment against the city, then allowed to rot, sink into the Bay and be covered over by landfill.

ENGLISH JIM'S POWERS OF PERSUASION must have been failing him. No one believed him, any more than they had believed Berdue. English Jim had claimed he had a cousin who baked at the Mission, John Stephens, who could vouch for him. In the afternoon, the Committee took Jim there by rented coach to check his story. For protection, four guards rode before and after the defendant's coach.

It was a wasted trip. No one at either of the two Mission bakeries knew a John Stephens. English Jim was returned to his cell. Bluxome, Stephen Payran, and Jacob Van Bokkelen had been appointed to examine those who came to the door of the Committee rooms. "We went out and found Frank Pixley, a notorious defender of criminals, and dragged him into the Committee Room," Bluxome said.

Pixley, now City Attorney of San Francisco, had gotten English Jim off twice in the past, once with paid perjured testimony by his confederate, Old Jack. "Pixley, will you say on your word of honor, if this is the man whom you have defended time and again in the lower courts?" Jake Van Bokkelen asked.

"I will, gentlemen," he replied.

Van Bokkelen administered the oath. Then, they all went into the prisoners room. English Jim was chained at the wrists and legs and sitting on a long oak bench. The moment he saw Pixley he started to stand. He thought his deliverance had come. Plainly, they recognized each other.

"Is that Stuart or not?"

"You have no authority to ask me any questions," Pixley said suddenly. "You are an illegal body."

The others heard what was going on through the thin partition. Grabbing ropes and tackle, they shouted, "Hang him! Hang Pixley!"

If Van Bokkelen had not pushed Pixley down the stairs and rolled him into the street, he would have been hanged. On Sunday, July 6, word that the Committee had arrested a man suspected of being English Jim reached Marysville. An *Alta* article reported that "a man suspected to be Stuart has fallen into the hands of the San Francisco Vigilance Committee and they have been collecting evidence against him. He has also been identified as one of the robbers of the Custom House at Monterey. It is pretty well settled that the man now in possession of the committee is the real Jim Stuart, the murderer of Moore and one of the worst desperadoes that ever was found in this or any other country. If the evidence becomes positive Berdue will be returned here to serve out his fourteen years imprisonment."

Berdue had less than twenty-four hours to live. Aud and a deputy headed for San Francisco.

While everyone was discussing the killer's possible fate, Pixley secured a warrant directing Devil Jack to bring English Jim to a lawful court where he would be safe from lynching. This brought the Sheriff into direct opposition with the Committee which refused to give up their prisoners with the view of extorting some clue to their other associates. Devil Jack searched their guardroom on the second floor with no success. The Committee had decided to shift English Jim to different locations all over San Francisco to keep him hidden from authorities.

Devil Jack trailed a carriage part way to Mission Dolores to get a bead on where the prisoner was secreted, but got nowhere. After telling the court he could not locate English Jim, the sheriff decided to question Ned Wakeman, the inefficient, former captain of the Citizen's Water Police. As the Vigilante's executioner, Wakeman had to know where English Jim was concealed. Devil Jack knew the Pirate was presently docked at Long Wharf. He knew Wakeman by sight since he had earlier attached his new side-wheeler steamer, *New Orleans*, for a $65,000 lien. At the time, the sheriff had been told of Wakeman's propensity to run his ship out of harbor after an official placed an attachment against him. Concerned Wakeman might flee, he stationed a lookout over the ship. "I want you to tell me when Wakeman has the steam up and is about to sneak out," Devil Jack ordered.

It was hard to keep track. Two years earlier the *McKim* out of New Orleans and the *Senator*, a speedy paddle-wheeler and greatest moneymaker boat on the Bay, and eight others had been the only steamers. Now, a hundred side-wheelers were humping up the harbor waters. Capt. Ned Wakeman, that wily Pirate, had spanked them all.

When the word came from a messenger that it looked as if Wakeman was going to take a trip aboard the *Orleans* and had a full head of steam up, Devil Jack had rushed to the scene.

"Let that line alone!" he ordered a young sailor handling the mooring.

"Who are you?" the sailor asked.

"I am the Sheriff of this county. Get away from there as quick as you can."

The sailor ran below and fetched Wakeman who came boiling onto deck and reached for the line. In a cold, even voice Devil Jack repeated his command.

"Wakeman, you must let that line remain where it is."

"Suppose I choose to cast it off, what then?"

"I will kill you," said Devil Jack, quietly.

There was no mistaking the look in the Texas Ranger's eye. As Wakeman kept his hand on the hawser, Devil Jack rested his on the butt of his famous original Colt that had gunned down so many foes. For a full minute both men locked eyes.

"I believe you would, by God!" Wakeman said, removing his hand. That had been the end of that.

Devil Jack obtained a rowboat and was pulling toward Wakeman's ship to question him again when he met him halfway in a large boat being pulled by several sailors. Wakeman was in a rush, so the two men conversed as the two boats raced each other. The Pirate did not want to be bothered and grew more irritated as they flew.

"Lay into your oars," Wakeman told his men.

In response, Devil Jack rowed faster.

"What's wanting," said Wakeman in a low voice.

He looked at the sheriff, making a trumpet with his hand at his ear as if to hear. The two boats pulled side by side for minutes as each of the combatants grew more obstinate and angrier. Devil Jack knew if he reached for his gun to force Wakeman's men to halt he would fall behind in the race, so he rowed faster. As they approached Long Wharf, Devil Jack put on a burst of speed, then sprang to the nearest pile and leaped into the other boat where he confronted Wakeman with his questions about English Jim's whereabouts. Wakeman did know, but was not telling. He was due at the Farallon Islands thirty miles off the Golden Gate to check on a rumor that gangs were using the islets as a rendezvous. He left Devil Jack unsatisfied and still needing answers.

At the Square, he asked the crowds for information about English Jim so he could rescue him from certain death at the hands of the Committee. Now the murderer was no longer a quarry but a man the sheriff had to save. Again, no one would aid him, mostly because English Jim was widely disliked and feared. English Jim wasn't worried. Berdue's time had run out.

On Monday, July 7, the day he was to be executed, Berdue resolved himself to being hanged for a fourth time for crimes committed by English Jim Stuart. Then, something English Jim hadn't counted on occurred. Key members of his gang who were being questioned by the Committee, began to turn informant to gain immunity for their confessions.

Sam Whittaker was first. His confession was not a simple recitation of crimes, but was interspersed with philosophical reflections on mankind and ethics. When he was brought into the Committee room, Payran examined him with his usual curt manner, but got nowhere. Whittaker was a gentleman and expected to be treated like one.

Garrett Ryckman could see that Payran had been drinking. The fifty-three year old drew him aside and said, "Payran, this won't do. That is no way to examine this man. You cannot intimidate him. Do you not see that he is strong-willed, fearless, and of iron nerves?"

Payran agreed.

"Whittaker," Ryckman began when they were alone in the same room, "what must be the feeling of your father, mother, sisters, when they learn of the awful acts and end of one they love: convicted and executed for infamous crimes in a foreign land? Think of it—misery, disgrace, death!"

"Oh, God!" he cried, and began to sob. "I have been bad, very bad, but let me tell you about it."

"Stop," Ryckman said, stunned. He raised his palm to tell him to halt. "Listen to me. Do not make any confession with the expectation that it will mitigate the least of your punishment if you are found guilty. I feel for you, but feeling and duty I divorced before entering upon this mission."

"I understand."

Ryckman left Whittaker alone in the Committee room, sent in a mug of ale, then stood where he could watch him unobserved. Whittaker seemed to be suffering "a great agony of mind," he said. After an hour, Whittaker sent word through the doorkeeper to Ryckman that he had to see him.

"What is the matter, Whittaker?" Ryckman asked as he entered and sat down beside him.

"My Ryckman," he said, "you are the first man who ever touched my heart. The world has hunted me as if I were a monster. You alone have spoken to me as to a human being. I must make a confession to you, if not I shall burst."

The first words out of his mouth were of others.

"As to the Jansen case," he told Ryckman, "Berdue and Windred are both innocent."

Ryckman wrote this down, and circled the comment.

"The man Stephens is Long Jim as I call him, or English Jim as you call him. To satisfy you, I will tell you about it. Long Jim struck the blow; the man who was shot in robbing the house at Sacramento was the man who entered Jansen's first. There were seven men concerned in the robbery of Jansen. They divided the money in the Hogan's parlor. After paying for drink, there was $246 left for each of them." Then, Whittaker told him of his life and his crimes in San Francisco, frankly and truthfully.

He spoke freely of his offenses. It is the most remarkable of all the Vigilante documents. English Jim had confessed in hopes of leniency. Whittaker had no hope of reprieve by his frankness at the expense of others.

Two men Whittaker refused to name had recently endeavored to get him to join them in robbing the El Dorado and the present Custom House using English Jim's plan. "I was afraid to trust them, otherwise I would have joined them." He wanted to unburden his conscience knowing full well "that even honesty would not save him from the penalty of his sins" Now that he had been warned it would have no effect, but spoke frankly all the same.

Once started, words flowed with fluency. Stuart's narrative was a plain recital of events, Whittaker's narrative was interspersed with reflections on the men that he described. At first he blamed society and gave instances of injustice to show that a thief had a better chance in life than an honest man.

He had become embittered because he had so often successfully and easily corrupted officials. Unlike English Jim, Whittaker spoke of his confederates in human terms, describing their moral and physical with equal facility. Little touches of personality came alive before his eyes "with startling realism."

He began with Belcher Kay. "He's ignorant, and a dandy. The others are bungling. One is a convict without doubt, and another might be an incendiary, but that report is a rumor. Now John Darke is a thief on his own hook. Dick Smith, is a friend of convicts and of police. He could be depended upon to provide straw bail. And Kitchen is worse, he is a rough, boatman-looking fellow, dirty, very dirty. unclean, and physically repulsive. George is round-shouldered, a thief, a receiver of stolen goods. Another was pockmarked and dirty-looking."

Finally, he came to Mrs. Hogan. His voice softened and filled with affection. He spoke of the lavish presents he had made her, and of her determination to never go back to her husband. "To do her justice," he said ardently, "I must say she done all in her power to break up my associations, and to lead a different life."

Mary Ann was recalled to headquarters and his confession was read to her. Compelled by Whittaker's frank avowals, she admitted the "intimacy that bound them together." On one point she was adamant. "I reject the insinuations that my affections were won by his gifts. I only handled his money as might a wife. I returned to him on various occasions such sums as he needed." Harriet Lang stated to the Committee that Mrs. Hogan was only guilty of loving a bad man.

"The examinations did not prove actual murder against either Whittaker or McKenzie, but that both were self-confessed robbers who did not hesitate at any violence, that they were a menace to the community, and that it wold be unsafe to hand them over to the authorities. It is therefore recommended that they should suffer death at the hands of the Committee of Vigilance."

With the real English Jim Stuart obviously captured, Governor John McDougal pardoned Berdue and rushed his executive document north to Marysville by horseback to save the innocent man from the noose. McDougal wasn't sure there was enough time to cover 40 miles. The hanging was now.

A mob had gathered as Berdue began climbing the thirteen steps to the scaffold. The noose was fitted over his neck, and tightened. Berdue closed his eyes. There was a clatter of hooves and Francis Aud, horse lathered, tongue hanging out, galloped into the courtyard. Aud swung from the saddle, waving the Governor's order to stop the execution. Berdue collapsed in relief, lay down on the planks and began to cry.

IN SAN FRANCISCO, Coffin heard the news and was relieved that a miscarriage of Justice had been averted. He went for a walk to ponder the workings of Fate and of the Law and the crimes of the hanging men. In the Cove, he studied ragged architecture poised to walk out over the water on shaky stilts. Clusters of shanty houses rose to flank the masts of arriving ships. Before dawn, he rowed toward the mud flats where enterprising merchants had pulled deserted Ghost Fleet hulks onto the shore and left them to decay.

"Some were scuttled or sank where they were anchored," Doris Muscatine wrote, "some became basements for buildings rising from their decks, some were made over into stores, saloons, and boarding houses, and later some were dismantled for their lumber, in a supreme effort to acquire building materials and clear the harbor at the same time."

Coffin completed his documentation of Graveyard Harbor ships. He glided past the *Panama, Garnet, Cordova, Alida,* and *Hardie.* Ahead, at anchor at the Pacific Street Wharf floated the *Bethal, Inez, Almandralina* and *Elmira.* On his starboard beam were the *Trescott* and several felucca. Full of energy, he weaved through alleys of rusted hulls and passed Clark's Point and the Vallejo Wharf where he saw the *Fortuna* anchored. He was feeling better with every turn.

"It was strange to see old ships built into the city streets," Amelia Ransome Neville wrote, "derelicts that had been left where they lay in the mud flats when the land was filled in, waves and lapping waters lost to them for good."

At Meigg's Wharf, Coffin headed due north for the Golden Gate where he could feel the wind in his hair. One of the ghostly Dark Watcher's ships supposedly rode the waves at night at the entrance to San Francisco Bay. It was dark by the time he reached the spot, but found no such ship there. Perhaps next time.

That night, he dined at the Bay Hotel, a ship-restaurant drawn up on the mud under a tall bank. Building on mud was difficult. With the first blow of a driver eighty-foot long piles disappeared below like magic. Another pile was put on top and still did not reach bottom. Finally, men drove bundles of piles, then the piles were capped and buildings laid on top. New brick warehouses on sandy fill fared poorly. In only a month the first brick home built on shifting ground collapsed in a heap of rubble. Inevitably, the shore must stretch out to meet the horizon, yearning for deep water and leaving behind the ship city. Stranded vessels still floated as bobbing warehouses, restaurants, saloons and lodging houses as buildings grew incongruously around them until they were imprisoned.

On July 8, the day after Berdue was to have been hanged, information reached Marysville confirming that the genuine English Jim was in San Francisco in the hands of the Vigilance Committee. When English Jim heard that, he concluded that further denials were useless. A mocking smile played around his lips as he looked his holiest and placed the tips of both hands together as if praying. Finally, he stood, rattled the bars of his cell with his cup, and asked to make a full confession of his nefarious career. His clever brain had worked out that an uncorroborated confession would later be set aside in a legal trial and buy him a little extra time.

Technicalities, playacting, and bravado got him nowhere before the hard-eyed men of the Vigilante Court. The men of the Committee could not forget that English Jim had been willing to let Berdue die in his place. Inflamed, they were eager to purge California of all Sydney convicts, even one that looked like Jesus Christ.

"Well, then may the devil damn you all, I am James Stuart. Now do your worst!"

"Stuart," Payran said, "you have got to die and speedily. Of that you may be assured. No earthly power can save you. It is in no spirit of revenge or hate that we will hang you. Between such as we and such as you there must of necessity be war. We must defend ourselves."

"But, sir," Stuart said, "this is no trial. You would not dare execute me on the strength of unlawful farce!"

"We will give you a further trial if you wish it," Payran said. "You may have your counsel, summon your witnesses, and prove yourself innocent if you can."

"Well, I will do it, damn 'em," he said. "There are some of them I will get even with anyway. Yes, I will make a full confession and incriminate my confederates."

English Jim had one requirement: After his confession, he was to then be handed over to a legal court in Yuba County for trial on the charge of murder. The black eyes glinted. If he were delivered to these authorities he could escape their ineffectual jails. He had done it before and could do it again. That could be his salvation.

There was one catch. The Vigilance Committee had their own proviso: if English Jim failed to fulfill the stipulated terms of the agreement to convict at least ten criminals with his confession, he was to remain in the hands of the Committee and at their tender mercies which mean instant hanging.

The General Committee met twice and the Executive Committee met three times to appoint James Spence, who assisted as one of the Executive Committee, to conduct the examination of the prisoner "Stephens," or "Stuart." It was ordered that questions should be put on paper and Spence should ask them.

"He went through the whole range of his many rascalities," said Coleman, who assisted in taking down his detailed, marathon confession. "He gave vivid descriptions of his adventures, entering with great zest into the details, and it was curious to see his eyes brighten and twinkle, and a smile play round his facile countenance, when describing his best successes, and recounting his best jobs. He threw off all restraint or reservation, and felt that he was bringing to light a brilliant record that had heretofore been necessarily kept in the dark."

"It now came out," Schenck added, "that Stuart was a leader of a gang of nine, who had been concerned in various robberies, assaults, and arsons. The gang was composed of Singing Billy, who was port warden at the time, Old Jack, Jack Edwards, Benjamin Lewis, Jemmy-from-town, and one other whose name I do not now remember. They had a plan to rob F. Argenti's bank and also F. W. Macondray's store."

The gang sat through the night as English Jim spoke and the recorder wrote until his hand cramped and the morning sun shone through the window and blinded him. Between Jim's confession and that of Whittaker, the two criminals had implicated a total of eighty-six persons, and only twenty of these were ex-convicts.

The confession did not reveal the prisoner's real name and touched only lightly on his early experiences. There was no doubt English Jim would have let Berdue die for his crimes, then exact revenge over the injustice in kind. That fit his perverse nature. "It was greatly to his credit," the recorder said, "that he and his gang had resolved to burn the city again if innocent men suffered unwarranted execution in consequence of the attempted murder of Jansen."

The recorder read over the transcription and saw that English Jim had painted a shocking picture of a dozen robberies, plunders and brutal beatings. Many of English Jim's gang were arsonists which allowed them to loot at will during the diversion of a huge fire.

"I never knew of anyone setting a place on fire in San Francisco," Sam Whittaker, the least heartless of the gang said, "except Billy Sweetcheese, whose real name is [Billy] Shears. I heard that he set the United States Exchange on fire [May 4, 1850] on the Plaza at the time it was vacant." Whittaker knew more about the fires, but kept his mouth shut. He only revealed things that would not incriminate him.

Finally, English Jim admitted the murderous assault upon Capt. Jones in the cabin of the *James Caskie*. "We left him nearly dead," he said proudly. Jones had defied him and so such brutality was perfectly warranted.

English Jim did not know that Sam Whittaker, whom he had barely implicated in the gang's crimes and who was his second in command, had confessed a day earlier. Now, the two confessions could be compared to uncover any discrepancies and then question him about them. Whittaker had also told Joseph Hetherington that English Jim had shot Moore and afterwards showed off a large $140 gold nugget he had taken off his body and later gave to Kitchen the Boatman.

Hetherington said he saw the prisoner at Mrs. Hogan's "for the first time a few days before the Jansen affair and several times after. Mrs. Hogan told me his name was Jim Stuart or English Jim or Long Jim, his constant companions were Jim Briggs, and Whittaker, all of whom used to hang around her house." He had not seen him since a row occurred at the house of Mr. Hogan three weeks after the Jansen affair. "I have seen the prisoner in your custody and know him to be the same man that I saw at the house of Mrs. Hogan. These men frequented the house, ate and slept there occasionally. I have frequently seen Sam Whittaker and Mrs. Hogan in bed together. Mrs. Hogan said she had done wrong and would not live with Mr. Hogan again."

At 9:00 AM the Monumental bell tolled for the assembling of the General Committee. The streets filled with members rushing to the Battery Street Headquarters. At 10:30 PM, Stuart formally signed his confession with his alias, "William Stephens," though he also went by the names James Campbell and James Carlisle and many others. After working all night on the document, English Jim ultimately named twenty-five confederates, details of more than a dozen robberies, and accounted for more than $9,000 in money in addition to the valuable plunder of horses and furniture. All the raids had been accompanied by brutal violence.

When Coffin learned that Stuart had made a full confession of "all his nefarious transactions," including the murderous assault upon Capt. Jones in the cabin of the *James Caskie*, he added it to his *Log*. "The public, or what I call the mobbish element was with the Committee," he noted. "The Committee room was guarded at night by portions of the members armed to the teeth. Like all excited multitudes, when once under headway, they knew not when to stop. Besides some of the most prominent members of that association are men as worthy of punishment as the wretched victims whom they have lawlessly sent, without a moment's preparation to meet their God."

English Jim had revealed abortive, uncommitted plots, and plots in progress such as his scheme to rob the City Vault of all its gold and incriminate the men of the El Dorado Saloon with a second tunnel. It was his most audacious plot. Had it succeeded, he would have wealth beyond his dreams. Carefully, he drew a simple diagram of the plan to tunnel into the Custom House bank in the Square and steal three million dollars worth of gold. English Jim never admitted the murder of Charles Moore.

Pixley attempted to get out a writ of habeas corpus for the surrender to the sheriff of his former client, English Jim, and asked the Supreme Court to grant a writ of habeas corpus to bring into court "one English Jim."

"We do not have said Stuart in our possession and have never had such custody as would have enabled us to comply," the Committee replied.

The writ specifically named and ordered W. H. Jones, A. J. McDuffee, J. L. Van Bookelen, Stephen Payran, and Isaac Bluxome, Jr, to produce English Jim. The Committee ordered these four to make themselves scarce to avoid the writ. Bluxome borrowed a slouched hat and shoved it down on English Jim's head. George Oakes located a long cloak and covered the prisoner with it. They thrust him into a carriage, and whipped away. At Endicott and Oaks' building on First Street between Market and Mission, they descended the stairs. First, they showed English Jim that they had two pistols.

"If you attempt to run," he was warned, "we will shoot you."

He nodded and was placed under guard in the cellar while Endicott, an alderman, went home to conduct some business. Soon, Endicott returned in distress.

"This won't do," he told them. "I am a city official and have taken the oath to support the government."

Rube Maloney offered to put English Jim up at his house to keep him clear of the writ. But, by noon, he decided he could not keep him any longer. They took English Jim to another place and another to keep him out of Devil Jack's hands.

Devil Jack, with a new warrant clenched in his fist, rushed to obtain the living body of the Jesus Christ lookalike. He charged into the Vigilante Headquarters to discover the members of the illegal Committee innocently sitting about chatting, smoking and reading. He conducted "a diligent search," but found no sign of English Jim in the guard room. When a grocery boy gave Dutch Charley the message that Brady had seen downtown at a house, he immediately went to find Devil Jack and found him in the Mission District. They began looking together without success. He had been moved again.

At a little after 9:00 AM on July 11, the toll of the Monumental Fire House bell rang out in the Plaza. On the first stroke, two hundred Vigilantes hurried toward their headquarters. On the second stroke, two hundred more hurried to the Committee Room. On the third, and most hollow stroke, a curious crowd congregated outside. The bell from the California Engine house rang and was passed on until the entire city was ringing with the sound of Death. Inside the Committee Room, four hundred members listened for the next three hours to the dreadful reading of English Jim's confession. In an adjoining room, the prisoner complained about the slow pace of the trial.

He placed his manacled hand over his mouth and yawned.

"This is damned tiresome," he said. "Give me a chew of tobacco."

He began to chew a quid placidly as a cow chewing her cud. English Jim's fine manners and eloquent speech had been discarded. Now, they were ineffective.

Mr. Selim Woodworth as Chair asked the assembled Committee Men: "Has the prisoner performed his contract or not?"

"No!" rang out unanimously.

"Has the prisoner being guilty of crimes rendering him liable to the punishment of death."

"Yes!" rang out unanimously.

The motion was carried as were the next five.

"On motion. Resolved that prisoner Stuart be hung."

"Resolved that the prisoner be hung at 2 o'clock."

"Resolved that Executive Committee make necessary arrangements."

"Resolved that no person be allowed to leave the room."

"Resolved that Colonel Stevenson inform the populace that at 2 o'clock the prisoner Stuart will be hung—"

A pause as the Chair reported that the Rev. F. S. Mines would be ministering to English Jim. Mines had been a communicant of the Church of England in his youth. Sullen at first, English Jim responded to Mines' appeals to his better instincts and received the absolution of the Church. He received his death sentence composedly. He had sensed that his failure to acknowledge Moore's murder had placed him beyond "the pale of clemency," and he saw no way back from that.

"I accept my fate," he said. "I can die without resentment toward anyone."

During the time it took to prepare the condemned murderer for execution, four hundred Vigilantes sat in the Committee Room like statues. Not a word was uttered. Not a sound was made to break the solemn stillness of the death watch. The Vigilantes, who dealt "eye-for-an-eye" justice without the bothersome expense of a pesky trial, had deliberated only two hours before deciding to string up English Jim. No longer would criminals escape punishment by "quibbles of the law," they said.

The silent moments slipped away as each man began to feel a "growing sense of personal responsibility for the approaching execution and with it some guilt."

"Things were coming to a pretty pass," Bancroft wrote of English Jim's confession, "when in addition to the trouble caused him by the people, every other man of them had turned thief-hunter, when a comrade would not suffer himself to be hanged in quiet, but must first tell all he knew and jeopardize the lives of his former companions. He is said to have been the instigator of the great fire of the 22nd of June." His assistants in that affair were Jemmy-from-town, Dutchy Betts, Adams, and Whittaker."

They were running late. At half past two, four hundred silent men shook themselves awake. As one, they emerged from the Committee Headquarters in platoons, eight abreast with Stuart in the center, bound and supported by two members. Outside, the crowd listened with keen attention to Col. Stevenson's account of English Jim's confession and his list of transgressions, "all painted up prettily," yet hideous.

Stevenson told the mob of the sentence, then put a question to them:

"Would you sustain the action of the Committee?"

The answer was a roar of affirmation.

"Would you sustain the action of the Committee?" Col. Stevenson asked.

The vote of endorsement was "almost unanimous," according to the *Herald*. Their tempers had cooled and they were beginning to look at what they were doing more responsibly.

Tim Burnham, who kept a butcher's shop on the northern side of Pacific Wharf, was commiserating with Capt. Coffin over Rev. Albert Williams who had been called in to pray for English Jim.

"Mr. Williams," Coffin elaborated, "is the worthy man who had so kindly volunteered to visit the prison to exhort and pray with the criminals. Williams was in the act of prayer, interceding for mercy on the guilty creatures, with particular reference to the culprits Stuart and his associates when his devotions were suspended by the Vigilance Committee delegation. He said no language can describe the horrified aspect of the wretch when he was so ruthlessly seized and dragged away to be executed."

Coffin hurried to his skiff.

ENGLISH JIM, WHO HAD BEEN GIVEN a liberal amount of brandy, was placed in the center of the Vigilante formation which moved slowly up the planked sidewalk of Battery Street. He was both preceded and followed by a mob so that most could see only his black hat bobbing up and down in the center. Some said he was too frightened to walk and was dragged to the Market Street Wharf. Others, such as James Dows, noted in the Sunday *Dispatch* that English Jim "marched as erect and with as firm tread as any innocent man and no one could see in his actions any indications of agitation."

When the ranks reached Long Wharf at its junction with Battery, two guards had to support English Jim. Along the five hundred feet or so of pier still ahead, there was not an available box, bale, or barrel, whiskey-filled or empty, that did not have someone standing on it for a better view. The decks and rigging of every ship were covered with people and the wharf crowded to overflowing. The boards were creaking and the planks strained to the utmost. The wharf threatened to break under all their weight. One man was shoved and tipped over the edge into the drink. Hands shot down and he was helped onto the pier again where he fought to regain his place. He did not want to miss a minute of "the entertainment."

Devil Jack and Dutch Charley had rushed to Committee Headquarters as soon as they heard the Vigilantes had tried English Jim and were marching their prisoner toward the waterfront. On the run, they pounded toward Battery Street.

A huge mob ahead blocked their way and Dutch Charley used his fists to batter through.

Devil Jack had never seen so many people or such a huge obstacle as they presented. Their ranks parted to the left and right only to give passage to English Jim's captors who locked arms and arranged themselves into a solid barrier, then closed again to keep the law out. Devil Jack and Dutch Charley quickened their pace. Ahead, they saw the biggest crowd ever assembled on the Market Street Wharf. Dutch Charley nudged Devil Jack and pointed over the assembled throng to something ahead. Devil Jack, not a tall man, craned his neck and then began to shove his way to the waterside where he could see ahead.

A derrick upon the pier had been selected for the place of execution. A gallows of plain uprights and two cross beams had been erected. There was a block with a rope in it with a ready-made noose in the hands of a man who had just climbed up onto the pier. Men of the Ghost Fleet watched from sharp-pointed row boats and from the decks of the *Salem, Autumn,* and *Tecumseh*. Whitehall boatmen sold space in their smaller, squarer boats and rowed offshore so their clients could observe the gruesome spectacle from just the right angle. The sky was light blue and filled with fluffy white clouds.

"By using the wharf," wrote policeman-historian Kevin J. Mullin, "the Vigilantes assured a good audience for their efforts and eliminated lines of approach for any intended rescue by officials."

English Jim began to laugh.

Fate was certainly having a horse laugh on him, he thought. A shirt! For a second time he had been unfairly arrested for stealing a shirt. In Marysville, he had put on a shirt in a trunk he found in a new house, one he had bought legitimately. It landed him in jail and had nearly gotten him hanged; the clothes had been reported stolen. Of course, he really was guilty of killing Charlie Moore, but was being hung for the murder of the Sheriff Echols, a homicide someone else had committed. English Jim shook his head. Hung for crimes he had not done, not for the ones he had, he thought. It seemed so unfair to him, yet he would have let Berdue hang in his place and then set fire to the city to show how outraged he was at that miscarriage of justice.

As Richard Hale later wrote, "The sudden clang of the bell! Who did not know what its ringing foretold! 'Death!' 'Death!' it generally pealed to the waiting listeners, while a body dangled from the derricks of the Sand Lot, the Plaza, or Russian Hill."

English Jim, with clasped hands and without a shroud over his head, only his hat, stood beneath the rope. A slight breeze gently stirred his long hair. English Jim looked up at the prepared gallows and began to shake all over. He squeezed his eyes shut.

The noose was slipped over his neck and adjusted behind his neck. Above him, he heard the loud *crack*! *crack*! *crack*! of a gigantic American flag in the gale. Its stars and bars stood straight out. Jim saw two pairs of eyes peering back at him from a watcher who had climbed to his level of fifteen feet and from another far above.

The crowd had fallen completely silent. A hush swept over the Ghost Fleet, except for the relentless creaking of the ships and the rising wind. In his bearing, English Jim had shown a remarkable degree of admirable qualities which many an honest and good man lacks. He had marched to execution, head erect, firm step and graceful carriage. At the end he had demonstrated coolness and courage.

"Yet, he was an audacious villain, and every inch a villain."

"The resemblance between Berdue and Stuart is most striking," the *Call* reported, "and it was not at all strange that one should have been taken for the other."

"Many witnesses swore particularly on the trial that the man in jail here was Jim Stuart," the reporter for the *Marysville Herald* who had covered Berdue's trial said. "Some swore that they had known him long and intimately, had worked with him on Foster's Bar, and could not be mistaken. Others swore to certain marks, and these were so numerous that it would seem almost impossible that two men should possess them in common. The bald spot on the top of the head, the finger on the right hand crooked in the first joint, on one of his fingers the shape of a star faintly impressed with the same sort of ink between the thumb and first finger. The scar on the side of the face, the peculiar shape of the nose, expression of the eyes, manner of action, singularity of voice and so on.

"And yet two men have been found who not only strongly resemble each other in general appearance, but each of whom has each and every one of these marks. It does seem, that after this, no one could positively identify his own brother. San Francisco persons who were before satisfied of the guilt of Berdue and who were satisfied that that name was but one of several aliases, have been completely bewildered in the matter. We presume that since these extraordinary developments have been brought to light by the Vigilance Committee, a new trial will be granted to Berdue. Justice and humanity both seem to require it, and in God's name, let justice be done, let it not be said that Berdue shall suffer the extreme penalty of the law if he be innocent."

"I die reconciled. My sentence is just," English Jim said loudly.

He heard the whispered word: "Now!"

"Stop!" Devil Jack shouted. He had unholstered his twin guns and was forcing his way through the human barrier. But he was too late. The illegal lynching had been carried out.

English Jim was dangling from a cargo derrick at the end of the pier by the time Devil Jack reached him. The wind off the Cove turned his body round and round. Now, he was staring with his face arched out into Graveyard Harbor. He had been jerked from his feet rapidly, but it was five minutes before his wide-brimmed hat had flown off and floated out among the Ghost Fleet ships. It drifted past Coffin's skiff. He watched it go and then sink. His face was etched in horror. He had wanted English Jim captured, but by the authorities and dealt with in a court of law. Not like this, for the love of God, not like this. He was sickened. Filled with horror at the scene, Coffin rowed away. The entire time, he kept his back to the dangling man until he reached a ship and climbed below.

On the pier, Ned Gallagher the coroner was trying to force his way through a platoon of men who had locked arms and were demanding of him permission to pass.

"Who are you?" Vigilante Middleton asked.

"By God," Gallagher cried, "you know I am a coroner!"

"By God," Middleton said, "you don't get through till that fellow's a fit subject for your administration."

"Get out of my way!"

Middleton feared some of Stuart's confederates would spirit English Jim away while he still breathed and resurrect him. As English Jim's body turned, his toes pointed toward the Ghost Fleet as if magnetically drawn there. The crane extended so that he was so far out over the water that he was part of Graveyard Harbor. His face was dark and his chin was thrust Westward. His eyes flickered as if absorbing the energy of the Cove. There was a gasp.

Stuart was still alive!

EDWARD BUFFUM SUGGESTED they send for Thomas Berdue who was in San Francisco. "He should be able to reach the wharf in half an hour," Buffum said. "Once there [Berdue] stood quietly for several minutes," he wrote, "and gazed upon his fixed features. It was like a living man looking at his own corpse. I never, before or since, seen such a resemblance between two men! English Jim Stuart was, perhaps, a triple stouter, but having seen either one, I think I should have unhesitatingly, at any time thereafter, been willing to swear to the other as that one. It scarcely seems possible that the men could have so perfectly resembled each other."

Stunned, Berdue looked up at the dangling man and walked slowly around the swinging figure. His boots were just above his head. Berdue was speechless. Solemnly, he was taken back to his horse and driven away. Buffam had never seen a more stricken man. It was as if Berdue had just watched his own execution.

Twenty-five minutes later they cut English Jim down. There was some life left in him, but all future efforts after that to revive him failed. English Jim was gone and this time for good.

The Vigilantes just could not get their illegal executions right, Sheriff Devil Jack thought.

The first man they hanged was dead before he was strung up.

The second was alive after he was cut down.

Hanged from a derrick at the end of the pier, English Jim Stuart had died like a dog. Thousands of erring mortals, whose wickedness had not yet been found out, had looked on and applauded.

"So perish every villain who would hurt his neighbor," said Father Taylor.

And all the people said, "Amen!"

AT DAWN, ON JULY 12, law-abiding citizens on their way to breakfast found English Jim still lying dead on the dock as a cautionary lesson to the inhabitants of Graveyard Harbor. After he was hanged, the Committee went after his gang with all their power.

Jim had provided the important names for them. It was a long list—Kitchen the Boatman, Dab the Horse-Thief, Big Bummy, Long Charley, Singing Billy, Jack Edwards, and two crooked San Francisco cops, R. C. McIntire and A. J. McCarty. Ben Lewis, ninth in the gang hierarchy, had by this time been freed twice on a technicality and his whereabouts were unknown and he was omitted from the roundup. Sam Whittaker who was seeking to redeem himself had, with little prompting, given the Committee the names of Jack Dandy, Big Bummy, Kitchen the Boatman, Jemmy-from-town, Joseph Turner, Richard Osman, Jim Briggs, and Old Jack Morgan (who was far more important than the Vigilantes suspected). Singing Billy, while they had him in custody, had provided other names—Billy Hughes, a man named Ryan, and, through his relationship, Mary Ann Hogan herself. The day English Jim was hanged, Singing Billy managed to escape to Panama where, three years later, he was still free and committing outrages in Valparaiso as one of a band of criminals.

Dr. Randall of the Custom House retired and borrowed several thousand dollars from Joseph Hetherington to buy a huge ranchero in Butte County. In 1856, when Randall refused to repay the money, Hetherington grabbed him by his long beard, flung him out of the office, and shot him to death as he lay below. The Vigilantes hanged Philander Brace who had killed Capt. West and, next to him, strung up

Hetherington for murdering Dr. Randall.

Jemmy-from-town was arrested on July 16, and put to work mixing the mortar for Devil Jack's new jail, only to escape before it was done. He was captured again, lashed, and sentenced to San Quentin for ten years. He escaped again, and eventually faded into the mists of history.

Marysville Vigilantes grabbed Dab the Horse-Thief on July 17, and delivered him to the Committee. Sam Brannan got him released. Over at the jail, Devil Jack, in spite of his good fortune finding backers for his jail overhaul, feared more lives might be lost in the meantime. He wrote the Committee to let them know that one of the heaviest items of expense about the prison were the doors and locks. Mrs. Biddy Gilligan, arrested fifty times in three months as a danger to herself, had been incarcerated in the unfinished jail. The over-fill of prisoners caused deputies to set her loose in the morning. She wandered into the street and promptly killed herself. The Vigilance Committee was also gearing up to hang more men. That troubled the sheriff too.

"I have not been able to find anyone who would make a suitable door for less than fifty cents per pound.," he wrote the Committee. "I am anxious to complete the ground story of the prison according to the plan now in the possession of the committee. To finish this building to the extent mentioned in my proposal could require $21,320."

On July 18, police nabbed Jack Dandy and Jemmy-from-town. Their sentences were very practical. Devil Jack put Dandy to work digging a twenty-seven foot deep hole and got him a twenty year sentence, and threw in Jemmy-from-town who ended up mixing concrete for the new jail.

Using English Jim's confession, the Vigilantes easily broke their alibis by making them believe they knew more than they knew. One by one, they admitted their guilt. Old Jack Morgan, who had helped bludgeon Jansen, ultimately avoided capture and never got to open the Custom House vault he had built. He still had the plans and combination if he ever had the chance again.

The day Jack Dandy was arrested, a large Sydney vessel, *Adirondack*, arrived carrying over 300 passengers. Immediately, Wakeman's Water Patrol detained and questioned 138 of them because they suspected the ship might contain more Australian ex-convicts to replace the ones they had hanged or arrested. Astonishingly, the Water Patrol searched none of the passengers, though some had shaved heads, tattoos and other indications they were convicts smuggled away from Australia. Ultimately, the Committee deported only one man off the *Adirondack*, but from then on sent a boat aboard every vessel coming in from Australia.

Thanks to the Pirate Wakeman, the Water Patrol had a secret weapon, an alphabetical list of all the convict ships that went from England to Australia. They called in passengers one at a time one and questioned each. Those that were on the list were sent back on the first vessel going to Australia. The Committee considered taking legal steps against shipmasters who brought convict passengers to California, but a year-old statute already existed prohibiting the immigration of criminals. Exasperated that they could not root out more immigrating felons, the Water Patrol was disbanded.

Berdue might as well have been disbanded too. When he was first arrested, he was well-heeled, well-liked, and though an unlucky miner and gambler, he had a total wealth of $15,000. Upon release, he was stone broke, having used up his life savings during the trial. His wife had been bilked of much of it by the lawyers. Jansen, who had recovered, offered to return the money taken from Berdue when a mob tried to wrest him from the police escorting him to jail, but there is no record of him actually doing so.

"Is not the case of Thomas Berdue, who was discharged in San Francisco a day or two ago," the *Sacramento Union* commented, "a sad commentary upon the times in which we are living? He and Windred twice escaped hanging by merest chance. And to show the influence of the press, it is only necessary to mention the course taken by the San Francisco Journals in this matter—they bitterly denounced Berdue and Windred, and probably did more towards effecting their conviction. I notice that the *Herald* of Tuesday expressed great sympathy for Berdue. A less violent course last winter would have done him more service." Some citizens collected $600 so Berdue could buy a horse and cart and in September the Committee would collect another $302 for him.

Touched, Berdue wrote a note of appreciation and gave it to the *California Courier* which printed it. "I have kindly to thank those gentlemen for what they have done for me," he wrote, "for certainly, though through their vigilance and the kind providence of Almighty

God, they succeeded in capturing the criminal for whom I have suffered so much." For a while, he set up shop on Montgomery north of Jackson Street, but an hour after getting the money was operating a monte pitch on Long Wharf.

On October 11, Berdue would lose the rest of the donations in an unfortunate mining venture and his friends would return to raising more money. All agreed that the "undeserved disgrace" and anxiety of his ordeal had broken Thomas Berdue in health and spirit. Next, he petitioned the legislature for an indemnity for $4000 for injuries suffered during his wrongful imprisonment and trial and the expenditures he had incurred in his fight to prove his innocence. The legislature refused his petition on grounds that, "To grant the prayer of the petitioner, would more than exhaust the entire revenue of the State. We know of no legislative precedent for such appropriation." Instead, they asked him to rejoice rather than seek remuneration from the government whose justice had protected him from ignominious death. Berdue left the United States for good and went to Ballarat, Victoria Australia, where he would start a hardware and general store in Plank Road selling mining supplies, remarry and have two more children.

When the late English Jim's confession exposed Sam Whittaker and Robb McKenzie as leaders of his gang, the Vigilantes went looking for them. It was a long and deadly search. A posse from the Vigilance Committees of Stockton and Sonora scoured Jamestown, Chinese Diggings, Georgetown, and Shaw's Flat without a sighting. McKenzie was finally discovered in Sacramento and arrested on July 29. By August 1, he was behind bars in the San Francisco Committee Headquarters.

Meanwhile, Whittaker remained at large and in plain sight at Mary Ann Hogan's House while her husband was at the mines. The lovely Mary Ann slipped onboard the *Cameo* for Sydney, but the Committee went onboard and removed her to their headquarters. They quickly released her hoping she might lead them to Whittaker's hiding place. She did not. As they searched the sloughs and creeks of the marshy Sacramento River, Mrs. Hogan secretly traveled to San Diego where Whittaker had by now fled and was waiting to join her via the coast route.

On August 8, Sheriff V. W. Hearne, acting on a tip, arrested Whittaker in Santa Barbara Harbor and escorted him back to San

Francisco onboard the *Ohio* steamer. Hearne left his prisoner onboard at Long Wharf and went to locate Sheriff Hays. First, though, he stopped at J. C. Palmer's office and bragged of his clever arrest of Whittaker. J. C. L. Wadsworth, a member of the Vigilance Committee, had an office in the same building. He overheard the news, rushed to Long Wharf, and induced the captain to deliver Whittaker to the Vigilantes.

When the Vigilantes recalled Mary Ann to testify, she readily admitted she and Whittaker were lovers, but indignantly repudiated the insinuation that her affections had been won by the value of his gifts.

"I handled his money as might a wife," she explained, "returning to him on various occasions such sums as needed."

When Whittaker was brought to see Mrs. Hogan, they spoke tenderly for an hour. Then she went downstairs, got into the same carriage the Vigilantes had hired to bring her to their rooms, and went away.

The couple never met again.

In the beginning the townsfolk judged her harshly, but ultimately forgave her. They decided she was "only guilty of loving a bad man."

On August 19, the governor learned that the Committee of Vigilance intended to hang both Whittaker and McKenzie on a Ghost Fleet vessel yardarm near shore on August 21. But, this time they met resistance. The governor got to San Francisco by midnight and dragged a judge out of bed to issue a warrant for immediate seizure. Mayor C. J. Brenham, who was determined not to let the Vigilantes hang another man, procured a writ of habeas corpus from the governor, and at 2:00 AM roused the exhausted sheriff from his bed. He was nothing without his coffee, but he forced himself awake.

"I want you to serve this," the Mayor told Devil Jack. "Take as many men with you as you want. I can provide a posse of police to go with you."

Devil Jack shook his head fiercely.

"That won't be necessary," he said, "I will only need my longtime friend and deputy, Maj. John Caperton, as support against as many armed Vigilantes which will be there." The Mayor understood. He was thinking of the saying: "One riot, one Ranger." These were the kind of odds he preferred. Devil Jack could be daring and he could be foolish, but not always at the same time. As he and his men went about their work, they were described as "like boys at play," and "racing daredevils." Jack had cultivated good relations with the Committee. He had asked them to his own jail, and they had promised financial assistance defraying the expenses he had assumed.

Accompanied by Caperton, the mayor, and the governor, he went to the rooms of the Committee. Van Bokkelen had completed arrangements for transferring the condemned to a vessel selected as the site of the hanging. He had stepped outside, when Hays and Caperton, hustled up the stairs, pushed past the guard at the door. Caperton ran directly to the prisoner's room, "Whittaker and McKenzie, I am an officer. I come to save you!" The three locked arms and raced back to where Devil Jack held the door open, then down the stairs after a brief struggle, and into the night. They met little resistance. Some of the Vigilance Police slept through the raid.

The twenty-nine guards at the Committee Headquarters had a coded system of security. At 3:00 AM a gigantic blacksmith, John A. Steele, was installed as doorkeeper. Chief of the Committee Police Van Bokkelen joined him. When Devil Jack and Caperton arrived they knocked. As the door opened, they sprang inside, and the sheriff slammed the door shut with his back.

"Don't resist me," Devil Jack said, "I am the Sheriff of the County."

Caperton called out to the two prisoners, "I am an officer! I've come to save you!"

The sheriff strolled down the path between the guards, barely pausing, but staring hard and calling out to them again. Whittaker and McKenzie dashed to Caperton and clutched his coat as if for dear life. Van Bokkelen and other guards had surrounded them, but Caperton shouted, "Resistance is useless! We are too strong!" giving the impression a squad of deputies was on the way. Devil Jack opened the door and the prisoners rushed through. Neither officer had drawn a gun and accomplished their raid only through their bearing and confident tone of voice. The secretary of the Vigilantes had been napping on a table and only when he awoke did he learn that Sheriff Devil Jack now had his two prisoners behind bars at his new jail. Well, two could play that game.

"In order to avoid any personal conflict with Jack Hays, George Schenck saw to it that the sheriff was invited to attend a bullfight at the Mission Dolores," writes historian Mary Floyd Williams, "Then in advance of the proposed raid, Isaac Bluxome inspected the jail ostensibly to see Burdue, who was lodged there awaiting a formal release from the sentence imposed on his as assailant of Jansen. The secretary's real errand was to discover whether a stand of muskets kept in the building was ready for emergency use. He accomplished this purpose by exhibiting his skill in the manual of arms to the old soldier, William Lambert, who acted as keeper, for he made excuses to pick up one gun after another during the drill and made certain none was loaded.

On Sunday afternoon, August 24, Capt. Cartwright stationed members of his guard of thirty near the front and rear entrances. The unsuspecting jailers even allowed a few of the men to enter the building and attend a religious service which was being held in the unroofed court. A vigilante hidden on Telegraph Hill commanded a view of the courtyard and watched for the signal that would indicate the best moment for attack. Capt. Lambert as guard was relaxed and unsuspecting. Caperton discussed his Sunday dinner. Sheriff Devil Jack was not there when thirty Vigilantes in three groups burst in the door and overpowered the few guards there.

At 2:30 Father Albert William completed his religious meeting. The signal was given from the hill. The doors without were forced, Whittaker and McKenzie were seized bodily and carried to a carriage only paces away outside the rear door. Their heads were forced down on the seats and held there. Cocked pistols were held at their heads. The driver lashed his mounts. Then came the toll of the bells. The First Vigilance Committee had agreed to meet upon the strokes of the bell sounding at either of two centrally located firehouses half a mile distant from each other—the California Engine Co. and the Monumental Engine Co.

The strokes would be repeated with an interval of one minute between each alarm and the passing of the whispered code word, "33 Secretary" from ear to ear. It was a slightly imperfect method, but effective. The Vigilantes waited no time at all before the death bell began to toll, its solemn notes rolling out over foggy Graveyard Harbor. What they heard was this: First came that of California Engine—a variation which was unfamiliar to the town—two measured taps, a pause, two taps, and then a much longer pause, and again two notes.

The call to death was enough to stop every man in his tracks. Then, came an answering call from the Monumental—if you listen, you can hear it now in the hot air. "Two strokes and silence, then silence: two and two, and two. It rose in the hot afternoon air—two and two and two—.

All were on their feet now—converging to murder and hanging. Though neither man had committed murder, they were doomed. Of the crowd, it was said that they did not seem like men, but like judges sent from the netherworld, so stern, and implacable were their expressions. It was the silence that was unnerving.

Coffin had become well acquainted with Rev. Williams at young Thurlo's funeral and gone to his home for dinner. Williams, who often volunteered to visit prisoners and pray with them, had been in a state of nervous excitement ever since he had watched horrified as Whittaker and MaKenzie were dragged away from his devotions in the open courtyard to be hanged.

Whittaker, according to witnesses, was calm and manly. Garritt Ryckman, one of the older members, said he was brave as Caesar, and won his admiration so that he regretted the necessity for the execution."

Whittaker whispered his last words to Ryckman as he placed the noose around his neck.

"You have to be careful," Whittaker said. "There is a plot against your life." He mentioned two names.

Whittaker's warning enabled the Vigilante leader to foil the would-be assassins.

Like everything in the story of Graveyard Harbor, it was one of the most unusual hangings in history. After Whittaker and MaKenzie were fitted with a noose, the other end of the rope of each was run through an opening to a large room, the Committee Room Headquarters. On the other side of the opening the room was filled with Vigilantes.

All took hold and began pulling, so that the two were hung by all.

"One of the Committee told me," Coffin said, "the men were more than half-dead before they were strung up. Twenty minutes later, Whittaker and McKenzie were dangling from a heavy redwood yardarm over the Cove water, which made them part of the Ghost Fleet. Hundreds of normally upstanding townsfolk cheered them on. Then they became silent by the horror of it all.

Mrs. Williams said her husband was brought home in a frightful state of nervous excitement, from which he had not wholly recovered." Over dinner, Coffin and Rev. Williams talked about the hangings and the madness the rush for gold seemed to incite.

When Coffin left that evening, he saw torch lights moving among the shadows of the Market Street Wharf and heard the great bell calling the Vigilance Committee to more murder. The hanging men held the waterfront and its assorted piers and gangways as their turf. Four days later, "Red Dick," a professional crimp in the Ghost Fleet, was trying to entice a crew to desert when the captain raised a pump handle, struck Red Dick's head, and sent him plummeting into the shallow Cove where he drowned. He was not prosecuted because the Pirate Wakeman considered this to be excusable behavior. Now that law and order, at least to his liking, had been restored to the Cove, the Pirate Wakeman traveled up the Sacramento River one last time on the *New World*, not as her skipper, but as a paying passenger. Near the Natural Bridge, he greeted some of his former *New World* crew who were dog-tired and "powerful glad," for a break from drudgery. That night he told them stirring forecastle tales, reinforcing each story with brandy toddies. Wakeman's strong cheery voice and animated countenance constructed enthralling tales that left his listeners gasping for breath.

One night, he baited a shark hook, hung it outside the nondescript bark and adobe cabin, and hooked a cougar. When the Pirate returned to Graveyard Harbor, San Francisco's leading citizens threw him a farewell banquet and presented him with a solid gold full-chronometer watch with double cases, a large, heavy silver speaking trumpet, and a weighty chain attached to large rings of California gold. As the city turned out to watch Wakeman pilot the *New Orleans* out the Golden Gate, Devil Jack, who had stopped him from leaving before, now smiled broadly and wished him on his way with a wave of his hand.

The Pirate sailed down to the Marquesas and Tahiti where he survived a fall over a waterfall and where his crew was mistaken for a gang of convicts who had stolen a whaleboat. After worming out of a number of messes, Wakeman and his men sailed on to Australia and a new gold strike.

Coffin watched Wakeman leave too. The colorful giant's departure officially marked the end of the Ghost Fleet to him.

COFFIN COMPLETED THE LAST section of his *Log* and was shading in some of the corners with his pen. He felt content. But, as the sun rose, depression seized him again. He had worked so hard, but all his efforts had been just so much scattered sand slipping between his fingers. "A constitutional melancholy, which has affected me though life at intervals," he explained, "now seized upon me with tenfold force." Completely prostrated, he dropped to his knees. As he said his prayers, he envisioned the real English Jim enjoying himself somewhere and planning more crimes. He sat up and lit his pipe. After a few puffs, he chastised himself for any vengeance he still harbored in his heart. There was no future in that. He went onshore for a snack. It was delicious. He went exploring and brought along his *Log*.

"Vessels are selling for dog cheap," a Sacramento trader told him. "Fine large barks bring $3,000 to $5,000 dollars. Schooners small enough to operate on the rivers and handle the heavy traffic to the mines are selling for good prices."

All around Graveyard Harbor vessels were being dismantled for scarce lumber for new houses and buildings. Nat Page was unloading some recovered lumber on the beach between California and Sacramento streets when he heard a voice boom, "Remove the lumber and vacate the premises." It was the dictatorial voice of Capt. Folsom. Before Page could speak, Folsom, accustomed to instant obedience, whipped out his revolver and fired a slug at Page's midsection. The bullet glanced off Page's watch in his waistband pocket, and put a hole in Folsom's boat fifty-yards away.

As the recovered planks were carted away, Coffin became pensive. "Such an abandoned fleet, biggest in the world," he thought, "yet San Franciscans look at the strange, vast floating land of desolation and mystery each morning and accept it as commonplace."

It was beyond him. Toward evening he took out his skiff and as he threaded in and out of the ship canyons he had a premonition of death. He stopped at the foot of the Jackson Street Wharf, let down his oars and wondered what this feeling could mean. He began rowing again. Soon he passed the moored bonded warehousing ship, *Edwin*, which had been deserted earlier today. Now only Jose Contreras and Clemente Sequel were staying onboard before the ship was moved to the Pacific Wharf.

Tonight the pair were having a high time, the best of friends, smiling, laughing in high-pitched caterwauls and waving at Coffin as he rowed past. He waved back. He passed the Washington and Clay Street Wharves and neared bustling Long Wharf—the tread of boots, bells chiming, and gulls calling. The fog was rolling in as he looked back at the Ghost Fleet. Had there ever been such a unique setting of fog-shrouded mystery, joy, hope, and tragedy? Well, he had recorded all he could learn of the harbor's ships, men and women, murder and lost treasure and would put them down on paper. He had his *Log*.

He returned after collecting a debt and earning another, then made for the northern part of the Cove. As he heard the drip of oarlocks behind, Coffin recalled his premonition. He listened, but heard only the moans of the decaying ships.

"It's only an echo," he reassured himself. Now, he quickened his pace. He needed to reach the *Talma*, get before a fire and have a drink to ward off the deathly night chill.

As he approached the end of a ship-corridor, he swung wide into a clearing. A ray of pale moonlight danced on the water—a swarm of silver and black fireflies. Soon a boat approached. Coffin waited, recalling his foreboding of death. In a moment he recognized Jose and his close friend Clemente as they crossed into the light, returning to the *Edwin* after buying more liquor on shore. They were already a little drunk and crooning in low, contented voices. They waved to him, laughing loudly and Coffin waved back. Relieved, he rowed on, glad that there had been nothing to his dread. At least in the Ghost Fleet there were some happy people. He heard their high-pitched laughter.

An hour later, on the deck of the *Edwin*, Jose stabbed Clemente to death.

The next morning Coffin floated across to the post office to mail a letter home. At Long Wharf he ate a chunk of sourdough bread and a wedge of Monterey Jack. Gulls darted at his breakfast leavings. An hour later, he went aboard the sinking paddle-wheeler. He had decided to leave San Francisco when the ship sank completely and so was keeping a careful vigil upon it. It was his nautical alarm clock.

Working below a swaying oil lamp, Coffin completed his map of the floating city. It would take up a double page. Taking up his pen, he dipped the nib into an ink well, and with a flourish drew a small border decoration of the city's inhabitants—Mexican gamblers, red-capped Malayans, robed Chinese, and tall black men from the Eastern deserts. He ran his finger along the parchment until he came to an area he had colored bright blue. It had dried perfectly flat. He put his pen down, studied the swath of blue and considered the unseen portion of the water city. Underwater, the Ghost Fleet was entwined in a huge spider web of cables, chains and anchors twisted around each other that caused the ships to pound each other or sway like cotillion dancing partners. Rats, kings of the water metropolis, swarmed on the rigging and watched guardedly. With each thump of the dancing ships the rodents were tossed into the water and, unfazed, paddled back to the ship.

Above the shrouds and lines of the paddle-wheeler, a fragile spiderwebbing of ratlines hung down. Forced to balance, he crossed the slanted deck to the hatch cover. The enormous hold was silent except for the swirl of rising water. A flash of movement and a huge shape cast a shadow on the clay floor of the shallow Cove. The undulant shape of a five-foot long moray glided past. The eel's jaw shifted side-to-side before it swam away. Coffin sat on the huge paddlewheel to watch boats pass. As he sat and thought on the great wheel, the day darkened.

The repaired *Apollo* storeship was alight. It was prosperous again, much to the relief of the Beach brothers. C. J. Mitchell was running a liquor store in a shed near the stern and Kashew and Bigley had opened a restaurant and grocery store in a small shed on the dock running alongside it. A coffee stand where pie and doughnuts were sold had also been cut into the *Apollo's* hull. In less than two years, the ship would be occupied for Lawrence and Company's boarding house and restaurant. When rising water lots surrounded the stranded ship, the square transom stern would be continued down to the ground level and a porch roof erected over the entrance and labeled "*Apollo* Saloon."

Buildings like Bubb Grub and the Eagle Saloon grew up incongruously around her. In the future the *Apollo* would become a gambling hall, and then a flophouse that drifted up down the front with the Bay tide—a strange fate for such a beloved, historically important vessel. While the water lots between Sansome and Battery streets and Washington and Jackson streets were still unfilled, the lots immediately south had been transformed into dry land with new structures being built over the burned remains of the *General Harrison*.

Rows of huge side-wheelers from the Isthmus were berthed at angles. Cheering crowds wagered on the outcome of races as skippers forced their boilers in a breathless, final dashes to the docks.

"We trust that this steamboat racing will not be persevered in," editorialized the *Alta*, "for if it be, we shall very soon have some horrible catastrophe [like the *Sagamore*] to chronicle which will chill the community with horror."

In Sacramento, the *La Grange*, a converted bark that had been anchored at the Sacramento waterfront as a county jail since the spring of 1850 and had briefly contained English Jim. The Legislature, in lieu of a state prison, leased the *La Grange's* prisoners to James M. Estell, a private contractor and corrupt politician. He and his partner, M. G. Vallejo, agreed to maintain the convicts on a brig, the *Waban*, in exchange for the use of their labor. In January 1852 the sheriff put the lesser prisoners to work cutting and grading the San Francisco streets as chain gangs. Forty of the more hardened prisoners were towed to Angel Island and put to work in a rock quarry."

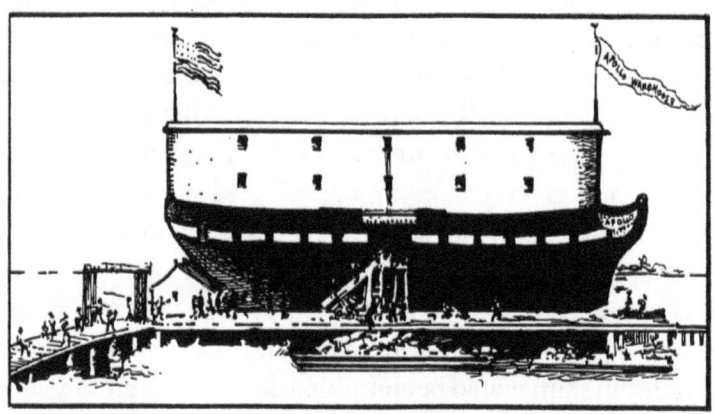

Apollo storeship

ABOUT THE MIDDLE OF AUGUST Coffin began looking over the ships in the harbor with the idea of acquiring a new vessel. It was still difficult to navigate the port, but he set about it anyway. "I fell in with a fine bark of three hundred tons, three years old. I found the captain was desirous of selling her, and, after bantering with him for about a week,

I got him to name a price in which I thought I could conscientiously propose to my friend to invest his money. He at once acceded to the purchase and I was placed in command of the *Arco Iris*. It was not as large a ship as I would have liked, but overall suited me more than any other I had seen."

On Sunday, September 7, Coffin attended Rev. Albert Williams's morning service at his new chapel. Williams's old church had been burned in the last great fire. Bulkheads were being built along the waterfront along with permanent brick warehouses. Speculators in frock coats, ties and glossy top hats were rubbing shoulders with deepwater sailors and sweetmeat vendors.

In the Cove southern coasters circled. Great three-skysail yarders, lumber schooners out of the Northwest, stood out against the blue-black clouds. A former storeship, the *Lucinda*, put out of business by a failing economy, grimly rode the swells. Thin lines of smoke curled from hundreds of Ghost Fleet decks. As evening fell, a stillness claimed the glasslike water. Coffin observed boats weaving among the rocking ships and vanishing into the fog banks beyond. Men were returning from the Farallones with their catches of giant pelican eggs. On the mud flats men polling barges passed double-ended whaling longboats, silently gliding over black water.

At the foot of Lumber St, Coffin looked mournfully over the Tonquin Shoal. Ships that had come from every port in the world packed with optimistic dreamers, had ended up beached along the shore of the Cove, or on land as ship-offices or reduced to lumber for churches and offices. Coffin had no desire to desert the Ghost Fleet. It was deserting him. Certainly, he would never find its like anywhere else. A gentle rain set up a patter on the high tin roofs as he came ashore. Fog bells chimed. A grave-like coldness swept in as the sun sank. His many friends hailed him and they all went into a saloon to discuss his future and toast him.

Coffin sipped from his mug and savored the warmth.

Graveyard Harbor was most beautiful by night.

Some saloons had lights, but on bright nights kept them extinguished to save money so that only moonlight lit the wharves. The effect of this moon-drenched city, against its forty-three hills, immense dunes, and blasted granite cliffs, was that of a stark cutout which flattened its inhabitants into two dimensions. Moonlight reflected brightly from the slanting pine decks of abandoned ships, but lay dull and dead on the nearby marshes and mud flats. Shadows of temporary dwellings stretched seaward over the hills and then slipped down into the Cove. Rooftops stood white between the hills. Oddly, more light blazed inside the Ghost Fleet than in the city. Coffin peered in that direction, searching for the *Talma*. The Fleet was casting its own shadows back against the docks and ship-auction houses. A flock of seabirds settled onto the water. Bright bubbles danced in the tide. A black current slid lugubriously by, carrying driftwood, yellow bone, and faded dreams far out to sea.

It was time for Coffin to join them.

The twilight faded, he dozed and when he awoke the tide was glowing red with marine life depositing a sheen of phosphoresce along the sand. The police boats were polling their way in and out of the deep shadows and shining their dark lanterns everywhere. Since the city was so volatile, everyone feared the hanging men who were organizing on every corner and in every room. Coffin listened to the creak of mat sails as stars rose over a red-tinted moon. The *Whang Ho's* cooking fires were sending smoke curling like a hangman's noose. Wind was whistling over the diminishing dunes and sand was whipping down the mud streets and tears began to run down his cheeks.

On September 8, Coffin obtained a mate, a cook, and four seaman at an average of $50 each and obtained freight for $700 for a run to the Sandwich Islands with three passengers. He got ready to sail. "My little bark did not sail so well as I expected from her reputed character and her model," he wrote. "This I attribute to her having lain so long in the mud in San Francisco. Her bottom is probably coated with barnacles and oyster, for I have seen attached to the copper on ships' bottoms lying there clusters of oysters that would fill a peck measure . . ."

He sat up all night. The Cove would soon be lost to him as an object of study but much of it still lived in his *Log*. At dawn he visited establishments rooted on both sides of the piers—shanties, grocery stores, saloons, commission houses and gambling dens, to say goodbye. He had a fine breakfast, then passed along the street fronting the waterfronts. The sawtoothed, jagged seaside boundary was moving outward with the new land.

The bowsprits of Ghost Fleet survivors pointed accusingly at him as he picked along the zig-zag path of East Street. Towering mountains of hay, grain, bricks, pyramids of lumber, and stacked merchandise peered down on him. At points, the street disappeared only to spring up again, and then melt into a maze of docks and alleyways. In the Cove, a few Ghost Fleet ships like the bark *Damariscotta* and the brig *Sussex* had been repaired to carry hundreds home, no wiser, no richer. Listing the ships with names on their hulls had been easy—the prison ship *Euphemia* and the rich store ships of the spectral fleet, the *Vallejo*, *Niantic*, and *Apollo*, floated near the *General Harrison*, *Roma*, *Othello*, and the *Georgean*.

He had even listed their fates. The *Othello* had become a casino near Law's Wharf until Michael Hart converted it to a storeship at Steuart Street. The *Edwin* was moored at Jackson Street Pier as a storehouse. The *Aurora*, *Hope*, *Dolores*, *Bonne Adela*, an unnamed galliot, several unnamed feluccas, the *Swallow* and *Cherie* floated nearby. The *Sara Sands* was converted into a cheap lodging house at Vallejo and Battery streets; a steamboat suddenly was transformed into a hotel. An unnamed emporium ship bulging with goods floated at Vallejo and Front streets alongside a vessel that later became a Chinese warehouse on the Jackson Street Wharf. An unnamed brig acted as a storehouse at California and Battery. The *Georgean's* hull would be incorporated into the building at 716-720 Montgomery Street as the Ship Building and the ship later moved west of Battery between Jackson and Washington streets.

Coffin decided that for now he would let the other ships keep their secrets. He would leave them to rock at anchor, decompose on the mud flats, or tower on a city street in a new guise and function. A few would be resurrected to transport thousands of failed miners back home and this set Coffin to wondering.

"Just how possible was escape from the Ghost Fleet?"

A ship trapped at the center of the morass of ships was logically a prisoner forever. As pilings and storehouses grew up around these unlucky craft and the land moved out and up and over them like a cresting wave, escape was truly impossible. He counted himself lucky. He could leave anytime he wished on a new ship; or could he? What if he could leave. Did he really wish to leave? Each time he left the Cove, something drew him back to the watery city of adventure, death, and unclaimed treasure.

On October 27, Coffin was preparing for his freight run to Honolulu and taking one last look. Floating warehouses were still anchored among a flotilla of small boats and barges. In eight months the Harbor Master would count 164 storehouses still in Cove, most off the Pacific and Market Street wharves. Though seemingly oblivious to the steady march of sand seaward, a water city has no stability. Its only permanence lies in its use as buildings or foundations.

Two-thirds of the Ghost Fleet had by now been dismantled—gone for lumber or sunk and buried for fill, or dragged onto land. One vessel was allowed to drift with the tide and constantly change locations along the waterfront. Streets that had not existed yesterday—Battery, Front, Davis, Drumm, and half of Sansome Street, presently extended the length of the shore. Fremont Street greedily encroached on the ship city each day, as did Beale, Spear, all of New East Street, and Steuart Street. Just think, Coffin recalled in wonderment—the Bay had once slapped against First and Montgomery streets and been such a hindrance to Collector of Customs James Collier.

Where auctioneer's quarters once stood, the Montgomery Block of fire-shuttered, iron-doored, granite buildings impervious to fire was rising. The new Philadelphia Market with sixty-eight saloons and a restaurant had already opened between Montgomery and Sansome streets. On land the industrious city had wedged 148 hulks between new buildings or possibly new buildings had grown around them. People would pass two or three houses, then the bow of a ship with cut-in hawsepipes serving as windows and a hole in the stern for a door. Then another ship and another and a house or two, then another ship. No one could fault the get-up-and-go spirit of the burgeoning metropolis that greedily reached out to engulf its roots. There was treasure here, Coffin thought, and so many mysteries he had been unable to solve, so many villains and strange creatures. The *Whang Ho* had secrets he would never know. But, he had decided, it was time to leave Graveyard Harbor.

It saddened Coffin to leave the Ghost Fleet behind. He studied the rows of orphaned vessels glistening as ivory bone—the spine upon which a new and exciting city was being erected. He beat out the harbor under double reefs, fighting against the usual fiery nor'wester. At sunset the wind fell calm, and a strong flood tide swept him back into the San Francisco Bay as if trying to hold him as it had more majestic vessels. He anchored in Sausalito Cove and at midnight started again with a light breeze from northeast, and finally headed out to sea.

"As I passed the Golden Gate," he recalled. "I thought of the strange career that had attended me since I passed in here in the *Alhambra* several years earlier. Before I left California, four streets built upon piles were run across the Cove in front and some of the largest commission houses located there . . . Here the cholera and dysentery raged with the greatest virulence, and it was here that Messrs. Carr, Williams, Tappan, and young Thurlo, and many of the Ladies of the Lake had breathed their last after enduring Panama's heat and terrible fever, quarrelsome passages on crowded steamers, and the thievery of dishonest sea-captains."

The killer who looked like Christ had died dangling over Graveyard Harbor. The rough framework was a cross of sorts. A pirate had stalked here. On the oldest ships, sails in long yellow strips and cargo not worth salvaging lay half-submerged and unsalable. Fresh, usable provisions still lay in the holds of freshly abandoned ships. More ships continued to come, drawn by fresh new veins of gold in the foothills and the dream of riches. Coffin went topside.

He heard Father Taylor preach one last time. "This country is a great rendezvous for the representatives of all nations," he roared. He was a lion too. "Which, in connection with the fact of its proximity to the Islands of the Pacific and the teeming millions of Asia and all others, constitutes the greatest missionary field in the world. Every fellow of them grabbed a pick and shovel, and went to digging, and here they are today. All of them are embraced in the covenant of promise."

The city rose up in the same frenzy of activity as it had after the six great fires when men rebuilt with smoking hammers and hot nails. Yet, Coffin thought, there were still so many ships, one could not pinpoint the exact location of all of them within the forest of masts. Coffin was on his way out and the Ghost Fleet was vanishing right behind him.

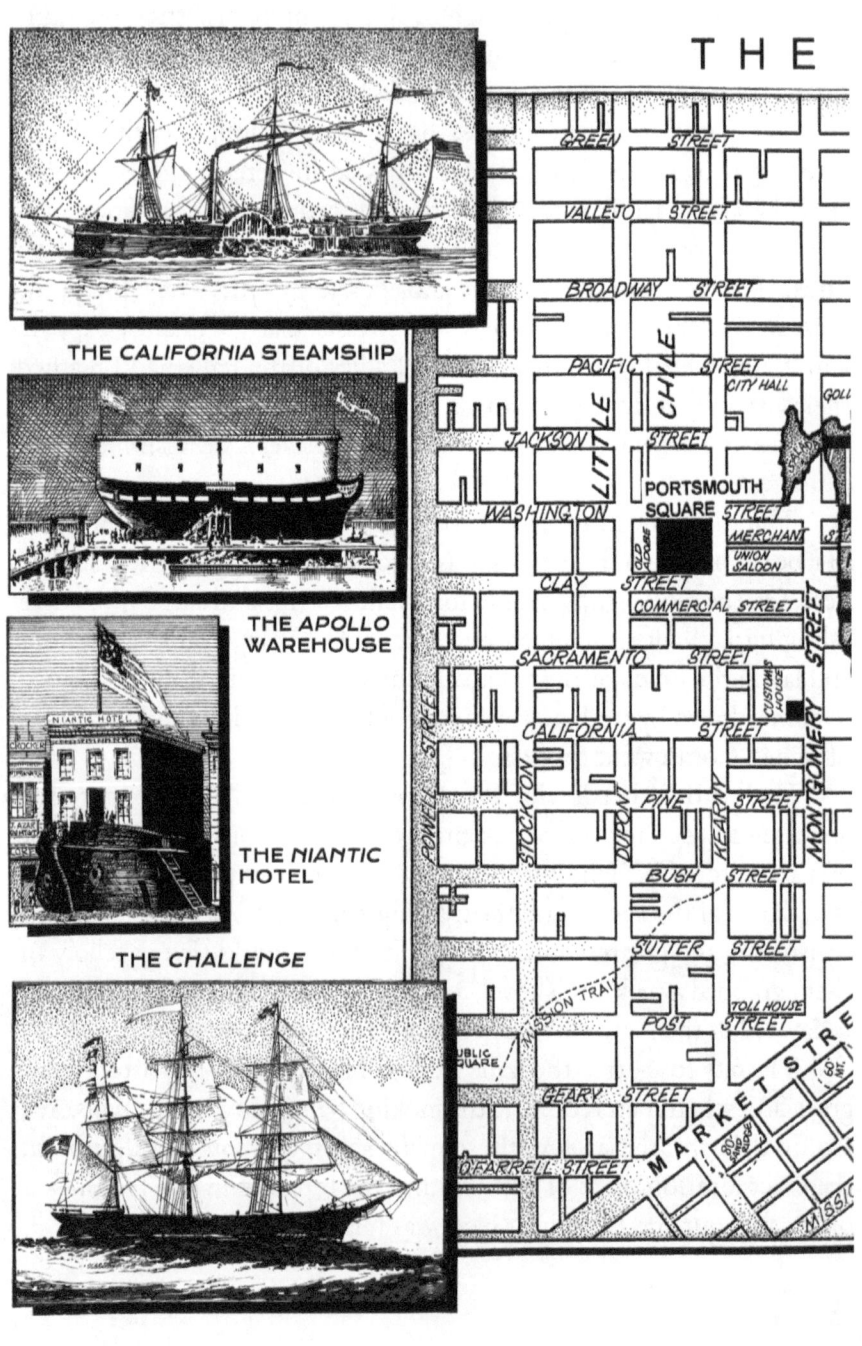

GHOST FLEET

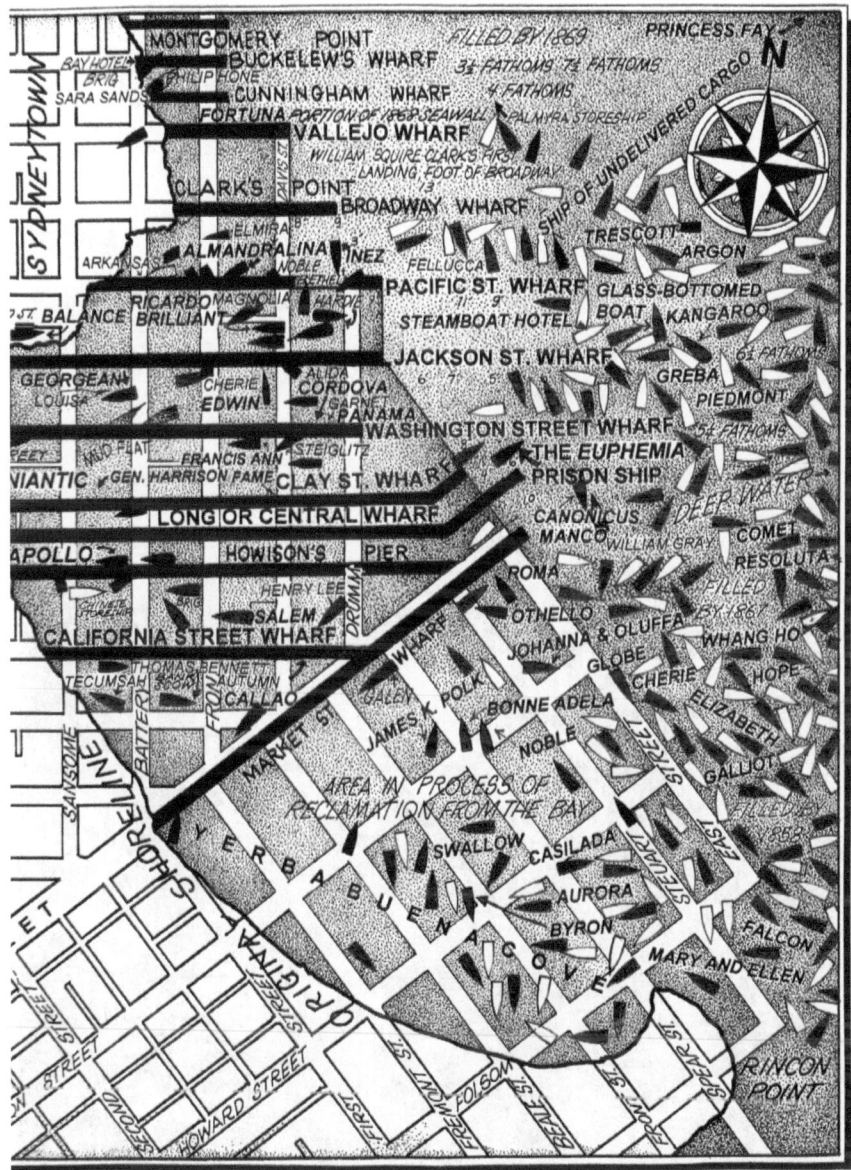

EPILOGUE

COFFIN WAS A DOZEN DAYS OUT when he made an island formed by a narrow entrance, a continuation of a ravine that came down from a steep mountain. A northeastern wind was prevailing. Seeing no land, he fumbled for his map which was wrapped in oilskin. According to his chart, his route lay directly across two positions where two small islands were laid down.

He tried to enter the narrow harbor on the lee (southwest) side. With the regular trade wind blowing out, he could not. He had never encountered such a thing. For several hours, his barque stood under a press of sail as he took it all in. Finally, he hauled short round the end of a coral reef, then beat out the harbor under double reefs, now fighting against a fiery nor'wester. He sailed on—to what?

He passed within two miles of a volcanic island which was issuing white smoke from a crater. He held up his palm to feel the heat. He could. He had a fine run down to where he anchored at dawn. Twenty days out, he delivered his passengers and cargo to Honolulu, then pushed on across the Pacific.

On January 8, 1852, without any official permit, he started on his retrograde voyage. The Northeast Monsoon, blowing directly down the China Sea, forced him to take the eastern route. He rushed through the Java Sea and doubled the end of Bouton Island on January 21.

"I found that a current or bad steerage had set me out of my course," Coffin explained. "I fell in with an extensive reef nearly even with the surface, with dry rocks visible in several places and the remains of numerous wrecks laying about on the reef, which extended to the Southeast and the extremity two miles on my weather bow."

At 4:00 PM that same day, he hove to wait for daylight so he would not wreck. He crept through the Bashee Passage. He tacked again and, seeing a clear passage to leeward passed through a strait two miles wide and came out into the Banda Sea on February 5, his birthday. He was a fortnight working his way out through the passages. Strong southeasterly breezes set the *Arco Iris* to dragging her anchors and clumping together to the beat.

On Tuesday, October 18, he became amused by a series of craft consistently passing his barque. "They generally go in pairs, two of a kind and exactly alike," he explained. "First come two fishing boats ... next come a pair of cargo boats, and then two lonely lorchas. Against the wind's howl, Coffin found his hearing oddly enhanced. He followed the sound and distinctly heard sails flapping—hulls pounding, and rudders bumping just as he had four years earlier when the Gold Rush made an international port of San Francisco. He studied the waves and dreamed of Graveyard Harbor and its mysteries, cooling fog, and hidden treasure and felt a pang. On the oldest ships there, sails in long yellow strips and cargo not worth salvaging lay half-submerged and unsalable. Fresh, usable provisions still lay in the holds of freshly abandoned ships. Yet, more vessels continued to come, drawn by fresh new veins of gold in the foothills and dreams of riches.

In his heart he knew the Ghost Fleet was no more and made a prayer. While his mind did not know, his heart did. "Now, when I look back on what has passed in the last few years," Coffin said, "it appears to me to have been a trance, a wonder dream, something unreal, a great blank in my existence.

"I had travelled about fifteen miles today when I opened out into a northwesterly direction and came to a towering mountain. The island is so rough and precipitous that a straight and level street of ten rods long is out of the question. A location for a home is hard to be found without digging down one side and leveling the other. My ship stands in under a press of sail and hauls short. Round the end of the reef every halyard is let go at once and sail taken in as quickly as possible. I had taken possession in a harbor fronted by a mountain that arose at least a half-mile out of the water."

Below, the mountain, Coffin made out a harbor packed with large western boats flying the flags of the United States and Britain. There were others too. On both sides of the mountain, ahead and behind, vessels stood as a spectral city in the fog and littered the harbor, so like "the rickety Venice hemmed in by a forest of masts," that he had left behind.

"Of all the places I have ever visited, this is the most heterogeneous and fantastic. As I came abreast of the city," he added, "the banks of the river were completely hidden from view by an absolute jam of boats, and I did not see how I was to effect a landing . . . I came to a narrow lane through the city of boats, which led to a small dock appropriated to the use of the common herd by a boom, which was drawn aside as I approached, and shot through into a beautiful little basin with granite steps. I threaded my way out through a narrow and crowded channel. As I ran into this yawning mouth it came out on a dark and rainy day.

"At early daylight I was taken possession in the harbor. Coffin sniffed the charcoal cooking fires and gazed thoughtfully upon paper lanterns glimmering in the fog. Tiny bats like swallows came out in the evening, swooping down on him as he ate his dinner.

On both sides, ahead and behind, were crowds of vessels. The river is full of boats of all sizes and shapes. Those living near the water can look down upon his neighbor for nearly one half the population live in boats. Coffin stood stock still. Many would be born and brought up and die on these floating homes. Perhaps so would he. Coffin studied how the boat homes rocked gently. He saw they were filled with happy families. Rows of junks and sampans were tied together as were the people. Clearly one-half the people, a grand total of half a million, were living altogether on the water, and scarcely ever putting foot upon the land.

"Children are born and brought up in a sampan," he added. Many would spend their lives on these floating homes. Perhaps so would he.

Again the glow of a pipe highlighted the straight line mouth and balding head of Capt. George B. Coffin. In his floating Oriental City he was content—for now. His book was almost done and someday his children would publish it. His feelings echoed those of Anne Booth—"I think I can never grow weary of living on the water, and feel as much reluctance to quit it as if it were my native element."

Amid the creaking of Asian boats, Coffin heard his own solitary footsteps striking his deck and sensed again the loneliness of the Ghost Fleet and for a moment expected it to rise from the sea and be reborn as one of the most unusual and mysterious places on earth.

Hong Kong Harbor as sketched by Capt. George Coffin.

ACKNOWLEDGMENTS

FIRST AND FOREMOST I'd like to thank my editor and sounding board Aaron Smith for his brilliant insight, flawless attention to detail, and endless patience. David & Lisa, Margot, Sow, Rayluk, Harmony, Zoe, Melanie, Rita Willaims, Kevin Fagan, Heather Taylor, Strephon Taylor, Steve Kellener, Leesa Gallentine, Zak Wilson, Mark DeVito, Diane Bodker, Gina Cafasso, Tiffany Hearsey, Bill Riling, Marge Dean, Marli Renfro Peterson, Alexandre O. Philippe, Kerry Deignan Roy, and Mike Medavoy who showed such great interest in these long forgotten tales of early San Francisco.

At the end of October Coffin wasn't present to witness the greatest manhunt within Graveyard Harbor since the search for English Jim. It began when Capt. "Bully" Waterman and his sadistic first mate, "Black" Douglass, sailed into Graveyard Harbor with much of their crew dead.

No doubt the sheriff would make certain any future jury learned all the facts. Devil Jack was relentless and a man of the truth in a city of lies.

DEVIL JACK AND THE CITY OF LIES

APPENDIX

KNOWN GHOST FLEET VESSELS AND THEIR CONFIRMED OR ESTIMATED SITES

This Appendix includes gold ships that arrived between 1848 and 1855 and were abandoned, burned, exploded, raided by gangs with fake lights, or scuttled in the Cove and Graveyard Harbor or dragged onto shore to become ship buildings. Before Clipper Ships, there were four predominant types of sailing vessels in the Gold Rush—Three-masted and square-rigged ships; barks on which the forward two masts were square-rigged and the rear (mizzen) mast rigged fore-and-aft; brigs with two square-rigged masts; schooners with two masts rigged fore-and aft.

ACASIA, off Rincon Point.

ADA, lay near Broadway Wharf.

ALIDA between Washington and Jackson Streets.

ADELAIDE, an old brig of Newburyport occupied inside the Ghost Fleet by Capt. Coffin's friends, Capt. George Noyes, Capt. E. Welch and Louis Martin [aka Martin Lewis].

ALCESTE, scuttled by Hulk Undertaker, Charles Hare.

ALEXANDER von HUMBOLDT, a German-built coal storeship, carried 358 gold seekers to San Francisco in May, 1849. It sold 440 berths at $200 each. Nine passengers were shoehorned into each six-foot-square compartment. "We were packed more densely, had less accommodations for sleeping and were served infinitely viler food and water than inmates of the worst jail," reported passenger Julius Pratt out of New England. Six passengers died of disease. George Payson observed the bark enter San Francisco Bay and described it as "an out-and-out vagrant, a beggar born and bred." Passengers swarmed black as ants out on the bowsprit, they clustered like bees in the rigging. [The] matted heads that looked at us over the bulwarks seemed almost as thick as a pile of coconuts." Once at dock it was condemned.

ALHAMBRA, 649-freighter, built in 1893 in Bristol Maine departed New Orleans on April 14, 1849 under Capt. George B. Coffin, refitted for $10.000. At 4:00 PM, October 11, she passed through the Golden Gate. During the great winter storms of 1849-50 When the storms passed Coffin brought the Alhambra up onto the mudflats near Long Wharf where it lay along with fifty other small craft for the next four months. On January 30, 1850, he let the old Alhambra go to the Pacific Steamship Company for $13,500. She was broken up and used as a storeship.

ALIDA, a storeship.

ALMANDRALINA, a storeship near Pacific Wharf on the corner of Pacific and Front.

ALMENA, Boston, carried a company of twenty-nine goldhunters who had paid six hundred dollars for a round-trip passage and share in the mining profits.

ALSOP, near Cunningham's Wharf.

AMELIA, a bark broken up by Charley Hare.

AMERIKA, a German craft.

ANDALUSIA, Anne Booth's Uncle Wes's merchant ship, provided lumber for the Booth's first land home in California.

ANNA REYNOLDS, bark out of Connecticut, sailed from New Haven, March 12, 1849 with the California & New Haven Joint Stock Company on board. On the night of November 18, 1849, she struck the *Amerika*, a German craft thirty miles off the Golden Gate, but both survived to reach the Cove.

ANDREW, a store hulk.

ANDREW SCOTT, near California Street Wharf.

MARY ANN, lay near Broadway Wharf.

ANN MCKIM, a Baltimore skysail yarder was the first to enter the Golden Gate. Between 1840-1851, the Harbor Mate reported that seventy-one clippers arrived in the Cove and departed. Clippers, unlike other vessels, rarely became marooned among the skeletons of the Ghost Fleet. Discipline aboard them was stern and the officers were able to hold their men. Soon, floating cities, enormous steamships and liners, would replace the clippers.

ANN PERRY, lay near Broadway Wharf.

ANNE THORPE

ANNA, lay near Pacific Wharf.

ANNA, a second ship of the same name.

ANTELOPE, English iron steamer at Long Wharf and Clark's Point

APOLLO, famous storeship, warehouse, boarding house and, finally, saloon. The *Apollo* left New York January 16, 1849, arrived in San Francisco September 18, 1849. Eventually, advancing wharves surrounded the *Apollo*. Burned badly in the May 3-4, 1851 city-destroying fire, but rebuilt, her final resting place at Battery and Sacramento Streets near the Federal Reserve Bank.

APTHORPE, a store hulk off Cunningham's Wharf.

ARK, a coal brig off Jackson Street.

ARK, a second ship of the same name, also a coal hulk, one of C. K. Garrison's.

ARKANSAS, American bark, 627-tons, a storage and tavern ship, the "Old Ship Tavern. A hotel was later built above the vessel on the north side of Pacific Wharf between Front and Battery, discovered at the corner of Battery and Pacific. She was consigned to George Wardle and Co. and heavily freighted. Later the US Hotel would be built over the ship on the north side of Pacific between Front and Battery Streets. She was disassembled in 1857 and sold for scrap, but the Old Ship Saloon stayed in the hotel for decades.

ATTILA

AUCLAND, owned by J. B. Thomas.

AUDLEY CLARK, off Rincon Point.

AUGUSTA

AURORA

AUTUMN, a storeship on Davis Street near Market Street, burned in May 3, 1851.

BACCHUS, a brig off Pacific Wharf.

BALANCE, a gold brig later found buried in mid-Gold Street at Balance Alley on Davis Street, near Jackson). This teak ship was already ninety-two years old when she arrived at the Cove.

BANK, a scow that served as the city's first bank, at the corner of California and

Battery.

BAY SLATE, a schooner.

BAY STATE, a brig.

BAZAAR, off Rincon Point.

BELFAST, 190-ton brig, took 76 passengers at $100 each to the harbor in mid-February, 1849. This brig was the first square-rigger to discharge cargo at a San Francisco dock, Broadway Wharf, in September, 1848.

BETHEL, a storeship deserted at the corner of Pacific and Drumm Streets.

BINGHAM, near California Street Wharf.

BIRMINGHAM, sunk between Goat and Sheep Islands.

BLACK EAGLE, a brig near California Street Wharf.

BONNE ADELA

BORDEAUX, storeship which lay near Broadway Wharf, lost on Columbia River Bar.

BRAMAH, coal hulk

BRANT, Russian storage ship off Long Wharf.

BREMEN, off Rincon Point.

BRIG, unknown ship, a vessel of six hundred tons, drawn up on the mud under a high bank and transformed into a restaurant and hotel. Bay Hotel built over the ship, placed in some records as being near the southeast corner of Battery and Green Streets near Balance and Globe and brigs Magnolia and Brilliant.

BRILLIANT, a warehouse ship and boarding house.

BRITISH SHIP, unnamed, sank in ten fathoms after being brought up against the Xylon, Alhambra and Canada.

BRONTES, storeship and lumber ship.

BROTHER JONATHAN, three decks, 269-feet by 40-feet by 30-feet wooden sidewheeler steamer. Left New York to San Francisco September 1851 and arrived November 19, 1851. One of the cholera ships. During an 1852 cholera outbreak a reported 84 passengers died. She went aground at Point Loma in 1854.

BRUNNER, a store hulk.

BURMAH, off Rincon Point.

BYRON a bark used as a lumber ship near California Street Wharf. Lost May 3, 1851 fire.

CABOT, lay near Broadway Wharf.

CACHALOT, French-owned brig.

CADMUS, off Rincon Point, the same ship that carried Lafayette to America in 1824, refitted for the Gold Rush as were hundreds of other derelicts.

CALEDONIA, lay near Law's Wharf.

CALIFORNIA, Statistics: Sidewheel steamer. L/B/D: 200' X 33' X 22'. Tons: 1057 grt. Hull: Wood/ live oak, 225 by 31 by 18-foot hull. A much abbreviated clipper bow with a horizontal bowsprit and a white band around her. 200 passengers; 75 crew. Machinery: Side-lever engine, 250-hp, 2 paddles. A single stack placed forward of the paddle blades. Square sails rigged fore and aft. Built: William H. Webb, New York; 1848, one of three sidewheeler steamships ordered (the *Panama* and *Oregon* being the others) for the Pacific Mail Steamship Company to carry passengers and mail. Launched on May 19, 1848, sailed from New York on October 6 under

Capt. Cleaveland Forbes carrying a cargo of coal. On November 11, 1875 the California made its last trip as a steamer from San Diego to San Francisco. Its machinery was removed and the hulk sold to N. Bichard, then bark-rigged and for years engaged in the coal and lumber trade. It ran aground at Pacasmayo, Peru in 1895. It spent eight of those years with the Mexican Coast Steamship Company from 1860-1868. In 1868 Goodall, Nelson & Perkins Steamship Company removed the California's engine and refitted it as a bark and the original Ghost Fleet ship sailed for twenty more years. It ran aground at Pacasmayo, Peru in 1895.

CALLAO, a storeship at the corner of Mission and Beale Streets. Burned May 3, 1851.

CALUMET, near California Street Wharf.

CAMILLA, a store hulk.

CANADA, a Nantucket ship lashed to the Alhambra during the winter storm of 1849-50.

CANDACE, a bark, went to San Blas. The long buried ship was displayed at San Francisco Mint in 2007, rare hull from 1818 whaling craft salvaged 20 feet of its stern, 17 feet of center. Location: Charles Hare who dismantled ships for a living, and never fully took the *Candace* apart. and part of its keel. buried a century and recovered, *Candace*, built in Boston in 1818 sailed as a trade ship in the Pacific before being transformed into a three-masted whaler. After a hunting trip to the Arctic in 1854 the ship set sail for homeport of New London, Conn, loaded with 400 barrels of whale oil and 2,000 pounds of whale bone. Leaking badly it docked in San Francisco on July 4, 1855 and was found buried beneath Hare's business. James Allan, an archeologist helped identify it from four other ships.

CANION, a bark.

CANONICUS, a storage brig often filled with gunpowder just off Sacramento Street Wharf, burned San Francisco Bay on July 25, 1853.

CANTERO, dropped anchor at the island of St. Catherine in December, 1849

CANTON, 93-feet long, 24-feet wide and ten-feet deep.The 198-ton bark carried forty- eight passengers of the Island City company and sailed from New York March, 1849 with the Island City Company on board. Joseph Kendall, a passenger, recalled their crossing of the Equator and the celebration that ensued: "When all was over, the drinking began...the sailors and the rest of passengers collected from thirty to forty bottles...and the heads of some by tomorrow will be aching badly indeed." On the *Canton*, heavy shutters were lashed over the cabin skylight against the heavy seas breaking over the deck.

CAPITOL, 700-tons, out of Boston in January, 1849 with almost 250 passengers who almost immediately laid plans to seize the *Capitol*. After rations were increased, the threat of mutiny disappeared.

CARDOVA

CARIB, of Salem.

CARIOLANUS, off Rincon Point.

CARIB, a bark, went to sea.

CAROLINE AUGUSTA, off Rincon Point.

CARLOTTA, wrecked at Tonquin Shoal in the Bay in 1850.

CARRIER PIGEON, 1849, lost within sight of the wharves.

CASILADA, a storeship at the end of Howison's Pier next to the Piedmont.

CHALLENGE, though only a visitor to the Ghost Fleet it was instrumental in the saga.

CHARLOTTE

CHATEAUBRIAND, of Le Havre.

CHERIE

CHINESE WAREHOUSE, on Long Wharf. Discovered at Battery and Sacramento Streets.

CHRISTOVAL COLON, made Rio in fifty-one days, arrived San Francisco on August 7, 1849.

CIVILIAN, schooner, sailed late 1849. Sixty members of the Cochituate Company each putting up only two hundred dollars provide the least expensive voyage on record.

COLONEL CROSS, a 160-ton side-wheeler, wrecked in the Bay on January 29, 1850.

COLORADO, anchored in the Cove on June 30, 1850.

COMMANCHE, collided with the *J. Bragdon* in the Carquinez Straits, the two miles wide passage leading to Suisun Bay, on January 5, 1853 with thirteen deaths.

CONTRA COSTA, a walking beam side-wheeler, suffered a boiler explosion in the Bay on April 4, 1859.

COPIAPO

CORDOVA, a water ship.

CORSAIR, a brig and storeship.

CORVO, off Jackson Street.

CROTON, out of New York.

CROWN PRINCESS, hit Blossom Rock in 1850 and run over to Goat Island.

CYCLOPS, lay between Jackson and Pacific Streets.

CYRUS, off Rincon Point.

DALMATIA, near California Street Wharf, Law's Wharf, and Cunningham's Wharf.

DAMARISCOTT, storeship near Long Wharf.

DASHING WAVE, 1849, lost within sight of the docks.

DELIA WALKER, off Rincon Point, broken up by J. Atkinson.

DETROIT, brig near California Street Wharf.

DIANTHE, near California Street Wharf, broken up by Hare.

DISDEM, off Rincon Point.

DOLORES

DOLPHIN, 100-ton schooner left New York, January, 1849 and left Panama, leaking and its rigging rotten in January with forty-five men aboard. Notable passengers, James McClatchy, later a major newspaper publisher.

DOMINGO, Russian ship broken up by Bichard.

DONNA MARIA, near California Street Wharf.

DOVER, a store hulk.

DRYADE, near Law's Wharf.

DUCHESS OF CLARENCE, a bark off Rincon Point.

DUKE OF WELLINGTON, fitted out and escaped the Ghost Fleet for Australia in 1852.

DUXBURY, of Boston, sailed into the Ghost Fleet on August 22, 1849. Newspaper published aboard and printed throughout the spring of 1849, reporting on the tedium and poor food.

EDWARD EVERETT, 700-tons, 150 passengers. This six-year old ship left Boston January, 1849, arrived Valparaiso, April 29 and San Francisco, July 6. She sold for $11,000. "Vessels are selling for dog cheap," said a Sacramento trader in the fall of 1849. "Fine large barks bring $3000 to $5000."

EDWIN, a storeship near Pacific Wharf, built over and eventually broken up.

ELEANOR, near California Street Wharf, storeship for Chile flour.

ELIZA, a crisp little bark constructed in Salem in 1822 by Thomas and David Magound. She was engaged in the Zanzibar trade for years under Capt. Augustine Staniford Perkins. On December 2, 1848, the *Eliza* sailed from Derby Wharf for San Francisco with six passengers and a cargo of flour, pork, sugar, dried apples, bread, butter, cheese, rice, figs, raisins, pickles, boots, shoes, stoves, axes, picks, a variety of small articles and lumber, materials for building a scow to dredge rivers or sand bars and a small steam engine. Everyone knew the "Liza ship" of the miner's "California Song"--"with a washboard on my knee." The *Eliza* reached San Francisco on June 1, 1849, sailed up river to Sacramento, arriving in time to prevent a famine. She finally became a storehouse there.

ELIDA, Norwegian laid off Jackson Street.

ELISA, bark broken up near Hashaway's Wharf.

ELIZABETH, bonded storeship used by Collector Collier near California Street Wharf.

ELLEN BROOKS, lay near Pacific Wharf.

ELMIRA, a storeship sunk at corner of Pacific and Davis Streets.

EMPRESS, British storeship near California Street Wharf, broken up by Hare.

EMPRESS (2), coal hulk.

ENVOY, near Law's Wharf, sunk near Vallejo Street, raised and broken up by Hare.

EQUATOR, whaler laid near California Street Wharf, sent to Costa Rica.

ERIE, sunk near Goat Island.

EUPHEMIA, (*Uphamer*), floating jail buried at Battery and Sacramento Streets.

EUROPE, sailed 20,000 miles over 222 days out of Philadelphia, arrived San Francisco, February 12, 1850.

FALEA, store hulk broken up by Hare.

FAME, a brig, corner of Clay and Front Streets broken up by Hare.

FALCON, a steamer which carried ninety-five passengers, (half its capacity) for the Isthmus, the first Panama-bound vessel to depart New York (March 8, 1849) since the Gold Rush began and the first to reach Panama City where passengers were awaiting the California's arrival. Passengers there paid $40 for the three day ride to Cruces. Five missionaries were on board, their spiritual goal to "recall to the attention of the multitudes rushing into El Dorado to the fact that there is something more valuable than gold."

FELLUCCAS, several unnamed.

FLAVINS, off Rincon Point.

FLORA, sank May, 1849 during a Bay squall. Capt. S. C. Reeves, a former Columbia Bar pilot, drowned.

FLORENCE, near Broadway Wharf, broken up by Hare.

FLYING DRAGON, 1849, lost within sight of the docks. 1127-tons, sailed from Newcastle, New South Wales to San Francisco with one thousand tons of coal. On the night of Jan 29, 1862, a squall and a flood tide drove her into Arch Rock in the Bay.

FORTUNA, a ship-hotel on bounded by Battery and Front, Vallejo and Green.

FRANCES, schooner.

Appendix A 345

FRANCIS, a brig and store hulk near Pacific Wharf.

FRANCIS ANN, a storeship at Clay and Front, broken up by Hare.

FRANCIS du PAU, coal hulk moored near Long Wharf, went to San Juan del Sur as Ghost Fleet filled in.

FRANKLIN, off Rincon Point.

FRIENDSHIP, off Rincon Point, fitted out in the end and went to sea.

GALEN, E. Travers' storeship "moored on Market Street in the center of six water lots."

GAILEO, off Rincon Point.

GALLATEA, off Rincon Point.

GALLIOT, unnamed.

GANGES, brig off Jackson Street broken up by Howgate.

GARNET, a storeship broken up by Lawson, fifteen feet behind Cordova.

GARRETT, lay near Long Wharf.

GENERAL CASTILLO, storeship for flour lay near Pacific Wharf.

GENERAL HARRISON, bow close to *Niantic's* stern on Clay Street, broken up by Hare. a three-masted, 409-ton ship built in Newburyport, Massachusetts and sailed around Cape Horn to San Francisco. Her solid oak hull was 126-feet, 2-inches in length and 26-feet, 7-inches wide. Listed in as a "fine and commodious storage facility" on May 30, 1850, but burned to the water line in the May 4, 1851 fire. Most of its copper and brass filings were picked off after salvage, then the hull buried. She was secured with pilings at Battery Street along the Clay Street as a storeship and warehouse, a floating warehouse owned by E. Mickle and Company. Bancroft places her at the northwest corner of Sacramento and Battery, but she was dug up at the southwest corner of Battery and Clay Streets.

GENERAL MORGAN, a sailing vessel which played host to curious Indians as they neared the Pacific. Among the passengers was Albert Lyman, one of the few prospectors to explore the Patagonian mainland.

GENERAL VERSEY, store hulk that ended up in Sydney.

GENERAL WORTH, left Newburyport on November 28, 1849,"After bidding our friends a hearty good-by, which was responded to with ringing cheers, the brig spread its wings, and flew down the harbor before a strong northwest breeze,"arrived San Francisco, May 6, 1850.

GENESSEE, lay near California Street Wharf, Joe Goldsmith had her.

GENETTA DE GOITO, a bark.

GEORGE RYAN, near California Street Wharf.

GEORGEAN a storeship south of Jackson Street and west of Battery, may be the hull incorporated into the building at 716-720 Montgomery, known as the Ship Building.

--Muscatine, Old San Francisco, between Jackson Street and Washington. Damaged by flames, May 3, 1851.

GEORGIA (GEORGIANA), steamer, exploded at Petaluma through negligence. owned by Howland and Aspinwall, left New York on May 13, 1849. Commander Capt. Parker H. French, 189 passengers who had paid $250 each to sail on his swift vessel, five killed on November 23, 1855.

GILBERT JAMESON, British brig off Rincon Point.

GINATE DE GOLA, broken up by Hare.

GLOBE, a storeship on Davis Street between Oregon and Jackson, cut up by Hare, 1851.

GLOUCHESTER, a British barque, capsized in the Bay on November 19, 1850.

GODDESS, struck Blossom Rock and sank in San Francisco Bay on July 18, 1856.

GOLCONDA, off Rincon Point, broken up by Hare.

GOLD HUNTER, steamship collided with the McKim in the Straits, June 25, 1850. By 1852 she had been renamed Active and was running as a US Survey steamer.

GOLDEN AGE, broken up by Howgate.

GRAY, cut up by Hare.

GRETRY, broken up by Howgate.

GROTIUS, near California Street Wharf near Ganges.

GRIFFON, built 1840, bark, 301 tons burthen, sold at auction on December 20, 1849, for $8000.

HAMILTON, off Rincon Point, broken up by Howgate.

HARDIE, a British storeship brig, twenty feet from *Noble*, opposite Clark Street.

HARDY, brig near Long Wharf.

HARRISON, on Battery between Clay and Sacramento, sold as whaler.

HARTFORD, burned at Central Wharf on March 18, 1851.

HARTLAND, near Broadway Wharf, British brig broken up by Hare.

HARRIET, broken up by Hare.

HARVEST, bark cut up near Long Wharf by Hare.

HECTOR, brig, command of Capt. Kemp.

HELEN HENSLEY, a Mississippi-style riverboat built in 1853. Her boiler exploded at the Jackson Street Wharf on January 19, 1854 with the loss of two.

HENRY EWBANK, store hulk for coal.

HENRY LEE, a little bark "of great antiquity, with rotten bottom, a miserable sailor" on California Street, broken up by Hare. Sailed February 17, 1849, via Cape Horn with 122 men of the Hartford Union Mining and Trading Company--New England landsmen--farmers and machinists, was three weeks out of New York headed toward Rio when storm splintered two of her masts on March 11, 1849, carried the Hartford Union Mining & Trading Company. Very religious passengers who had signed a solemn pledge of temperance. They had transformed their ship into a floating New England village. Brought printing supplies. An eighty-eight page book was printed while the ship lay in the Bay. The Henry Lee "lay for a long time on the site now (1882) occupied by Selby's store."

HERCULES, a tug.

HOPE

HURON, near Cunningham's Wharf.

HYCONIUM, taken apart by Howgate.

IANTHE, Liverpool packet near California Street Wharf.

IDA FERRIS, (*Louise*) a German vessel at foot of Jackson Street, broken up by Bichard.

INEZ, a whaler off Rincon Point, sunk on Pacific and Drumm Streets by Lawson.

ITALIAN RESTAURANT SHIP, beached at Davis and Pacific Streets. Under direction of Giuseppe Bazzuro from Genova. Bazzuro gave up the ship-restaurant as San Francisco reclaimed

Appendix A 347

the Bay.

IWANONA, near California Street, afterward a lumber droger.

IZETTE, schooner near California Street Wharf, cut up by Hare.

JAMES, hulk cut up by Howgate.

JAMES CASKIE, brig anchored off Clark's Point, the farthest northern point of the Ghost Fleet. Capt. Jones, a friend of Coffin, and his wife lived aboard and were beaten and robbed by "English Jim" Stuart and three ruffians from his gang.

JAMES K. POLK, an iron-clad revenue steamer. Just before the arrival of the *California* the *Polk* was hauled high up on the beach at Vallejo and Battery and remained there for many months. It became an unloading station where passengers were discharged into small boats in the stream and rowed to the shallow water where the old iron hulk was stuck. There they climbed up the steep gangway of the old Polk, across her deck to the plank which had been laid from her rail across the water to the shore.

JAMES STUART, off Jackson Street owned by Capt. Coffin, storekeeper, broken up by Hare.

JAMES W. PAIGE, bound from Bangor to San Francisco under Capt. Jackson. Dropped anchor in the Cove on September 7, 1852. Practical jokes aboard were "as thick as weevils in the ship's bread." One passenger, John Dolliff resembled Capt. Jackson, and sometimes put on the skipper's cap and coat and went around ordering the stewards and giving a variety of orders. Notable passenger: J. Lamson who chronicled the voyage.

JEANETTE, laid at Clark's Point, broken up by Hare. Only ship laying here when gold was discovered.

JANET, brig near California Street Wharf.

JAPAN, laid near Pacific Street Wharf and owned by "Emperor" Joshua Norton.

JAPAN (2), first heaving down hulk, bark broken up by Batchelder at Cowell's Wharf.

JAVA, lay near Broadway Wharf, Hare broke her up.

J. BRAGDON, on January 3, 1853 collided with the Commanche in the Straits.

JOHANNA & OLUFFA, a Danish brig deserted within three days of arrival.

JOHN ADAMS, a bark near California Street, taken apart by Hare.

JOHN ALLYN, of New Bedford.

JOHN BREWER, lay near Pacific Wharf, sent to China, "burnt by Chinese pardones."

JOHN CALVIN, off Rincon Point.

JOSEPHINE, lay near Broadway Wharf, settled by Hare.

JOSHUA MUNN, settled by Hare.

JULIA HELEN, lay near Pacific Wharf.

JUSTINE, near Long Wharf, coal hulk once near Cunningham's Wharf.

KANGAROO, the first ferryboat on San Francisco Bay, smokestack lowered and abandoned in 1851. Capt. Thomas Gray ran his small ship between San Francisco and the east shore of the Bay in San Antonio Creek (now Oakland Estuary).

LADY ADAMS, brig off Rincon Point and broken up by Hare.

LE BARON, lay near Long Wharf, sunk near North Point dock.

LaGRANGE, out of Salem. Her cargo of live chickens sold for $25 each.

LAURA ANN, a one hundred-ton "old fashioned tub of a vessel, and slower than justice." The menu featured wormy hardtack, hard beans. The badly crowded *Laura Ann* reached San

Francisco on October 4, 1849. A voyage that had been estimated at fifty to sixty days at most, had taken eight months!

LE BARON

LEONORE, New England ship off Vallejo Street, broken up by Howgate. carried a fireproof safe, and a case of swords. Dropped anchor off Clark's Point in August, 1849 with a hold full of tools and hardware. Owned by the New England Mining and Trading Company. During negotiations to sell the cargo other ships arrived just behind and made it a glut on the market. She had cleared Boston Harbor two weeks after the Everett, but she was a fast sailer and sailed into the Cove on July 5, a record time of 149 days. Like the other ships she was sold. Even the steamboat they had brought out for river use at $1,700 got an offer of $30.000 which they turned down. When she was finally sold, it was for little and the Lenore ended up as one of the Cove storeships.

LINDSAYS, storeship.

LITTLE SITKA, Russian, used by Russian Officers as a party boat and the first steamer on the Bay; thirty-seven-foot steam side-wheeler, sank at the Cove dock on February 12, 1848. Owned by William Leidesdorff.

LOO CHOO, ended her days July 15, 1855 in the Umpqua River Bar, Oregon.

LOUISA, former yacht of the King of the Hawaiian Islands at Washington and Battery. Heath Davis first visited California aboard the Louisa in 1831. Deserted at Washington and Battery Streets.

LOUISE, a storeship.

LUCINDA, a storeship.

LYDIA, dismantled and sunk at Howard Street.

MAGNOLIA, out of New Bedford, sunk close to *Magnolia*, *Brilliant*, *Balance* and *Globe*. Raced with the Sweden which Moses Cogswell recounted: "The moon shone very bright and the white sails reflected its pale light, casting a bright shadow on the rushing waves beyond. I never expected to see a more beautiful sight." The *Magnolia*, to cheers on both ships, pulled ahead to stay.

MALLORY, lay off Jackson Street.

MANCO, burned, then a storage vessel later fitted up for sea. She was often a storeship of gun powder kegs, moored just off the Sacramento Street Wharf. The *Manco* was burned Tuesday, May 24, 1853 in the same fire as the *Canonicus*. Nahl captured the burning of both ships in a celebrated oil painting.

MARGARSI, smashed by Hare.

MARIA, a bark.

MARIE, broken up by Hare.

MARIPOSA, rammed and sunk at New York of the Pacific by the West Point on October 28, 1850.

MARTHA, London packet which lay near California Street Wharf, broken up by Hare.

MARTHA WATSON, a storeship.

MARY AND ELLEN, The first sailing vessel to put into the Cove, a brig from Salem, Massachusetts. Its Capt. John H. Eagleston had bought the *Zemo* for $7,000 dollars from Hooper and Cheesbury and renamed her for his daughters. While he was in Salem, Eagleston learned that gold had been discovered. He sailed for San Francisco on October 28, 1848 with a full cargo- -flour and other cargo from Salem merchants. John Henry Proctor died of an infected finger

Appendix A   349

during the voyage. *The Mary and Ellen* reached the Cove at 3:00 PM on March 28, 1849. After disposing of his cargo and passengers, the Capt. was unable to find a crew to sail on to Oregon. Sailors wanted "three hundred dollars per month, ham, eggs, butter, soft tack, and canned meats, and all the liberty we want in port." When the captain could get no one to sail it the ship was sold on March 28, 1849, making a profit of eight thousand dollars above what Eagleston had paid.

MAGNOLIA, a storeship and boarding house.

MANILLA, abandoned ship that Louisa and Fayette Clappe lived upon.

MASON, Salem ship off Jackson Street which took a lumber cargo to Australia.

MAYFLOWER, near California Street Wharf.

MAZEPPA, a barque, left January 27, 1849 and reached San Francisco on December 2.

MAZEPPA, a brig, sailed on June 8, 1849, one of the first of forty-eight ships from Australia to reach the Bay. By the time William Shaw, an English midshipman, arrived the harbor was filled with ships. The crew deserted in boats or on floating planks, leaving the passengers to fend for themselves.

McKIM, the 327-ton side-wheeler out of New Orleans in 1849, collided with the Gold Hunter on June 25, 1850.

MEISER, broken up by Hare.

MELAN, storeship broken up.

MEMNON, storeship broken up.

MENTOR, ship which stored quicksilver off Rincon Point.

MERSEY, did service near Law's Wharf.

METROPOLIS, of Beverly, Massachusetts, New England ship struck Arch Rock in the Bay 1855.

MINER, Capt. Clark's sternwheeler of 75-tons, burned to the waters edge on October 9, 1851.

MINERVA, off Sacramento Street, broken up by Hare.

MONSOON, was off Rincon, off Market Street, broken up by Hare.

MONTANE, French packet, sold to Bichard who broke it up.

MONTANIA.

MONTASO, near California Street Wharf, in stream.

MONUMENT, broken up by Hare.

MORRISON, near California Street Wharf, broken up by Hare.

MOUNT VERNON, settled by Hare.

MUVOY, lay near Law's Wharf.

NAUMKEAG, of Providence.

NEPTUNE, off Rincon Point, broken up.

NEW ORLEANS, one of the Howard Line of steamers.

NEW WORLD, sidewheeler steamer sent to the boneyard on the Oakland mud flats, abandoned and stripped of its brass and iron. Her last charred timbers were buried in the silt of Oakland Creek. Launched February 10, 1850 from New York. The flat-bottomed sidewheeler steamboat, powered by vertical-beam engine, was 220-feet long and weighed 525 gross tons. Capt. Ned Wakeman sailed his stolen ship through the Golden Gate on July 11, 1850 and anchored at Cunningham's Wharf. By August she was a steamer between Sacramento and the Bay. Sold in 1851 and plied the Sacramento River until the mid-1870s when the great engine was failing. In

1875 it was a ferryboat between Vallejo Junction and South Vallejo. Four years later the Amelia replaced the *New World*.

NEW ENGLAND, a barque wrecked at Angel Island in the 1850s.

NIANTIC, ship-hotel, at the northwest corner of Clay and Sansome Streets. Most famous of the ship-buildings. The *Niantic* had brought 248 miners to the city in July of 1849, then was converted into a storeship. The May 3-4, 1851 fire left it little more than a burned hull, but she became a hotel, served as a general office and hotel saloon. The large floating storeship was moored only a block from the *Apollo* and *General Harrison* storeships. The difference was that the *Niantic* contained nearly 2000 tons of merchandise, most of it of an extraordinary combustible nature, including 200 casks of gunpowder.

Capt. Henry Cleaveland had sailed the ship from Liverpool to Valparaiso and hove into sight of Paita, Chile. Cleaveland realized the *Niantic* could rescue these stranded immigrants from fever and death and in the bargain make more money as an immigrant ship than as a whale hunter. He took her on to Panama and saw thousands who had crossed the Isthmus of Panama crowding the west side and clamoring for passage to San Francisco.

After suffering in the sickly climate for weeks they were ready to pay any amount for a berth. The *Niantic* anchored five miles out, and "bungoes" set out from shore to reach her. Moorhead, Whitehead & Waddington, a Chilean merchant firm, purchased her and spent three weeks in fitting out. Cleaveland packed aboard 248 passengers at $150 each and was able to send an extra $45,000 in gold coin back to the ship's owners. He caught a good breeze which carried her on for a few hours, but several hours out from Panama becalmed and dysentery, scurvy and cholera broke out aboard.

On July 3, after a voyage of sixty-eight days, the passengers saw weeds and floating logs around the ship that morning. As the summer fogs cleared later in the day they fixed their position as sixty miles off San Francisco. As they approached land, "The passengers are all engaged in packing up," wrote passenger, J. M. Letts. "The retorts, crucibles, gold tests, pickaxes, shovels, and tin pans...each determined to be first off for the mines. Each one having conceived a different mode of keeping his gold, one would exhibit and ingenious box with a secret lock, another, a false bottom to his trunk, a third a huge belt, while a fourth was at work on a fifteenth buckskin bag, each of twenty pounds capacity."

Cleaveland saw his crew jump ship in accordance with the established local manner, and head for the diggings along with all the passengers. Without a crew, the consignees, Cook, Baker & Company, were left with only a "useless elephant" on their hands. A few months later she was purchased by Gildmeister, De Fremesy and Company who ran the bluff-bowed cargo vessel into a berth on the northwest corner of Clay and Sansome Streets. They set the *Niantic* out as a floating warehouse, constructed a few houses on deck and rented these out as sleeping quarters.

The *Niantic* prospered so that for the rest of 1849 and beginning of 1850 she earned her delighted owners $20,000 a month in rental income! She was covered with a shingle roof, with offices and stores on the deck, at the level of which was constructed a wide balcony surmounted by a verandah. The hull was divided into warehouses, entered by doorways on the sides. The *Niantic* floated so far inland that buildings sprouted around it as the shore began to fill in and move outward toward deeper water to accommodate larger ships unloading. After a while, the ship store no longer appeared unusual nestled among the more conventional land buildings crowding the water-locked vessel.

The fire of May 3, 1851, destroyed all but the submerged hulk which later was utilized as the foundation for the *Niantic* Hotel, a famous hostelry which stood until 1872. The *Niantic* Block a four-story building was erected on the site where the ship was anchored in the mud. A

Appendix A   351

tablet placed in September, 1919 read: "Site of the Ship 'Niantic' The emigrant ship *Niantic* stood on this spot in the early days when the water came up to Montgomery Street. Converted to other uses it was covered with a shingle roof, with offices and stores on the deck, at the level of which was constructed a wide balcony surmounted by a verandah. The hull was divided into warehouses, entered by doorways on the sides.

NOBLE, a storeship off Clark's Point, lay in the block bounded by Pacific, Jackson, Davis and Drumm Streets with her bow near Pacific.

NONANTUM, July 27, 1850 of Boston.

NONPAREIL, storeship broken up by Hare.

NOONDAY, 1849, lost within sight of the piers.

NORTHENER, one of the Howard Line of steamers.

OCEAN BIRD, afterwards a lumbership.

OHIO, lay near Pacific Wharf.

ONYX, near California Street Wharf.

OPORTE (OPORTO) a brig broken up by Hare.

ORATOR, British bark, for many years a storeship near California Street Wharf.

ORION, lay near Law's Wharf.

ORB, bark. Overloaded with supplies, shipped water badly. Left part of her cargo in Rio, and, seven inches higher in the water arrived San Francisco in September 1849, after a seven month voyage.

OREGON, the second Ghost Ship. It left Panama behind the California on May 23, 1849 and arrived in San Francisco on June 17, 1849 with enough coal to rescue the California. It was sold for scrap in 1869 to a local lumber firm. Then the *Oregon* was converted into a bark for carrying lumber. It was wrecked as it was sailing from Pugent Sound to San Francisco.

ORPHEUS, storeship.

OSCEOLA, brig, left January and sailed via Cape Horn, 201- day trip, 176 of them at sea. Arrived August 5, 1849 in San Francisco. The 19,308-mile trip was so trying that passenger Samuel Upham returned home a year and a half later.

OTHELLO, lay near Law's Wharf in the stream, became a storeship on Steuart Street.

PACIFIC, sailing vessel. Left New York, January 23, 1849 under Capt. Tibbits in the midst of a blizzard, arrived San Francisco, August 5, 1849. Notable

PALESTRO, a Havre packet, broken up by Hare.

PALLADIUM, lay near Long Wharf.

PALMYRA, a small brig storeship, inside of India Dock, now Battery between Greenwich and Filbert.

PANAMA, taken to Beale and Mission and cut up.

left Panama trailing her sister ships, the *California* and *Oregon* steamers on May 18, 1849. Bayard Taylor, Gold Rush chronicler, was onboard. The ship entered the Bay on June 4, 1849. Aspinwall's ship was converted into a church, the Seaman's Bethal or Bethal Methodist Episcopal Church. Its machinery was removed in 1865. The hulk was sent to Central America for storage purposes in connection with the coffee trade. Some of the Panama was dismantled for lumber, a valuable commodity in treeless San Francisco.

PANTHEON, near California Street Wharf, broken up by Hare.

PATRIOT, lay off Jackson Street, broken up by Hare.

PAULINE, carried members of the Bunker Hill Mining and Trading Company. They vowed "to abstain from all the vices and temptations incident to the expedition" such as gambling, profanity and drinking.

PEMBROKE.

PERA, lay near California Street Wharf.

PERSIA

PERU, a bark.

PHILADELPHIA, on June 24, 1849, Capt. Weare's 513-ton sail ship burned at the water's edge at the Wharf. Weare ordered her cables cut and the Philadelphia drifted off with the tide containing a full cargo. This was considered a foreshadowing of the great fire to come, as was the burning of the Shades Hotel in January.

PHILLIP HONE, a warehouse ship south of Union Street near Law's Wharf, filled over.

PHOENIX, carried sixty passengers, took 115 days to reach San Francisco.

PIEDMONT, a storeship next to the *Casilada* at the end of Howison's Pier.

PILGRIM, near Long Wharf.

PIONEER, first ship hove down by the Japan.

PLOVER, a bark which once sailed in search of Sir John Franklin.

PLEIDES, a bark off Jackson Street, broken up by Hare.

POLYNESIA, broken up by Hare.

POTOMAC, lay near Pacific Wharf in stream.

POWHATTEN, broken up by Howgate.

PRESCOTT

PRINCE de JOINVILLE, went to the Ohinchas where she was condemned.

RALPH BERNAL, near California Street Wharf. *Resoluta* (aka *Resolutis* and *Resolute*)

RESOLUTA, a French ship in care of the pilot agent Nelson.

RESOLUTE (*RESOLUTIS*), Dutch vessel, coal hulk near Cunningham's Wharf.

REGULUS, off California Street Wharf in the stream, broken up by Hare.

RHINE, a store hulk and brig.

RHODE, off Rincon Point, sold and broken up by Hare.

RHONE, storeship near Law's Wharf.

RICARDO, a storeship and then hotel-ship at Pacific and Front Streets near the *Almandrilina's* ruins.

RICHMOND (two ships) one near Broadway Wharf, broken up by Hare.

ROANOKE, a schooner.

ROBERT, lay off Jackson Street.

ROBERT ROLLA, near Cunningham's Wharf.

ROJAH, teakwood ship, went to China.

ROLAND, coal hulk near California Street Wharf.

ROME, Salem ship.

ROMA, a coal ship, big Russian vessel, sunk by Lawson at the southwest corner of Market and East Streets. Lost during the May 3, 1851 burning. Today, the Muni Metro runs right through the remains of the Russian *Roma* near what is now the foot of Mission Street.

ROSE, a brig near Griffin's Wharf.

ROWENA, Cove lumberman, later lost between Liverpool and New Orleans.

RUSSELL, bark broken up by Hare.

SACRAMENTO, coal bark, broken up by Hare.

SAGAMORE, steamer exploded while leaving the Central Wharf on October 29, 1850. Side wheel, 66-tons, 75 to 100 dead and wounded. Her engines were removed and installed on the Secretary where they detonated a second time and killed another thirty victims.

SALEM, a warehouse ship that "lay for several years on California Street. Dismantled by Hare for wood at Rincon Point.

SAMSON, 500-ton schooner from Philadelphia, October, 1849. Under command of Capt. Blanchard.

SANGE

SAN FRANCISCO, bark, Beverly, Massachusetts, left in August, 1849 with eight pre- fab houses, 63,000 feet of lumber and 10,000 bricks. Command of Capt. Baker. Carried twenty pigs housed in a stout pen. One pig perished after a sadistic seaman cut off the animal's tail and it bled to death. Another pig became a "good sea pie." Their July Fourth band consisted of bass and kettle drums, cymbals, tambourine, accordion, and bells. Lost within sight of the Cove.

SAN MATEO, Capt. Lambert's schooner, capsized in a storm in the Bay on February 14, 1854 with the loss of two.

SANTA CLARA, burned to the water's edge at Central Wharf on March 3, 1851 with the death of three.

SARA PARKER, of Nantucket.

SARA SANDS, one of the first iron steamships constructed. It became a cheap lodging house at Vallejo and Battery Streets.

SEA WITCH, a pilot boat, sank at Arch Rock on January 6, 1853.

SELA, storeship broken up by Howgate.

SISTERS, bark broken up by Hare.

SONORA, a steamer broken up by Hare.

STAR OF CHINA, steamer lost on Coos Bay Bar.

SITKA, see *Little Sitka*.

STEAMBOAT HOTEL.

STIEGLITZ, a storeship on the south side of Washington Street settled by Hare.

STOCKTON, on October 18, 1853, the steamer Stockton exploded at New York landing. Capt. Sharp and one other lost, eight injured.

STORESHIP, at Vallejo and First Streets.

SULLA, storeship brig broken up by Howgate.

SULTAN, a New York and Charleston packet.

SUPERIOR, broken up.

SUSAN ABIGAIL, storeship, burnt later in the Arctic.

SUSAN DREW, at the foot of Sacramento Street. Went to sea afterward.

SUSAN STURGESS, taken by natives and burnt at Queen Charlotte's Island.

SWALLOW

SWEDEN, 650-ton ship, cleared Boston in March, 1849. Under Capt. Cutter.

SYLPH, a three-hundred-ton ex-whaler out of Fair Haven, Massachusetts. She left Panama on May 9, 1849 and on July 26 sailed into the Ghost Fleet. Cal Gardiner was a passenger.

TALCA, brig.

TALMA, out of Boston, lay near Pacific Wharf in stream. under command of Capt. Stephen Haskel, Capt. Coffin's generous friend, who had formally been his mate in the ship *Arragon*. Coffin slept onboard in the Cove 1850-1851.

TAROLITA

TARTAR, lay near Pacific Wharf, in stream.

TECUMSEH, a storeship at southwest corner of California Street between Sansome and Battery, broken up.

TENNESSEE. Her purser sent Lillie Coit, the only girl firefighter, a model of a Chinese junk carved in ivory. The *Tennessee* was the first Pacific mail steamer to be lost, 1,275-ton, operated between Panama and San Francisco from March, 1850 until March 6, 1853 when she was wrecked a few miles north of the Golden Gate near Benicia after colliding with the Northerner.

THAMES, near Cunningham's Wharf, broken up by Howgate.

THOMAS BENNETT, a grocery store between Sacramento and California after Battery Street, then a storeship on the south side of Howison's Pier at the corner of Sansome Street with a building over her. Out of Charleston, South Carolina, she became controlled by Trowbridge, Morrison and Company. According to Bancroft she once lay at the Sansome Street corner.

THOMAS BURNETT, sank at Alcatraz in 1850.

THOMAS H. BENTON, 200-ton brig, went ashore at Angel Island with complete loss on December 12, 1849.

THOMAS JONES, near Long Wharf.

THRECIAN, off Rincon Point.

TIGRESS, 150-tons, from Beverly, Massachusetts, under command of Capt. Howe. She brought shotgun shells and tobacco in large containers, but San Franciscans were only buying tobacco in small packages at eighty-five cents a pound. "If our seeds had been packed in air-tight tins they would have paid a handsome profit; as they cannot sell them," wrote Howe.

TOBACCO PLANT, part of the US Arctic Expedition under Commodore Wilkes, sunk in the vicinity of Cunningham's Wharf.

TOCCAO, schooner of Cape Cod, carried five passengers and a crew of four. At 28-tons it was the smallest ship to negotiate the Horn in 1849.

TONQUIN, on November 20, 1849, she struck Whalesman Shoal and was lost but the cargo of bricks, lumber and stoves was saved. The site today is filled over and near the San Francisco Maritime Museum.

TREATY, brig at Clark's Point, broken up.

TRESCOTT, a storeship near California Street Wharf, broken up.

TRITON, store hulk.

TUSKENA, near Long Wharf.

TWO FRIENDS, with 164 passengers, a five month voyage.

UGARTE, coal hulk.

UNICORN, steamer that arrived on February 12, 1850, "a foreign bottom."

UNKNOWN BRIG, a storeship at California and Battery.

UNKNOWN BARK on Battery Street near Jackson. Batchelder moved her.

UNKNOWN BRIG at southeast Battery and California Streets closed in. The Bay Hotel built over her.

UNKNOWN, one of Cushing's brigs near Euphemia.

UNKNOWN, planking of Griffin's Wharf laid over this vessel.

UNKNOWN, four sunken ships shown on 1853 map as being on Davis, near Market (possibly the *Autumn*) on Market near Davis, on Market between Beale and Fremont, and on Market near Beale.

URANIA, ship.

UTICA, July 1850 Havre packet ship burned at Clay Street Wharf and towed to Goat Island to sink.

VALHALLA

VARIOUS LORCHAS, coastal craft of the Orient.

VITULA, broken up by Hare.

WABAN, brig. Authorites towed the overcrowded *Euphemia* to San Quentin Point where the prisoners would work for a time as slave laborers to construct California's first land penitentiary. The *Euphemia* was pulled around to North Beach in June 1851 and became the town's first "lunatic house" and "receptacle for the insane." Its final resting place is Battery and Sacramento allowed to rot and sink into the Bay and covered by landfill. In 1921 her remains would be discovered while excavating the construction site for the Federal Reserve Bank. The *Euphemia* was not the only prison ship, a converted bark, *La Grange*, anchored at the Sacramento waterfront as a county jail for eleven years.

In December 1851 the authorities asked private contractor and corrupt politician Jim Estrill to use convict labor. In January he had an old brig, The *Waban*, tugged to Angel Island and put forty cons to work in a rock quarry there. The lesser offenders were sent to cut and regrade San Francisco city streets. At the same time seventeen prisoners overpowered guards and escaped from the brig. They rowed toward Contra Costa. Devil Jack was on their trail, but they separated into three groups and escaped into the Coast Range near Livermore's ranch. Devil Jack could not recapture them and returned to the brig, where he fired the three keepers. A year later the *Waban* packed with 150 convicts was towed to Point San Quentin where land had been purchased for the prison—two story cells. In 1854 the prison was completed with accommodations for 300 prisoners in 48 cells. All the convict workers were housed on the *Waban* to relieve overcrowded county jail, would serve in the meantime as the first state prison. In early 1851 the county began construction of a prison, but the overcrowded land jail remained the main jail for the next five years.

WASHINGTON, steamer broken up by Hare.

WASHINGTON IRVING, packet, left New York on December 8, 1850 under Capt. Plumer. Notable passenger, the elderly Mr Whippet, a Bostonian and constant complainer. Garrett W. Low kept a Log of the trip. For some time the Irving lay becalmed less than two hundred miles from San Francisco.

WILLIAM GRAY, discovered at Levi Square.

WILLIAM IVY, left New York harbor on January 25, 1849, reached Rio in a fleet forty-two days. Arrived in San Francisco in the company of the Edward Everett.

WILSON G.HUNT, a 450-ton steamer which came to California in 1850 via the Strait of

Magellan and traded between San Francisco and Sacramento until 1858. After years of operation in the Pacific Northwest she returned to San Francisco Bay and was scrapped in 1890.

WHANG HO, a one hundred year old Chinese Pirate junk arrived in the Cove July, 1849. Chinese and Japanese junks had been seen off the California coast as early as 1814.

WINDSOR FAY, lay at the foot of Sacramento Street, broken up by Hare.

WILLIAM BRANT, in the stream near Long Wharf.

WILLIAM GRAY, near Griffin's Wharf, tentatively identified as lying in Levi's Plaza.

YORK, near California Street Wharf.

XYLON, involved in the crash between an unnamed British ship, the *Canada* and the *Alhambra*.

ZUID POOL, a ship off Rincon Point, in stream, broken up by Hare.

RELATED SINKINGS IN THE COVE AND BAY

CONTRA COSTA, a walking beam side-wheeler , suffered a boiler explosion in the Bay on April 4, 1859.

ELLEN BURKE, a scow schooner, sank off Bird Island in the Bay in 1860.

ISCA, went aground in a gale in the Cove on November 16, 1863.

J. A. MacCLELLAND, boiler exploded on August 27, 1861 and flew 350 yards to shore three miles below Knight's Landing. Fourteen lives were lost. Owner, Capt. C. Mills.

JENNY LIND, boiler exploded near Pulgas Ranch on April 11, 1853 with thirty injured and thirty-one dead.

NEVADA, sank in Cache Slough.

PAUL PRY, the 330-ton side-wheeler struck Alcatraz and sank December 12, 1862.

POLYNESIA, a clipper ship of 1084-tons, went ashore at South Beach in the Bay on March 3, 1863. The crew set her afire and the wreck was sold at auction.

SHAWMUT, struck Bird Island in the Bay in 1863.

UNDERWRITER, sank in the Sacramento River in 1857.

NOTABLE GOLD-SHIP WRECKS AND PLAGUE-SHIPS

AMERICAN EAGLE, lost along the San Joaquin River, October 18, 1853. Barrels of brandy were lashed on her deck, her hold packed with gunpowder. As the American Eagle strove for an extra pound of pressure, she was torn apart amidships. Fire broke out forward of the wheelhouse and the gunpowder caught, killing nine people.

BELLE, a sidewheeler steam boat that exploded just above Sacramento at Russian Ford, with thirty dead or missing.

BENICIA, steamer sank eight miles north of Fremont after hitting a snag. Commander, Capt. Hight.

FAWN, steamer that exploded near Sacramento, with two deaths on August 16, 1851.

JACK HAYES, snagged on the Sacramento River in February, 1851.

MONTAGUE, out of New Haven, lay in quarantine in Bay in 1850, twenty men on board, including the Capt, second mate and six passengers, died of cholera.

NEW WORLD, sank October 10, 1854, nine miles below Sacramento.

PEARL, sidewheeler steamboat, 78-tons, boiler exploded and killed fifty-five people including Capt. Davis. Many of the dead were Chinese workmen.

RANGER, boiler explosion killed three on January 8, 1854.

R. K. PAGE, (the rebuilt *JACK HAYES*) river steamer boiler exploded during race with the *Governor Dana* on March 22, 1853. Capt. Moore and his son and twenty-two others were fatalities.

UNCLE SAM, debarked from the Nicaraguan coast with 750 passengers, 104 perished en route from cholera and nine more on arrival in San Francisco.

UNION, en route home from California gold fields with forty-five passengers, struck a reef.

THE MARTHA SANGER, commanded by Capt. Robinson, out of Charges for New Orleans with ninety California passengers, hung up on the Quita Sueno Reef.

YANKEE BLADE, in the fall of 1854, went down with a loss of thirty lives and $153,000.

CENTRAL AMERICA, sank with 423 persons and eight million dollars of gold from California in 1857.

CAPTAIN COFFIN'S UNNAMED AND NICKNAMED LEGENDARY VESSELS

ARGON, a ship of gloom.
GREBA, a light ship.
SHIP OF NETS, a Japanese Ship.
PADDLEWHEELER #573
THE ORNATE SHIP
A SHIP OF UNDELIVERED CARGO
THE MIWOK'S FRIGATE
COMET, an abandoned clipper not fully explored.
THE NOISY SHIP, a Chilean craft of joyful men.
ADDER, a plague ship of the steamer class.

NAVAL BAY SHIPS

ANITA, U. S. bark, for a time, under past midshipman Selim E Woodworth, was down to only six crewmen in just a minute." She was armed with two guns to be used as a man-of-war on the upper California coast.

OHIO, flagship The firm-handed Pacific Squadron Commander Thomas Ap Catesby Jones wrote Secretary of the Navy, J. J. Mason from the Flagship Ohio on December 28, 1848. As late as October 1849 the bodies of deserting seamen were hung limply from the yardarms as an example to deserters.

LAWRENCE, Coast Guard ship.

SELECTED REFERENCES

Andrews. Ralph W. *Historic Fires of the West*: 1865 to 1915. New York: Bonanza Books. 1966.
Asbury, Herbert. *The Barbary Coast*. New York: Alfred A. Knopf,Inc., 1933.
Bacon, Daniel. *Walking San Francisco on the Barbary Coast Trail*. San Francisco: Quicksilver Press, 1996.
Bancroft, Hubert Howe. *The Works, Volume XXIII, History of California Vol. IV. 1849-1859*. San Francisco: The History Company, Publishers, 1888.
Barker, Malcolm E. *San Francisco Memoirs 1835-1851*. San Francisco: London born Publications, 1996.—*More San Francisco Memoirs 1852-1899*. San Francisco: London born Publications, 1994.
Barnett, S. Anthony. *The Story of Rats*. Australia: Allen & Unwin, 2001.
Barry, T. A., and Patten, B. A. *Men and Memories: in the Spring of '50*. San Francisco: A. L. Bancroft and Company, Publishers, Booksellers And Stationers, 1873.
Boessenecker, John. *Gold Dust & Gunsmoke*. New York: John Wiley & Sons, Inc, 1999. From published edition and advance uncorrected proofs.
Beebe, Lucius and Clegg, Charles. *San Francisco's Golden Era*. Berkeley: Howell-North, 1960.
Beilharz, Edwin and Lopez, Carlos U. *We Were '49ers! Chilean Accounts of the California Gold Rush*. Pasadena, California: Ward Ritchie Press, 1976, p. 146.
Benemann, William. *A Year of Mud and Gold, San Francisco in Letters and Diaries 1849-1850*. Lincoln: University of Nebraska Press, 1999
Brady, Matthew Brady. *The Old Town, Real Life in Early Frisco*. San Francisco: Independent Books, 1992.
Braynard, Frank O. *Famous American Ships*. New York: Hastings House Publishers, 1956.
Brooks, Van Wyck. *The Times of Melville and Whitman*. New York: E.P. Dutton & Co., Inc., 1947.
Browning, Peter. *Yerba Buena San Francisco*. Lafayette, California: Great West Books, 1998.
Bruff, J. Goldsborough. *Gold Rush, The Journals, Drawings & Other Papers of J. Goldsborough Bruff, April 2, 1849-July 20, 1851*. New York, Columbia University Press, 1949.
Calkins, Carroll C. Project Editor. *Mysteries of the Unexplained*. New York: the Reader's Digest Association, Inc., 1982.
Camp, William Martin. *San Francisco, Port of Gold*. Garden City, New York: Doubleday & Company, 1947.
Carlisle, Henry C. *San Francisco Street Names*. San Francisco: The American Trust Company, 1954.
Clark, Arthur. H. *The Clipper Ship Era*. New York: G.P. Putnam's Sons, 1910. (Riverside Connecticut: Seven C's, 1970 reprint of 1910 edition)
Coffin, George B. *Pioneer Voyage to California and around the World 1849-1852*. Chicago: Gorham Bartlett Coffin, privately printing of Capt Coffin's original handwritten manuscript, Chicago: June 1908.
Cole, Tom. *A Short History of San Francisco*. San Francisco: Don't Call It Frisco Press, 1981.
Dana, Richard Henry. *Two Years before the Mast*. New York: Harper & Brothers,1840.
Dando-Collins, Steven. *Mistaken Identity, The Trials of Joe Windred*. Australia: Random House, a Vintage Book, 2012. Excellent Australian history and a source for Joe Windred.

Davis, William Heath. *Seventy-Five Years in California*.
Delgado, James P., *To California by Sea, A Maritime History of the California Gold Rush*. Columbia South Carolina: University of South Carolina, 1990. Wonderful account filling in the missing pieces of the burying of the Ghost Fleet and the workings of the Coast Guard cruiser, *Lawrence*.
—*Gold Rush Port, the Maritime Archaeology of San Francisco's Waterfront*. University of California Press, 2009. This history is another of Delgado's remarkable feats of archaeology, added immensely to an understanding of the history of Yerba Buena Cove's storeships and provided some elusive dates. This book, the last the author consulted as he completed his story of the Ghost Fleet, provided a layer of detail like the finest silt on the floor of the Cove. Marvelous and well-written. Bravo to Delgado and his team.
Dickson, Samuel. *Tales of San Francisco*. Stanford, California: Stanford University Press, 1965.
—*Tales of Love and Hate in Old San Francisco*. San Francisco: Chronicle Books, 1971.
Dillon, Richard H. Shanghaiing Days. New York: Coward-McCann, Inc. 1961.
—The Challenge, New York: Coward-McCann, Inc. 1961. Dillon is my favorite descriptive writer of the Bay next to Harold Gilliam.
J. Ross Browne: Confidential Agent in Old California. Norman, Oklahoma: University of Oklaholma Press, 1965.
Dobie, Charles Caldwell. *San Francisco, A Pageant*. New York: D. Appleton-Century Co., 1934.
Dow, Robert Gerald. *Thesis "Bay Fill."* California State University, July 1973. Excellent detail and valuable.
Drago, Harry Sinclair. *The Steamboaters*. New York: Dodd, Mead & Company, 1967.
Driesbach, Janice T., Jones, Harvey L., Holland, Katherine Church, editors. *Art of the Gold Rush*. Oakland and Berkeley: University of California Press, 1998.
Emerson, Everett. *Mark Twain, A Literary Life*. Philadelphia: University of Pennsylvania Press, 2000.
Dunshee, Kenneth Holcomb. *As You Pass By*. New York: Hastings House, 1952. This history is just a joy with maps of important buildings showing elevations and landmarks.
Fracchia, Charles A. *Fire & Gold*. Encinitas, California: Heritage Media, 1996.
Gilliam, Harold. *San Francisco Bay*. Garden City, New York: Doubleday & Company, Inc., 1957. A terrific book! I read it for pleasure.
Hale, Richard Lunt. *Log*. Privately printed.
Harlan, George. *San Francisco Bay Ferryboats*. San Diego: Howell-North Books, 19 .
Hart, Ann Clark. *Clark's Point*. San Francisco: Pioneer Press, Publishers, 1937.
Hazen, Margaret Hindle and Hazen, Robert M. *Keepers of the Flame*. Princeton: Princeton University Press, 1992.
Hill, Mary. *Gold*. Berkeley: University of California Press, 1999.
Hoffman, Andrew. *Inventing Mark Twain, the Lives of Samuel Langhorne Clemens*. New York: William Morrow and Company, Inc., 1997
Holdredge, Helen. *Firebelle Lillie*. New York: Meredith Press, 1967.
Holliday, J. S. *Rush For Riches*. Oakland Museum of California. Berkeley: University of California Press, 1999.
Issel, William, and Cherney, Robert W. *San Francisco 1865-1932*. Berkeley: University of California Press, 1986.
Jackson, Donald Dale. *Gold Dust*. New York: University of Nebraska Press, 1980.
Jackson, Joseph Henry. *Bad Company*. New York: Harcourt, Brace and Company, 1939, 1940.
—. *Anybody's Gold*. San Francisco: Chronicle Books, 1970.
Jacobson, Pauline. *City of the Golden 'Fifties*. Berkeley: University of California Press, 1941.
Johnson, Paul C. *Pictorial History of California*. New York: Doubleday & Co., 1970.
Johnson, Paul C. and Reinhardt, Richard. *San Francisco, As It Is, As It Was*. San Francisco: Doubleday & Company, Inc., 1979.

Sources   361

Johnson, William Weber. *The Forty-Niners*. New York: Time-Life Books, 1974.
Jurmain, Claudia, and Rawls, James J., editors. *California, A Place, A People, A Dream*. Oakland: Chronicle Books, 1986 and Oakland Museum Exhibition of 1998.
Kaplin, Justin. *Mark Twain and His World*. New York: Harmony Books, 1974.
Kemble, John Haskell. *San Francisco Bay, A Pictorial Maritime History*. Cambridge, Maryland: Cornell Maritime Press, 1957.
Kowalewski, Michael, editor. *Gold Rush*. Berkeley, California: Heyday Books, 1997.
Levy, JoAnn. *They Saw the Elephant: Women in the California Gold Rush*. Hamden, Connecticut: Archon Books, 1990.
Lewis, Oscar. *This Was San Francisco*. New York: David McKay Co., Inc., 1962.
—. *San Francisco: Mission to Metropolis*. San Diego: Howell-North Books, 1980.
Lockwood, Charles. *Suddenly San Francisco*. San Francisco: The Hearst Corporation, 1978.
Mayer, Robert, editor and compiler. *San Francisco, A Chronological and Documentary History, 1542-1970*. New York: Oceana Publications, Inc., 1974.
McGloin, S. J., John Bernard. *San Francisco, The Story of A City*. San Rafael, California: Presidio Press, 1978.
Mullen, Kevin J. *Let Justice Be Done, Crime and Politics in Early San Francisco*. Reno and Las Vegas: University of Nevada Press, 1989.
Muscatine, Doris. *Old San Francisco, the Biography of a City*. New York: G.P. Putnam's Sons, 1975.
Myrick, David F. *San Francisco's Telegraph Hill*. Berkeley: Howell-North Books, 1972.
Neville, Amelia Ransome. *The Fantastic City*. Boston and New York: Houghton Mifflin Company, 1932.
O'Brien, Robert. *This Is San Francisco*. New York: McGraw-Hill Book Co., Inc., 1948.
Quinn, Arthur. *The Rivals*. Lincoln: University of Nebraska Press, 1994.
Rathmell, George. *Realms of Gold*. Berkeley, California: Creative Arts Book Company, 1998.
Richards, Rand. *Historic San Francisco*. San Francisco: Heritage House Publishers, 1991.
Riesenberg, Felix, Jr. *Golden Gate*. New York: Alfred A. Knopf, 1940.
Russ, Carolyn Hale. *The Log of a Forty-Niner*, edited from the original manuscript. Boston Massachusettes: B. J. Brimmer Co., 1923.
Scott, Mel. *The San Francisco Bay Area*. Berkeley: University of California at Berkeley, 1959.
Senkewicz, Robert M. *Vigilantes In Gold Rush San Francisco*. Stanford, California: Stanford University Press, 1985.
Stellman, Louis J. *Sam Brannan, Builder of San Francisco*. Fairfield, California: James Stevenson Publisher, 1996.
Stewart, George R. *Committee of Vigilance*. Boston: Houghton Mifflin Co., 1964.
Taper, Bernard, edit. *Mark Twain's San Francisco*. New York: McGraw-Hill Book Co., Inc. 1963.
Taylor, Rev. William. *Seven Years' Street Preaching in San Francisco, California*. New York, published for the author by Carlton & Porter, 1856.
Taylor, William. *California Life Illustrated*. New York, published for the author by Carlton & Porter, 1858.
Utley, Robert M. *Lone Star Justice*. New York: Berkley Books 2002.
Walkins, T. H. and Olmstead, R.R. *Mirror of the Dreams, an Illustrated History of San Francisco*. San Francisco: Scrimshaw Press, 1976.
Water Trails West. Garden City, New York: Doubleday & Co., Inc., 1978.
Whipple, A.B.C. *The Challenge*. Norwalk, Connecticut: The Easton Press, 1987.
Williams, George J. III. *On The Road with Mark Twain in California and Nevada*. Tree by The River Publishing. Dayton, Nevada, 1994.
Williams, Mary Floyd. *History of the San Francisco Committee of Vigilance of 1851*. Berkeley: University of California Publications in History, 1921.

Periodicals 1850-56:

Argonaut
San Francisco *Call*
San Francisco *Chronicle*
The Daily Alta California
Perrigan, Dana. "Beneath the City." San Francisco *Examiner*, March 16, 1998, p. A-1 and A-10.
Moulder, A.J. "Broderick's Moral Courage." *Argonaut* 3, no. 24 (1878): 9--12.
Brady, Matthew. "The Torch Boys," p. 20. October 29, 1990. San Francisco *Independent* column: "The Old Town."
Engravings: "The Life of a Fireman." Currier and Ives portfolio.
Coffin, George B. *Pioneer. Voyage to California and around the World, 1849-1852*. Chicago: Gorham B. Coffin, 1908.
Neville, Amelia Ransome. *The Fantastic City*. Boston and New York: Houghton Mifflin Company, 1932.
"Riptides," O'Brien, Robert. May 11, 2008, *SFGate.com*. English Jim's hanging.
San Francisco *Call*, Volume 73, Number 116, 26 March 1893. In 1893, a passenger on the Niantic had taken offense at the *Call* saying she was a "old rotten hulk." He tells the inside story.
Daily Alta California, May 6, 1852, p. 2. The May Fire
Daily Alta California, May 6, 1852, August 18, 1851, Whittaker and Mackenzie and Mary Ann Hogan's confession. Very important. Jansen robbery. *Caskie*.
Daily Alta California, July 12, 1851 Stuart's hanging. "Intense Excitement!"
Daily Alta California, July 12, 1851, English Jim Stuart's Long Confession.
Daily Alta California, Berdue, June 24, 1867 "Accused by Mistake." Reporter Buffram
Daily Alta California, Volume 2, No. 97, March 16, 1851. The Trial of Thomas Berdue
Daily Alta California, October 11, 1851. Tom Berdue aftermath
Sacramento *Transcript*, March 26, 1851. Story on English Jim
Daily Alta California, August 26, 1851. Discharge of Tom Berdue.
Daily Alta California, February 23, 1851. Examination in court of Windred and Berdue.
Alta California, February 23, 1851.
Alta California, February 22, 1951, Jansen's watch and chain.
Alta March 16, 1851 Windred and Berdue verdict.
Alta, March 1, 1851. Recorder Washington's testimony
March 5, 1851 Alta Editorial page. goes with waterlots
"San Francisco is still constantly enlarging her borders
March 14, 1851 Alta Editorial page.
March 17, 1851 Warning to police.
"How is it with San Francisco!
March 15, 1851, Alta, Jansen's testimony.
Alta March 16, 1851 James Utting testifies.
Alta July 18, 1851 English Jim and the New Star testimony.
Alta March 19, 1851, Robert Reed's testimony
Marysville Daily Herald, June 24, 1851
Marysville Herald, March 1, 1851, "Stuart the prisoner—There seems to be a mystery hanging over the identity of this man that is most difficult to fathom.
Marysville Daily Herald, July 3, 1851. The People vs. James Stuart alias Thomas Berdue.
Marysville Herald, March 27, 1951, "Another Man Hung."
Marysville Herald, July 8, 1851. Woman hung at Downieville.
Daily Alta California August18, 1851. Arrentrue and plan to rob the Custom Houses

Marysville Daily Herald July 15, 1851. Detailed descriptions of Berdue and Stuart

Author Robert Graysmith at the edge of Graveyard Harbor.
(*Photo by Margot Graysmith*)

ABOUT THE AUTHOR

ROBERT GRAYSMITH is an author and illustrator. He was the political cartoonist for the *San Francisco Chronicle* when the letters and cryptograms from the infamous Zodiac killer began arriving to the paper. He was present when they were opened in the morning editorial meetings, and has been investigating & writing ever since. He lives in San Francisco where he continues to write and illustrate.

www.robertgraysmith.com
www.facebook.com/RobertGraysmithInk

MONKEY'S PAW PUBLISHING, INC.

www.monkeyspawpublishing.com

follow us on social media at

www.facebook.com/MonkeysPawPub
www.instagram.com/MonkeysPawPub
twitter.com/MonkeysPawPub

www.ingramcontent.com/pod-product-compliance
Lightning Source LLC
Chambersburg PA
CBHW031931160426
43209CB00037B/1964/J